THE ULTIMATE PUBLIC CAMP

## *American West*

**Discover 1,902 places where you can camp for free!**

Published by:

Roundabout Publications
P.O. Box 569
LaCygne, KS 66040

Phone: 800-455-2207
Internet: www.RoundaboutPublications.com

Library of Congress Control Number: 2020940378
ISBN-10: 1-885464-77-0
ISBN-13: 978-1-885464-77-4

# Table of Contents

# Introduction

## About the Ultimate Public Campground Project

The Ultimate Public Campground Project was conceived in 2008 to provide a consolidated and comprehensive source for public campgrounds of all types. It all began with a simple POI (Point of Interest) list of GPS coordinates and names, nothing more, totaling perhaps 5,000 locations. As the list grew in size and information provided, a website was designed to display the data on a map. Next came mobile apps, first iOS and Mac apps and more recently Android versions.

Ultimate Campgrounds is NOT the product of some large company with deep pockets. We are a team of three, all working on this as a part-time avocation: Ted is the founder of Ultimate Campgrounds and its Data Meister, Bill is our iOS and Mac developer and Geoff is our Android guy. Both Ted and Bill have been camping for many years and Ultimate Campgrounds reflects their interest in accurate and useful campground information.

Please note that despite our best efforts, there will always be errors to be found in the data. With over 43,000 records in our database, it is impossible to ensure that each one is always up-to-date. Ted tries to work his way through the data at least once a year to pick up things like increased fees and URL's that always seem to be changing. On an annual basis, it requires reviewing over 115 locations each and every day of the year – that's a pretty tall order.

Thus we always appreciate input from users who have found errors…or would like to submit a new location. Our goal is accuracy and we will gratefully accept any and all input.

We decided some years ago to focus on just one thing, publicly-owned camping locations, and try to be the best at it.

You can find a lot more information about Ultimate Campgrounds on our website: www.ultimatecampgrounds.com.

Feel free to address any questions or comments to us at info@ultimatecampgounds.com.

Happy Camping!

## About This Guide

### State Maps

Each state begins with a map of that state. The towns shown on the map indicate that camping areas are nearby. Lines of latitude and longitude are also indicated on each map, which can help in locating the camping areas.

### Abbreviations Chart

Following each state map is a list, in chart form, showing the abbreviations used in the camping area names for that state.

### Camping Area Details

Free camping areas in each state are listed alphabetically under a town name. The towns within the state are also presented in alphabetical order.

Details of each camping area include most or all of the information listed below using the following "headings" and in the same order as shown:

- Name of the camping area
- Agency: managing agency or organization
- Tel: phone number for information
- Location: miles from camping area to town
- GPS: latitude and longitude coordinates
- Open: the season of operation
- Stay Limit: restrictions on length of stay
- Total Sites: number of sites or "dispersed" camping
- RV Sites: number of sites or "undefined" for dispersed
- Max RV Length: any known length limits
- RV Fee: all are free but some will accept donations
- Electric Sites: number of sites with hookups
- Water: comment on availability
- Toilet: comment on availability and type
- Notes: area specific comments
- Activities: list of the popular activities
- Elevation: camping area elevation

## Using This Guide

You have the opportunity to discover many wonderful and scenic areas ranging from small remote settings offering peace and quiet to larger lakeside recreation areas complete with all the sights and sounds of people in motion. Knowing how to use this guide will help you receive the most from it.

### Camping Area Locations

Only towns with camping areas nearby are shown on the state maps. Town selection was based on the roads traveled to reach the camping area and not a straight line aerial path. When possible, towns that offer services for the traveler were chosen over towns with no services. So the referenced town will not always be the closest town to the camping area.

Keep in mind that lakes, rivers, mountains and access roads can make the camping area a greater distance away (in miles) from town than it would appear on a map. Sometimes camping areas can be fairly close to each other but have different reference towns because of the access roads used to reach each location.

### Getting There

This guide is best used in conjunction with Google Maps or similar mapping programs that can provide detailed driving directions. Satellite images can also be helpful in showing the surrounding area and the type of camping experience available.

We have attempted to omit locations with access roads that require a 4x4 vehicle or similar challenging road conditions but it is always advisable to inquire locally with any concerns about your specific rig setup.

### Helpful Tips

In the descriptions for each camping area, nearby towns with limited or no services available for the traveler have been tagged with "limited services" and a second nearby town with more traveler services is provided.

A wide variety of camping areas are offered and many are located around or near water. Some are in or near a population center and many are in remote locations. Always plan ahead for a safe and enjoyable visit.

## Agencies

This directory includes camping areas managed and operated by a variety of agencies including federal, state, local, and others. Below is a list of the abbreviations used when identifying the various agencies.

| Abbreviation | Description |
|---|---|
| BLM | Bureau of Land Management |
| BR | US Bureau of Reclamation |
| COE | Corps of Engineers |
| CP | County/Regional Park |
| FWS | US Fish & Wildlife Service |
| IND | Indian Reservation |
| MISC | Miscellaneous |
| MU | Municipal |
| NP | National Park Service |
| PRIV | Non-profit, such as museums or conservation groups |
| ST | State |
| TVA | Tennessee Valley Authority |
| USFS | US Forest Service |
| UT | Utility Company |

# Arizona

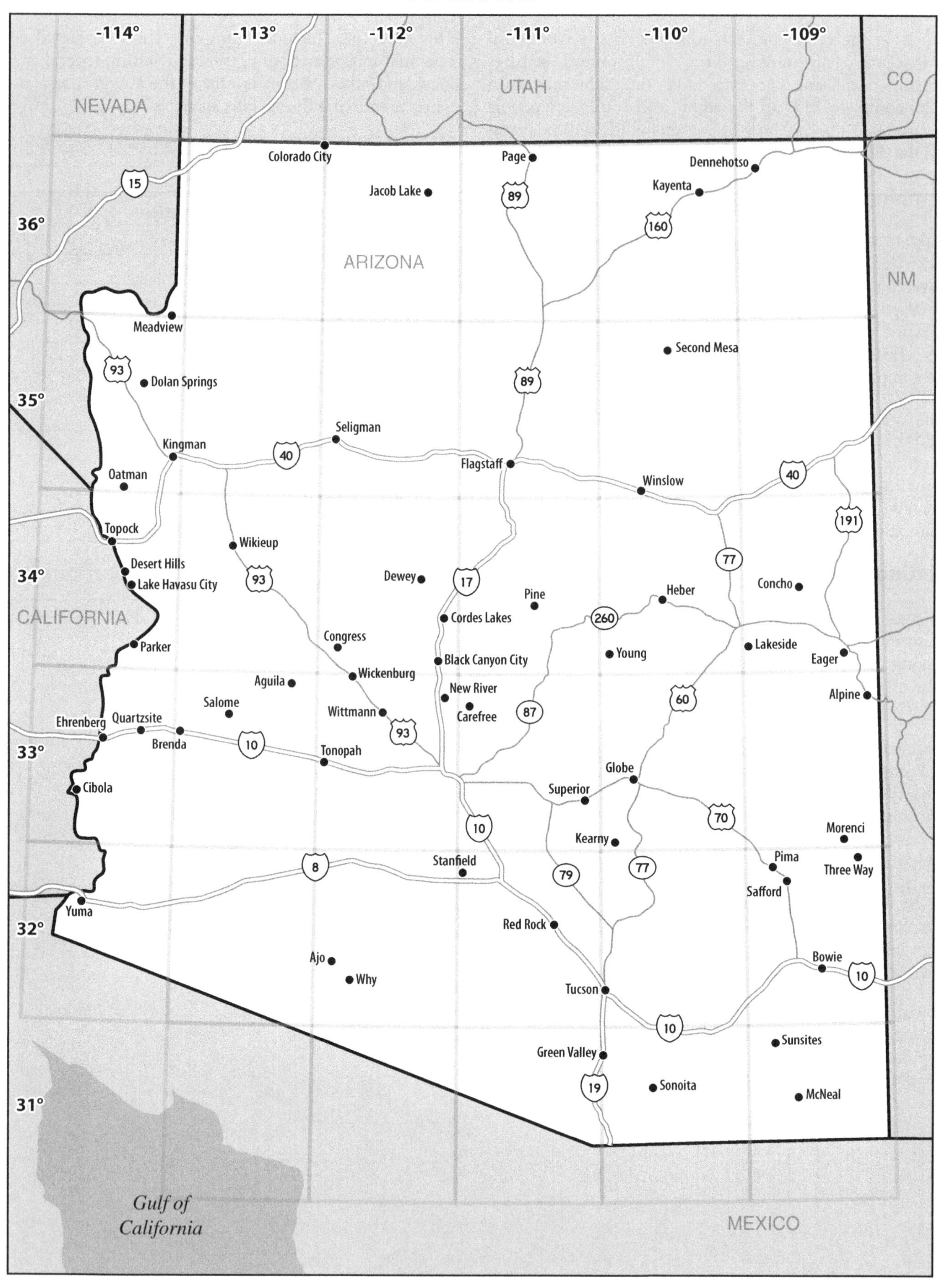
-114°
-113°
-112°
-111°
-110°
-109°
36°
35°
34°
33°
32°
31°
NEVADA
UTAH
CO
NM
ARIZONA
CALIFORNIA
MEXICO
Gulf of California
Colorado City
Page
Dennehotso
Kayenta
Jacob Lake
Meadview
Second Mesa
Dolan Springs
Seligman
Kingman
Flagstaff
Oatman
Winslow
Topock
Wikieup
Desert Hills
Lake Havasu City
Dewey
Pine
Heber
Concho
Cordes Lakes
Parker
Congress
Young
Lakeside
Eager
Black Canyon City
Wickenburg
Aguila
New River
Alpine
Salome
Carefree
Wittmann
Ehrenberg
Quartzsite
Brenda
Tonopah
Globe
Cibola
Superior
Morenci
Kearny
Pima
Three Way
Stanfield
Safford
Yuma
Red Rock
Bowie
Ajo
Why
Tucson
Sunsites
Green Valley
Sonoita
McNeal
15
89
160
93
40
17
77
191
260
60
87
10
70
8
79
19

# Arizona — Camping Areas

| Abbreviation | Description |
|---|---|
| ASTL | Arizona State Trust Land |
| CG | Campground |
| NCA | National Conservation Area |
| NF | National Forest |
| NM | National Monument |
| NRA | National Recreation Area |
| OHV | Off-Highway Vehicle |
| WA | Wildlife Area |

## Aguila

**Harquahala Mountains - Eagle Eye Road** • Agency: Bureau of Land Management • Location: 18 miles S of Aguila (limited services), 40 miles SW of Wickenburg • GPS: Lat 33.729497 Lon -113.296919 • Total sites: Dispersed • RV sites: Undefined • RV fee: Free • No water • No toilets • Elevation: 1843

## Ajo

**Alley Road** • Agency: Bureau of Land Management • Location: 3 miles SW of Ajo • GPS: Lat 32.353639 Lon -112.887503 • Total sites: Dispersed • RV sites: Undefined • RV fee: Free • No water • No toilets • Elevation: 2095

**Darby Wells Road** • Agency: Bureau of Land Management • Location: 4 miles S of Ajo • GPS: Lat 32.341354 Lon -112.843637 • Total sites: Dispersed • RV sites: Undefined • RV fee: Free • No water • No toilets • Elevation: 1788

## Alpine

**Blue Crossing** (Apache-Sitgreaves NF) • Agency: US Forest Service • Tel: 928-339-5000 • Location: 23 miles S of Alpine • GPS: Lat 33.627892 Lon -109.098102 • Open: Apr-Nov • Stay limit: 14 days • Total sites: 4 • RV sites: 4 • Max RV Length: 16 • RV fee: Free • No water • Vault toilets • Activities: Hiking • Elevation: 5824

**Gabaldon Horse Camp** (Apache-Sitgreaves NF) • Agency: US Forest Service • Tel: 928 333-4301 • Location: 25 miles W of Alpine • GPS: Lat 33.929199 Lon -109.487469 • Open: Jun-Sep • Stay limit: 14 days • Total sites: 5 • RV sites: 5 • Max RV Length: 16 • RV fee: Free • No water • Vault toilets • Activities: Hiking, motor sports, equestrian area • Elevation: 9419

**Hannagan** (Apache-Sitgreaves NF) • Agency: US Forest Service • Tel: 928-339-5000 • Location: 23 miles S of Alpine • GPS: Lat 33.635859 Lon -109.322315 • Open: May-Sep • Stay limit: 14 days • Total sites: 8 • RV sites: 8 • Max RV Length: 16 • RV fee: Free (donation appreciated) • Central water • Vault toilets • Activities: Hiking • Elevation: 9262

**KP Cienega** (Apache-Sitgreaves NF) • Agency: US Forest Service • Tel: 928-339-5000 • Location: 29 miles S of Alpine • GPS: Lat 33.576183 Lon -109.355957 • Open: May-Sep • Stay limit: 14 days • Total sites: 5 • RV sites: 5 • Max RV Length: 16 • RV fee: Free • Central water • Vault toilets • Activities: Fishing • Elevation: 8986

**Strayhorse** (Apache-Sitgreaves NF) • Agency: US Forest Service • Tel: 928-687-8600 • Location: 32 miles S of Alpine • GPS: Lat 33.550321 Lon -109.318093 • Open: Apr-Nov • Total sites: 7 • RV sites: 7 • Max RV Length: 16 • RV fee: Free • Central water • Vault toilets • Elevation: 7802

**Upper Blue** (Apache-Sitgreaves NF) • Agency: US Forest Service • Tel: 928-339-5000 • Location: 17 miles S of Alpine • GPS: Lat 33.694001 Lon -109.071863 • Open: Apr-Nov • Stay limit: 14 days • Total sites: 3 • RV sites: 3 • Max RV Length: 16 • RV fee: Free • No water • Vault toilets • Activities: Fishing • Elevation: 6335

## Black Canyon City

**Table Mesa OHV Little Pan** • Agency: Bureau of Land Management • Tel: 623-580-5500 • Location: 10 miles S of Black Canyon City • GPS: Lat 34.004123 Lon -112.161272 • Open: All year • Total sites: Dispersed • RV sites: Undefined • RV fee: Free • No water • Vault toilets • Activities: Motor sports • Elevation: 1932

**Table Mesa OHV Remote** • Agency: Bureau of Land Management • Tel: 623-580-5500 • Location: 4 miles S of Black Canyon City • GPS: Lat 34.014698 Lon -112.156062 • Open: All year • Total sites: Dispersed • RV sites: Undefined • RV fee: Free • No water • Vault toilets • Activities: Motor sports • Elevation: 2055

## Bowie

**Indian Bread Rocks** • Agency: Bureau of Land Management • Tel: 928-348-4400 • Location: 7 miles S of Bowie (limited services), 31 miles E of Wilcox • GPS: Lat 32.238443 Lon -109.499676 • Open: All year • Total sites: 5 • RV sites: 5 • Max RV Length: 25 • RV fee: Free • No water • Vault toilets • Activities: Hiking • Elevation: 4167

## Brenda

**Ramsey Mine Road** • Agency: Bureau of Land Management • Location: 1 mile W of Brenda (limited services), 14 miles E of Quartzsite • GPS: Lat 33.674656 Lon -113.961122 • Total sites: Dispersed • RV sites: Undefined • RV fee: Free • No water • No toilets • Activities: Hiking • Elevation: 1365

## Carefree

**Bronco Trailhead** (Tonto NF) • Agency: US Forest Service • Tel: 480-595-3300 • Location: 8 miles N of Carefree • GPS: Lat 33.934822 Lon -111.820501 • Open: All year • Total sites: 40 • RV sites: 40 • Max RV Length: 32 • RV fee: Free • No water (water for stock) • Vault toilets • Activities: equestrian area • Elevation: 3707

## Cibola

**Hippie Hole - ASTL** • Agency: State • Tel: 928-857-3568 • Location: 2 miles W of Cibola (limited services), 23 miles S of Ehrenberg • GPS: Lat 33.378496 Lon -114.706148 • Total sites: Dispersed • RV sites: Undefined • RV fee: Free • No water • Vault toilets • Elevation: 229

**S Cibola Lake Road** • Agency: Bureau of Land Management • Location: 2 miles S of Cibola (limited services), 21 miles S of Ehrenberg • GPS: Lat 33.362718 Lon -114.661085 • Open: All year • Total sites: Dispersed • RV sites: Undefined • RV fee: Free • No water • No toilets • Notes: The first 1000' is state trust land requiring a permit so go in a little way to hit BLM property • Elevation: 279

## Colorado City

**Black Mountain Rock Art** • Agency: Bureau of Land Management • Tel: 435-688-3200 • Location: 47 miles W of Colorado City, 9 miles S of St George, UT • GPS: Lat 36.982706 Lon -113.502915 • Open: All year • Total sites: Dispersed • RV sites: Undefined • RV fee: Free • No water • Vault toilets • Activities: Hiking • Elevation: 2897

## Concho

**Concho Lake - AZ Game and Fish** • Agency: State • Location: In Concho (limited services), 26 miles NE of Show Low • GPS: Lat 34.441411 Lon -109.632201 • Total sites: Dispersed • RV sites: Undefined • RV fee: Free • No water • No toilets • Notes: 7 day maximum stay • Activities: Hiking, fishing • Elevation: 6312

## Congress

**Ghost Town Rd** • Agency: Bureau of Land Management • Tel: 623-580-5500 • Location: In Congress (limited services), 17 miles N of Wickenburg • GPS: Lat 34.18882 Lon -112.85422 • Total sites: Dispersed • RV sites: Undefined • RV fee: Free • No water • No toilets • Elevation: 3196

**South of North Ranch** • Agency: Bureau of Land Management • Location: 5 miles S of Congress (limited services), 9 miles N of Wickenburg • GPS: Lat 34.089406 Lon -112.819489 • Total sites: Dispersed • RV sites: Undefined • RV fee: Free • No water • No toilets • Elevation: 2707

## Cordes Lakes

**Agua Fria NM - Badger Spring** • Agency: Bureau of Land Management • Location: 7 miles S of Cordes Lakes • GPS: Lat 34.232655 Lon -112.099418 • Open: All year • Total sites: Dispersed • RV sites: Undefined • RV fee: Free • No water • No toilets • Elevation: 3135

**Crown King Road 1** (Prescott NF) • Agency: Bureau of Land Management • Location: 4 miles W of Cordes Lakes • GPS: Lat 34.296345 Lon -112.142466 • Total sites: Dispersed • RV sites: Undefined • RV fee: Free • No water • No toilets • Elevation: 3805

**Crown King Road Dispersed 2** • Agency: Bureau of Land Management • Location: 4 miles W of Cordes Lakes • GPS: Lat 34.290172 Lon -112.141084 • Total sites: Dispersed • RV sites: Undefined • RV fee: Free • No water • No toilets • Elevation: 3692

**Crown King Road Dispersed 3** • Agency: Bureau of Land Management • Location: 4 miles W of Cordes Lakes • GPS: Lat 34.287353 Lon -112.141197 • Total sites: Dispersed • RV sites: Undefined • RV fee: Free • No water • No toilets • Elevation: 3657

**FSR 259 Dispersed 1** • Agency: Bureau of Land Management • Location: 4 miles W of Cordes Lakes • GPS: Lat 34.294961 Lon -112.139699 • Total sites: Dispersed • RV sites: Undefined • RV fee: Free • No water • No toilets • Elevation: 3926

**FSR 259 Dispersed 2** • Agency: Bureau of Land Management • Location: 4 miles W of Cordes Lakes • GPS: Lat 34.298993 Lon -112.140034 • Total sites: Dispersed • RV sites: Undefined • RV fee: Free • No water • No toilets • Elevation: 3863

**FSR 259 Dispersed 3** • Agency: Bureau of Land Management • Location: 5 miles W of Cordes Lakes • GPS: Lat 34.300554 Lon -112.146756 • Total sites: Dispersed • RV sites: Undefined • RV fee: Free • No water • No toilets • Elevation: 3870

**FSR 259 Dispersed 4** • Agency: Bureau of Land Management • Location: 7 miles W of Cordes Lakes • GPS: Lat 34.290138 Lon -112.175556 • Total sites: Dispersed • RV sites: Undefined • RV fee: Free • No water • No toilets • Elevation: 3947

### Dennehotso

**Round Top Mesa** • Agency: Bureau of Land Management • Location: 6 miles N of Dennehotso (limited services), 32 miles NE of Kayenta • GPS: Lat 36.917778 Lon -109.762615 • Total sites: Dispersed • RV sites: Undefined • RV fee: Free • No water • No toilets • Activities: Hiking, mountain biking, non-power boating, equestrian area • Elevation: 5128

### Desert Hills

**Havasu Heights** • Agency: Bureau of Land Management • Location: 9 miles N of Desert Hills • GPS: Lat 34.664812 Lon -114.308965 • Total sites: Dispersed • RV sites: Undefined • RV fee: Free • No water • No toilets • Elevation: 1402

**Lake Havasu** • Agency: Bureau of Land Management • Location: 8 miles N of Desert Hills • GPS: Lat 34.644835 Lon -114.316253 • Total sites: Dispersed • RV sites: Undefined • RV fee: Free • No toilets • Elevation: 1518

**Lone tree** • Agency: Bureau of Land Management • Location: 8 miles N of Desert Hills • GPS: Lat 34.626704 Lon -114.327325 • Open: All year • Total sites: Dispersed • RV sites: Undefined • RV fee: Free • No water • No toilets • Activities: Motor sports • Elevation: 1379

### Dewey

**Powell Springs** (Prescott NF) • Agency: US Forest Service • Tel: 928-567-4121 • Location: 14 miles NE of Dewey • GPS: Lat 34.578051 Lon -112.068914 • Open: All year • Stay limit: 14 days • Total sites: 11 • RV sites: 11 • Max RV Length: 40 • RV fee: Free • No water • Vault toilets • Elevation: 5331

### Dolan Springs

**Lake Mead NRA - Bonelli Bay** • Agency: National Park Service • Tel: 702-293-8990 • Location: 48 miles N of Dolan Springs (limited services), 43 miles E of Boulder City, NV • GPS: Lat 36.062182 Lon -114.474159 • Total sites: Dispersed • RV sites: Undefined • RV fee: Free • No water • No toilets • Elevation: 1243

**Lake Mead NRA - Bonelli Landing** • Agency: National Park Service • Tel: 702-293-8990 • Location: 48 miles N of Dolan Springs (limited services), 43 miles E of Boulder City, NV • GPS: Lat 36.083538 Lon -114.485144 • Total sites: Dispersed • RV sites: Undefined • RV fee: Free • No water • No toilets • Elevation: 1227

**Lake Mead NRA - Greg's Hideout** • Agency: National Park Service • Tel: 702-293-8990 • Location: 34 miles N of Dolan Springs (limited services), 57 miles N of Kingman • GPS: Lat 36.001272 Lon -114.230704 • Total sites: Dispersed • RV sites: Undefined • RV fee: Free • No water • No toilets • Elevation: 1257

### Eagar

**Carnero Lake - AZ Game and Fish** • Agency: State • Location: 20 miles W of Eagar • GPS: Lat 34.114422 Lon -109.530787 • Total sites: Dispersed • RV sites: Undefined • RV fee: Free • No water • No toilets • Activities: Hiking, fishing • Elevation: 9055

### Ehrenberg

**Ehrenberg Sandbowl** • Agency: Bureau of Land Management • Tel: 928-317-3200 • Location: 2 miles S of Ehrenberg • GPS: Lat 33.590908 Lon -114.522312 • Total sites: Dispersed • RV sites: Undefined • RV fee: Free • No water • Vault toilets • Activities: Motor sports • Elevation: 288

**Ox Bow Road** • Agency: Bureau of Land Management • Location: 4 miles S of Ehrenberg • GPS: Lat 33.570475 Lon -114.532319 • Stay limit: 14 days • Total sites: Dispersed • RV sites: Undefined • RV fee: Free • No water • No toilets • Elevation: 266

**Ox Bow Road** • Agency: Bureau of Land Management • Location: 5 miles S of Ehrenberg • GPS: Lat 33.548048 Lon -114.530443 • Total sites: Dispersed • RV sites: Undefined (numerous spots along Colorado River) • RV fee: Free • No water • No toilets • Elevation: 259

**Ehrenburg-Cibola Road** • Agency: Bureau of Land Management • Location: 3 miles SE of Ehrenburg • GPS: Lat 33.590454 Lon -114.483597 • Total sites: Dispersed • RV sites: Undefined • RV fee: Free • No water • No toilets • Elevation: 485

**Tom Wells Road** • Agency: Bureau of Land Management • Location: 6 miles E of Ehrenburg • GPS: Lat 33.616538 Lon -114.432455 • Open: All year • Total sites: Dispersed • RV sites: Undefined (numerous sites along road) • RV fee: Free • No water • No toilets • Elevation: 648

### Flagstaff

**Freidlein Prairie** (Coconino NF) • Agency: US Forest Service • Tel: 928-526-0866 • Location: 6 miles N of Flagstaff • GPS: Lat 35.282792 Lon -111.718957 • Total sites: 14 • RV sites: 14 • RV fee: Free • No water • No toilets • Activities: Hiking • Elevation: 7552

### Globe

**Jones Water** (Tonto NF) • Agency: US Forest Service • Tel: 928-402-6200 • Location: 17 miles N of Globe • GPS: Lat

33.592046 Lon -110.642811 • Open: All year • Stay limit: 14 days • Total sites: 12 • RV sites: 12 • Max RV Length: 20 • RV fee: Free • No water • Vault toilets • Elevation: 4193

**Lower Pinal** (Tonto NF) • Agency: US Forest Service • Tel: 928-402-6200 • Location: 17 miles S of Globe • GPS: Lat 33.287354 Lon -110.830322 • Open: May-Nov • Stay limit: 14 days • Total sites: 16 • RV sites: 16 • Max RV Length: 20 • RV fee: Free • Central water • Vault toilets • Notes: Narrow winding mountain gravel road • Activities: Hiking • Elevation: 7539

**Pioneer Pass** (Tonto NF) • Agency: US Forest Service • Tel: 928-4-2-6200 • Location: 10 miles S of Globe • GPS: Lat 33.279701 Lon -110.796712 • Open: May-Nov • Stay limit: 14 days • Total sites: 23 • RV sites: 23 • Max RV Length: 18 • RV fee: Free • No water • Vault toilets • Activities: Hiking • Elevation: 5886

**Sulphide Del Ray** (Tonto NF) • Agency: US Forest Service • Tel: 928-402-6200 • Location: 12 miles S of Globe • GPS: Lat 33.292725 Lon -110.86792 • Open: All year • Stay limit: 14 days • Total sites: 10 • RV sites: 10 • Max RV Length: 20 • RV fee: Free • No water • Vault toilets • Elevation: 6024

**Upper Pinal** (Tonto NF) • Agency: US Forest Service • Tel: 928-402-6200 • Location: 17 miles S of Globe • GPS: Lat 33.284227 Lon -110.821267 • Open: May-Nov • Stay limit: 14 days • Total sites: 3 • RV sites: 3 • Max RV Length: 20 • RV fee: Free • Notes: Narrow winding mountain gravel road • Activities: Hiking • Elevation: 7687

## Green Valley

**White House Canyon Road** • Agency: Bureau of Land Management • Location: 8 miles SE of Green Valley • GPS: Lat 31.787596 Lon -110.871729 • Total sites: Dispersed • RV sites: Undefined • RV fee: Free • No water • No toilets • Elevation: 3774

## Heber

**Airplane Flat** (Tonto NF) • Agency: US Forest Service • Tel: 928-462-4300 • Location: 27 miles SW of Heber • GPS: Lat 34.283375 Lon -110.809621 • Open: May-Oct • Stay limit: 14 days • Total sites: 12 • RV sites: 12 • Max RV Length: 16 • RV fee: Free • No water • Vault toilets • Activities: Fishing • Elevation: 6608

**Colcord Ridge** (Tonto NF) • Agency: US Forest Service • Tel: 928-462-4300 • Location: 22 miles NE of Heber • GPS: Lat 34.262172 Lon -110.843822 • Open: May-Oct • Stay limit: 14 days • Total sites: 8 • RV sites: 8 • Max RV Length: 32 • RV fee: Free • No water • Vault toilets • Activities: Motor sports • Elevation: 7615

**Upper Canyon Creek** (Tonto NF) • Agency: US Forest Service • Tel: 928-462-4300 • Location: 28 miles SW of Heber • GPS: Lat 34.288308 Lon -110.803339 • Open: May-Oct • Stay limit: 14 days • Total sites: 10 • RV sites: 10 • Max RV Length: 16 • RV fee: Free • No water • Vault toilets • Activities: Fishing • Elevation: 6591

## Jacob Lake

**Indian Hollow** (Kaibab NF) • Agency: US Forest Service • Tel: 928 643-7395 • Location: 34 miles SW of Jacob Lake (limited services), 54 miles S of Knab, UT • GPS: Lat 36.461789 Lon -112.484467 • Open: All year • Total sites: 3 • RV sites: 3 (not suitable for large RV's) • RV fee: Free • No water • Vault toilets • Activities: Hiking • Elevation: 6332

## Kayenta

**Navajo NM -Sunset View** • Agency: National Park Service • Tel: 928-672-2700 • Location: 28 miles W of Kayenta • GPS: Lat 36.676352 Lon -110.542432 • Open: All year • Total sites: 31 • RV sites: 31 • Max RV Length: 28 • RV fee: Free • Central water • Flush toilets • Notes: No open fires • Activities: Hiking • Elevation: 7306

## Kearny

**Kearny Lake City CG** • Agency: Municipal • Tel: 520-363-5547 • Location: In Kearny • GPS: Lat 33.050795 Lon -110.897913 • Total sites: 12 • RV sites: 12 • RV fee: Free • Central water • Flush toilets • Activities: Hiking • Elevation: 1854

**Mescal Mountain OHV Area** • Agency: State • Location: In Kearny • GPS: Lat 33.062317 Lon -110.896191 • Total sites: Dispersed • RV sites: Undefined • RV fee: Free • No water • No toilets • Activities: Hiking, motor sports • Elevation: 2074

## Kingman

**County Road 193** • Agency: Bureau of Land Management • Location: 15 miles E of Kingman • GPS: Lat 35.148288 Lon -113.810092 • Total sites: Dispersed • RV sites: Undefined • Max RV Length: 20 • RV fee: Free • No water • No toilets • Activities: Hiking, mountain biking, motor sports • Elevation: 4659

## Lake Havasu City

**Standard Wash Dispersed 1** • Agency: Bureau of Land Management • Location: 5 miles SE of Lake Havasu City • GPS: Lat 34.419622 Lon -114.198854 • Open: All year • Total sites: Dispersed • RV sites: Undefined • RV fee: Free • No water • No toilets • Elevation: 1063

**Standard Wash Dispersed 2** • Agency: Bureau of Land Management • Location: 3 miles E of Lake Havasu City • GPS: Lat 34.437556 Lon -114.215621 • Open: All year • Total sites: Dispersed • RV sites: Undefined • RV fee: Free • No water • No toilets • Elevation: 1212

## Lakeside

**Los Burros** (Apache-Sitgreaves NF) • Agency: US Forest Service • Tel: 928-368-2100 • Location: 13 miles E of Lakeside • GPS: Lat 34.140878 Lon -109.777324 • Open: May-Oct • Stay limit: 14 days • Total sites: 10 • RV sites: 10 • Max RV Length: 22 • RV fee: Free • No water • Vault toilets • Elevation: 7890

**Scott Reservoir** (Apache-Sitgreaves NF) • Agency: US Forest Service • Tel: 928-368-2100 • Location: In Lakeside • GPS: Lat 34.176715 Lon -109.961051 • Open: Apr-Oct • Stay limit: 5 days • Total sites: 12 • RV sites: 12 • RV fee: Free • No water • Vault toilets • Activities: Fishing • Elevation: 6742

## McNeal

**Whitewater Draw** • Agency: Bureau of Land Management • Location: 5 miles SW of McNeal (limited services), 20 miles NE of Bisbee • GPS: Lat 31.560721 Lon -109.718967 • Stay limit: 3 days • Total sites: Dispersed • RV sites: Undefined • RV fee: Free • No water • Vault toilets • Elevation: 4078

## Meadview

**Lake Mead NRA - Pearce Ferry** • Agency: National Park Service • Tel: 702-293-8990 • Location: 12 miles N of Meadview (limited services), 65 miles N of Kingman • GPS: Lat 36.116231 Lon -114.001611 • Total sites: Dispersed • RV sites: Undefined • RV fee: Free • No water • No toilets • Elevation: 1220

## Morenci

**Granville** (Apache-Sitgreaves NF) • Agency: US Forest Service • Tel: 928-687-8600 • Location: 15 miles N of Morenci • GPS: Lat 33.188315 Lon -109.383288 • Open: Apr-Nov • Stay limit: 14 days • Total sites: 11 • RV sites: 11 • Max RV Length: 16 • RV fee: Free • Central water • Vault toilets • Elevation: 6713

**Honeymoon** (Apache-Sitgreaves NF) • Agency: US Forest Service • Tel: 928-687-8600 • Location: 46 miles N of Morenci • GPS: Lat 33.475351 Lon -109.481205 • Open: All year • Stay limit: 14 days • Total sites: 4 • RV sites: 4 • Max RV Length: 16 • RV fee: Free • No water • Vault toilets • Activities: Fishing • Elevation: 5456

**Lower Juan Miller** (Apache-Sitgreaves NF) • Agency: US Forest Service • Tel: 928-687-8600 • Location: 26 miles N of Morenci • GPS: Lat 33.267362 Lon -109.340611 • Open: All year • Stay limit: 14 days • Total sites: 4 • RV sites: 4 • Max RV Length: 16 • RV fee: Free • No water • Vault toilets • Activities: Motor sports • Elevation: 5718

## New River

**North Little Grand Canyon Rd Site 1** • Agency: Bureau of Land Management • Location: 8 miles N of New River • GPS: Lat 33.989558 Lon -112.174003 • Total sites: Dispersed • RV sites: Undefined • RV fee: Free • No water • No toilets • Activities: Hiking • Elevation: 1886

**North Little Grand Canyon Rd Site 2** • Agency: Bureau of Land Management • Location: 8 miles N of New River • GPS: Lat 33.988202 Lon -112.170237 • Total sites: Dispersed • RV sites: Undefined • RV fee: Free • No water • No toilets • Activities: Hiking • Elevation: 1916

## Oatman

**Oatman-Topock Road Site 5** • Agency: Bureau of Land Management • Location: 10 miles S of Oatman • GPS: Lat 34.900895 Lon -114.427191 • Total sites: Dispersed • RV sites: Undefined • RV fee: Free • No water • No toilets • Elevation: 1300

**Oatman-Topock Road Site 6** • Agency: Bureau of Land Management • Location: 8 miles S of Oatman • GPS: Lat 34.927636 Lon -114.424609 • Total sites: Dispersed • RV sites: Undefined • RV fee: Free • No water • No toilets • Elevation: 1426

**Oatman-Topock Road Site 7** • Agency: Bureau of Land Management • Location: 8 miles S of Oatman • GPS: Lat 34.936917 Lon -114.419908 • Total sites: Dispersed • RV sites: Undefined • RV fee: Free • No water • No toilets • Elevation: 1498

**Oatman-Topock Road Site 8** • Agency: Bureau of Land Management • Location: 6 miles S of Oatman • GPS: Lat 34.953697 Lon -114.409448 • Total sites: Dispersed • RV sites: Undefined • RV fee: Free • No water • No toilets • Elevation: 1799

## Page

**Glen Canyon NRA - Beehive** • Agency: National Park Service • Tel: 928-645-1059 • Location: 3 miles W of Page • GPS: Lat 36.936028 Lon -111.503523 • Open: All year • Total sites: Dispersed • RV sites: Undefined • RV fee: Free • No water • No toilets • Elevation: 3938

**Slickrock Corral** • Agency: National Park Service • Location: 10 miles NW of Page • GPS: Lat 36.994208 Lon -111.600989 • Open: All year • Total sites: Dispersed • RV sites: Undefined • RV fee: Free • No water • No toilets • Activities: Hiking, motor sports • Elevation: 4191

## Parker

**Gibraltar Mountain** • Agency: Bureau of Land Management • Location: 16 miles E of Parker • GPS: Lat 34.121305 Lon -114.061893 • Total sites: Dispersed • RV sites: Undefined • RV fee: Free • No water • No toilets • Elevation: 1043

**Shea Road Dispersed 1** • Agency: Bureau of Land Management • Location: 7 miles E of Parker • GPS: Lat 34.146957 Lon -114.194157 • Total sites: Dispersed • RV sites: Undefined • RV fee: Free • No water • No toilets • Activities: Hiking • Elevation: 587

**Shea Road Dispersed 2** • Agency: Bureau of Land Management • Location: 10 miles E of Parker • GPS: Lat 34.123806 Lon -114.153406 • Total sites: Dispersed • RV sites: Undefined • RV fee: Free • No water • No toilets • Elevation: 768

## Pima

**Red Knolls Amphitheater** • Agency: Bureau of Land Management • Location: 8 miles NW of Pima (limited services), 13 miles NW of Safford • GPS: Lat 32.961665 Lon -109.939325 • Total sites: Dispersed • RV sites: Undefined • RV fee: Free • No water • No toilets • Activities: Motor sports • Elevation: 2797

## Pine

**Clint's Well** (Coconino NF) • Agency: US Forest Service • Tel: 928-477-2255 • Location: 22 miles NE of Pine • GPS: Lat 34.554162 Lon -111.311846 • Open: All year • Total sites: 7 • RV sites: 7 • Max RV Length: 22 • RV fee: Free • No water • Vault toilets • Activities: Hiking • Elevation: 6900

**Kehl Springs Camp** (Coconino NF) • Agency: US Forest Service • Tel: 928-477-2255 • Location: 19 miles E of Pine • GPS: Lat 34.435053 Lon -111.317574 • Open: All year • Total sites: 8 • RV sites: 8 • Max RV Length: 22 • RV fee: Free • No water • Vault toilets • Activities: Hiking • Elevation: 7477

## Quartzite

**Dome Rock** • Agency: Bureau of Land Management • Location: 5 miles W of Quartzite • GPS: Lat 33.642022 Lon -114.313832 • Total sites: Dispersed • RV sites: Undefined • RV fee: Free • No toilets • Elevation: 1161

**Dome Rock Mountain** • Agency: Bureau of Land Management • Tel: 928-317-3250 • Location: 3 miles W of Quartzite • GPS: Lat 33.648725 Lon -114.279206 • Stay limit: 14 days • Total sites: Dispersed • RV sites: Undefined • RV fee: Free • No water • No toilets • Activities: Motor sports • Elevation: 1025

**Gold Nugget Road** • Agency: Bureau of Land Management • Location: 7 miles E of Quartzite • GPS: Lat 33.675482 Lon -114.078084 • Total sites: Dispersed • RV sites: Undefined • RV fee: Free • No toilets • Elevation: 1503

**Road Runner** • Agency: Bureau of Land Management • Tel: 928-317-3200 • Location: 6 miles S of Quartzite • GPS: Lat 33.581503 Lon -114.227473 • Stay limit: 14 days • Total sites: Dispersed • RV sites: Undefined • RV fee: Free • No water • No toilets • Elevation: 1058

## Red Rock

**Ironwood Forest NM** • Agency: Bureau of Land Management • Location: 10 miles SW of Red Rock (limited services), 33 miles NW of Tucson • GPS: Lat 32.496937 Lon -111.498826 • Total sites: Dispersed • RV sites: Undefined • RV fee: Free • No water • No toilets • Elevation: 2064

## Safford

**Clark Creek Corrals Horse Camp** (Coronado NF) • Agency: US Forest Service • Tel: 928-428-4150 • Location: 36 miles SW of Safford • GPS: Lat 32.717116 Lon -109.977026 • Open: Apr-Nov • Total sites: 2 • RV sites: 2 • Max RV Length: 22 • RV fee: Free • No water • Activities: Equestrian area • Elevation: 8901

**Hackel Road** • Agency: Bureau of Land Management • Location: 10 miles SE of Safford • GPS: Lat 32.778655 Lon -109.572236 • Total sites: Dispersed • RV sites: Undefined • RV fee: Free • No water • No toilets • Elevation: 3178

**Hackle Road** • Agency: Bureau of Land Management • Tel: 928-348-4400 • Location: 9 miles SE of Safford • GPS: Lat 32.782233 Lon -109.605522 • Total sites: Dispersed • RV sites: Undefined • RV fee: Free • No water • No toilets • Elevation: 3054

**Stockton Pass** (Coronado NF) • Agency: US Forest Service • Tel: 928-428-4150 • Location: 27 miles SW of Safford • GPS: Lat 32.591697 Lon -109.850151 • Open: All year • Stay limit: 14 days • Total sites: 7 • RV sites: 7 • Max RV Length: 22 • RV fee: Free • No water • Vault toilets • Elevation: 5705

## Salome

**Vicksburg** • Agency: Bureau of Land Management • Location: 11 miles W of Salome (limited services), 28 miles E of

Quartzsite • GPS: Lat 33.749361 Lon -113.739943 • Open: All year • Total sites: Dispersed • RV sites: Undefined • RV fee: Free • No water • No toilets • Elevation: 1447

## Second Mesa

**Hopi Cultural Center** • Agency: Indian Reservation • Tel: 928-734-6650 • Location: 5 miles N of Second Mesa (limited services), 65 miles N of Winslow • GPS: Lat 35.843448 Lon -110.528251 • Total sites: Dispersed • RV sites: Undefined • RV fee: Free • No water • No toilets • Elevation: 6316

## Seligman

**Historic Route 66** (Chicken Fry) • Agency: State • Location: 11 miles E of Seligman • GPS: Lat 35.278611 Lon -112.693178 • Total sites: Dispersed • RV sites: Undefined • RV fee: Free • No water • No toilets • Elevation: 5619

## Sonoita

**Gardner Canyon** (Coronado NF) • Agency: US Forest Service • Location: 5 miles N of Sonoita • GPS: Lat 31.734566 Lon -110.677012 • Open: All year • Total sites: Dispersed • RV sites: Undefined • RV fee: Free • No water • No toilets • Elevation: 4744

**Las Cienegas NCA - Cieneguita** • Agency: Bureau of Land Management • Location: 11 miles N of Sonoita • GPS: Lat 31.766666 Lon -110.627132 • Open: All year • Total sites: Dispersed • RV sites: Undefined (several spots along the road) • RV fee: Free • No water • No toilets • Elevation: 4607

**Las Cienegas NCA - Road Canyon** • Agency: Bureau of Land Management • Tel: 520-439-6400 • Location: 7 miles NE of Sonoita • GPS: Lat 31.739234 Lon -110.585718 • Open: Jul-Mar • Total sites: 6 • RV sites: 6 • RV fee: Free • No water • No toilets • Activities: Hiking, mountain biking • Elevation: 4578

## Stanfield

**Vekol Valley** • Agency: Bureau of Land Management • Location: 20 miles W of Stanfield (limited services), 26 miles SW of Maricopa • GPS: Lat 32.806601 Lon -112.253108 • Total sites: Dispersed • RV sites: Undefined • RV fee: Free • No water • No toilets • Elevation: 1814

## Sunsites

**Sycamore** (Coronado NF) • Agency: US Forest Service • Tel: 520-364-3468 • Location: 32 miles E of Sunsites (limited services), 52 miles SE of Wilcox • GPS: Lat 31.859799 Lon -109.334303 • Open: All year • Stay limit: 14 days • Total sites: 7 • RV sites: 7 • Max RV Length: 16 • RV fee: Free • No water • Vault toilets • Activities: Hiking • Elevation: 6355

## Superior

**Oak Flat** (Tonto NF) • Agency: US Forest Service • Tel: 928-402-6200 • Location: 4 miles E of Superior • GPS: Lat 33.307879 Lon -111.050359 • Open: All year • Stay limit: 14 days • Total sites: 16 • RV sites: 16 • Max RV Length: 30 • RV fee: Free • Vault toilets • Elevation: 3934

## Three Way

**Blackjack** (Apache-Sitgreaves NF) • Agency: US Forest Service • Tel: 928-687-8600 • Location: 14 miles NE of Three Way (limited services), 45 miles NE of Safford • GPS: Lat 33.056422 Lon -109.080427 • Open: All year • Stay limit: 14 days • Total sites: 10 • RV sites: 10 • RV fee: Free • No water • Vault toilets • Elevation: 6276

**Coal Creek** (Apache-Sitgreaves NF) • Agency: US Forest Service • Tel: 928-687-8600 • Location: 18 miles NE of Three Way (limited services), 50 miles NE of Safford • GPS: Lat 33.103033 Lon -109.060386 • Open: All year • Stay limit: 14 days • Total sites: 5 • RV sites: 5 • Max RV Length: 16 • RV fee: Free • No water • Vault toilets • Elevation: 5814

## Tonopah

**Saddle Mountain** • Agency: Bureau of Land Management • Tel: 623-580-5500 • Location: 11 miles SW of Tonopah (limited services), 47 miles W of Phoenix • GPS: Lat 33.447899 Lon -113.046571 • Total sites: Dispersed • RV sites: Undefined • RV fee: Free • No water • No toilets • Activities: Hiking • Elevation: 1387

**Saddle Mountain** • Agency: Bureau of Land Management • Location: 10 miles SW of Tonopah (limited services), 47 miles W of Phoenix • GPS: Lat 33.451081 Lon -113.036827 • Open: All year • Total sites: Dispersed • RV sites: Undefined • RV fee: Free • No water • No toilets • Elevation: 1433

## Topock

**Needle Mountain Road** • Agency: Bureau of Land Management • Location: 7 miles S of Topock (limited services), 21 miles N of Lake Havasu City • GPS: Lat 34.714164 Lon -114.435406 • Total sites: Dispersed • RV sites: Undefined • RV fee: Free • No water • No toilets • Elevation: 830

**Oatman-Topock Road Site 1** • Agency: Bureau of Land Management • Location: 3 miles N of Topock (limited services), 15 miles E of Needles, CA • GPS: Lat 34.816031 Lon -114.467838 • Total sites: Dispersed • RV sites: Undefined • RV fee: Free • No water • No toilets • Elevation: 722

**Oatman-Topock Road Site 2** • Agency: Bureau of Land Management • Location: 4 miles N of Topock (limited services), 16 miles E of Needles, CA • GPS: Lat 34.824316 Lon -114.466454 • Total sites: Dispersed • RV sites: Undefined • RV fee: Free • No water • No toilets • Elevation: 756

**Oatman-Topock Road Site 3** • Agency: Bureau of Land Management • Location: 4 miles N of Topock (limited services), 16 miles E of Needles, CA • GPS: Lat 34.834032 Lon -114.462687 • Total sites: Dispersed • RV sites: Undefined • RV fee: Free • No water • No toilets • Elevation: 817

**Oatman-Topock Road Site 4** • Agency: Bureau of Land Management • Location: 6 miles N of Topock (limited services), 18 miles E of Needles, CA • GPS: Lat 34.855483 Lon -114.449305 • Total sites: Dispersed • RV sites: Undefined • RV fee: Free • No water • No toilets • Elevation: 977

## Tucson

**Snyder Hill** • Agency: Bureau of Land Management • Location: 7 miles W of Tucson • GPS: Lat 32.158031 Lon -111.115385 • Open: All year • Stay limit: 14 days • Total sites: Dispersed • RV sites: Undefined • RV fee: Free • No water • No toilets • Elevation: 2493

**West Mile Wide Road** • Agency: Bureau of Land Management • Location: 15 miles W of Tucson • GPS: Lat 32.248436 Lon -111.275578 • Total sites: Dispersed • RV sites: Undefined • RV fee: Free • No water • No toilets • Elevation: 2218

## Why

**Gunsite Wash** • Agency: Bureau of Land Management • Tel: 623-580-5500 • Location: 2 miles S of Why (limited services), 13 miles S of Ajo • GPS: Lat 32.238056 Lon -112.751393 • Total sites: Dispersed • RV sites: Undefined • RV fee: Free • No water • No toilets • Elevation: 1801

**Wild Woman** • Agency: Bureau of Land Management • Location: 3 miles SW of Why (limited services), 14 miles S of Ajo • GPS: Lat 32.241228 Lon -112.765296 • Total sites: Dispersed • RV sites: Undefined • RV fee: Free • No water • No toilets • Activities: Hiking • Elevation: 1764

## Wickenburg

**Vulture Mine Road** • Agency: Bureau of Land Management • Tel: 623-580-5500 • Location: 7 miles S of Wickenburg • GPS: Lat 33.88118 Lon -112.821226 • Total sites: Dispersed • RV sites: Undefined • RV fee: Free • No water • No toilets • Elevation: 2543

## Wikieup

**17 Mile Road** • Agency: Bureau of Land Management • Location: 18 miles SE of Wikieup (limited services), 54 miles NW of Wickenburg • GPS: Lat 34.505972 Lon -113.414432 • Total sites: Dispersed • RV sites: Undefined • RV fee: Free • No water • No toilets • Elevation: 2240

## Winslow

**McHood** • Agency: County • Tel: 928-289-4792 • Location: 6 miles SE of Winslow • GPS: Lat 34.972074 Lon -110.642898 • Open: All year • Stay limit: 14 days • Total sites: 12 • RV sites: 12 • Max RV Length: 40+ • RV fee: Free • Central water • Vault toilets (bathroom closed in winter) • Activities: Fishing, swimming, non-power boating • Elevation: 4889

## Wittmann

**Boulders OHV** • Agency: Bureau of Land Management • Location: 11 miles NE of Wittmann (limited services), 20 miles N of Surprise • GPS: Lat 33.843795 Lon -112.441924 • Open: All year • Total sites: Dispersed • RV sites: Undefined • RV fee: Free • No water • Vault toilets • Activities: Motor sports • Elevation: 2022

## Young

**Alderwood** (Tonto NF) • Agency: US Forest Service • Tel: 480-595-3300 • Location: 12 miles N of Young (limited services), 34 miles E of Payson • GPS: Lat 34.205825 Lon -110.980587 • Open: All year • Stay limit: 14 days • Total sites: 5 • RV sites: 5 • Max RV Length: 16 • RV fee: Free • No water • Vault toilets • Notes: Inaccessible during/after inclement weather • Activities: Hiking, mountain biking, fishing, swimming • Elevation: 5243

**Rose Creek** (Tonto NF) • Agency: US Forest Service • Tel: 928-462-4300 • Location: 23 miles S of Young (limited services), 38 miles N of Claypool • GPS: Lat 33.829667 Lon -110.979623 • Open: May-Oct • Stay limit: 14 days • Total sites: 5 • RV sites: 5 • Max RV Length: 16 • RV fee: Free • No water • Vault toilets • Activities: Hiking • Elevation: 5472

**Sawmill Flats** (Tonto NF) • Agency: US Forest Service • Tel: 928-462-4300 • Location: 24 miles S of Young (limited services), 38 miles N of Claypool • GPS: Lat 33.813672 Lon -110.983472 • Open: May-Oct • Stay limit: 14 days • Total sites: 5 • RV sites: 5 • Max RV Length: 16 • RV fee: Free • Vault toilets • Elevation: 5817

**Valentine Ridge** (Tonto NF) • Agency: US Forest Service • Tel: 928-462-4300 • Location: 21 miles N of Young (limited services), 35 miles E of Payson • GPS: Lat 34.244005 Lon -110.798245 • Open: May-Oct • Stay limit: 14 days • Total sites: 10 • RV sites: 10 • Max RV Length: 16 • RV fee: Free • No water • Vault toilets • Activities: Mountain biking, fishing • Elevation: 6647

## Yuma

**Fortuna Pond** • Agency: Bureau of Land Management • Tel: 928-317-3200 • Location: 8 miles E of Yuma • GPS: Lat 32.724183 Lon -114.453452 • Open: All year • Stay limit: 14 days • Total sites: Dispersed • RV sites: Undefined • RV fee: Free • No water • No toilets • Activities: Fishing • Elevation: 138

**Mittry Lake WA** • Agency: Bureau of Land Management • Tel: 928-317-3200 • Location: 10 miles N of Yuma • GPS: Lat 32.817314 Lon -114.472315 • Total sites: Dispersed • RV sites: Undefined • RV fee: Free • No water • Vault toilets • Elevation: 158

**Yuma VFW** • Agency: Bureau of Land Management • Tel: 928-317-3200 • Location: 6 miles E of Yuma • GPS: Lat 32.72845 Lon -114.42334 • Open: All year • Total sites: 150 • RV sites: 150 • RV fee: Free • No water • No toilets • Notes: Near RR tracks • Elevation: 171

# California

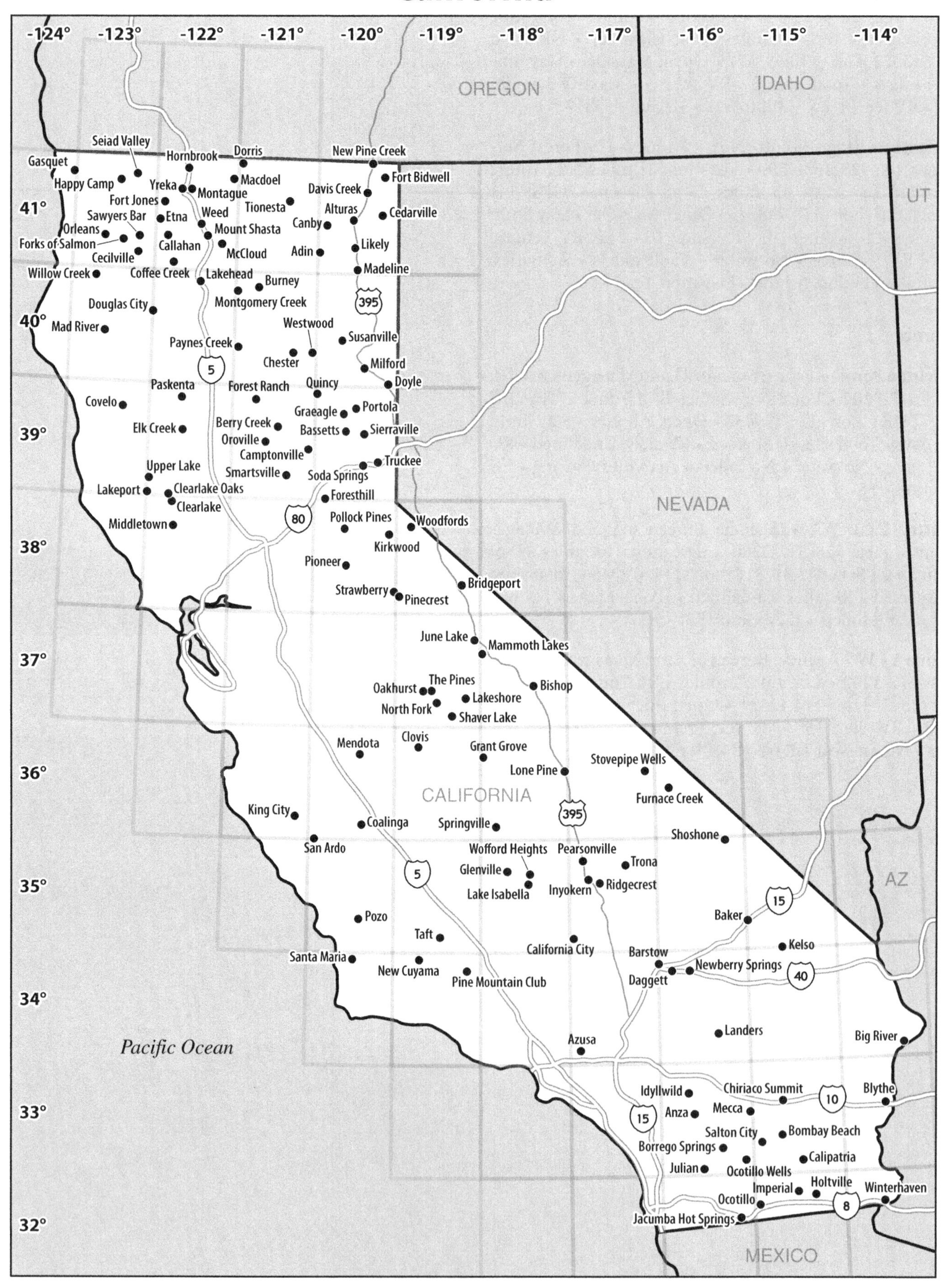

-124° -123° -122° -121° -120° -119° -118° -117° -116° -115° -114°
41° 40° 39° 38° 37° 36° 35° 34° 33° 32°
OREGON
IDAHO
UT
NEVADA
AZ
MEXICO
CALIFORNIA
Pacific Ocean
Seiad Valley
Gasquet
Hornbrook
Dorris
New Pine Creek
Happy Camp
Yreka
Montague
Macdoel
Davis Creek
Fort Bidwell
Fort Jones
Tionesta
Alturas
Cedarville
Sawyers Bar
Etna
Weed
Canby
Orleans
Mount Shasta
Forks of Salmon
Callahan
McCloud
Adin
Likely
Cecilville
Willow Creek
Coffee Creek
Lakehead
Madeline
Burney
Montgomery Creek
Douglas City
Mad River
Westwood
Susanville
Paynes Creek
Chester
Milford
Paskenta
Forest Ranch
Quincy
Doyle
Covelo
Graeagle
Portola
Berry Creek
Bassetts
Sierraville
Elk Creek
Oroville
Camptonville
Truckee
Upper Lake
Smartsville
Soda Springs
Lakeport
Clearlake Oaks
Foresthill
Clearlake
Pollock Pines
Woodfords
Middletown
Kirkwood
Pioneer
Strawberry
Bridgeport
Pinecrest
June Lake
Mammoth Lakes
The Pines
Bishop
Oakhurst
Lakeshore
North Fork
Shaver Lake
Clovis
Mendota
Grant Grove
Stovepipe Wells
Lone Pine
Furnace Creek
King City
Coalinga
Springville
Shoshone
San Ardo
Wofford Heights
Pearsonville
Trona
Glenville
Ridgecrest
Lake Isabella
Inyokern
Baker
Pozo
Taft
Kelso
California City
Santa Maria
Barstow
New Cuyama
Newberry Springs
Pine Mountain Club
Daggett
Landers
Big River
Azusa
Idyllwild
Chiriaco Summit
Blythe
Anza
Mecca
Salton City
Bombay Beach
Borrego Springs
Calipatria
Julian
Ocotillo Wells
Holtville
Imperial
Winterhaven
Ocotillo
Jacumba Hot Springs
5
395
80
15
40
10
8

# California — Camping Areas

| Abbreviation | Description |
| --- | --- |
| CDFW | California Department of Fish and Wildlife |
| CG | Campground |
| DSF | Demonstration State Forest |
| LTVA | Long Term Visitors Area |
| NF | National Forest |
| NM | National Monument |
| NNL | National Natural Location |
| NP | National Park |
| OHV | Off-Highway Vehicle |
| OHVA | Off-Highway Vehicle Area |
| RA | Recreation Area |
| SP | State Park |
| SVRA | State Vehicular Recreation Area |
| SWA | State Wildlife Area |

## Adin

**Ash Creek** (Modoc NF) • Agency: US Forest Service • Tel: 530-299-3215 • Location: 8 miles E of Adin (limited services), 45 miles SE of Alturas • GPS: Lat 41.160959 Lon -120.828823 • Open: All year • Stay limit: 14 days • Total sites: 5 • RV sites: 5 • Max RV Length: 22 • RV fee: Free • No water • Vault toilets • Notes: Rough road • Activities: Fishing • Elevation: 4895

**Lava Camp** (Modoc NF) • Agency: US Forest Service • Tel: 530-299-3215 • Location: 35 miles NW of Adin (limited services), 52 miles W of Alturas • GPS: Lat 41.402091 Lon -121.338554 • Open: May-Oct • Stay limit: 14 days • Total sites: 12 • RV sites: 12 • Max RV Length: 32 • RV fee: Free • Central water • Vault toilets • Activities: Hunting • Elevation: 4426

**Lower Rush Creek** (Modoc NF) • Agency: US Forest Service • Tel: 530-299-3215 • Location: 8 miles N of Adin (limited services), 32 miles SW of Alturas • GPS: Lat 41.292655 Lon -120.878836 • Open: All year • Stay limit: 14 days • Total sites: 10 • RV sites: 5 • Max RV Length: 22 • RV fee: Free • No water • Vault toilets • Activities: Fishing • Elevation: 4751

**Red Tail Rim South Trailhead** (Modoc NF) • Agency: US Forest Service • Tel: 530-233-5811 • Location: 9 miles E of Adin (limited services), 47 miles SW of Alturas • GPS: Lat 41.167513 Lon -120.829682 • Open: Jun-Oct • Stay limit: 14 days • Total sites: 6 • RV sites: 6 • RV fee: Free • No water • Vault toilets • Activities: Hiking • Elevation: 4938

## Alturas

**Big Sage** (Modoc NF) • Agency: US Forest Service • Tel: 530-233-5811 • Location: 12 miles N of Alturas • GPS: Lat 41.579841 Lon -120.629174 • Open: May-Oct • Stay limit: 14 days • Total sites: 11 • RV sites: 11 • Max RV Length: 22 • RV fee: Free • No water • Vault toilets • Activities: Fishing, power boating, hunting, non-power boating • Elevation: 4905

**Janes Reservoir** (Modoc NF) • Agency: US Forest Service • Tel: 530-233-5811 • Location: 33 miles N of Alturas • GPS: Lat 41.88 Lon -120.764 • Open: May-Oct • Stay limit: 14 days • Total sites: 8 • RV sites: 8 • Max RV Length: 22 • RV fee: Free • No water • Vault toilets • Activities: Fishing • Elevation: 5121

**Lassen Creek** (Modoc NF) • Agency: US Forest Service • Tel: 530-279-6116 • Location: 36 miles N of Alturas • GPS: Lat 41.826733 Lon -120.296228 • Open: May-Oct • Stay limit: 14 days • Total sites: 4 • RV sites: 4 • RV fee: Free • No water • Vault toilets • Activities: Hiking • Elevation: 5463

**Reservoir C** (Modoc NF) • Agency: US Forest Service • Tel: 530-233-5811 • Location: 19 miles NW of Alturas • GPS: Lat 41.660135 Lon -120.775258 • Open: May-Oct • Stay limit: 14 days • Total sites: 11 • RV sites: 11 • Max RV Length: 22 • RV fee: Free • No water • Vault toilets • Activities: Fishing, power boating, non-power boating • Elevation: 4954

## Anza

**Tool Box Springs** (San Bernardino NF) • Agency: US Forest Service • Location: 15 miles N of Anza (limited services), 31 miles W of Palm Desert • GPS: Lat 33.611682 Lon -116.661558 • Open: All year • Total sites: 6 • RV sites: 6 • RV fee: Free • No water • Vault toilets • Elevation: 6122

**Snowslide Canyon** (Angeles NF) • Agency: US Forest Service • Location: 24 miles N of Azusa • GPS: Lat 34.325396 Lon -117.837086 • Stay limit: 14 days • Total sites: 20 • RV sites: 20 • RV fee: Free • No water • Vault toilets • Elevation: 5693

## Baker

**Hollow Hills** • Agency: Bureau of Land Management • Tel: 760-252-6000 • Location: 13 miles N of Baker • GPS: Lat 35.410324 Lon -116.061485 • Total sites: Dispersed • RV sites: Undefined • RV fee: Free • No water • No toilets • Activities: Hiking, hunting, equestrian area • Elevation: 1825

**Mojave National Preserve - Cross on the Rock** • Agency: National Park Service • Location: 35 miles E of Baker • GPS:

Lat 35.315198 Lon -115.550823 • Total sites: 2 • RV sites: Undefined • RV fee: Free • No water • No toilets • Elevation: 5035

## Barstow

**Black Mountain Wilderness - Black Canyon** • Agency: Bureau of Land Management • Tel: 760-252-6000 • Location: 27 miles NW of Barstow • GPS: Lat 35.141115 Lon -117.261162 • Total sites: Dispersed • RV sites: Undefined • RV fee: Free • No water • No toilets • Activities: Hiking • Elevation: 2609

**Black Mountain Wilderness - Opal** • Agency: Bureau of Land Management • Tel: 760-252-6000 • Location: 29 miles NW of Barstow • GPS: Lat 35.156385 Lon -117.182037 • Total sites: Dispersed • RV sites: Undefined • RV fee: Free • No water • No toilets • Activities: Hiking • Elevation: 3339

**Sawtooth Canyon** • Agency: Bureau of Land Management • Tel: 760-252-6000 • Location: 15 miles S of Barstow • GPS: Lat 34.670249 Lon -116.983713 • Open: All year • Total sites: 13 • RV sites: 13 • RV fee: Free • No water • Vault toilets • Activities: Hiking, rock climbing • Elevation: 3607

**Sawtooth Canyon** • Agency: Bureau of Land Management • Tel: 760-252-6000 • Location: 15 miles S of Barstow • GPS: Lat 34.671541 Lon -116.990266 • Total sites: Dispersed • RV sites: Undefined • RV fee: Free • No water • No toilets • Activities: Hiking • Elevation: 3635

**Stoddard Valley OHV** • Agency: Bureau of Land Management • Tel: 760-252-6000 • Location: 6 miles S of Barstow • GPS: Lat 34.812727 Lon -117.083377 • Stay limit: 14 days • Total sites: Dispersed • RV sites: Undefined • RV fee: Free • No water • No toilets • Activities: Motor sports • Elevation: 2615

## Bassetts

**Snag Lake** (Tahoe NF) • Agency: US Forest Service • Tel: 530-265-4531 • Location: 5 miles N of Bassetts (limited services), 11 miles S of Graeagle • GPS: Lat 39.670795 Lon -120.626904 • Open: May-Sep • Total sites: 12 • RV sites: 12 • RV fee: Free • No water • Vault toilets • Activities: Fishing, non-power boating • Elevation: 6713

## Berry Creek

**Little North Fork** (Plumas NF) • Agency: US Forest Service • Tel: 530-534-6500 • Location: 16 miles NE of Berry Creek (limited services), 29 miles NE of Oroville • GPS: Lat 39.782 Lon -121.26 • Stay limit: 14 days • Total sites: 6 • RV sites: 6 • RV fee: Free • Central water • Vault toilets • Activities: Fishing, motor sports • Elevation: 4032

**Rogers Cow Camp** (Plumas NF) • Agency: US Forest Service • Tel: 530-534-6500 • Location: 13 miles NE of Berry Creek (limited services), 26 miles NE of Oroville • GPS: Lat 39.766905 Lon -121.312547 • Open: All year • Total sites: 6 • RV sites: 6 • RV fee: Free • Central water • Vault toilets • Activities: Mountain biking, motor sports • Elevation: 4131

## Big River

**Blue Cloud** • Agency: Bureau of Land Management • Tel: 760-326-7000 • Location: 3 miles N of Big River (limited services), 4 miles W of Parker, AZ • GPS: Lat 34.166516 Lon -114.371843 • Total sites: Dispersed • RV sites: Undefined • RV fee: Free • No water • No toilets • Elevation: 643

**Earp 2 Dispersed** • Agency: Bureau of Land Management • Location: 4 miles N of Big River (limited services), 6 miles W of Parker, AZ • GPS: Lat 34.177372 Lon -114.391191 • Total sites: Dispersed • RV sites: Undefined • RV fee: Free • No water • No toilets • Elevation: 751

**Earp 3 Dispersed** • Agency: Bureau of Land Management • Location: 5 miles N of Big River (limited services), 7 miles W of Parker, AZ • GPS: Lat 34.187875 Lon -114.40348 • Total sites: Dispersed • RV sites: Undefined • RV fee: Free • No water • No toilets • Elevation: 820

## Bishop

**Volcanic Tablelands 1** • Agency: Bureau of Land Management • Location: 4 miles N of Bishop • GPS: Lat 37.423267 Lon -118.416778 • Total sites: Dispersed • RV sites: Undefined • RV fee: Free • No water • No toilets • Elevation: 4363

**Volcanic Tablelands 2** • Agency: Bureau of Land Management • Location: 5 miles NW of Bishop • GPS: Lat 37.426543 Lon -118.421493 • Total sites: Dispersed • RV sites: Undefined • RV fee: Free • No water • No toilets • Elevation: 4406

**Volcanic Tablelands 3** • Agency: Bureau of Land Management • Location: 5 miles NW of Bishop • GPS: Lat 37.430723 Lon -118.423212 • Total sites: Dispersed • RV sites: Undefined • RV fee: Free • No water • No toilets • Elevation: 4465

**Volcanic Tablelands 4** • Agency: Bureau of Land Management • Location: 6 miles NW of Bishop • GPS: Lat 37.437751 Lon -118.430211 • Total sites: Dispersed • RV sites: Undefined • RV fee: Free • No water • No toilets • Elevation: 4468

## Blythe

**Blythe-Vidal** • Agency: Bureau of Land Management • Tel: 760-326-7000 • Location: 24 miles N of Blythe • GPS: Lat 33.929058 Lon -114.541758 • Total sites: Dispersed • RV sites: Undefined • RV fee: Free • No water • No toilets • Elevation: 409

**Horace Miller** • Agency: County • Tel: 760-921-7900 • Location: 18 miles S of Blythe • GPS: Lat 33.433821 Lon -114.627921 • Open: All year • Total sites: Dispersed • RV sites: Undefined • RV fee: Free • No water • No toilets • Activities: Fishing • Elevation: 233

**Miller Park** • Agency: County • Location: 18 miles S of Blythe • GPS: Lat 33.434829 Lon -114.627461 • Total sites: 5 • RV sites: 5 • RV fee: Free • No water • No toilets • Activities: Fishing, non-power boating • Elevation: 233

## Bombay Beach

**Niland Boat Ramp** • Agency: County • Location: 8 miles E of Bombay Beach (limited services), 20 miles NW of Calipatria • GPS: Lat 33.340596 Lon -115.663542 • Total sites: Dispersed • RV sites: Undefined • RV fee: Free • No water • No toilets • Elevation: -226

## Borrego Springs

**Anza-Borrego Desert SP - Arroyo Salado** • Agency: State • Tel: 760-767-5311 • Location: 16 miles E of Borrego Springs • GPS: Lat 33.280449 Lon -116.147974 • Open: All year • Total sites: Dispersed • RV sites: Undefined • Max RV Length: 35 • RV fee: Free • No water • Vault toilets • Notes: Ground fires prohibited • Activities: Hiking, motor sports • Elevation: 851

**Anza-Borrego Desert SP - Culp Valley** • Agency: State • Tel: 760-767-5311 • Location: 8 miles SW of Borrego Springs • GPS: Lat 33.223717 Lon -116.454961 • Open: All year • Total sites: Dispersed • RV sites: Undefined • Max RV Length: 20 • RV fee: Free • No water • Vault toilets • Notes: Ground fires prohibited • Activities: Hiking • Elevation: 3340

**Anza-Borrego Desert SP - Peg Leg Smith** • Agency: State • Location: 7 miles NE of Borrego Springs • GPS: Lat 33.295502 Lon -116.298293 • Open: Oct-Mar • Stay limit: 30 days • Total sites: Dispersed • RV sites: Undefined • RV fee: Free • No water • No toilets • Activities: Hiking, mountain biking • Elevation: 633

**Anza-Borrego Desert SP - Yaqui Pass** • Agency: State • Tel: 760-767-5311 • Location: 9 miles S of Borrego Springs • GPS: Lat 33.149046 Lon -116.349139 • Open: All year • Total sites: Dispersed • RV sites: Undefined • Max RV Length: 35 • RV fee: Free • No water • No toilets • Notes: Ground fires prohibited • Activities: Hiking • Elevation: 1696

## Bridgeport

**Chemung Mine** • Agency: Bureau of Land Management • Location: 9 miles NE of Bridgeport • GPS: Lat 38.349707 Lon -119.150441 • Open: All year • Total sites: Dispersed • RV sites: Undefined • RV fee: Free • No water • No toilets • Activities: Hiking • Elevation: 8156

## Burney

**Latour DSF - Old Cow Meadows** • Agency: State • Tel: 530-225-2438 • Location: 19 miles S of Burney • GPS: Lat 40.661724 Lon -121.676145 • Open: Jun-Oct • Total sites: 3 • RV sites: 3 • Max RV Length: 25 • RV fee: Free • Central water • Vault toilets • Activities: Hiking • Elevation: 5837

**Latour DSF - South Cow Creek Meadows** • Agency: State • Tel: 530-225-2438 • Location: 23 miles S of Burney • GPS: Lat 40.627738 Lon -121.677813 • Open: Jun-Oct • Total sites: 4 • RV sites: 4 • Max RV Length: 30 • RV fee: Free • Central water • Vault toilets • Activities: Hiking • Elevation: 5647

## California City

**Dove Springs** • Agency: Bureau of Land Management • Tel: 760-384-5400 • Location: 22 miles N of California City • GPS: Lat 35.423855 Lon -118.011453 • Total sites: Dispersed • RV sites: Undefined • RV fee: Free • No water • Vault toilets • Activities: Motor sports • Elevation: 3287

**Dove Springs OHV** • Agency: Bureau of Land Management • Tel: 760-384-5400 • Location: 20 miles N of California City • GPS: Lat 35.417969 Lon -117.988592 • Total sites: Dispersed • RV sites: Undefined • RV fee: Free • No water • Vault toilets • Notes: 2nd area few hundreds yards to the NW • Activities: Motor sports • Elevation: 3200

**Dove Springs Strip** • Agency: Bureau of Land Management • Tel: 760-384-5400 • Location: 23 miles N of California City • GPS: Lat 35.433484 Lon -117.996312 • Total sites: Dispersed • RV sites: Undefined • RV fee: Free • No water • No toilets • Activities: Motor sports • Elevation: 3377

**Jawbone Canyon OHV Primitive Area 1** • Agency: Bureau of Land Management • Tel: 760-384-5400 • Location: 19 miles N of California City • GPS: Lat 35.317444 Lon -118.078091 • Open: All year • Total sites: Dispersed • RV sites: Undefined • RV fee: Free • No water • Vault toilets • Activities: Motor sports • Elevation: 2591

**Jawbone Canyon OHV Primitive Area 2** • Agency: Bureau of Land Management • Tel: 760-384-5400 • Location: 21 miles N of California City • GPS: Lat 35.305318 Lon -118.106217 • Open: All year • Total sites: Dispersed • RV sites: Undefined • RV fee: Free • No water • Vault toilets • Activities: Motor sports • Elevation: 2774

**Jawbone Canyon OHV Staging Area 1** • Agency: Bureau of Land Management • Tel: 760-384-5400 • Location: 17 miles N of California City • GPS: Lat 35.315949 Lon -118.055112 • Open: All year • Total sites: Dispersed • RV sites: Undefined • RV fee: Free • No water • Vault toilets • Activities: Motor sports • Elevation: 2482

**Jawbone Canyon OHV Staging Area 2** • Agency: Bureau of Land Management • Tel: 760-384-5400 • Location: 18 miles N of California City • GPS: Lat 35.313539 Lon -118.057995 • Open: All year • Total sites: Dispersed • RV sites: Undefined • RV fee: Free • No water • Vault toilets • Activities: Motor sports • Elevation: 2478

**Jawbone Canyon OHV Staging Area 3** • Agency: Bureau of Land Management • Tel: 760-384-5400 • Location: 19 miles N of California City • GPS: Lat 35.320362 Lon -118.077988 • Open: All year • Total sites: Dispersed • RV sites: Undefined • RV fee: Free • No water • Vault toilets • Activities: Motor sports • Elevation: 2597

**Jawbone Canyon OHV Staging Area 4** • Agency: Bureau of Land Management • Tel: 760-384-5400 • Location: 19 miles N of California City • GPS: Lat 35.324217 Lon -118.077715 • Open: All year • Total sites: Dispersed • RV sites: Undefined • RV fee: Free • No water • Vault toilets • Activities: Motor sports • Elevation: 2630

**Jawbone Canyon OHV Staging Area 5** • Agency: Bureau of Land Management • Tel: 760-384-5400 • Location: 20 miles N of California City • GPS: Lat 35.317836 Lon -118.092616 • Open: All year • Total sites: Dispersed • RV sites: Undefined • RV fee: Free • No water • Vault toilets • Activities: Motor sports • Elevation: 2648

## Calipatria

**Imperial Wildlife Area - Finney Lake** • Agency: State • Location: 4 miles S of Calipatria • GPS: Lat 33.065417 Lon -115.500786 • Total sites: Dispersed • RV sites: Undefined • RV fee: Free • No water • Vault toilets • Elevation: -158

## Callahan

**Scott Mountan** (Shasta-Trinity NF) • Agency: US Forest Service • Tel: 530-623-2121 • Location: 8 miles SE of Callahan (limited services), 53 miles N of Weaverville • GPS: Lat 41.275 Lon -122.698 • Open: All year • Total sites: 7 • RV sites: 7 • Max RV Length: 15 • RV fee: Free • No water • Vault toilets • Activities: Hiking, equestrian area • Elevation: 5443

## Camptonville

**Burnt Bridge** (Plumas NF) • Agency: US Forest Service • Tel: 530-534-6500 • Location: 16 miles SW of Camptonville (limited services), 31 miles NW of Nevada City • GPS: Lat 39.420342 Lon -121.172944 • Total sites: 31 • RV sites: 13 • RV fee: Free • Central water • Vault toilets • Elevation: 2264

## Canby

**Reservoir F** (Modoc NF) • Agency: US Forest Service • Tel: 530-233-5811 • Location: 19 miles N of Canby (limited services), 36 miles NW of Alturas • GPS: Lat 41.580881 Lon -120.874511 • Open: May-Oct • Stay limit: 14 days • Total sites: 9 • RV sites: 9 • Max RV Length: 22 • RV fee: Free • No water • Vault toilets • Activities: Fishing, non-power boating • Elevation: 4961

## Cecilville

**East Fork** (Grasshopper Ridge) (Klamath NF) • Agency: US Forest Service • Tel: 530-468-5351 • Location: 2 miles NE of Cecilville (limited services), 66 miles SW of Yreka • GPS: Lat 41.153992 Lon -123.108632 • Open: May-Oct • Stay limit: 14 days • Total sites: 6 • RV sites: 6 • RV fee: Free • No water • Vault toilets • Activities: Hiking, fishing, swimming • Elevation: 2461

**Shadow Creek** (Klamath NF) • Agency: US Forest Service • Tel: 530-468-5351 • Location: 7 miles NE of Cecilville (limited services), 61 miles SE of Yreka • GPS: Lat 41.201631 Lon -123.069169 • Open: May-Oct • Total sites: 5 • RV sites: 5 • RV fee: Free • No water • Vault toilets • Activities: Hiking, fishing • Elevation: 2976

## Cedarville

**Cedar Pass** (Modoc NF) • Agency: US Forest Service • Location: 7 miles NW of Cedarville (limited services), 14 miles NE of Alturas • GPS: Lat 41.559055 Lon -120.298784 • Open: May-Oct • Stay limit: 14 days • Total sites: 17 • RV sites: 17 • Max RV Length: 17 • RV fee: Free • No water • Vault toilets • Elevation: 5791

**Pepperdine** (Modoc NF) • Agency: US Forest Service • Tel: 530-279-6116 • Location: 11 miles SW of Cedarville (limited services), 21 miles E of Alturas • GPS: Lat 41.450229 Lon -120.242219 • Open: Jul-Oct • Stay limit: 14 days • Total sites: 5 • RV sites: 5 (not suitable for large RV's) • RV fee: Free • Central water • Vault toilets • Activities: Hiking, equestrian area • Elevation: 6844

**Pepperdine Horse Camp** (Modoc NF) • Agency: US Forest Service • Tel: 530-279-6116 • Location: 10 miles SW of Cedarville (limited services), 21 miles E of Alturas • GPS: Lat 41.456011 Lon -120.244147 • Open: Jul-Oct • Stay limit: 14 days • Total sites: 7 • RV sites: 7 • Max RV Length: 25 • RV fee: Free • No water • Vault toilets • Activities: Hiking, equestrian area • Elevation: 6788

**Stough Reservoir** (Modoc NF) • Agency: US Forest Service • Tel: 530-279-6116 • Location: 4 miles NW of Cedarville (limited services), 17 miles NE of Alturas • GPS: Lat 41.562543 Lon -120.255189 • Open: May-Oct • Stay limit: 14 days • Total sites: 4 • RV sites: 4 • Max RV Length: 22 • RV fee: Free • Central water • Vault toilets • Activities: Fishing, non-power boating • Elevation: 6375

**Surprise Valley Wildlife Area** • Agency: State • Tel: 530-233-3581 • Location: 11 miles S of Cedarville (limited services), 33 miles SE of Alturas • GPS: Lat 41.369389 Lon -120.125944 • Open: Aug-Mar • Total sites: Dispersed • RV sites: Undefined • RV fee: Free • No water • No toilets • Elevation: 4612

## Chester

**Benner Creek** (Lassen NF) • Agency: US Forest Service • Tel: 530-258-2141 • Location: 7 miles N of Chester • GPS: Lat 40.395335 Lon -121.268047 • Open: May-Oct • Total sites: 9 • RV sites: 9 • RV fee: Free • No water • Vault toilets • Activities: Fishing • Elevation: 5614

**Willow Springs** (Lassen NF) • Agency: US Forest Service • Tel: 530-258-2141 • Location: 11 miles W of Chester • GPS: Lat 40.306288 Lon -121.377532 • Open: Apr-Oct • Total sites: 14 • RV sites: 14 • RV fee: Free • No water • Vault toilets • Activities: Fishing • Elevation: 5184

## Chiriaco Summit

**Chiriaco Summit - Patton Museum** • Agency: Non-Profit Organization • Tel: 760-227-3227 • Location: In Chiriaco Summit (limited services), 27 miles E of Indio • GPS: Lat 33.663348 Lon -115.723119 • Open: All year • Total sites: 23 • RV sites: 23 • RV fee: Free • No toilets • Elevation: 1722

**Summit** • Agency: Bureau of Land Management • Location: 16 miles SE of Chiriaco Summit (limited services), 43 miles SE of Indio • GPS: Lat 33.603716 Lon -115.532372 • Total sites: Dispersed • RV sites: Undefined • RV fee: Free • No water • No toilets • Notes: Near RR tracks • Elevation: 1663

## Clearlake

**Knoxville RA - Cedar Creek** • Agency: Bureau of Land Management • Tel: 707-468-4000 • Location: 23 miles SE of Clearlake • GPS: Lat 38.812203 Lon -122.382374 • Total sites: Dispersed • RV sites: Undefined • RV fee: Free • No water • No toilets • Elevation: 1299

**Knoxville RA - Cement Creek** • Agency: Bureau of Land Management • Tel: 707-468-4000 • Location: 21 miles SE of Clearlake • GPS: Lat 38.772034 Lon -122.411952 • Total sites: Dispersed • RV sites: Undefined • RV fee: Free • No water • No toilets • Elevation: 892

**Knoxville RA - Lower Hunting Creek** • Agency: Bureau of Land Management • Tel: 707-468-4000 • Location: 22 miles SE of Clearlake • GPS: Lat 38.808812 Lon -122.374913 • Total sites: 8 • RV sites: 8 • RV fee: Free • No water • Vault toilets • Elevation: 1119

**Knoxville RA - Pocock Creek** • Agency: Bureau of Land Management • Tel: 707-468-4000 • Location: 21 miles SE of Clearlake • GPS: Lat 38.794892 Lon -122.407797 • Total sites: Dispersed • RV sites: Undefined • RV fee: Free • No water • No toilets • Activities: Fishing • Elevation: 935

## Clearlake Oaks

**Indian Valley RA - Blue Oaks** • Agency: Bureau of Land Management • Tel: 707-468-4000 • Location: 22 miles NE of Clearlake Oaks • GPS: Lat 39.069533 Lon -122.508668 • Open: All year • Total sites: 6 • RV sites: 6 • RV fee: Free • No water • Vault toilets • Elevation: 1818

## Clovis

**Kirch Flat** (Sierra NF) • Agency: US Forest Service • Tel: 559-885-5355 • Location: 40 miles E of Clovis • GPS: Lat 36.879737 Lon -119.150459 • Open: All year • Stay limit: 14 days • Total sites: 17 • RV sites: 17 • Max RV Length: 30 • RV fee: Free • No water • Vault toilets • Activities: Non-power boating • Elevation: 1047

## Coalinga

**Jade Mill** • Agency: Bureau of Land Management • Tel: 831-582-2200 • Location: 38 miles NW of Coalinga • GPS: Lat 36.368068 Lon -120.754211 • Total sites: 5 • RV sites: 5 • RV fee: Free • No water • Vault toilets • Elevation: 2815

**Oak Flat** • Agency: Bureau of Land Management • Tel: 831-582-2200 • Location: 37 miles NW of Coalinga • GPS: Lat 36.361524 Lon -120.760717 • Open: All year • Total sites: 6 • RV sites: 6 • RV fee: Free • No water • Vault toilets • Elevation: 2593

## Coffee Creek

**Big Flat** (Klamath NF) • Agency: US Forest Service • Tel: 530-468-5351 • Location: 19 miles W of Coffee Creek (limited services), 55 miles N of Weaverville • GPS: Lat 41.068035 Lon -122.934505 • Open: May-Oct • Stay limit: 14 days • Total sites: 9 • RV sites: 9 • RV fee: Free • No water • Vault toilets • Activities: Hiking, equestrian area • Elevation: 5184

**Clear Creek** (Shasta-Trinity NF) • Agency: US Forest Service • Tel: 530-623-2121 • Location: 18 miles SE of Coffee Creek (limited services), 38 miles NW of Shasta Lake • GPS: Lat 40.931275 Lon -122.586341 • Open: All year • Total sites: 6 • RV sites: 6 • Max RV Length: 22 • RV fee: Free • No water • Vault toilets • Elevation: 3540

**Goldfield** (Shasta-Trinity NF) • Agency: US Forest Service • Tel: 530-623-2121 • Location: 5 miles W of Coffee Creek (limited services), 41 miles N of Weaverville • GPS: Lat 41.1 Lon -122.779 • Open: All year • Total sites: 6 • RV sites: 6 • Max RV Length: 16 • RV fee: Free • No water • Vault toilets • Elevation: 3032

**Horse Flat** (Shasta-Trinity NF) • Agency: US Forest Service • Tel: 530-623-2121 • Location: 7 miles N of Coffee Creek (limited services), 40 miles SW of Weed • GPS: Lat 41.165968 Lon -122.691955 • Open: May-Oct • Total sites: 10 • RV sites: 10 • Max RV Length: 16 • RV fee: Free • No water • Vault toilets • Elevation: 3458

**Jackass Spring** (Shasta-Trinity NF) • Agency: US Forest Service • Tel: 530-623-2121 • Location: 20 miles S of Coffee Creek (limited services), 51 miles NE of Weaverville • GPS: Lat 40.961585 Lon -122.646591 • Open: All year • Total sites: 10 • RV sites: 10 • Max RV Length: 32 • RV fee: Free • No water • Vault toilets • Elevation: 3501

## Covelo

**Boardman Camp** (Mendocino NF) • Agency: US Forest Service • Location: 20 miles E of Covelo (limited services), 65 miles W of Orland • GPS: Lat 39.847079 Lon -123.012889 • Total sites: 3 • RV sites: 3 • RV fee: Free • No water • Vault toilets • Elevation: 4525

**Howard Meadows** (Mendocino NF) • Agency: US Forest Service • Tel: 530-934-3316 • Location: 25 miles NE of Covelo (limited services), 63 miles W of Corning • GPS: Lat 39.877914 Lon -122.992256 • Open: May-Oct • Total sites: 6 • RV sites: 6 • RV fee: Free • No water • Vault toilets • Activities: Fishing • Elevation: 3930

## Daggett

**Rodman Mts Wilderness** • Agency: Bureau of Land Management • Tel: 760-252-6000 • Location: 27 miles SE of Daggett (limited services), 32 miles SE of Barstow • GPS: Lat 34.675803 Lon -116.608612 • Total sites: Dispersed • RV sites: Undefined • RV fee: Free • No water • No toilets • Elevation: 4484

## Davis Creek

**Plum Valley** (Modoc NF) • Agency: US Forest Service • Tel: 530-279-6116 • Location: 5 miles SE of Davis Creek (limited services), 25 miles NE of Alturas • GPS: Lat 41.711837 Lon -120.325772 • Open: Jun-Oct • Stay limit: 14 days • Total sites: 7 • RV sites: 7 • Max RV Length: 16 • RV fee: Free • No water • Vault toilets • Activities: Hiking • Elevation: 5748

## Dorris

**Stateline on the Klamath River** • Agency: Bureau of Land Management • Tel: 530-224-2100 • Location: 19 miles W of Dorris • GPS: Lat 42.006602 Lon -122.188023 • Open: All year • Total sites: Dispersed • RV sites: Undefined • RV fee: Free • No water • Vault toilets • Elevation: 2785

## Douglas City

**Steiner Flat** • Agency: Bureau of Land Management • Tel: 530-224-2100 • Location: Just W of Douglas City (limited services), 6 miles S of Weaverville • GPS: Lat 40.654555 Lon -122.953746 • Open: All year • Total sites: 8 • RV sites: 8 • Max RV Length: 18 • RV fee: Free • No water • No toilets • Elevation: 1618

## Doyle

**Fort Sage OHVA** • Agency: Bureau of Land Management • Tel: 530-257-0456 • Location: 7 miles NE of Doyle (limited services), 51 miles SE of Susanville • GPS: Lat 40.060392 Lon -120.072667 • Total sites: Dispersed • RV sites: Undefined • RV fee: Free • No toilets • Notes: 3 ton weight limit for a bridge on the access road • Activities: Hiking, hunting, rock climbing, motor sports, equestrian area • Elevation: 4738

**Meadow View Equestrian Camp** (Plumas NF) • Agency: US Forest Service • Tel: 530-836-2575 • Location: 7 miles W of Doyle (limited services), 46 miles SE of Susanville • GPS: Lat 40.036 Lon -120.213 • Open: Apr-Sep • Stay limit: 14 days • Total sites: 6 • RV sites: 6 • RV fee: Free • No water • Vault toilets • Activities: Equestrian area • Elevation: 6096

## Elk Creek

**Stony Gorge Reservoir** • Agency: US Bureau of Reclamation • Location: 3 miles SE of Elk Creek (limited services), 22 miles NW of Willows • GPS: Lat 39.579373 Lon -122.522469 • Total sites: Dispersed • RV sites: Undefined • RV fee: Free • No water • No toilets • Elevation: 892

## Etna

**Mulebridge** (Klamath NF) • Agency: US Forest Service • Tel: 530-468-5351 • Location: 21 miles SW of Etna • GPS: Lat 41.356313 Lon -123.075388 • Open: May-Oct • Stay limit: 14 days • Total sites: 4 • RV sites: 4 • RV fee: Free • No water • Vault toilets • Activities: Hiking, fishing • Elevation: 2907

## Forest Ranch

**Butte Creek Recreation Area** • Agency: Bureau of Land Management • Location: 7 miles S of Forest Ranch (limited services), 12 miles NE of Chico • GPS: Lat 39.836022 Lon -121.666665 • Total sites: Dispersed • RV sites: Undefined • RV fee: Free • No toilets • Elevation: 2231

## Foresthill

**Parker Flat Staging Area** (Tahoe NF) • Agency: US Forest Service • Tel: 530-478-0248 • Location: 12 miles N of Foresthill • GPS: Lat 39.127425 Lon -120.760353 • Open: Apr-Dec • Total sites: 6 • RV sites: 6 • Max RV Length: 20 • RV fee: Free • No water • Vault toilets • Activities: Motor sports • Elevation: 3940

## Forks of Salmon

**Hotelling** (Klamath NF) • Agency: US Forest Service • Tel: 530-468-5351 • Location: 4 miles SE of Forks of Salmon (limited services), 69 miles SW of Yreka • GPS: Lat 41.239544 Lon -123.275314 • Open: May-Oct • Stay limit: 14 days • Total sites: 4 • RV sites: 4 • RV fee: Free • No water • Vault toilets • Activities: Fishing, swimming, non-power boating • Elevation: 1401

## Fort Bidwell

**Fee Reservoir** • Agency: Bureau of Land Management • Tel: 530-233-4666 • Location: 7 miles E of Fort Bidwell (limited services), 55 miles NE of Alturas • GPS: Lat 41.835107 Lon -120.028776 • Open: All year • Total sites: 7 • RV sites: 7 • Max RV Length: 24 • RV fee: Free • No water • Vault toilets • Activities: Hiking, mountain biking, fishing, power boating • Elevation: 5269

## Fort Jones

**Bridge Flat** (Klamath NF) • Agency: US Forest Service • Tel: 530-468-5351 • Location: 17 miles W of Fort Jones • GPS: Lat 41.650108 Lon -123.113116 • Open: May-Oct • Total sites: 4 • RV sites: 4 • RV fee: Free • No water • Vault toilets • Activities: Hiking, swimming, non-power boating • Elevation: 2205

## Furnace Creek

**Desert CG** • Agency: Bureau of Land Management • Location: 19 miles SE of Furnace Creek (limited services), 32 miles W of Pahrump, NV • GPS: Lat 36.338643 Lon -116.601784 • Open: All year • Total sites: Dispersed • RV sites: Undefined (over 60 concrete pads) • RV fee: Free • No water • No toilets • Elevation: 3005

## Gasquet

**Doe Flat Trailhead** (Six Rivers NF) • Agency: US Forest Service • Location: 24 miles E of Gasquet (limited services), 42 miles E of Crescent City • GPS: Lat 41.816933 Lon -123.699139 • Total sites: 3 • RV sites: 3 • RV fee: Free • No water • Vault toilets • Activities: Hiking • Elevation: 4167

## Glenville

**Frog Meadow** (Sequoia NF) • Agency: US Forest Service • Tel: 559-539-2607 • Location: 8 miles N of Glenville (limited services), 52 miles SE of Porterville • GPS: Lat 35.874118 Lon -118.575265 • Open: Jun-Oct • Total sites: 10 • RV sites: 10 • Max RV Length: 16 • RV fee: Free • No water • Vault toilets • Notes: Cabin can be reserved • Elevation: 7710

## Graeagle

**Gold Lake 4X4** (Plumas NF) • Agency: US Forest Service • Tel: 530-836-2575 • Location: 12 miles S of Graeagle • GPS: Lat 39.668632 Lon -120.662843 • Total sites: 16 • RV sites: 16 • RV fee: Free • No water • No toilets • Activities: Motor sports • Elevation: 6450

## Grant Grove

**Abbott Creek** (Sequoia NF) • Agency: US Forest Service • Location: 6 miles N of Grant Grove (limited services), 48 miles E of Fresno • GPS: Lat 36.768003 Lon -118.974786 • Total sites: 2 • RV sites: 2 • RV fee: Free • No water • No toilets • Activities: Motor sports • Elevation: 6004

**Buck Rock** (Sequoia NF) • Agency: US Forest Service • Tel: 559-338-2251 • Location: 11 miles E of Grant Grove (limited services), 56 miles E of Fresno • GPS: Lat 36.722406 Lon -118.850873 • Total sites: 8 • RV sites: 8 • Max RV Length: 16 • RV fee: Free • No water • Vault toilets • Elevation: 7779

**Camp 4 1/2** (Sequoia NF) • Agency: US Forest Service • Tel: 559-338-2251 • Location: 28 miles NW of Grant Grove (limited services), 52 miles NE of Fresno • GPS: Lat 36.861834 Lon -119.122033 • Open: All year • Total sites: 4 • RV sites: 4 • Max RV Length: 25 • RV fee: Free • No water • Vault toilets • Activities: Hiking, swimming, non-power boating • Elevation: 1027

**Convict Flat** (Sequoia NF) • Agency: US Forest Service • Tel: 559-338-2251 • Location: 18 miles NE of Grant Grove (limited services), 53 miles E of Fresno • GPS: Lat 36.818497 Lon -118.832174 • Open: May-Nov • Total sites: 5 • RV sites: 5 • Max RV Length: 24 • RV fee: Free • No water • Vault toilets • Activities: Fishing • Elevation: 3225

**Green Cabin Flat** (Sequoia NF) • Agency: US Forest Service • Tel: 559-338-2251 • Location: 27 miles NW of Grant Grove (limited services), 53 miles NE of Fresno • GPS: Lat 36.859925 Lon -119.102895 • Open: All year • Total sites: 5 • RV sites: 5 • Max RV Length: 25 • RV fee: Free • No water • Vault toilets • Activities: Hiking, mountain biking, fishing, non-power boating, equestrian area • Elevation: 1063

**Horse Camp** (Sequoia NF) • Agency: US Forest Service • Tel: 559-338-2251 • Location: 11 miles E of Grant Grove (limited services), 56 miles E of Fresno • GPS: Lat 36.716919 Lon -118.849716 • Open: Jun-Oct • Total sites: 5 • RV sites: 5 • RV fee: Free • No water • Vault toilets • Activities: Equestrian area • Elevation: 7648

**Mill Flat** (Sequoia NF) • Agency: US Forest Service • Tel: 559-338-2251 • Location: 27 miles NW of Grant Grove (limited services), 53 miles NE of Fresno • GPS: Lat 36.856581 Lon -119.096994 • Open: All year • Total sites: 5 • RV sites: 5 • Max RV Length: 25 • RV fee: Free • No water • Vault toilets • Activities: Hiking, fishing, motor sports, non-power boating • Elevation: 1083

## Happy Camp

**Frog Pond** (Klamath NF) • Agency: US Forest Service • Tel: 530-627-3291 • Location: 31 miles SW of Happy Camp • GPS: Lat 41.487464 Lon -123.541769 • Open: May-Oct • Total sites: 3 • RV sites: 3 • RV fee: Free • No water • Vault toilets • Activities: Fishing, non-power boating • Elevation: 1932

**Norcross** (Klamath NF) • Agency: US Forest Service • Tel: 530-493-2243 • Location: 26 miles S of Happy Camp (limited services), 95 miles W of Yreka • GPS: Lat 41.647372 Lon -123.311371 • Open: May-Oct • Stay limit: 14 days • Total sites: 6 • RV sites: 6 • RV fee: Free • No water • Vault toilets • Activities: Hiking, fishing, swimming • Elevation: 2428

**Ten Bear Trailhead** (Six Rivers NF) • Agency: US Forest Service • Location: 40 miles S of Happy Camp (limited services), 70 miles NW of Willow Creek • GPS: Lat 41.529463 Lon -123.438368 • Total sites: 2 • RV sites: 2 • RV fee: Free • No water (water for stock) • Vault toilets • Activities: Hiking, equestrian area • Elevation: 4895

**West Branch** (Klamath NF) • Agency: US Forest Service • Tel: 530-493-2243 • Location: 12 miles NW of Happy Camp (limited services), 82 miles NW of Yreka • GPS: Lat 41.931885 Lon -123.477539 • Open: May-Oct • Stay limit: 14 days • Total sites: 10 • RV sites: 10 • Max RV Length: 28 • RV fee: Free • No water • Vault toilets • Activities: Hiking, swimming • Elevation: 2241

## Holtville

**Holtville Hot Springs North LTVA** • Agency: Bureau of Land Management • Location: 7 miles SE of Holtville • GPS: Lat 32.768612 Lon -115.269856 • Total sites: Dispersed • RV sites: Undefined • RV fee: Free • No water • No toilets • Elevation: 38

**Holtville Hot Springs South LTVA** • Agency: Bureau of Land Management • Location: 8 miles SE of Holtville • GPS: Lat 32.759895 Lon -115.265635 • Total sites: Dispersed • RV sites: Undefined • RV fee: Free • No water • No toilets • Elevation: 32

## Hornbrook

**Copco Cove** (Copco Reservoir) • Agency: Bureau of Land Management • Tel: 530-224-2100 • Location: 15 miles NE of Hornbrook (limited services), 29 miles NE of Yreka • GPS: Lat 41.976546 Lon -122.398874 • Open: All year • Total sites: Dispersed • RV sites: Undefined • RV fee: Free • No water • Vault toilets • Activities: Fishing, swimming, non-power boating • Elevation: 2338

**Mallard Cove** (Copco Reservoir) • Agency: Bureau of Land Management • Tel: 530-224-2100 • Location: 19 miles NE of Hornbrook (limited services), 33 miles NE of Yreka • GPS: Lat 41.973548 Lon -122.29894 • Open: All year • Total sites: 4 • RV sites: 4 • RV fee: Free • No water • Vault toilets • Activities: Fishing, swimming, non-power boating • Elevation: 2616

## Idyllwild

**Little Thomas Mountain - Yellow Post #1** (San Bernardino NF) • Agency: US Forest Service • Location: 15 miles SE of Idyllwild • GPS: Lat 33.579653 Lon -116.624299 • Total sites: 5 • RV sites: 5 • RV fee: Free • No water • No toilets • Elevation: 5064

**Morris Ranch Road Yellow Post** (San Bernardino NF) • Agency: US Forest Service • Location: 15 miles SE of Idyllwild • GPS: Lat 33.63948 Lon -116.59249 • Total sites: 6 • RV sites: 6 • RV fee: Free • No water • No toilets • Notes: 1/2 mile past gate • Elevation: 5359

### Imperial

**Superstition Mt OHV** • Agency: Bureau of Land Management • Tel: 760-337-4400 • Location: 15 miles W of Imperial • GPS: Lat 32.888895 Lon -115.765581 • Open: All year • Total sites: Dispersed • RV sites: Undefined • RV fee: Free • No water • No toilets • Activities: Motor sports • Elevation: 42

### Inyokern

**Long Valley** • Agency: Bureau of Land Management • Tel: 661-391-6000 • Location: 40 miles NW of Inyokern • GPS: Lat 35.844727 Lon -118.151611 • Open: All year • Total sites: 13 • RV sites: 13 • RV fee: Free (donation appreciated) • No water • Vault toilets • Elevation: 5397

### Jacumba Hot Springs

**Valley of the Moon - Elliot Mine Area** • Agency: Bureau of Land Management • Location: 7 miles W of Jacumba Hot Springs (limited services), 38 miles W of El Centro • GPS: Lat 32.625232 Lon -116.081864 • Open: All year • Total sites: Dispersed • RV sites: Undefined • RV fee: Free • No water • No toilets • Activities: Hiking, rock climbing • Elevation: 3852

### Julian

**Anza-Borrego Desert SP - Blair Valley** • Agency: State • Tel: 760-767-5311 • Location: 16 miles SE of Julian • GPS: Lat 33.037685 Lon -116.409559 • Open: All year • Total sites: Dispersed • RV sites: Undefined • Max RV Length: 25 • RV fee: Free • No water • Vault toilets • Notes: Ground fires prohibited • Activities: Hiking • Elevation: 2540

**Anza-Borrego Desert SP - Sunrise Trailhead** • Agency: State • Tel: 760-767-5311 • Location: 9 miles SE of Julian • GPS: Lat 32.977808 Lon -116.524658 • Open: All year • Total sites: Dispersed • RV sites: Undefined • Max RV Length: 35 • RV fee: Free • No water • Vault toilets • Notes: Ground fires prohibited • Activities: Hiking, equestrian area • Elevation: 5003

### June Lake

**Hartley Springs** (Inyo NF) • Agency: US Forest Service • Tel: 760-647-3044 • Location: 6 miles E of June Lake • GPS: Lat 37.771921 Lon -119.037386 • Open: Jun-Oct • Stay limit: 14 days • Total sites: 20 • RV sites: 20 • RV fee: Free • No water • Vault toilets • Elevation: 8448

### Kelso

**Mojave National Preserve - Banshee Canyon** • Agency: National Park Service • Tel: 760 928-2572 • Location: 30 miles E of Kelso (limited services), 61 miles NW of Needles • GPS: Lat 35.038782 Lon -115.398532 • Total sites: Dispersed • RV sites: Undefined • RV fee: Free • No water • No toilets • Activities: Hiking, rock climbing, equestrian area • Elevation: 4200

**Mojave National Preserve - Kelso Dunes** • Agency: National Park Service • Tel: 760 928-2572 • Location: 12 miles S of Kelso (limited services), 46 miles SE of Baker • GPS: Lat 34.888212 Lon -115.716767 • Open: All year • Total sites: Dispersed • RV sites: Undefined • RV fee: Free • No water • No toilets • Activities: Hiking • Elevation: 2526

### King City

**Laguna Mountain** • Agency: Bureau of Land Management • Tel: 831-582-2200 • Location: 31 miles NE of King City • GPS: Lat 36.367411 Lon -120.830327 • Open: All year • Total sites: Dispersed • RV sites: Undefined • RV fee: Free • No water • Vault toilets • Activities: Hiking, mountain biking • Elevation: 2858

**Upper Sweetwater** • Agency: Bureau of Land Management • Tel: 831-630-5000 • Location: 29 miles NE of King City • GPS: Lat 36.360436 Lon -120.849341 • Open: All year • Total sites: 6 • RV sites: 6 • RV fee: Free • No water • Vault toilets • Activities: Hiking, mountain biking • Elevation: 2841

### Kirkwood

**Martin Meadows** (Eldorado NF) • Agency: US Forest Service • Location: 4 miles W of Kirkwood (limited services), 28 miles SW of Meyers • GPS: Lat 38.696476 Lon -120.122656 • Stay limit: 14 days • Total sites: 13 • RV sites: 13 • RV fee: Free • No water • Vault toilets • Elevation: 7641

### Lake Isabella

**Keyesville Recreation Site** • Agency: Bureau of Land Management • Tel: 661-391-6112 • Location: 1 mile W of Lake Isabella • GPS: Lat 35.634392 Lon -118.491874 • Total sites: Dispersed • RV sites: Undefined • RV fee: Free • No water • Vault toilets • Activities: Motor sports • Elevation: 2506

### Lakehead

**Oak Grove** • Agency: US Forest Service • Location: 5 miles S of Lakehead (limited services), 15 miles N of Shasta Lake • GPS: Lat 40.849476 Lon -122.353343 • Total sites: 10 • RV sites: 5 • RV fee: Free • No water • No toilets • Elevation: 1207

## Lakeport

**Cow Mountain RA - Buckhorn** • Agency: Bureau of Land Management • Tel: 707-468-4000 • Location: 15 miles W of Lakeport • GPS: Lat 39.038426 Lon -123.039234 • Open: All year • Total sites: 4 • RV sites: 4 (no large RV's) • RV fee: Free • No water • Vault toilets • Elevation: 2868

**Cowboy Camp Horse CG** • Agency: Bureau of Land Management • Tel: 707-468-4000 • Location: 15 miles W of Lakeport • GPS: Lat 38.998453 Lon -122.354526 • Open: Apr-Nov • Total sites: 6 • RV sites: 6 • RV fee: Free • Vault toilets • Activities: equestrian area • Elevation: 1086

## Lakeshore

**Sample Meadow** (Sierra NF) • Agency: US Forest Service • Tel: 559-855-5355 • Location: 14 miles N of Lakeshore (limited services), 33 miles NE of Shaver Lake • GPS: Lat 37.335862 Lon -119.156009 • Open: Jun-Oct • Stay limit: 14 days • Total sites: 16 • RV sites: 16 (not recommended for large RV's) • Max RV Length: 20 • RV fee: Free • No water • Vault toilets • Activities: Hiking, equestrian area • Elevation: 7897

**West Kaiser** (Sierra NF) • Agency: US Forest Service • Tel: 559-855-5355 • Location: 22 miles N of Lakeshore (limited services), 31 miles N of Shaver Lake • GPS: Lat 37.344842 Lon -119.240181 • Open: Jun-Dec • Total sites: 8 • RV sites: 8 • Max RV Length: 25 • RV fee: Free • No water • Vault toilets • Activities: Hiking • Elevation: 5564

## Landers

**Bighorn Mountain Wilderness - Barnes Rd** • Agency: Bureau of Land Management • Tel: 760-252-6000 • Location: 12 miles N of Landers (limited services), 22 miles N of Yucca Valley • GPS: Lat 34.39371 Lon -116.5262 • Total sites: Dispersed • RV sites: Undefined • RV fee: Free • No water • No toilets • Activities: Hiking, hunting, equestrian area • Elevation: 2684

**Boone Road** • Agency: Bureau of Land Management • Location: 13 miles N of Landers (limited services), 23 miles N of Yucca Valley • GPS: Lat 34.410761 Lon -116.516435 • Total sites: Dispersed • RV sites: Undefined • RV fee: Free • No water • No toilets • Elevation: 2579

## Likely

**East Creek Horse Camp** (Modoc NF) • Agency: US Forest Service • Tel: 530-279-6116 • Location: 23 miles E of Likely (limited services), 41 miles SE of Alturas • GPS: Lat 41.196173 Lon -120.195599 • Open: May-Oct • Stay limit: 14 days • Total sites: 5 • RV sites: 5 • Max RV Length: 22 • RV fee: Free • No water • Vault toilets • Activities: equestrian area • Elevation: 7119

**Patterson** (Modoc NF) • Agency: US Forest Service • Tel: 530-279-6116 • Location: 24 miles E of Likely (limited services), 41 miles SE of Alturas • GPS: Lat 41.197916 Lon -120.186206 • Open: May-Oct • Stay limit: 14 days • Total sites: 6 • RV sites: 6 • Max RV Length: 16 • RV fee: Free • Central water • Vault toilets • Activities: Hiking, fishing • Elevation: 7274

## Lone Pine

**Alabama Hills - Movie Road** • Agency: Bureau of Land Management • Tel: 760-872-5000 • Location: 4 miles W of Lone Pine • GPS: Lat 36.604938 Lon -118.122129 • Total sites: Dispersed • RV sites: Undefined • RV fee: Free • No water • No toilets • Elevation: 4613

**Alabama Hills RA** • Agency: Bureau of Land Management • Tel: 760-872-5000 • Location: 2 miles W of Lone Pine • GPS: Lat 36.606285 Lon -118.094571 • Total sites: Dispersed • RV sites: Undefined • RV fee: Free • Elevation: 4429

## Macdoel

**Butte Valley Wildlife Area** • Agency: State • Tel: 530-398-4627 • Location: 5 miles W of Macdoel (limited services), 16 miles SW of Dorris • GPS: Lat 41.837546 Lon -122.096888 • Total sites: Dispersed • RV sites: Undefined • RV fee: Free • Vault toilets • Activities: Hiking, hunting • Elevation: 4342

**Orr Lake** (Klamath NF) • Agency: US Forest Service • Tel: 530-398-4391 • Location: 18 miles S of Macdoel (limited services), 32 miles NE of Weed • GPS: Lat 41.667571 Lon -121.992377 • Open: May-Oct • Stay limit: 14 days • Total sites: 8 • RV sites: 8 • RV fee: Free • No water • Vault toilets • Notes: Low-hanging branches • Elevation: 4682

## Mad River

**Scotts Flat** (Shasta-Trinity NF) • Agency: US Forest Service • Tel: 530-628-5227 • Location: 15 miles SE of Mad River (limited services), 65 miles SE of Fortuna • GPS: Lat 40.365738 Lon -123.309397 • Total sites: 10 • RV sites: 10 • RV fee: Free • No water • Vault toilets • Activities: Hiking, fishing, swimming • Elevation: 2354

## Madeline

**Dodge Reservoir** • Agency: Bureau of Land Management • Tel: 530-257-0456 • Location: 28 miles E of Madeline (limited services), 75 miles NE of Susanville • GPS: Lat 40.974156 Lon -120.13295 • Open: All year • Total sites:

11 • RV sites: 11 • RV fee: Free (donation appreciated) • No water • Vault toilets • Elevation: 5758

**Ramhorn Springs** • Agency: Bureau of Land Management • Tel: 530-257-0456 • Location: 32 miles SE of Madeline (limited services), 44 miles NE of Susanville • GPS: Lat 40.707154 Lon -120.25231 • Open: All year • Total sites: 10 • RV sites: 10 • RV fee: Free (donation appreciated) • No water • Vault toilets • Elevation: 5745

## Mammoth Lakes

**Benton Crossing Road** • Agency: Bureau of Land Management • Location: 11 miles E of Mammoth Lakes • GPS: Lat 37.660389 Lon -118.788874 • Total sites: Dispersed • RV sites: Undefined • RV fee: Free • No water • No toilets • Elevation: 6886

**Big Springs** (Inyo NF) • Agency: US Forest Service • Tel: 760-647-3044 • Location: 11 miles N of Mammoth Lakes • GPS: Lat 37.748779 Lon -118.940918 • Open: Jun-Oct • Stay limit: 21 days • Total sites: 26 • RV sites: 26 • RV fee: Free • No water • Vault toilets • Notes: Bear boxes must be used for food storage • Activities: Fishing • Elevation: 7290

**Glass Creek** (Inyo NF) • Agency: US Forest Service • Tel: 760-647-3044 • Location: 10 miles N of Mammoth Lakes • GPS: Lat 37.752693 Lon -118.990749 • Open: Jun-Oct • Total sites: 50 • RV sites: 50 • Max RV Length: 45 • RV fee: Free • No water • Vault toilets • Activities: Hiking • Elevation: 7546

**Hot Creek Hatchery Road** • Agency: Bureau of Land Management • Location: 8 miles E of Mammoth Lakes • GPS: Lat 37.645889 Lon -118.839474 • Total sites: Dispersed • RV sites: Undefined • RV fee: Free • No water • No toilets • Elevation: 7074

**Lower Deadman** (Inyo NF) • Agency: US Forest Service • Location: 8 miles N of Mammoth Lakes • GPS: Lat 37.720485 Lon -119.009028 • Stay limit: 14 days • Total sites: 15 • RV sites: 15 • RV fee: Free • No water • Vault toilets • Elevation: 7818

**Upper Deadman** (Inyo NF) • Agency: US Forest Service • Tel: 760-873-2400 • Location: 8 miles N of Mammoth Lakes • GPS: Lat 37.721182 Lon -119.011747 • Stay limit: 14 days • Total sites: 15 • RV sites: 15 • Max RV Length: 45 • RV fee: Free • No water • No toilets • Elevation: 7802

**Whitmore Tubs Road** • Agency: Bureau of Land Management • Location: 11 miles E of Mammoth Lakes • GPS: Lat 37.660678 Lon -118.811618 • Total sites: Dispersed • RV sites: Undefined • RV fee: Free • No water • No toilets • Elevation: 6984

**Whitmore Tubs Road** • Agency: Bureau of Land Management • Location: 11 miles E of Mammoth Lakes • GPS: Lat 37.648029 Lon -118.804884 • Total sites: Dispersed • RV sites: Undefined • RV fee: Free • No water • No toilets • Elevation: 6986

**Whitmore Tubs Road** • Agency: Bureau of Land Management • Location: 10 miles E of Mammoth Lakes • GPS: Lat 37.648279 Lon -118.812336 • Total sites: Dispersed • RV sites: Undefined • RV fee: Free • No water • No toilets • Elevation: 7020

## McCloud

**Algoma** (Shasta-Trinity NF) • Agency: US Forest Service • Tel: 530-964-2184 • Location: 14 miles E of McCloud (limited services), 26 miles E of Mt Shasta • GPS: Lat 41.256047 Lon -121.883773 • Open: May-Oct • Total sites: 8 • RV sites: Undefined • Max RV Length: 24 • RV fee: Free • No water • Vault toilets • Elevation: 3848

**Bullseye Lake** (Modoc NF) • Agency: US Forest Service • Tel: 530-667-2246 • Location: 46 miles NE of McCloud (limited services), 56 miles NE of Mt Shasta • GPS: Lat 41.554672 Lon -121.573793 • Open: May-Oct • Stay limit: 14 days • Total sites: 10 • RV sites: 10 • Max RV Length: 22 • RV fee: Free • No water • Vault toilets • Activities: Fishing, non-power boating • Elevation: 6798

**Harris Spring** (Shasta-Trinity NF) • Agency: US Forest Service • Tel: 530-964-2184 • Location: 27 miles NE of McCloud (limited services), 37 miles NE of Mt Shasta • GPS: Lat 41.454346 Lon -121.785156 • Open: Aug-Oct • Total sites: 15 • RV sites: 15 • Max RV Length: 32 • RV fee: Free • No water • Vault toilets • Elevation: 4882

**Payne Springs** (Modoc NF) • Agency: US Forest Service • Tel: 530-667-2246 • Location: 47 miles NE of McCloud (limited services), 57 miles NE of Mt Shasta • GPS: Lat 41.555082 Lon -121.562137 • Open: Jul-Oct • Stay limit: 14 days • Total sites: 5 • RV sites: 5 • Max RV Length: 20 • RV fee: Free • No water • Vault toilets • Activities: Fishing • Elevation: 6539

**Schonichin Springs** (Modoc NF) • Agency: US Forest Service • Tel: 530-667-2246 • Location: 50 miles NE of McCloud (limited services), 59 miles NE of Mt Shasta • GPS: Lat 41.591564 Lon -121.617552 • Open: Jul-Oct • Stay limit: 14 days • Total sites: 10 • RV sites: 10 • Max RV Length: 20 • RV fee: Free • No water • Vault toilets • Elevation: 6782

**Trout Creek** (Shasta-Trinity NF) • Agency: US Forest Service • Tel: 530-964-2184 • Location: 22 miles NE of McCloud (limited services), 32 miles NE of Mt Shasta • GPS: Lat 41.445285 Lon -121.885922 • Open: Jun-Oct • Total sites: 10 • RV sites: 10 • Max RV Length: 24 • RV fee: Free • No water • Vault toilets • Elevation: 4941

### Mecca

**Painted Canyon** • Agency: Bureau of Land Management • Tel: 760-833-7100 • Location: 10 miles NE of Mecca (limited services), 20 miles SE of Indio • GPS: Lat 33.619198 Lon -115.999448 • Total sites: Dispersed • RV sites: Undefined • RV fee: Free • No water • No toilets • Activities: Hiking • Elevation: 627

### Mendota

**Tumey Hills** • Agency: Bureau of Land Management • Tel: 831-630-5000 • Location: 20 miles SW of Mendota • GPS: Lat 36.624894 Lon -120.659271 • Open: Oct-Apr (closed to vehicle access during fire season) • Total sites: Dispersed • RV sites: Undefined • Max RV Length: 20 • RV fee: Free • No toilets • Elevation: 554

### Middletown

**Cedar Creek** • Agency: Bureau of Land Management • Tel: 707-468-4000 • Location: 17 miles W of Middletown • GPS: Lat 38.773071 Lon -122.391915 • Total sites: Dispersed • RV sites: Undefined • RV fee: Free • No water • No toilets • Elevation: 1512

### Milford

**Laufman** (Plumas NF) • Agency: US Forest Service • Tel: 530-836-2575 • Location: 3 miles S of Milford (limited services), 25 miles SE of Susanville • GPS: Lat 40.135 Lon -120.348 • Open: Apr-Oct • Stay limit: 14 days • Total sites: 6 • RV sites: 6 • RV fee: Free • No water • Vault toilets • Elevation: 5098

### Montague

**Shasta Valley Wildlife Area** • Agency: State • Tel: 530-459-3926 • Location: 9 miles SE of Montague (limited services), 15 miles SE of Yreka • GPS: Lat 41.689237 Lon -122.484118 • Total sites: Dispersed • RV sites: Undefined • RV fee: Free • No water • Activities: Hiking, fishing, hunting • Elevation: 2599

### Montgomery Creek

**Deadlun** (Shasta-Trinity NF) • Agency: US Forest Service • Tel: 530-275-1587 • Location: 27 miles N of Montgomery Creek (limited services), 38 miles NW of Burney • GPS: Lat 41.061087 Lon -121.975684 • Open: All year • Total sites: 25 • RV sites: 25 • Max RV Length: 24 • RV fee: Free • No water • Vault toilets • Activities: Fishing, hunting, motor sports • Elevation: 2746

**Madrone** (Shasta-Trinity NF) • Agency: US Forest Service • Tel: 530-275-1587 • Location: 22 miles NW of Montgomery Creek (limited services), 40 miles W of Burney • GPS: Lat 40.924361 Lon -122.095473 • Open: All year • Total sites: 10 • RV sites: 10 • Max RV Length: 16 • RV fee: Free • No water • Vault toilets • Elevation: 1552

### Mount Shasta

**Gumboot Lake** (Shasta-Trinity NF) • Agency: US Forest Service • Tel: 530-926-4511 • Location: 15 miles SW of Mount Shasta • GPS: Lat 41.213 Lon -122.509 • Open: May-Oct • Total sites: 4 • RV sites: 4 • Max RV Length: 12 • RV fee: Free • No water • Vault toilets • Elevation: 6010

**Castle Lake** (Shasta-Trinity NF) • Agency: US Forest Service • Tel: 530-926-4511 • Location: 11 miles SW of Mt Shasta • GPS: Lat 41.23528 Lon -122.37889 • Open: All year • Total sites: 6 • RV sites: 6 • Max RV Length: 10 • RV fee: Free • No water • Vault toilets • Elevation: 5331

### New Cuyama

**Aliso** (Los Padres NF) • Agency: US Forest Service • Tel: 661-245-3731 • Location: 9 miles SW of New Cuyama (limited services), 39 miles SW of Taft • GPS: Lat 34.907715 Lon -119.768555 • Open: All year • Total sites: 10 • RV sites: 10 • Max RV Length: 28 • RV fee: Free • No water • Vault toilets • Activities: Hiking • Elevation: 2884

**Carrizo Plains NM - Selby CG** • Agency: Bureau of Land Management • Location: 23 miles NW of New Cuyama (limited services), 33 miles W of Taft • GPS: Lat 35.127851 Lon -119.841862 • Open: All year • Total sites: 13 • RV sites: 13 • RV fee: Free • No water • Vault toilets • Elevation: 2510

### New Pine Creek

**Cave Lake** (Modoc NF) • Agency: US Forest Service • Tel: 530-279-6116 • Location: 7 miles E of New Pine Creek (limited services), 20 miles SE of Lakeview, OR • GPS: Lat 41.978187 Lon -120.205818 • Open: Jul-Oct • Stay limit: 14 days • Total sites: 3 • RV sites: 3 • RV fee: Free • No water • Vault toilets • Activities: Hiking, fishing • Elevation: 6801

### Newberry Springs

**Camp Cady Wildlife Area** - Harvard Road Dove Field • Agency: State • Tel: 760-257-0900 • Location: 7 miles S of Newberry Springs (limited services), 25 miles E of Barstow • GPS: Lat 34.922943 Lon -116.644857 • Total sites: Dispersed • RV sites: Undefined • RV fee: Free • Vault toilets • Activities: Hiking, hunting • Elevation: 1755

**Camp Cady Wildlife Area - Main Parking Lot** • Agency: State • Tel: 760-257-0900 • Location: 8 miles S of Newberry

Springs (limited services), 26 miles E of Barstow • GPS: Lat 34.936031 Lon -116.613232 • Total sites: Dispersed • RV sites: Undefined • RV fee: Free • Flush toilets • Activities: Hiking, hunting • Elevation: 1720

## North Fork

**Whiskey Falls** (Sierra NF) • Agency: US Forest Service • Tel: 559-877-2218 • Location: 12 miles NE of North Fork (limited services), 28 miles SE of Oakhurst • GPS: Lat 37.285756 Lon -119.441554 • Open: Jun-Nov • Total sites: 14 • RV sites: 14 • RV fee: Free • No water • Vault toilets • Activities: Fishing • Elevation: 5902

## Oakhurst

**Clover Meadow** (Sierra NF) • Agency: US Forest Service • Tel: 209-966-3638 • Location: 39 miles NE of Oakhurst • GPS: Lat 37.527022 Lon -119.277625 • Open: Jun-Oct • Stay limit: 14 days • Total sites: 7 • RV sites: 7 • Max RV Length: 20 • RV fee: Free • Central water • Vault toilets • Activities: Hiking, equestrian area • Elevation: 7047

**Granite Creek** (Sierra NF) • Agency: US Forest Service • Tel: 559-877-2218 • Location: 41 miles NE of Oakhurst • GPS: Lat 37.538647 Lon -119.263963 • Open: Jun-Oct • Total sites: 20 • RV sites: 20 • Max RV Length: 20 • RV fee: Free • No water • Vault toilets • Activities: Hiking, equestrian area • Elevation: 6982

**Nelder Grove** (Sierra NF) • Agency: US Forest Service • Tel: 559-877-2218 • Location: 11 miles NE of Oakhurst • GPS: Lat 37.431043 Lon -119.583468 • Open: May-Dec • Total sites: 7 • RV sites: 7 • Max RV Length: 20 • RV fee: Free • No water • Vault toilets • Activities: Hiking • Elevation: 5430

## Ocotillo

**Anza-Borrego Desert SP - Carrizo Badlands Overlook** • Agency: State • Tel: 760-767-5311 • Location: 12 miles NW of Ocotillo (limited services), 36 miles W of El Centro • GPS: Lat 32.828855 Lon -116.167253 • Open: All year • Total sites: Dispersed • RV sites: Undefined • Max RV Length: 35 • RV fee: Free • No water • No toilets • Notes: Ground fires prohibited • Activities: Hiking • Elevation: 1142

## Ocotillo Wells

**Ocotillo Wells SVRA** • Agency: State • Tel: 760-767-5391 • Location: 1 mile N of Ocotillo Wells (limited services), 32 miles E of Julian • GPS: Lat 33.157227 Lon -116.149658 • Open: All year • Total sites: Dispersed • RV sites: Undefined • RV fee: Free • No water • No toilets • Activities: Motor sports • Elevation: 256

## Orleans

**Aikens Creek West** (Six Rivers NF) • Agency: US Forest Service • Tel: 530-627-3291 • Location: 10 miles SW of Orleans (limited services), 28 miles N of Willow • GPS: Lat 41.228795 Lon -123.654856 • Open: May-Sep • Total sites: 10 • RV sites: 10 • Max RV Length: 35 • RV fee: Free • Central water • No toilets • Activities: Fishing • Elevation: 312

**Beans Camp** (Klamath NF) • Agency: US Forest Service • Tel: 530-627-3291 • Location: 18 miles N of Orleans (limited services), 43 miles SW of Happy Camp • GPS: Lat 41.443717 Lon -123.613089 • Open: May-Oct • Total sites: 6 • RV sites: 6 • RV fee: Free • No water • Vault toilets • Activities: Hunting • Elevation: 4324

## Oroville

**Oroville SWA** • Agency: State • Tel: 530-538-2236 • Location: 6 miles SW of Oroville • GPS: Lat 39.457293 Lon -121.634761 • Open: All year • Total sites: Dispersed • RV sites: Undefined • RV fee: Free • No water • Vault toilets • Notes: Permit required • Activities: Fishing, non-power boating • Elevation: 118

## Paskenta

**Dead Mule** (Mendocino NF) • Agency: US Forest Service • Location: 26 miles W of Paskenta (limited services), 46 miles W of Corning • GPS: Lat 39.846136 Lon -122.828245 • Open: Jun-Oct • Total sites: 2 • RV sites: 2 • RV fee: Free • No water • Vault toilets • Elevation: 5148

**Kingsley Glade** (Mendocino NF) • Agency: US Forest Service • Tel: 530-934-3316 • Location: 22 miles W of Paskenta (limited services), 42 miles W of Corning • GPS: Lat 39.903807 Lon -122.764613 • Open: May-Nov • Total sites: 6 • RV sites: 6 • RV fee: Free • No water • Vault toilets • Activities: Equestrian area • Elevation: 4577

**Rocky Cabin** (Mendocino NF) • Agency: US Forest Service • Location: 20 miles NW of Paskenta (limited services), 40 miles W of Corning • GPS: Lat 39.954494 Lon -122.739613 • Open: Jun-Oct • Total sites: 3 • RV sites: 3 • RV fee: Free • No water • Vault toilets • Elevation: 6246

**Sugarfoot Glade** (Mendocino NF) • Agency: US Forest Service • Tel: 530-934-3316 • Location: 24 miles W of Paskenta (limited services), 44 miles W of Corning • GPS: Lat 39.885038 Lon -122.777093 • Open: Jun-Nov • Total sites: 6 • RV sites: 6 • Max RV Length: 16 • RV fee: Free • No water • Vault toilets • Elevation: 3812

**Three Prong** (Mendocino NF) • Agency: US Forest Service • Tel: 530-934-3316 • Location: 25 miles N of Paskenta (limited services), 44 miles W of Corning • GPS: Lat 39.920713 Lon -122.791721 • Open: Jun-Dec • Total sites: 6 • RV sites: 3 • Max RV Length: RV-24/Trailer-16 • RV fee: Free • No water • Vault toilets • Activities: Hiking • Elevation: 6014

**Toomes Camp** (Mendocino NF) • Agency: US Forest Service • Location: 25 miles NW of Paskenta (limited services), 38 miles SW of Red Bluff • GPS: Lat 40.002985 Lon -122.759041 • Open: Jun-Oct • Total sites: 2 • RV sites: 2 • RV fee: Free • No water • Vault toilets • Activities: Hiking • Elevation: 6001

**Whitlock** (Mendocino NF) • Agency: US Forest Service • Tel: 530-934-3316 • Location: 13 miles N of Paskenta (limited services), 33 miles W of Corning • GPS: Lat 39.920028 Lon -122.687032 • Open: May-Nov • Total sites: 5 • RV sites: 5 • RV fee: Free • No water • Vault toilets • Elevation: 4249

## Paynes Creek

**South Antelope** (Lassen NF) • Agency: US Forest Service • Tel: 530-258-2141 • Location: 17 miles SE of Paynes Creek (limited services), 37 miles E of Red Bluff • GPS: Lat 40.253027 Lon -121.758434 • Open: All year • Total sites: 4 • RV sites: 4 • RV fee: Free • No water • Vault toilets • Activities: Fishing • Elevation: 2861

## Pearsonville

**Chimney Creek** • Agency: Bureau of Land Management • Tel: 661-391-6000 • Location: 17 miles W of Pearsonville (limited services), 29 miles NW of Inyokern • GPS: Lat 35.8396 Lon -118.039307 • Open: All year • Total sites: 32 • RV sites: 32 • RV fee: Free • No water • No toilets • Elevation: 5738

## Pine Mountain Club

**Toad Springs** (Los Padres NF) • Agency: US Forest Service • Tel: 661-245-3731 • Location: 4 miles W of Pine Mountain Club • GPS: Lat 34.860721 Lon -119.228178 • Total sites: 5 • RV sites: 5 • RV fee: Free • Central water • Vault toilets • Activities: Hiking, hunting, motor sports • Elevation: 5676

## Pinecrest

**Kerrick Corral Horse Camp** (Stanislaus NF) • Agency: US Forest Service • Tel: 209-965-3434 • Location: 5 miles E of Pinecrest (limited services), 32 miles NE of Sonora • GPS: Lat 38.174292 Lon -119.956079 • Open: May-Dec • Stay limit: 14 days • Total sites: 9 • RV sites: 9 • RV fee: Free • No water • Vault toilets • Activities: Equestrian area • Elevation: 7050

## Pioneer

**Mokelumne** (Eldorado NF) • Agency: US Forest Service • Tel: 209-295-4251 • Location: 29 miles E of Pioneer (limited services), 45 miles NE of Jackson • GPS: Lat 38.478221 Lon -120.270822 • Open: All year • Stay limit: 14 days • Total sites: 13 • RV sites: 8 • RV fee: Free • No water • Vault toilets • Activities: Fishing, swimming • Elevation: 3343

## Pollock Pines

**Airport Flat** (Eldorado NF) • Agency: US Forest Service • Tel: 530-644-2349 • Location: 34 miles NE of Pollock Pines • GPS: Lat 38.985357 Lon -120.380174 • Open: May-Oct • Stay limit: 14 days • Total sites: 16 • RV sites: 16 • RV fee: Free • No water • Vault toilets • Activities: Hiking • Elevation: 5407

**Camino Cove** (Eldorado NF) • Agency: US Forest Service • Tel: 530-647-5415 • Location: 25 miles NE of Pollock Pines • GPS: Lat 38.880347 Lon -120.428115 • Open: May-Oct • Stay limit: 14 days • Total sites: 32 • RV sites: 32 • RV fee: Free • No water • Vault toilets • Activities: Mountain biking, fishing, swimming, power boating, non-power boating • Elevation: 4905

**West Point** (Eldorado NF) • Agency: US Forest Service • Tel: 530-647-5415 • Location: 23 miles NE of Pollock Pines • GPS: Lat 38.871111 Lon -120.441168 • Open: May-Oct • Stay limit: 14 days • Total sites: 8 • RV sites: 8 • RV fee: Free • No water • Vault toilets • Activities: Swimming, power boating, non-power boating • Elevation: 5016

## Portola

**Conklin Park** (Plumas NF) • Agency: US Forest Service • Tel: 530-836-2575 • Location: 23 miles N of Portola • GPS: Lat 40.047 Lon -120.368 • Open: All year • Stay limit: 14 days • Total sites: 9 • RV sites: 9 • RV fee: Free • No water • Vault toilets • Elevation: 5974

**Crocker** (Plumas NF) • Agency: US Forest Service • Tel: 530-836-2572 • Location: 10 miles N of Portola • GPS: Lat 39.891 Lon -120.423 • Open: May-Oct • Stay limit: 14 days • Total sites: 10 • RV sites: 10 • RV fee: Free • No water • Vault toilets • Elevation: 5771

## Pozo

**Navajo** (Los Padres NF) • Agency: US Forest Service • Tel: 805-925-9538 • Location: 8 miles NE of Pozo (limited services), 25 miles E of Santa Margarita • GPS: Lat 35.368674 Lon -120.312399 • Total sites: 2 • RV sites: 2 • RV fee: Free • No water • Vault toilets • Activities: Motor sports • Elevation: 2221

## Quincy

**Deanes Valley** (Plumas NF) • Agency: US Forest Service • Tel: 530-283-0555 • Location: 9 miles SW of Quincy • GPS: Lat 39.889545 Lon -121.024617 • Open: Apr-Sep • Total sites: 7 • RV sites: 7 • RV fee: Free • No water • Vault toilets • Activities: Hunting, motor sports, equestrian area • Elevation: 4322

**Meadow Camp** (Plumas NF) • Agency: US Forest Service • Tel: 530-283-0555 • Location: 8 miles W of Quincy • GPS: Lat 39.930435 Lon -121.041738 • Open: All year (no services in winter) • Total sites: 7 • RV sites: 7 • RV fee: Free • No water • Vault toilets • Activities: Mountain biking, hunting, motor sports • Elevation: 3747

**Snake Lake** (Plumas NF) • Agency: US Forest Service • Tel: 530-283-0555 • Location: 9 miles NW of Quincy • GPS: Lat 39.980787 Lon -121.006064 • Open: All year (no services in winter) • Total sites: 9 • RV sites: 9 • RV fee: Free • No water • Vault toilets • Activities: Hiking, mountain biking, fishing, non-power boating, equestrian area • Elevation: 4010

## Ridgecrest

**Spangler Hills OHVA - Searles Station** • Agency: Bureau of Land Management • Tel: 760-384-5400 • Location: 12 miles S of Ridgecrest • GPS: Lat 35.484871 Lon -117.626757 • Total sites: Dispersed • RV sites: Undefined • RV fee: Free • No toilets • Activities: Motor sports • Elevation: 3202

**Spangler Hills OHVA - Teagle Wash** • Agency: Bureau of Land Management • Tel: 760-384-5400 • Location: 16 miles SE of Ridgecrest • GPS: Lat 35.514407 Lon -117.555961 • Total sites: Dispersed • RV sites: Undefined • RV fee: Free • No water • No toilets • Activities: Motor sports • Elevation: 2628

**Spangler Hills OHVA - Wagon Wheel** • Agency: Bureau of Land Management • Tel: 760-384-5400 • Location: 10 miles SE of Ridgecrest • GPS: Lat 35.572665 Lon -117.548393 • Total sites: Dispersed • RV sites: Undefined • RV fee: Free • No water • Vault toilets • Activities: Motor sports • Elevation: 3235

**Walker Pass** • Agency: Bureau of Land Management • Tel: 661-391-6000 • Location: 23 miles W of Ridgecrest • GPS: Lat 35.664025 Lon -118.037851 • Open: All year • Total sites: 13 • RV sites: 2 • RV fee: Free (donation appreciated) • No water • Vault toilets • Activities: Equestrian area • Elevation: 5039

## Salton City

**Anza Borego Desert** • Agency: Bureau of Land Management • Location: 5 miles W of Salton City • GPS: Lat 33.278953 Lon -116.058357 • Total sites: Dispersed • RV sites: Undefined • RV fee: Free • No water • No toilets • Activities: Hiking • Elevation: 408

## San Ardo

**Williams Hill RA** • Agency: Bureau of Land Management • Tel: 831-630-5000 • Location: 10 miles W of San Ardo (limited services), 25 miles S of King City • GPS: Lat 35.978291 Lon -121.009757 • Open: All year • Total sites: 7 • RV sites: 7 • RV fee: Free • No water • Vault toilets • Elevation: 2289

## Santa Maria

**Baja** (Los Padres NF) • Agency: US Forest Service • Tel: 805-925-9538 • Location: 30 miles NE of Santa Maria • GPS: Lat 35.139186 Lon -120.137827 • Total sites: 1 • RV sites: 1 • RV fee: Free • No water • Vault toilets • Activities: Mountain biking, motor sports • Elevation: 1411

**Colson** (Los Padres NF) • Agency: US Forest Service • Tel: 805-925-9538 • Location: 20 miles E of Santa Maria • GPS: Lat 34.94 Lon -120.17 • Total sites: 5 • RV sites: 5 • RV fee: Free • No water • No toilets • Activities: Hiking, fishing • Elevation: 2067

## Sawyers Bar

**Red Bank** (Klamath NF) • Agency: US Forest Service • Tel: 530-468-5351 • Location: 7 miles W of Sawyers Bar (limited services), 32 miles SW of Etna • GPS: Lat 41.297842 Lon -123.230272 • Open: May-Oct • Stay limit: 14 days • Total sites: 5 • RV sites: 5 • RV fee: Free • No water • Vault toilets • Activities: Hiking, fishing, swimming • Elevation: 1752

## Seiad Valley

**Grider Creek** (Klamath NF) • Agency: US Forest Service • Tel: 530-493-2243 • Location: 6 miles S of Seiad Valley (limited services), 55 miles W of Yreka • GPS: Lat 41.806631 Lon -123.217908 • Open: May-Oct • Stay limit: 14 days • Total sites: 10 • RV sites: 10 • Max RV Length: 16 • RV fee: Free • No water • Vault toilets • Activities: Hiking, fishing, swimming, hunting, equestrian area • Elevation: 1708

## Shaver Lake

**Bretz Mill** (Sierra NF) • Agency: US Forest Service • Tel: 559-855-5355 • Location: 16 miles SE of Shaver Lake • GPS: Lat 37.037897 Lon -119.240066 • Open: All year • Stay limit: 14 days • Total sites: 10 • RV sites: 10 • Max RV Length: 24 • RV fee: Free • No water • Vault toilets • Activities: Motor sports • Elevation: 3356

**Sawmill Flat** (Sierra NF) • Agency: US Forest Service • Tel: 559-855-5355 • Location: 27 miles SE of Shaver Lake • GPS: Lat 36.969583 Lon -119.017023 • Open: Jun-Nov • Stay limit: 14 days • Total sites: 15 • RV sites: 15 • RV fee: Free • No water • Vault toilets • Activities: Hiking, fishing • Elevation: 6811

## Shoshone

**Kingston Mts - Horse Thief** • Agency: Bureau of Land Management • Tel: 760-326-7000 • Location: 31 miles SE of Shoshone (limited services), 53 miles N of Baker • GPS: Lat 35.773108 Lon -115.888294 • Open: All year • Total sites: 4 • RV sites: 4 • RV fee: Free • No water • Vault toilets • Activities: Hiking • Elevation: 4721

## Sierraville

**Bear Valley** (Tahoe NF) • Agency: US Forest Service • Tel: 530-994-3401 • Location: 14 miles E of Sierraville (limited services), 20 miles N of Truckee • GPS: Lat 39.557373 Lon -120.236816 • Total sites: 10 • RV sites: 5 • RV fee: Free • Central water • Vault toilets • Activities: Hiking, mountain biking • Elevation: 6608

## Smartsville

**Spenceville Wildlife Area** • Agency: State • Tel: 530-538-2236 • Location: 10 miles S of Smartsville (limited services), 25 miles E of Yuba City • GPS: Lat 39.110833 Lon -121.276516 • Open: Sep-Mar • Total sites: Dispersed • RV sites: Undefined • RV fee: Free • No water • No toilets • Activities: Hiking, mountain biking, fishing, hunting, equestrian area • Elevation: 325

## Soda Springs

**Woodchuck** (Tahoe NF) • Agency: US Forest Service • Tel: 530-265-4531 • Location: 12 miles W of Soda Springs (limited services), 24 miles W of Truckee • GPS: Lat 39.332913 Lon -120.519406 • Open: May-Sep • Total sites: 8 • RV sites: 8 • RV fee: Free • No water • Vault toilets • Activities: Swimming, motor sports • Elevation: 6299

## Springville

**Mountain Home State Forest - Frazier Mill** • Agency: State • Tel: 559-539-2321 • Location: 21 miles NE of Springville (limited services), 36 miles NE of Porterville • GPS: Lat 36.237236 Lon -118.689566 • Total sites: 49 • RV sites: 49 • Max RV Length: 20 • RV fee: Free • Central water • Vault toilets • Activities: Hiking • Elevation: 6362

**Mountain Home State Forest - Hedrick Pond** • Agency: State • Tel: 559-539-2321 • Location: 20 miles NE of Springville (limited services), 35 miles NE of Porterville • GPS: Lat 36.229668 Lon -118.680647 • Total sites: 14 • RV sites: 14 • Max RV Length: 20 • RV fee: Free • Central water • Vault toilets • Activities: Hiking • Elevation: 6368

**Mountain Home State Forest - Hidden Falls** • Agency: State • Tel: 559-539-2321 • Location: 21 miles NE of Springville (limited services), 36 miles NE of Porterville • GPS: Lat 36.258008 Lon -118.663404 • Total sites: 8 • RV sites: 8 • Max RV Length: 20 • RV fee: Free • Central water • Vault toilets • Activities: Hiking • Elevation: 6145

**Mountain Home State Forest - Moses Gulch** • Agency: State • Tel: 559-539-2321 • Location: 21 miles NE of Springville (limited services), 36 miles NE of Porterville • GPS: Lat 36.246 Lon -118.655 • Total sites: 10 • RV sites: 10 • Max RV Length: 20 • RV fee: Free • No water • Vault toilets • Activities: Hiking • Elevation: 5627

**Mountain Home State Forest - Shake Camp** • Agency: State • Tel: 559-539-2321 • Location: 21 miles NE of Springville (limited services), 36 miles NE of Porterville • GPS: Lat 36.249242 Lon -118.671054 • Total sites: 11 • RV sites: 11 (no large RV's) • Max RV Length: 20 • RV fee: Free • Central water • Vault toilets • Activities: Hiking • Elevation: 6562

## Stovepipe Wells

**Death Valley NP - Wildrose** • Agency: National Park Service • Tel: 760-786-3200 • Location: 30 miles S of Stovepipe Wells (limited services), 63 miles NE of Ridgecrest • GPS: Lat 36.265895 Lon -117.188276 • Open: All year • Stay limit: 30 days • Total sites: 23 • RV sites: 11 • RV fee: Free • Central water • Vault toilets • Elevation: 4239

## Strawberry

**Herring Creek** (Stanislaus NF) • Agency: US Forest Service • Tel: 209-965-3434 • Location: 9 miles NE of Strawberry (limited services), 37 miles NE of Sonora • GPS: Lat 38.244461 Lon -119.932471 • Open: May-Oct • Stay limit: 14 days • Total sites: 7 • RV sites: 7 • RV fee: Free (donation appreciated) • No water • Vault toilets • Activities: Fishing • Elevation: 7392

**Herring Reservoir** (Stanislaus NF) • Agency: US Forest Service • Tel: 209-965-3434 • Location: 9 miles NE of Strawberry (limited services), 37 miles NE of Sonora • GPS: Lat 38.248961 Lon -119.934786 • Open: May-Sep • Stay limit: 14 days • Total sites: 42 • RV sites: 42 • RV fee: Free (donation appreciated) • No water • Vault toilets • Activities: Hiking, fishing, equestrian area • Elevation: 7448

## Susanville

**Goumaz** (Lassen NF) • Agency: US Forest Service • Tel: 530-825-3212 • Location: 15 miles W of Susanville • GPS:

Lat 40.413916 Lon -120.862025 • Open: May-Sep • Total sites: 6 • RV sites: 6 • Max RV Length: 18 • RV fee: Free • Central water • Vault toilets • Activities: Hiking, mountain biking, equestrian area • Elevation: 5249

**Rice Canyon OHVA** • Agency: Bureau of Land Management • Tel: 530-257-0456 • Location: 8 miles E of Susanville • GPS: Lat 40.422112 Lon -120.526392 • Total sites: Dispersed • RV sites: Undefined • RV fee: Free • No water • Vault toilets • Activities: Motor sports • Elevation: 4335

**Rocky Point East** • Agency: Bureau of Land Management • Tel: 530-257-0456 • Location: 36 miles N of Susanville • GPS: Lat 40.673572 Lon -120.745552 • Open: All year • Total sites: Dispersed • RV sites: Undefined • RV fee: Free (donation appreciated) • No water • No toilets • Elevation: 5112

**Rocky Point West** • Agency: Bureau of Land Management • Tel: 530-257-0456 • Location: 37 miles N of Susanville • GPS: Lat 40.682601 Lon -120.757589 • Open: All year • Total sites: Dispersed • RV sites: Undefined • RV fee: Free (donation appreciated) • No water • No toilets • Elevation: 5249

## Taft

**Carrizo Plains NM - KCL CG** • Agency: Bureau of Land Management • Location: 35 miles W of Taft • GPS: Lat 35.090583 Lon -119.734886 • Open: All year • Total sites: 12 • RV sites: 12 • RV fee: Free • No water • Vault toilets • Elevation: 2280

## The Pines

**Bowler** (Sierra NF) • Agency: US Forest Service • Tel: 559-877-2218 • Location: 27 miles NE of The Pines (limited services), 35 miles NE of Oakhurst • GPS: Lat 37.509257 Lon -119.328103 • Open: Jul-Oct • Stay limit: 14 days • Total sites: 12 • RV sites: 12 • Max RV Length: 20 • RV fee: Free • No water • Vault toilets • Activities: Hiking, equestrian area • Elevation: 7110

## Tionesta

**Blanche Lake** (Modoc NF) • Agency: US Forest Service • Tel: 530-667-2246 • Location: 22 miles SW of Tionesta (limited services), 46 miles NE of Mc Cloud • GPS: Lat 41.557 Lon -121.57 • Open: Jul-Oct • Stay limit: 14 days • Total sites: 6 • RV sites: 6 • RV fee: Free • No water • Vault toilets • Activities: Fishing • Elevation: 6818

## Trona

**Trona Pinnacles NNL** • Agency: Bureau of Land Management • Tel: 760-384-5400 • Location: 11 miles S of Trona (limited services), 22 miles E of Ridgecrest • GPS: Lat 35.619093 Lon -117.370247 • Total sites: Dispersed • RV sites: Undefined • RV fee: Free • No water • Vault toilets • Notes: Road may be closed after heavy rains • Elevation: 1772

## Truckee

**Annie McCloud** • Agency: US Forest Service • Location: 4 miles NE of Truckee • GPS: Lat 39.380723 Lon -120.135419 • Total sites: 10 • RV sites: 10 • Max RV Length: 20 • RV fee: Free • No water • Vault toilets • Elevation: 5833

**Sagehen Creek** (Tahoe NF) • Agency: US Forest Service • Tel: 530-994-3401 • Location: 11 miles N of Truckee • GPS: Lat 39.434371 Lon -120.257461 • Open: May-Nov • Total sites: 10 • RV sites: 3 (not suitable for large RV's) • Max RV Length: 18 • RV fee: Free • No water • Vault toilets • Activities: Mountain biking • Elevation: 6526

## Upper Lake

**Bear Creek** (Mendocino NF) • Agency: US Forest Service • Tel: 707-275-2361 • Location: 30 miles NE of Upper Lake • GPS: Lat 39.322687 Lon -122.836399 • Total sites: 16 • RV sites: 16 • RV fee: Free • No water • Vault toilets • Activities: Hiking, fishing • Elevation: 2274

## Weed

**Deer Mt Snowpark** (Klamath NF) • Agency: US Forest Service • Tel: 530-398-4391 • Location: 20 miles NE of Weed • GPS: Lat 41.570447 Lon -122.132071 • Open: All year • Stay limit: 14 days • Total sites: 8 • RV sites: 8 • Max RV Length: 30 • RV fee: Free • No water • Vault toilets • Activities: Skiing • Elevation: 5763

## Westwood

**Bogard** (Lassen NF) • Agency: US Forest Service • Tel: 530-257-4188 • Location: 23 miles N of Westwood (limited services), 28 miles NW of Susanville • GPS: Lat 40.575297 Lon -121.098381 • Open: All year (not maintained in winter - often inaccessible) • Stay limit: 14 days • Total sites: 10 • RV sites: 10 • Max RV Length: 25 • RV fee: Free • Central water • Vault toilets • Activities: Mountain biking • Elevation: 5692

**McCoy Flat Reservoir Bridge - CDFW** • Agency: State • Location: 11 miles N of Westwood (limited services), 17 miles W of Susanville • GPS: Lat 40.446008 Lon -120.94413 • Total sites: Dispersed • RV sites: Undefined • RV fee: Free • No water • No toilets • Elevation: 5542

**McCoy Flat Reservoir Dam - CDFW** • Agency: State • Location: 11 miles N of Westwood (limited services), 17 miles W of Susanville • GPS: Lat 40.453193 Lon -120.941966 • Total sites: Dispersed • RV sites: Undefined • RV fee: Free • No water • No toilets • Elevation: 5565

## Willow Creek

**Groves Prairie** (Six Rivers NF) • Agency: US Forest Service • Tel: 530-629-2118 • Location: 21 miles E of Willow Creek (limited services), 60 miles E of Arcata • GPS: Lat 40.966182 Lon -123.487157 • Open: May-Oct • Total sites: 5 • RV sites: 5 • RV fee: Free • No water • Vault toilets • Activities: Hiking, hunting • Elevation: 4268

## Winterhaven

**Fergusen Lake** • Agency: Bureau of Land Management • Tel: 928-317-3200 • Location: 28 miles NE of Winterhaven (limited services), 28 miles N of Yuma, AZ • GPS: Lat 32.969803 Lon -114.497536 • Open: All year • Total sites: Dispersed • RV sites: Undefined • RV fee: Free • No water • No toilets • Activities: Hiking, fishing, power boating, non-power boating • Elevation: 177

## Wofford Heights

**Alder Creek** (Alta Sierra, Sequoia NF) • Agency: US Forest Service • Tel: 760-376-3781 • Location: 15 miles W of Wofford Heights • GPS: Lat 35.719825 Lon -118.611871 • Total sites: 13 • RV sites: 13 • Max RV Length: 20 • RV fee: Free • No water • Vault toilets • Elevation: 3950

**Evans Flat** (Sequoia NF) • Agency: US Forest Service • Tel: 760-379-5646 • Location: 13 miles SW of Wofford Heights • GPS: Lat 35.642804 Lon -118.589455 • Total sites: 20 • RV sites: 20 (4 horse sites) • Max RV Length: 20 • RV fee: Free • No water • Vault toilets • Activities: Equestrian area • Elevation: 6145

## Woodfords

**Snowshoe Springs** (Humboldt-Toiyabe NF) • Agency: US Forest Service • Location: 4 miles W of Woodfords • GPS: Lat 38.776878 Lon -119.884264 • Open: May-Sep • Stay limit: 14 days • Total sites: 5 • RV sites: 4 • RV fee: Free • No toilets • Activities: Hiking, fishing • Elevation: 6657

## Yreka

**Beaver Creek** (Klamath NF) • Agency: US Forest Service • Tel: 530-493-2243 • Location: 28 miles NW of Yreka • GPS: Lat 41.927669 Lon -122.829174 • Open: May-Oct • Stay limit: 14 days • Total sites: 8 • RV sites: 8 • RV fee: Free • No water • Vault toilets • Activities: Fishing, swimming • Elevation: 2246

# Colorado

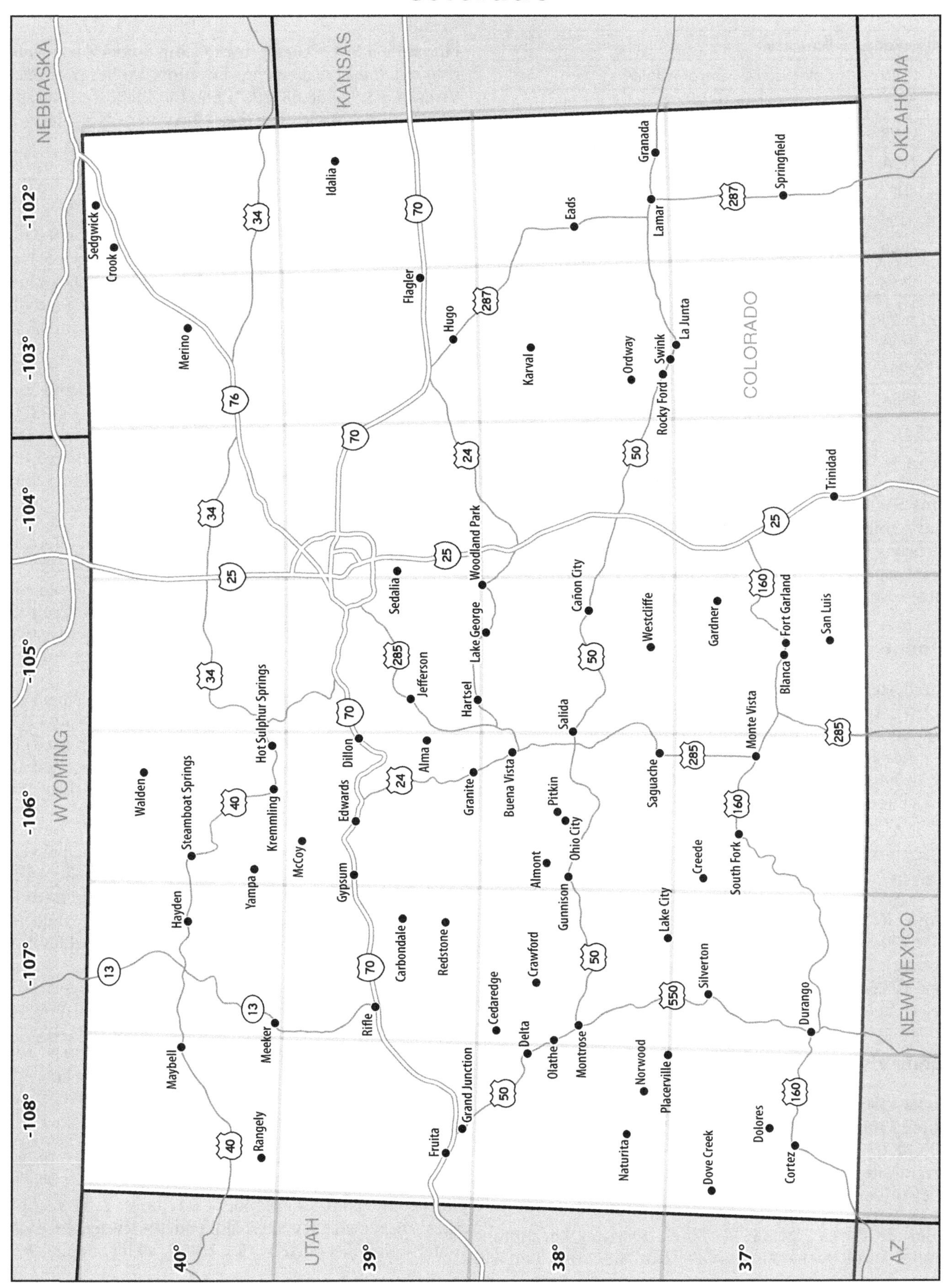
NEBRASKA
KANSAS
OKLAHOMA
WYOMING
UTAH
NEW MEXICO
AZ
COLORADO
-102°
-103°
-104°
-105°
-106°
-107°
-108°
40°
39°
38°
37°
Sedgwick
Crook
Idalia
Granada
Springfield
Eads
Lamar
Merino
Flagler
Hugo
Karval
Ordway
Swink
La Junta
Rocky Ford
Trinidad
Sedalia
Woodland Park
Lake George
Cañon City
Westcliffe
Gardner
Fort Garland
San Luis
Blanca
Jefferson
Hartsel
Salida
Monte Vista
Hot Sulphur Springs
Dillon
Alma
Granite
Buena Vista
Saguache
Walden
Steamboat Springs
Kremmling
Edwards
Pitkin
Ohio City
McCoy
Yampa
Gypsum
Almont
Gunnison
Creede
South Fork
Hayden
Carbondale
Redstone
Crawford
Lake City
Silverton
Cedaredge
Meeker
Rifle
Delta
Olathe
Montrose
Norwood
Placerville
Durango
Maybell
Grand Junction
Rangely
Fruita
Naturita
Dove Creek
Dolores
Cortez
13
40
34
76
70
25
24
50
287
285
160
550

# Colorado — Camping Areas

| Abbreviation | Description |
|---|---|
| CDW | Colorado Division of Wildlife |
| DOW | Divison of Wildlife |
| DWB | Denver Water Board |
| NCA | National Conservation Area |
| NF | National Forest |
| NM | National Monument |
| NWR | National Wildlife Refuge |
| OHV | Off-Highway Vehicle |
| SWA | State Wildlife Area |
| TMA | Travel Management Area |
| WMA | Wildlife Management Area |
| WSA | Wilderness Study Area |

## Alma

**Alma SWA** • Agency: State • Tel: 303-291-7227 • Location: 2 miles N of Alma (limited services), 8 miles N of Fairplay • GPS: Lat 39.319256 Lon -106.058032 • Total sites: Dispersed • RV sites: Undefined • RV fee: Free • No water • No toilets • Activities: Fishing • Elevation: 10499

## Almont

**Dorchester** (Grand Mesa-Uncompahgre-Gunnison NF) • Agency: US Forest Service • Tel: 970-874-6600 • Location: 37 miles NE of Almont (limited services), 47 miles NE of Gunnison • GPS: Lat 38.965683 Lon -106.660955 • Open: May-Oct • Total sites: 10 • RV sites: 10 • RV fee: Free (donation appreciated) • No water • Vault toilets • Elevation: 9933

## Blanca

**Smith Reservoir SWA** • Agency: State • Tel: 719-587-6900 • Location: 5 miles S of Blanca (limited services), 23 miles E of Alamosa • GPS: Lat 37.388345 Lon -105.531768 • Total sites: 15 • RV sites: 15 • RV fee: Free • Vault toilets • Activities: Fishing • Elevation: 7713

## Buena Vista

**Buena Vista** • Agency: Bureau of Land Management • Location: 2 miles N of Buena Vista • GPS: Lat 38.872347 Lon -106.147037 • Total sites: Dispersed • RV sites: Undefined (several sites along the road) • RV fee: Free • No water • No toilets • Elevation: 8070

**Colorado Pass** • Agency: US Forest Service • Location: 9 miles W of Buena Vista • GPS: Lat 38.813189 Lon -106.283709 • Total sites: 10 • RV sites: 10 • RV fee: Free • No water • No toilets • Activities: Hiking • Elevation: 9364

**Fourmile TMA - Turtle Rock Camp Spur** • Agency: Bureau of Land Management • Location: 3 miles N of Buena Vista • GPS: Lat 38.881897 Lon -106.144801 • Total sites: 20 • RV sites: 20 • RV fee: Free • No water • No toilets • Elevation: 8298

## Canon City

**Oak Creek** (Pike & San Isabel NF) • Agency: US Forest Service • Tel: 719-553-1400 • Location: 13 miles S of Canon City • GPS: Lat 38.296335 Lon -105.267209 • Open: All year • Total sites: 15 • RV sites: 15 • RV fee: Free • No water • Vault toilets • Activities: Hiking, mountain biking, fishing, motor sports • Elevation: 7680

**Penrose Commons WSA** • Agency: Bureau of Land Management • Location: 4 miles N of Canon City • GPS: Lat 38.493347 Lon -105.031589 • Open: Sep-May • Total sites: Dispersed • RV sites: Undefined • RV fee: Free • No water • No toilets • Activities: Hiking, mountain biking, motor sports, equestrian area • Elevation: 5817

**Red Canyon Park - Site 3** • Agency: Municipal • Tel: 719-269-9028 • Location: 10 miles N of Canon City • GPS: Lat 38.592487 Lon -105.253526 • Total sites: Dispersed • RV sites: Undefined • RV fee: Free • No water • Vault toilets • Notes: 72-hour limit • Activities: Hiking • Elevation: 6455

**Red Canyon Park - Sites 1-2** • Agency: Municipal • Tel: 719-269-9028 • Location: 10 miles N of Canon City • GPS: Lat 38.585925 Lon -105.248665 • Total sites: Dispersed • RV sites: Undefined • RV fee: Free • No water • Vault toilets • Notes: 72-hour limit • Activities: Hiking • Elevation: 6236

**Red Canyon Park - Sites 4-5** • Agency: Municipal • Tel: 719-269-9028 • Location: 10 miles N of Canon City • GPS: Lat 38.591336 Lon -105.254842 • Total sites: Dispersed • RV sites: Undefined • RV fee: Free • No water • Vault toilets • Notes: 72-hour limit • Activities: Hiking • Elevation: 6435

**Seep Springs WSA** • Agency: Bureau of Land Management • Location: 10 miles N of Canon City • GPS: Lat 38.557221 Lon -105.271448 • Open: Sep-Jun • Total sites: Dispersed • RV sites: Undefined • RV fee: Free • No water • No toilets • Activities: Hiking, mountain biking, motor sports, equestrian area • Elevation: 6332

**Temple Canyon Park** • Agency: Municipal • Tel: 719-269-9028 • Location: 6 miles SW of Canon City • GPS: Lat 38.406851 Lon -105.311406 • Stay limit: 3 days • Total sites: Dispersed • RV sites: Undefined • RV fee: Free • No water • No toilets • Activities: Hiking • Elevation: 6096

**Texas Creek** • Agency: Bureau of Land Management • Tel: 719-269-8500 • Location: 26 miles W of Canon City • GPS: Lat 38.415728 Lon -105.586324 • Open: Sep-May • Total sites: Dispersed • RV sites: Undefined • RV fee: Free • No water • No toilets • Activities: Hiking, mountain biking, motor sports • Elevation: 6291

## Carbondale

**Avalanche** (White River NF) • Agency: US Forest Service • Tel: 970-945-2521 • Location: 12 miles S of Carbondale • GPS: Lat 39.235855 Lon -107.202797 • Open: May-Sep • Total sites: 13 • RV sites: 13 • Max RV Length: 25 • RV fee: Free (donation appreciated) • Vault toilets • Activities: Hiking • Elevation: 7507

**Prince Creek Rd** • Agency: Bureau of Land Management • Location: 5 miles S of Carbondale • GPS: Lat 39.339897 Lon -107.159602 • Total sites: 5 • RV sites: 5 • RV fee: Free • No water • Vault toilets • Elevation: 7187

## Cedaredge

**Carson Lake** (Grand Mesa-Uncompahgre-Gunnison NF) • Agency: US Forest Service • Tel: 970-874-6600 • Location: 25 miles NW of Cedaredge • GPS: Lat 38.997025 Lon -108.111435 • Open: Jul-Sep • Total sites: 4 • RV sites: 4 • RV fee: Free • No water • Vault toilets • Activities: Hiking, fishing, equestrian area • Elevation: 9915

**Kiser Creek** (Grand Mesa-Uncompahgre-Gunnison NF) • Agency: US Forest Service • Location: 15 miles N of Cedaredge • GPS: Lat 39.037473 Lon -107.948123 • Open: Jul-Sep • Total sites: 12 • RV sites: 12 • Max RV Length: 16 • RV fee: Free • Vault toilets • Elevation: 10121

## Cortez

**Hovenweep NM - Canyon of the Ancients** • Agency: Bureau of Land Management • Tel: 970-882-5600 • Location: 36 miles NW of Cortez • GPS: Lat 37.44563 Lon -108.973315 • Total sites: Dispersed • RV sites: Undefined • RV fee: Free • No water • No toilets • Notes: Camp no closer than 300' to ruins • Activities: Hiking • Elevation: 6878

**McElmo Dome Sand Creek Overlook** • Agency: Bureau of Land Management • Location: 16 miles W of Cortez • GPS: Lat 37.383253 Lon -108.803658 • Total sites: Dispersed • RV sites: Undefined • Max RV Length: 25 • RV fee: Free • No water • No toilets • Activities: Hiking • Elevation: 7054

**Mesa Verde** • Agency: Bureau of Land Management • Location: 7 miles E of Cortez • GPS: Lat 37.360258 Lon -108.426089 • Total sites: 13 • RV sites: 13 • RV fee: Free • No water • No toilets • Elevation: 6707

## Crawford

**Mesa Creek** (Grand Mesa-Uncompahgre-Gunnison NF) • Agency: US Forest Service • Location: 21 miles S of Crawford (limited services), 32 miles S of Hotchkiss • GPS: Lat 38.475338 Lon -107.523574 • Total sites: 4 • RV sites: 4 • RV fee: Free • No toilets • Elevation: 8995

## Creede

**Hansons Mill** (Rio Grande NF) • Agency: US Forest Service • Tel: 719-658-2556 • Location: 16 miles E of Creede • GPS: Lat 37.813 Lon -106.737 • Total sites: 3 • RV sites: 3 • RV fee: Free • No water • Vault toilets • Activities: Hiking, fishing, motor sports, equestrian area • Elevation: 10935

**Ivy Creek** (Rio Grande NF) • Agency: US Forest Service • Tel: 719-657-3321 • Location: 15 miles S of Creede • GPS: Lat 37.682097 Lon -106.999589 • Open: Apr-Sep • Total sites: 4 • RV sites: 2 • Max RV Length: 25 • RV fee: Free • No water • Vault toilets • Activities: Hiking, fishing • Elevation: 9264

**Lost Trail** (Rio Grande NF) • Agency: US Forest Service • Tel: 719-657-3321 • Location: 37 miles W of Creede • GPS: Lat 37.768619 Lon -107.349813 • Total sites: 7 • RV sites: 7 • Max RV Length: 20 • RV fee: Free • Central water • Vault toilets • Activities: Hiking, mountain biking • Elevation: 9619

**Road Canyon** (Rio Grande NF) • Agency: US Forest Service • Tel: 719-657-3321 • Location: 26 miles W of Creede • GPS: Lat 37.754996 Lon -107.192111 • Total sites: 6 • RV sites: 6 • Max RV Length: 25 • RV fee: Free • No water • Vault toilets • Elevation: 9318

## Crook

**Tamarack Ranch SWA** • Agency: State • Tel: 970-842-6300 • Location: 2 miles S of Crook (limited services), 27 miles NE of Sterling • GPS: Lat 40.836279 Lon -102.804436 • Total sites: Dispersed • RV sites: Undefined • RV fee: Free • No water • Vault toilets • Activities: Hiking • Elevation: 3720

## Delta

**Cottonwood Grove** • Agency: Bureau of Land Management • Tel: 970-240-5300 • Location: 13 miles E of Delta • GPS: Lat 38.779104 Lon -107.853145 • Total sites: 6 • RV sites: 6 • Max RV Length: 25 • RV fee: Free • No water • Vault toilets • Activities: Non-power boating • Elevation: 5125

**Escalante Canyon Road** • Agency: Bureau of Land Management • Tel: 970-244-3000 • Location: 13 miles W of Delta • GPS: Lat 38.763711 Lon -108.244987 • Total sites:

Dispersed • RV sites: Undefined • RV fee: Free • No water • No toilets • Elevation: 4961

**Escalante Canyon Road** • Agency: Bureau of Land Management • Tel: 970-244-3000 • Location: 12 miles W of Delta • GPS: Lat 38.778569 Lon -108.250816 • Total sites: Dispersed • RV sites: Undefined • RV fee: Free • No water • No toilets • Elevation: 5293

## Dillon

**Keystone/Loveland Pass** • Agency: US Forest Service • Location: 7 miles E of Dillon • GPS: Lat 39.616912 Lon -105.929926 • Total sites: 6 • RV sites: 6 • Max RV Length: 25 • RV fee: Free • No water • No toilets • Elevation: 9670

## Dolores

**Groundhog Reservoir SWA** • Agency: State • Location: 31 miles N of Dolores • GPS: Lat 37.792859 Lon -108.290598 • Total sites: Dispersed • RV sites: Undefined • RV fee: Free • No water • Vault toilets • Elevation: 8750

## Dove Creek

**Aggregate** • Agency: Bureau of Land Management • Location: 7 miles NE of Dove Creek (limited services), 32 miles N of Cortez • GPS: Lat 37.804294 Lon -108.818986 • Total sites: Dispersed • RV sites: Undefined • RV fee: Free • No water • No toilets • Activities: Hiking, fishing • Elevation: 6087

**Box Elder** • Agency: Bureau of Land Management • Tel: 970-882-7296 • Location: 7 miles NE of Dove Creek (limited services), 32 miles N of Cortez • GPS: Lat 37.801119 Lon -108.824266 • Total sites: 11 • RV sites: 11 • RV fee: Free • No water • Vault toilets • Activities: Hiking, fishing • Elevation: 6087

**Cabin Canyon** (San Juan NF) • Agency: US Forest Service • Location: 18 miles SE of Dove Creek (limited services), 30 miles N of Cortez • GPS: Lat 37.628199 Lon -108.692988 • Total sites: 11 • RV sites: 11 • Max RV Length: 45 • RV fee: Free • Central water • No toilets • Activities: Fishing • Elevation: 6555

## Durango

**Miners Cabin** (San Juan NF) • Agency: US Forest Service • Location: 17 miles NW of Durango • GPS: Lat 37.381294 Lon -108.076952 • Total sites: 7 • RV sites: 7 • RV fee: Free • No water • Vault toilets • Activities: Hiking, fishing • Elevation: 8959

## Eads

**Queens SWA - Nee Gronda Reservoir** • Agency: State • Location: 16 miles S of Eads • GPS: Lat 38.295496 Lon -102.741622 • Total sites: Dispersed • RV sites: Undefined • RV fee: Free • Vault toilets • Activities: Fishing, power boating, non-power boating • Elevation: 3932

**Queens SWA - Nee Noshe Reservoir** • Agency: State • Location: 11 miles S of Eads • GPS: Lat 38.345456 Lon -102.707392 • Total sites: Dispersed • RV sites: Undefined • RV fee: Free • No toilets • Activities: Fishing, power boating, non-power boating • Elevation: 3924

**Queens SWA - Queens Reservoir** • Agency: State • Location: 18 miles S of Eads • GPS: Lat 38.296401 Lon -102.659925 • Total sites: Dispersed • RV sites: Undefined • RV fee: Free • No water • Vault toilets • Activities: Fishing, power boating, non-power boating • Elevation: 3884

## Edwards

**Bocco Mountain Recreation Area** • Agency: Bureau of Land Management • Tel: 970-876-9000 • Location: 10 miles NW of Edwards • GPS: Lat 39.742715 Lon -106.705977 • Total sites: Dispersed • RV sites: Undefined • RV fee: Free • No water • Vault toilets • Activities: Hiking, mountain biking, motor sports • Elevation: 7525

## Flager

**Flager Reservoir SWA** • Agency: State • Location: 5 miles E of Flager (limited services), 38 miles W of Burlington • GPS: Lat 39.290705 Lon -102.984358 • Total sites: Dispersed • RV sites: Undefined • RV fee: Free • No toilets • Elevation: 4721

## Fruita

**BLM Road 209** • Agency: Bureau of Land Management • Tel: 970-244-3000 • Location: 10 miles N of Fruita • GPS: Lat 39.305555 Lon -108.704494 • Total sites: 28 • RV sites: 28 (sites along 1 mile of road) • RV fee: Free • No water • No toilets • Notes: Firepans required • Activities: Hiking • Elevation: 5071

**Kokopelli's Trail - Jouflas** • Agency: Bureau of Land Management • Tel: 970-244-3000 • Location: 19 miles W of Fruita • GPS: Lat 39.175964 Lon -109.022171 • Total sites: 10 • RV sites: 4 • RV fee: Free • No water • No toilets • Activities: Hiking, motor sports • Elevation: 4696

**Kokopelli's Trail - Rabbit Valley** • Agency: Bureau of Land Management • Tel: 970-244-3000 • Location: 19 miles W of Fruita • GPS: Lat 39.179838 Lon -109.021429 • Total sites: Dispersed • RV sites: Undefined • RV fee: Free • No water • No toilets • Activities: Hiking, motor sports • Elevation: 4669

## Ft Garland

**Mountain Home Reservoir SWA - North** • Agency: State • Tel: 719-587-6900 • Location: 5 miles SE of Ft Garland • GPS: Lat 37.398782 Lon -105.386404 • Total sites: Dispersed • RV sites: Undefined • RV fee: Free • No water • Vault toilets • Activities: Fishing • Elevation: 8225

**Mountain Home Reservoir SWA - South** • Agency: State • Tel: 719-587-6900 • Location: 6 miles SE of Ft Garland • GPS: Lat 37.388922 Lon -105.384179 • Total sites: Dispersed • RV sites: Undefined • RV fee: Free • No water • No toilets • Activities: Fishing • Elevation: 8173

## Gardner

**Huerfano SWA - Site 1** • Agency: State • Tel: 719-561-5300 • Location: 16 miles SW of Gardner (limited services), 42 miles W of Walsenburg • GPS: Lat 37.687925 Lon -105.397849 • Total sites: Dispersed • RV sites: Undefined • RV fee: Free • No water • Vault toilets • Activities: Hiking, fishing • Elevation: 8793

**Huerfano SWA - Site 2** • Agency: State • Tel: 719-561-5300 • Location: 14 miles SW of Gardner (limited services), 40 miles W of Walsenburg • GPS: Lat 37.701266 Lon -105.382935 • Total sites: Dispersed • RV sites: Undefined • RV fee: Free • No water • Vault toilets • Activities: Hiking, fishing • Elevation: 8652

## Granada

**Deadman SWA** • Agency: State • Tel: 719-336-6600 • Location: 6 miles NE of Granada (limited services), 22 miles E of Lamar • GPS: Lat 38.085012 Lon -102.263278 • Total sites: Dispersed • RV sites: Undefined • RV fee: Free • No water • Elevation: 3472

## Grand Junction

**Divide Fork** (Uncompahgre NF) • Agency: US Forest Service • Tel: 970-874-6600 • Location: 36 miles S of Grand Junction • GPS: Lat 38.684429 Lon -108.689542 • Open: Apr-Nov • Total sites: 11 • RV sites: 11 • RV fee: Free • No water • Vault toilets • Activities: Motor sports • Elevation: 8740

**Dominguez-Escalante NCA - Big Dominguez** • Agency: Bureau of Land Management • Tel: 970-244-3000 • Location: 31 miles S of Grand Junction • GPS: Lat 38.745 Lon -108.55 • Open: May-Oct • Total sites: 9 • RV sites: 9 • RV fee: Free • No water • Vault toilets • Elevation: 7136

**Dominguez-Escalante NCA - Dominguez Creek** • Agency: Bureau of Land Management • Tel: 970-244-3000 • Location: 19 miles S of Grand Junction • GPS: Lat 38.829413 Lon -108.379162 • Total sites: Dispersed • RV sites: Undefined • RV fee: Free • No water • Vault toilets • Activities: Non-power boating • Elevation: 4765

**Dominguez-Escalante NCA - Triangle Mesa** • Agency: Bureau of Land Management • Tel: 970-244-3000 • Location: 20 miles S of Grand Junction • GPS: Lat 38.857154 Lon -108.398068 • Total sites: Dispersed • RV sites: Undefined • RV fee: Free • No water • Vault toilets • Activities: Non-power boating • Elevation: 4724

**Grand Valley OHV** • Agency: Bureau of Land Management • Tel: 970-244-3000 • Location: 3 miles N of Grand Junction • GPS: Lat 39.156361 Lon -108.541565 • Total sites: Dispersed • RV sites: Undefined • RV fee: Free • No water • No toilets • Activities: Motor sports • Elevation: 4884

## Granite

**Clear Creek SWA** • Agency: State • Tel: 719-530-5520 • Location: 4 miles S of Granite (limited services), 17 miles N of Buena Vista • GPS: Lat 39.020196 Lon -106.277599 • Open: All year • Total sites: Dispersed • RV sites: Undefined • RV fee: Free • No water • Vault toilets • Activities: Fishing, power boating, non-power boating • Elevation: 8914

## Gunnison

**Cochetopa** • Agency: Bureau of Land Management • Tel: 970-642-4940 • Location: 21 miles S of Gunnison • GPS: Lat 38.355024 Lon -106.781784 • Total sites: 14 • RV sites: 14 • Max RV Length: 25 • RV fee: Free • No water • Vault toilets • Elevation: 8369

**Gunnison SWA** • Agency: State • Tel: 970-641-7060 • Location: 7 miles W of Gunnison • GPS: Lat 38.527443 Lon -107.045123 • Total sites: Dispersed • RV sites: Undefined • RV fee: Free • No water • No toilets • Activities: Fishing • Elevation: 7854

**Hartman Rocks Recreation Area** • Agency: Bureau of Land Management • Tel: 970-642-4940 • Location: 3 miles S of Gunnison • GPS: Lat 38.496697 Lon -106.945371 • Total sites: Dispersed • RV sites: Undefined • RV fee: Free • No water • No toilets • Activities: Hiking, mountain biking, rock climbing, motor sports • Elevation: 8146

**Tomichi Dome State Trust Land** • Agency: State • Location: 24 miles E of Gunnison • GPS: Lat 38.511924 Lon -106.542858 • Total sites: Dispersed • RV sites: Undefined • RV fee: Free • No water • No toilets • Elevation: 8796

**Van Tuyl SWA** • Agency: State • Tel: 970-641-7060 • Location: 9 miles NE of Gunnison • GPS: Lat 38.611259 Lon -106.802283 • Total sites: Dispersed • RV sites: Undefined • RV fee: Free • No water • No toilets • Activities: Fishing, hunting • Elevation: 9066

## Gypsum

**Pinball Point** • Agency: Bureau of Land Management • Location: 25 miles N of Gypsum • GPS: Lat 39.841852 Lon -106.940927 • Open: All year • Total sites: 1 • RV sites: Undefined • RV fee: Free • No water • Vault toilets • Activities: Hiking, fishing, non-power boating • Elevation: 6463

## Hartsel

**Antero Reservoir - CDW** • Agency: State • Location: 8 miles W of Hartsel (limited services), 25 miles S of Fairplay • GPS: Lat 38.982765 Lon -105.896293 • Total sites: Dispersed • RV sites: Undefined • RV fee: Free • No toilets • Elevation: 8953

## Hayden

**Indian Run SWA - Beaver Creek** • Agency: State • Tel: 970-870-2197 • Location: 25 miles S of Hayden • GPS: Lat 40.253663 Lon -107.410554 • Total sites: Dispersed • RV sites: Undefined • RV fee: Free • Activities: Hiking, fishing • Elevation: 7198

**Indian Run SWA - Horse Camp** • Agency: State • Tel: 970-870-2197 • Location: 24 miles S of Hayden • GPS: Lat 40.268262 Lon -107.420933 • Total sites: Dispersed • RV sites: Undefined • RV fee: Free • Activities: Hiking, fishing, equestrian area • Elevation: 6926

## Hot Sulphur Springs

**Hot Sulphur Springs SWA - Joe Gerrans** • Agency: State • Tel: 970-725-6200 • Location: 3 miles SW of Hot Sulphur Springs • GPS: Lat 40.050801 Lon -106.130134 • Total sites: Dispersed • RV sites: Undefined • RV fee: Free • No water • Vault toilets • Activities: Hiking • Elevation: 7631

**Hot Sulphur Springs SWA - Lone Buck** • Agency: State • Tel: 970-725-6200 • Location: 3 miles SW of Hot Sulphur Springs • GPS: Lat 40.048957 Lon -106.139793 • Total sites: Dispersed • RV sites: Undefined • RV fee: Free • No water • Vault toilets • Activities: Hiking • Elevation: 7612

**Pioneer Park - City** • Agency: Municipal • Location: In Hot Sulphur Springs • GPS: Lat 40.07427 Lon -106.10816 • Total sites: 20 • RV sites: 20 • RV fee: Free • Central water • Vault toilets • Notes: Near RR tracks • Activities: Hiking, mountain biking, fishing • Elevation: 7678

**Williams Fork Reservoir - East Ramp - DWB** • Agency: Utility Company • Location: 8 miles SW of Hot Sulphur Springs • GPS: Lat 40.019872 Lon -106.199572 • Open: All year • Total sites: 16 • RV sites: 13 • RV fee: Free • No water • Vault toilets • Elevation: 7832

**Williams Fork Reservoir - West Ramp - DWB** • Agency: Utility Company • Location: 12 miles SW of Hot Sulphur Springs • GPS: Lat 40.007085 Lon -106.222308 • Open: All year • Total sites: 11 • RV sites: 11 • RV fee: Free • No water • Vault toilets • Elevation: 7841

## Hugo

**Hugo SWA - Clingingsmith #2 Reservoir** • Agency: State • Tel: 719-227-5200 • Location: 16 miles S of Hugo (limited services), 30 miles SE of Limon • GPS: Lat 38.935184 Lon -103.431517 • Total sites: Dispersed • RV sites: Undefined • RV fee: Free • No water • Vault toilets • Activities: Fishing • Elevation: 5003

**Hugo SWA - Middle** • Agency: State • Tel: 719-227-5200 • Location: 17 miles S of Hugo (limited services), 31 miles SE of Limon • GPS: Lat 38.923267 Lon -103.430772 • Total sites: Dispersed • RV sites: Undefined • RV fee: Free • No water • Vault toilets • Activities: Fishing • Elevation: 4970

**Hugo SWA - South** • Agency: State • Tel: 719-227-5200 • Location: 19 miles S of Hugo (limited services), 33 miles SE of Limon • GPS: Lat 38.896922 Lon -103.426867 • Total sites: Dispersed • RV sites: Undefined • RV fee: Free • No water • Vault toilets • Activities: Fishing • Elevation: 4980

**Kinney Lake SWA** • Agency: State • Location: 13 miles S of Hugo (limited services), 27 miles SE of Limon • GPS: Lat 38.972723 Lon -103.461492 • Total sites: Dispersed • RV sites: Undefined • RV fee: Free • No toilets • Activities: Fishing • Elevation: 5072

## Idalia

**South Republican (aka Bonny) SWA - Hale Corner** • Agency: State • Tel: 719-227-5200 • Location: 13 miles SE of Idalia (limited services), 28 miles N of Burlington • GPS: Lat 39.630101 Lon -102.142471 • Total sites: Dispersed • RV sites: Undefined • RV fee: Free • No water • Vault toilets • Elevation: 3612

**South Republican (aka Bonny) SWA - Hale Ponds** • Agency: State • Tel: 719-227-5200 • Location: 18 miles SE of Idalia (limited services), 34 miles N of Burlington • GPS: Lat 39.645341 Lon -102.057623 • Total sites: Dispersed • RV sites: Undefined • RV fee: Free • No water • Vault toilets • Activities: Fishing • Elevation: 3530

**South Republican SWA - East Beach** • Agency: State • Tel: 719-227-5200 • Location: 15 miles SE of Idalia (limited services), 26 miles N of Burlington • GPS: Lat 39.614337 Lon -102.170415 • Total sites: Dispersed • RV sites: 14 • RV fee: Free • No water • No toilets • Notes: Lake drained • Elevation: 3714

**South Republican SWA - North Cove** • Agency: State • Tel: 719-227-5200 • Location: 11 miles SE of Idalia (limited services), 32 miles N of Burlington • GPS: Lat 39.637331 Lon -102.186444 • Total sites: Dispersed • RV sites: 14 • RV fee: Free • No water • No toilets • Notes: Lake drained • Elevation: 3714

## Jefferson

**Tarryall Reservoir SWA - Derbyshire** • Agency: State • Tel: 303-291-7227 • Location: 17 miles SE of Jefferson (limited services), 32 miles E of Fairplay • GPS: Lat 39.230049 Lon -105.608738 • Total sites: 8 • RV sites: 8 • RV fee: Free • No water • No toilets • Activities: Fishing, power boating, hunting, non-power boating • Elevation: 8898

**Tarryall Reservoir SWA - Parker Gulch** • Agency: State • Tel: 303-291-7227 • Location: 18 miles SE of Jefferson (limited services), 33 miles E of Fairplay • GPS: Lat 39.222255 Lon -105.609707 • Total sites: 11 • RV sites: 11 • RV fee: Free • No water • No toilets • Activities: Fishing, power boating, hunting, non-power boating • Elevation: 8871

## Karval

**Karval Reservoir SWA - North** • Agency: State • Tel: 719-227-5200 • Location: 3 miles SE of Karval (limited services), 50 miles S of Limon • GPS: Lat 38.716544 Lon -103.507822 • Total sites: Dispersed • RV sites: Undefined • RV fee: Free • No water • No toilets • Activities: Fishing • Elevation: 5003

**Karval Reservoir SWA - South** • Agency: State • Tel: 719-227-5200 • Location: 3 miles SE of Karval (limited services), 50 miles S of Limon • GPS: Lat 38.715375 Lon -103.505948 • Total sites: Dispersed • RV sites: Undefined • RV fee: Free • No water • Vault toilets • Activities: Fishing • Elevation: 4980

## Kremmling

**Radium SWA - Sheephorn Unit** • Agency: State • Tel: 970-725-6200 • Location: 17 miles SW of Kremmling • GPS: Lat 39.950963 Lon -106.542146 • Total sites: Dispersed • RV sites: Undefined • RV fee: Free • No water • Vault toilets • Activities: Fishing, rock climbing • Elevation: 7037

**Wolford Mountain Recreation Area** • Agency: Bureau of Land Management • Tel: 970-724-3000 • Location: 2 miles N of Kremmling • GPS: Lat 40.073309 Lon -106.367377 • Total sites: Dispersed • RV sites: Undefined • RV fee: Free • No water • No toilets • Activities: Motor sports • Elevation: 7412

## La Junta

**Timpas Creek SWA** (Rocky Ford) • Agency: State • Tel: 719-336-6600 • Location: 9 miles W of La Junta • GPS: Lat 37.968217 Lon -103.705578 • Total sites: Dispersed • RV sites: Undefined • RV fee: Free • No water • No toilets • Activities: Fishing • Elevation: 4209

## Lake City

**Big Blue** (Grand Mesa-Uncompahgre-Gunnison NF) • Agency: US Forest Service • Location: 21 miles N of Lake City • GPS: Lat 38.217285 Lon -107.385498 • Open: Jun-Sep • Total sites: 11 • RV sites: 11 • RV fee: Free (donation appreciated) • No water • Vault toilets • Activities: Hiking • Elevation: 9652

**Mill Creek** • Agency: Bureau of Land Management • Location: 12 miles S of Lake City • GPS: Lat 37.906254 Lon -107.380846 • Total sites: Dispersed • RV sites: Undefined • RV fee: Free • No water • No toilets • Activities: Hiking, fishing • Elevation: 9414

**Rito Hondo** (Rio Grande NF) • Agency: US Forest Service • Tel: 719-852-5941 • Location: 26 miles SE of Lake City • GPS: Lat 37.892353 Lon -107.178379 • Open: All year • Total sites: 30 • RV sites: 30 • RV fee: Free • No water • Vault toilets • Activities: Fishing, non-power boating • Elevation: 10253

**Spruce** (Grand Mesa-Uncompahgre-Gunnison NF) • Agency: US Forest Service • Tel: 970-641-0471 • Location: 17 miles E of Lake City • GPS: Lat 38.047277 Lon -107.117029 • Open: Jun-Oct • Total sites: 9 • RV sites: 9 • Max RV Length: 15 • RV fee: Free (donation appreciated) • Central water • Vault toilets • Activities: Hiking, fishing • Elevation: 9346

## Lake George

**Tarryall Reservoir SWA - Potato Gulch** • Agency: State • Tel: 303-291-7227 • Location: 17 miles SE of Lake George (limited services), 32 miles E of Fairplay • GPS: Lat 39.226406 Lon -105.606333 • Total sites: 10 • RV sites: 10 • RV fee: Free • No water • No toilets • Activities: Fishing, power boating, hunting, non-power boating • Elevation: 8891

## Lamar

**Mike Higbee SWA** • Agency: State • Tel: 719-336-6600 • Location: 4 miles E of Lamar • GPS: Lat 38.084486 Lon -102.534558 • Total sites: Dispersed • RV sites: Undefined • RV fee: Free • No water • No toilets • Activities: Hiking, fishing, hunting • Elevation: 3597

**Thurston Reservoir SWA** • Agency: State • Location: 10 miles N of Lamar • GPS: Lat 38.219831 Lon -102.633395 • Total sites: Dispersed • RV sites: Undefined • RV fee: Free • No water • Vault toilets • Activities: Fishing, power boating, non-power boating • Elevation: 3806

## Maybell

**Browns Park NWR - Crook Camp** • Agency: US Fish & Wildlife • Tel: 970-365-3613 • Location: 53 miles NW of Maybell (limited services), 80 miles NW of Craig • GPS: Lat 40.809253 Lon -108.922304 • Total sites: Dispersed • RV sites: Undefined • RV fee: Free • No water • No toilets • Elevation: 5390

**Browns Park NWR - Swinging Bridge** • Agency: US Fish & Wildlife • Tel: 970-365-3613 • Location: 62 miles NW of Maybell (limited services), 91 miles NW of Craig • GPS: Lat 40.829642 Lon -109.035104 • Total sites: Dispersed • RV sites: Undefined • RV fee: Free • No water • No toilets • Elevation: 5453

**Irish Canyon** • Agency: Bureau of Land Management • Location: 50 miles NW of Maybell (limited services), 78 miles NW of Craig • GPS: Lat 40.829422 Lon -108.735592 • Total sites: 6 • RV sites: 6 • Max RV Length: 25 • RV fee: Free • No water • Vault toilets • Activities: Hiking, mountain biking • Elevation: 6643

**Rocky Reservoir** • Agency: Bureau of Land Management • Location: 69 miles NW of Maybell (limited services), 97 miles NW of Craig • GPS: Lat 40.959387 Lon -108.904992 • Total sites: 5 • RV sites: 5 • RV fee: Free • No water • Vault toilets • Elevation: 8468

**Sand Wash Basin** • Agency: Bureau of Land Management • Tel: 970-826-5000 • Location: 19 miles NW of Maybell (limited services), 47 miles NW of Craig • GPS: Lat 40.627231 Lon -108.380918 • Total sites: Dispersed • RV sites: Undefined • RV fee: Free • No water • No toilets • Activities: Motor sports • Elevation: 5827

## McCoy

**Catamount Bridge** • Agency: Bureau of Land Management • Tel: 970-876-9000 • Location: 8 miles W of McCoy (limited services), 36 miles NW of Edwards • GPS: Lat 39.890591 Lon -106.832303 • Open: All year • Total sites: 9 • RV sites: 9 • RV fee: Free • No water • Vault toilets • Notes: Near RR tracks • Activities: Fishing, non-power boating • Elevation: 6581

## Meeker

**Jensen SWA - Horse Camp 1** • Agency: State • Tel: 970-878-6090 • Location: 11 miles N of Meeker • GPS: Lat 40.146093 Lon -107.793714 • Total sites: Dispersed • RV sites: Undefined • RV fee: Free • Activities: Equestrian area • Elevation: 7658

**Jensen SWA - Horse Camp 2** • Agency: State • Tel: 970-878-6090 • Location: 12 miles NE of Meeker • GPS: Lat 40.130441 Lon -107.765727 • Total sites: Dispersed • RV sites: Undefined • RV fee: Free • Activities: Equestrian area • Elevation: 7234

**Jensen SWA - West Entrance** • Agency: State • Tel: 970-878-6090 • Location: 10 miles N of Meeker • GPS: Lat 40.146339 Lon -107.807649 • Total sites: Dispersed • RV sites: Undefined • RV fee: Free • Elevation: 7582

**Lake Avery #1 - DOW** • Agency: State • Location: 20 miles E of Meeker • GPS: Lat 39.970812 Lon -107.650204 • Total sites: Dispersed • RV sites: Undefined • RV fee: Free • No toilets • Elevation: 7008

**Lake Avery #2 - DOW** • Agency: State • Location: 20 miles E of Meeker • GPS: Lat 39.980279 Lon -107.641297 • Total sites: Dispersed • RV sites: Undefined • RV fee: Free • No toilets • Elevation: 7149

**Lake Avery #3 - DOW** • Agency: State • Location: 20 miles E of Meeker • GPS: Lat 39.982303 Lon -107.642213 • Total sites: Dispersed • RV sites: Undefined • RV fee: Free • No toilets • Elevation: 7152

**Lake Avery #4 - DOW** • Agency: State • Location: 20 miles E of Meeker • GPS: Lat 39.984785 Lon -107.643313 • Total sites: Dispersed • RV sites: Undefined • RV fee: Free • No toilets • Elevation: 7103

**Piceance SWA - Little Hills Unit** • Agency: State • Tel: 970-878-6090 • Location: 29 miles W of Meeker • GPS: Lat 40.008868 Lon -108.209677 • Total sites: Dispersed • RV sites: Undefined • RV fee: Free • No water • Vault toilets • Activities: Fishing • Elevation: 6106

**Piceance SWA - Square S Ranch Unit** • Agency: State • Tel: 970-878-6090 • Location: 30 miles W of Meeker • GPS: Lat 39.964236 Lon -108.266195 • Total sites: Dispersed • RV sites: Undefined • RV fee: Free • No water • No toilets • Elevation: 6030

**Rio Blanco Lake SWA** • Agency: State • Tel: 303-297-1192 • Location: 19 miles W of Meeker • GPS: Lat 40.092 Lon -108.21 • Total sites: Dispersed • RV sites: Undefined • RV fee: Free • No water • No toilets • Activities: Fishing • Elevation: 5784

## Merino

**Prewitt Reservoir SWA - Boat Ramp** • Agency: State • Location: 6 miles S of Merino (limited services), 17 miles S of Sterling • GPS: Lat 40.418133 Lon -103.381832 • Total sites: Dispersed • RV sites: Undefined • RV fee: Free • No water • Vault toilets • Activities: Fishing, power boating, non-power boating • Elevation: 4108

**Prewitt Reservoir SWA - North End** • Agency: State • Location: 3 miles S of Merino (limited services), 14 miles S of Sterling • GPS: Lat 40.439027 Lon -103.349847 • Total sites: Dispersed • RV sites: Undefined • RV fee: Free • No water • Vault toilets • Activities: Fishing • Elevation: 4072

**Prewitt Reservoir SWA - South End** • Agency: State • Location: 6 miles S of Merino (limited services), 17 miles S of Sterling • GPS: Lat 40.411506 Lon -103.385874 • Total sites: Dispersed • RV sites: Undefined • RV fee: Free • No water • Vault toilets • Activities: Fishing • Elevation: 4101

## Monte Vista

**Alamosa** (Rio Grande NF) • Agency: US Forest Service • Tel: 719-274-8971 • Location: 25 miles SW of Monte Vista • GPS: Lat 37.379395 Lon -106.345215 • Open: May-Sep • Total sites: 5 • RV sites: 5 • Max RV Length: 25 • RV fee: Free • No water • No toilets • Activities: Hiking, motor sports • Elevation: 8684

**Comstock** (Rio Grande NF) • Agency: US Forest Service • Tel: 719-657-3321 • Location: 19 miles SW of Monte Vista • GPS: Lat 37.445309 Lon -106.362832 • Open: May-Dec • Total sites: 7 • RV sites: 7 • Max RV Length: 35 • RV fee: Free • No water • Vault toilets • Activities: Hiking, fishing, motor sports • Elevation: 9718

**Rio Grande SWA** • Agency: State • Tel: 719-587-6900 • Location: 2 miles E of Monte Vista • GPS: Lat 37.575535 Lon -106.087615 • Total sites: Dispersed • RV sites: Undefined (camping only in parking lots with toilets) • RV fee: Free • No water • Vault toilets • Activities: Fishing, hunting • Elevation: 7643

**Rock Creek** (Greenie Mt, Rio Grande NF) • Agency: US Forest Service • Tel: 719-657-3321 • Location: 16 miles SW of Monte Vista • GPS: Lat 37.468506 Lon -106.332275 • Open: Apr-Dec • Total sites: 10 • RV sites: 10 • Max RV Length: 40 • RV fee: Free • No water • Vault toilets • Activities: Hiking, fishing • Elevation: 9219

## Montrose

**Flat Top OHV** • Agency: Bureau of Land Management • Tel: 970-240-5300 • Location: 4 miles N of Montrose • GPS: Lat 38.521346 Lon -107.859268 • Total sites: Dispersed • RV sites: Undefined • RV fee: Free • No water • Vault toilets • Activities: Hiking, mountain biking, motor sports, equestrian area • Elevation: 5900

## Naturita

**Dolores River - Bedrock Access** • Agency: Bureau of Land Management • Tel: 970-240-5300 • Location: 22 miles W of Naturita • GPS: Lat 38.304135 Lon -108.895086 • Total sites: 4 • RV sites: 4 • Max RV Length: 60 • RV fee: Free • No water • No toilets • Notes: 1-day limit • Activities: Non-power boating • Elevation: 4967

## Norwood

**Dan Noble SWA - Northeast** (Miramonte Reservoir) • Agency: State • Location: 18 miles S of Norwood (limited services), 47 miles W of Telluride • GPS: Lat 37.974813 Lon -108.333821 • Total sites: Dispersed • RV sites: Undefined • RV fee: Free • Central water • Vault toilets • Elevation: 7746

**Dan Noble SWA - Northwest** (Miramonte Reservoir) • Agency: State • Tel: 970-252-6000 • Location: 20 miles S of Norwood (limited services), 49 miles W of Telluride • GPS: Lat 37.976675 Lon -108.345344 • Total sites: Dispersed • RV sites: Undefined • RV fee: Free • No water • Vault toilets • Activities: Fishing, power boating, non-power boating • Elevation: 7713

**Dan Noble SWA - Southeast** (Miramonte Reservoir) • Agency: State • Location: 18 miles S of Norwood (limited services), 47 miles W of Telluride • GPS: Lat 37.964844 Lon -108.333863 • Total sites: Dispersed • RV sites: Undefined • RV fee: Free • Vault toilets • Elevation: 7716

**Dan Noble SWA - Southwest** (Miramonte Reservoir) • Agency: State • Location: 21 miles S of Norwood (limited services), 50 miles W of Telluride • GPS: Lat 37.967223 Lon -108.342367 • Total sites: Dispersed • RV sites: Undefined • RV fee: Free • Vault toilets • Elevation: 7720

**Lower Beaver** • Agency: Bureau of Land Management • Tel: 970-240-5300 • Location: 6 miles E of Norwood (limited services), 26 miles W of Telluride • GPS: Lat 38.109524 Lon -108.188844 • Total sites: 5 • RV sites: 5 • Max RV Length: 25 • RV fee: Free • No water • Vault toilets • Activities: Non-power boating • Elevation: 6696

## Ohio City

**Gold Creek** (Grand Mesa-Uncompahgre-Gunnison NF) • Agency: US Forest Service • Tel: 970-874-6600 • Location: 7 miles N of Ohio City (limited services), 26 miles NE of Gunnison • GPS: Lat 38.655175 Lon -106.574499 • Open: May-Oct • Total sites: 6 • RV sites: 6 • Max RV Length: 25 • RV fee: Free (donation appreciated) • No water • Vault toilets • Notes: Campers are required to store food and other items in a hard sided vehicle or camping unit constructed of solid non-pliable material • Activities: Hiking • Elevation: 10069

## Olathe

**Peach Valley OHV** • Agency: Bureau of Land Management • Tel: 970-240-5300 • Location: 6 miles E of Olathe • GPS: Lat 38.595108 Lon -107.889987 • Total sites: Dispersed • RV sites: Undefined • RV fee: Free • No water • Vault toilets • Activities: Motor sports • Elevation: 5630

## Ordway

**Lake Henry SWA** • Agency: State • Location: 4 miles NE of Ordway • GPS: Lat 38.25092 Lon -103.71143 • Total sites: Dispersed • RV sites: Undefined • RV fee: Free • No water • Vault toilets • Activities: Fishing, power boating, non-power boating • Elevation: 4380

**Lake Meredith SWA** • Agency: State • Location: 3 miles E of Ordway • GPS: Lat 38.212299 Lon -103.692423 • Total sites: Dispersed • RV sites: Undefined • RV fee: Free • No water • Vault toilets • Activities: Fishing, power boating, non-power boating • Elevation: 4275

**Ordway Reservoir SWA** • Agency: State • Location: 3 miles N of Ordway • GPS: Lat 38.250758 Lon -103.753474 • Total sites: Dispersed • RV sites: Undefined • RV fee: Free • No water • Vault toilets • Activities: Fishing • Elevation: 4400

## Pitkin

**Middle Quartz** (Grand Mesa-Uncompahgre-Gunnison NF) • Agency: US Forest Service • Tel: 970-641-0471 • Location: 6 miles E of Pitkin (limited services), 32 miles E of Gunnison • GPS: Lat 38.623 Lon -106.425 • Open: May-Sep • Total sites: 7 • RV sites: 7 • RV fee: Free (donation appreciated) • No water • Vault toilets • Elevation: 10348

## Placerville

**Caddiz Flats** • Agency: Bureau of Land Management • Tel: 970-240-5300 • Location: 2 miles W of Placerville (limited services), 17 miles NW of Telluride • GPS: Lat 38.027246 Lon -108.092968 • Total sites: 3 • RV sites: 3 • Max RV Length: 60 • RV fee: Free • No water • Vault toilets • Activities: Non-power boating • Elevation: 7303

## Rangely

**Canyon Pintado Historic District** • Agency: Bureau of Land Management • Tel: 970-878-3800 • Location: 13 miles S of Rangely • GPS: Lat 39.925968 Lon -108.737626 • Total sites: Dispersed • RV sites: Undefined • RV fee: Free • No water • No toilets • Activities: Hiking • Elevation: 5796

## Redstone

**McClure** (Grand Mesa-Uncompahgre-Gunnison NF) • Agency: US Forest Service • Tel: 970-527-4131 • Location: 10 miles S of Redstone (limited services), 25 miles S of Carbondale • GPS: Lat 39.123713 Lon -107.313118 • Open: May-Nov • Total sites: 10 • RV sites: 10 • Max RV Length: 35 • RV fee: Free • No water • Vault toilets • Elevation: 8205

## Rifle

**West Rifle Creek SWA** • Agency: State • Tel: 970-255-6100 • Location: 10 miles N of Rifle • GPS: Lat 39.662845 Lon -107.813748 • Total sites: Dispersed • RV sites: Undefined • RV fee: Free • No water • No toilets • Activities: Hiking • Elevation: 6368

## Rocky Ford

**Rocky Ford SWA - County Road FF** • Agency: State • Tel: 719-336-6600 • Location: 4 miles E of Rocky Ford • GPS: Lat 38.051973 Lon -103.653685 • Total sites: Dispersed • RV sites: Undefined • RV fee: Free • No water • No toilets • Elevation: 4180

## Saguache

**Lake Russell WMA** • Agency: State • Tel: 719-587-6900 • Location: 10 miles S of Saguache • GPS: Lat 37.938176 Lon -106.144024 • Total sites: Dispersed • RV sites: Undefined (must be self-contained) • RV fee: Free • No water • Vault toilets • Activities: Hunting • Elevation: 7595

## Salida

**CR 194** • Agency: Bureau of Land Management • Location: 9 miles N of Salida • GPS: Lat 38.638765 Lon -106.076023 • Total sites: Dispersed • RV sites: Undefined • RV fee: Free • No water • No toilets • Elevation: 7557

**Rincon** • Agency: Bureau of Land Management • Location: 8 miles SE of Salida • GPS: Lat 38.471351 Lon -105.871043 • Total sites: Dispersed • RV sites: Undefined • RV fee: Free • No water • Vault toilets • Elevation: 6788

## San Luis

**Sanchez Reservoir SWA** • Agency: State • Tel: 719-587-6900 • Location: 9 miles S of San Luis • GPS: Lat 37.097369 Lon -105.394542 • Total sites: Dispersed • RV sites: Undefined • RV fee: Free • No toilets • Notes: No camping in launch parking lot • Activities: Fishing • Elevation: 8320

## Sedalia

**Dutch Fred** (Pike & San Isabel NF) • Agency: US Forest Service • Location: 17 miles SW of Sedalia • GPS: Lat 39.290192 Lon -105.092383 • Open: May-Sep • Total sites: 11 • RV sites: 11 • RV fee: Free • No water • Vault toilets • Activities: Motor sports • Elevation: 8501

## Sedgwick

**Jumbo Reservoir SWA - Site 1** • Agency: State • Location: 9 miles W of Sedgwick (limited services), 36 miles NE of Sterling • GPS: Lat 40.920955 Lon -102.659954 • Total sites: Dispersed • RV sites: Undefined • RV fee: Free • Vault toilets • Activities: Fishing • Elevation: 3714

**Jumbo Reservoir SWA - Site 2** • Agency: State • Tel: 970-842-6300 • Location: 8 miles W of Sedgwick (limited services), 37 miles NE of Sterling • GPS: Lat 40.923855 Lon -102.646846 • Total sites: Dispersed • RV sites: Undefined • RV fee: Free • No water • Vault toilets • Activities: Fishing • Elevation: 3711

**Jumbo Reservoir SWA - Site 3** • Agency: State • Location: 8 miles W of Sedgwick (limited services), 37 miles NE of Sterling • GPS: Lat 40.932623 Lon -102.634854 • Total sites: Dispersed • RV sites: Undefined • RV fee: Free • No water • Vault toilets • Elevation: 3714

**Jumbo Reservoir SWA - Site 4** • Agency: State • Tel: 970-842-6300 • Location: 6 miles W of Sedgwick (limited services), 38 miles NE of Sterling • GPS: Lat 40.941846 Lon -102.634366 • Total sites: Dispersed • RV sites: Undefined • RV fee: Free • No water • Vault toilets • Activities: Fishing • Elevation: 3707

## Silverton

**Little Molas Lake** (San Juan NF) • Agency: US Forest Service • Location: 7 miles S of Silverton • GPS: Lat 37.744656 Lon -107.709869 • Total sites: 10 • RV sites: 5 • RV fee: Free • No water • Vault toilets • Activities: Fishing, power boating, non-power boating • Elevation: 11004

## South Fork

**Cathedral** (Rio Grande NF) • Agency: US Forest Service • Tel: 719-657-3321 • Location: 19 miles N of South Fork • GPS: Lat 37.822266 Lon -106.60498 • Open: Apr-Dec • Total sites: 22 • RV sites: 22 • Max RV Length: 45 • RV fee: Free • No water • Vault toilets • Activities: Hiking, mountain biking, fishing, motor sports • Elevation: 9475

**Stunner** (Rio Grande NF) • Agency: US Forest Service • Tel: 719-274-8971 • Location: 34 miles S of South Fork • GPS: Lat 37.377803 Lon -106.574129 • Open: May-Sep • Total sites: 5 • RV sites: 5 • Max RV Length: 25 • RV fee: Free • No water • Vault toilets • Activities: Motor sports • Elevation: 9866

## Springfield

**Two Buttes Reservoir SWA** • Agency: State • Tel: 719-336-6600 • Location: 19 miles N of Springfield • GPS: Lat 37.635616 Lon -102.544504 • Total sites: Dispersed • RV sites: Undefined • RV fee: Free • No water • Vault toilets • Activities: Hiking, fishing, rock climbing • Elevation: 4226

**Two Buttes Reservoir SWA** • Agency: State • Tel: 719-336-6600 • Location: 17 miles N of Springfield • GPS: Lat 37.622167 Lon -102.560531 • Total sites: Dispersed • RV sites: Undefined • RV fee: Free • No water • Vault toilets • Activities: Hiking, fishing, rock climbing • Elevation: 4252

## Steamboat Springs

**Middle Fork Elk River** (Medicine Bow-Routt NF) • Agency: US Forest Service • Location: 28 miles N of Steamboat Springs • GPS: Lat 40.772756 Lon -106.767631 • Total sites: 8 • RV sites: 8 • RV fee: Free • No water • Vault toilets • Elevation: 8076

## Swink

**Holbrook Reservoir SWA** • Agency: State • Location: 3 miles N of Swink (limited services), 7 miles E of Rocky Ford • GPS: Lat 38.055948 Lon -103.616874 • Total sites: Dispersed • RV sites: Undefined • RV fee: Free • No toilets • Activities: Fishing, power boating, non-power boating • Elevation: 4170

## Trinidad

**Lake Dorothey SWA** • Agency: State • Tel: 719-561-5300 • Location: 31 miles S of Trinidad, 10 miles N of Raton, NM • GPS: Lat 36.998685 Lon -104.365517 • Total sites: Dispersed • RV sites: Undefined • RV fee: Free • No water • Vault toilets • Activities: Fishing • Elevation: 7615

**Spanish Peaks SWA** • Agency: State • Tel: 719-561-5300 • Location: 20 miles NW of Trinidad • GPS: Lat 37.239466 Lon -104.786194 • Total sites: Dispersed • RV sites: Undefined • RV fee: Free • No water • No toilets • Elevation: 7405

## Walden

**Cowdrey Lake SWA** • Agency: State • Location: 8 miles N of Walden • GPS: Lat 40.83917 Lon -106.311947 • Total sites: Dispersed • RV sites: Undefined • RV fee: Free • No water • Vault toilets • Activities: Fishing • Elevation: 7976

**Diamond J/Brownlee SWA** • Agency: State • Tel: 970-870-2197 • Location: 2 miles W of Walden • GPS: Lat 40.742268 Lon -106.307369 • Total sites: Dispersed • RV sites: Undefined • RV fee: Free • No water • Vault toilets • Activities: Fishing, hunting • Elevation: 8116

**East Delaney SWA** (East Delaney Lake) • Agency: State • Location: 11 miles W of Walden • GPS: Lat 40.703127 Lon -106.454722 • Total sites: Dispersed • RV sites: Undefined • RV fee: Free • No water • No toilets • Elevation: 8127

**Hohnholz Lakes SWA** • Agency: State • Location: 51 miles NE of Walden, 40 miles SW of Laramie, WY • GPS: Lat 40.936189 Lon -105.968188 • Total sites: Dispersed • RV sites: Undefined • RV fee: Free • No water • No toilets • Activities: Fishing • Elevation: 6878

**Lake John SWA - East** • Agency: State • Tel: 970-870-2197 • Location: 15 miles NW of Walden • GPS: Lat 40.785619 Lon -106.46932 • Total sites: Dispersed • RV sites: Undefined • RV fee: Free • No water • No toilets • Activities: Fishing • Elevation: 8061

**Lake John SWA - North** • Agency: State • Tel: 970-870-2197 • Location: 16 miles NW of Walden • GPS: Lat 40.787711 Lon -106.483004 • Total sites: Dispersed • RV sites: Undefined • RV fee: Free • No water • Vault toilets • Activities: Fishing, power boating, non-power boating • Elevation: 8074

**Lake John SWA - South** • Agency: State • Tel: 970-870-2197 • Location: 15 miles NW of Walden • GPS: Lat 40.765961 Lon -106.470341 • Total sites: Dispersed • RV sites: Undefined • RV fee: Free • No water • Vault toilets • Activities: Fishing • Elevation: 8087

**Lake John SWA - West** • Agency: State • Tel: 970-870-2197 • Location: 17 miles NW of Walden • GPS: Lat 40.780831 Lon -106.477362 • Total sites: Dispersed • RV sites: Undefined • RV fee: Free • No water • Vault toilets • Activities: Fishing • Elevation: 8077

**North Delaney Lake SWA** • Agency: State • Location: 12 miles W of Walden • GPS: Lat 40.716704 Lon -106.469133 • Total sites: Dispersed • RV sites: Undefined • RV fee: Free • No toilets • Activities: Fishing, power boating, non-power boating • Elevation: 8179

**North Sand Hills Recreation Area** • Agency: Bureau of Land Management • Tel: 970-724-3000 • Location: 16 miles NE of Walden • GPS: Lat 40.870983 Lon -106.200034 • Total sites: 13 • RV sites: 13 • RV fee: Free • No water • Vault toilets • Activities: Motor sports • Elevation: 8619

**South Delaney Lake SWA - DOW** • Agency: State • Location: 11 miles W of Walden • GPS: Lat 40.702101 Lon -106.465403 • Total sites: Dispersed • RV sites: Undefined • RV fee: Free • No toilets • Elevation: 8127

**Walden Reservoir** • Agency: State • Location: 1 mile W of Walden • GPS: Lat 40.734254 Lon -106.301002 • Total sites: Dispersed • RV sites: Undefined • RV fee: Free • No water • No toilets • Elevation: 8062

## Westcliffe

**DeWeese Reservoir SWA** • Agency: State • Location: 8 miles N of Westcliffe • GPS: Lat 38.210127 Lon -105.453485 • Total sites: Dispersed • RV sites: Undefined • RV fee: Free • Central water • Vault toilets • Elevation: 7684

## Woodland Park

**Big Turkey** (Pike & San Isabel NF) • Agency: US Forest Service • Tel: 303-275-5610 • Location: 17 miles NW of Woodland Park • GPS: Lat 39.119992 Lon -105.227175 • Total sites: 10 • RV sites: 10 • RV fee: Free • Central water • Vault toilets • Activities: Fishing, motor sports • Elevation: 8032

## Yampa

**Crosho Lake** (Medicine Bow-Routt NF) • Agency: US Forest Service • Tel: 307-745-2300 • Location: 10 miles W of Yampa (limited services), 31 miles SW of Steamboat Springs • GPS: Lat 40.17 Lon -107.052 • Open: May-Nov • Total sites: 10 • RV sites: 10 • RV fee: Free • No water • Vault toilets • Activities: Hiking, fishing • Elevation: 8914

# Idaho

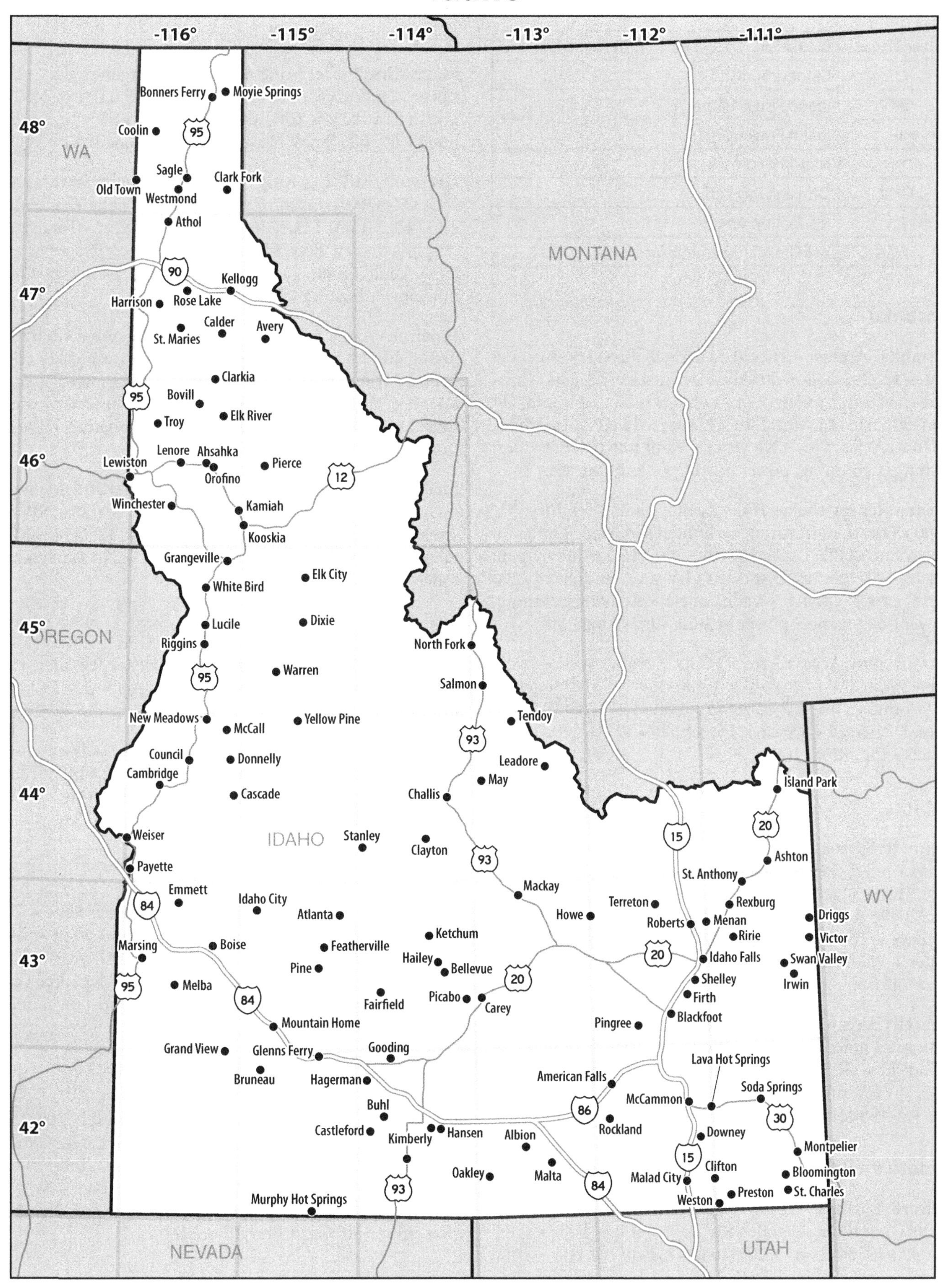
-116°
-115°
-114°
-113°
-112°
-111°
48°
47°
46°
45°
44°
43°
42°
WA
MONTANA
OREGON
IDAHO
WY
NEVADA
UTAH
Bonners Ferry
Moyie Springs
Coolin
Sagle
Old Town
Westmond
Clark Fork
Athol
Kellogg
Harrison
Rose Lake
Calder
St. Maries
Avery
Clarkia
Bovill
Troy
Elk River
Lenore
Ahsahka
Lewiston
Orofino
Pierce
Winchester
Kamiah
Kooskia
Grangeville
Elk City
White Bird
Lucile
Dixie
Riggins
North Fork
Warren
Salmon
New Meadows
Yellow Pine
McCall
Tendoy
Council
Donnelly
Cambridge
Leadore
May
Cascade
Challis
Island Park
Weiser
Stanley
Clayton
Payette
Ashton
St. Anthony
Mackay
Emmett
Terreton
Rexburg
Idaho City
Atlanta
Howe
Roberts
Menan
Driggs
Ketchum
Ririe
Victor
Marsing
Boise
Featherville
Hailey
Idaho Falls
Swan Valley
Pine
Bellevue
Shelley
Irwin
Melba
Picabo
Carey
Firth
Fairfield
Blackfoot
Mountain Home
Pingree
Grand View
Glenns Ferry
Gooding
Bruneau
Lava Hot Springs
Hagerman
American Falls
Soda Springs
McCammon
Buhl
Rockland
Castleford
Kimberly
Hansen
Albion
Downey
Montpelier
Clifton
Oakley
Malta
Malad City
Bloomington
Preston
St. Charles
Weston
Murphy Hot Springs
95
90
12
93
84
20
15
86
30

# Idaho — Camping Areas

| Abbreviation | Description |
|---|---|
| CG | Campground |
| IFG | Idaho Fish & Game |
| IP | Idaho Power |
| NF | National Forest |
| OHV | Off-Highway Vehicle |
| RA | Recreation Area |
| WMA | Wildlife Management Area |

## Ahsahka

**Ahsahka Access - IFG** (Clearwater River) • Agency: State • Tel: 208-334-3700 • Location: Just E of Ahsahka (limited services), 3 miles W of Orofino • GPS: Lat 46.500834 Lon -116.316116 • Total sites: Dispersed • RV sites: Undefined • RV fee: Free • No water • Vault toilets • Activities: Fishing, swimming, power boating • Elevation: 996

**Clearwater Hatchery - IFG** • Agency: State • Tel: 208-334-3700 • Location: In Ahsahka (limited services), 4 miles W of Orofino • GPS: Lat 46.505108 Lon -116.330368 • Open: All year • Total sites: Dispersed • RV sites: Undefined • RV fee: Free • No water • Vault toilets • Activities: Fishing, power boating, non-power boating • Elevation: 988

**McGill Spur Access Area - IFG** • Agency: State • Location: 2 miles W of Ahsahka (limited services), 6 miles W of Orofino • GPS: Lat 46.500456 Lon -116.374587 • Total sites: Dispersed • RV sites: Undefined • RV fee: Free • No toilets • Elevation: 1099

## Albion

**Bennett Springs** (Sawtooth NF) • Agency: US Forest Service • Tel: 208-678-0439 • Location: 12 miles S of Albion (limited services), 28 miles SE of Burley • GPS: Lat 42.326496 Lon -113.601639 • Open: Jun-Oct • Stay limit: 14 days • Total sites: 6 • RV sites: 6 • RV fee: Free • No water • Vault toilets • Activities: Hiking, fishing • Elevation: 7421

**Howell Canyon Sno-Park** • Agency: US Forest Service • Location: 12 miles S of Albion (limited services), 28 miles SE of Burley • GPS: Lat 42.327564 Lon -113.608842 • Total sites: 2 • RV sites: 2 • RV fee: Free • No water • Vault toilets • Activities: Hiking • Elevation: 7614

## American Falls

**Gifford Springs - IFG** • Agency: State • Tel: 208-334-3700 • Location: 24 miles SW of American Falls • GPS: Lat 42.640384 Lon -113.191946 • Open: All year • Total sites: Dispersed • RV sites: Undefined • RV fee: Free • No water • No toilets • Activities: Fishing, power boating, non-power boating • Elevation: 4216

**Mary Mine/Placer Mine Access - IFG** • Agency: State • Location: 5 miles SW of American Falls • GPS: Lat 42.743206 Lon -112.901735 • Total sites: Dispersed • RV sites: Undefined • RV fee: Free • No toilets • Elevation: 4245

**Oregon Trail Crossing - IFG** • Agency: State • Tel: 208-334-3700 • Location: In American Falls • GPS: Lat 42.774217 Lon -112.873695 • Open: All year • Total sites: Dispersed • RV sites: Undefined • RV fee: Free • No water • Vault toilets • Activities: Fishing, power boating, non-power boating • Elevation: 4276

**Pipeline** • Agency: Bureau of Land Management • Tel: 208-478-6340 • Location: 4 miles SW of American Falls • GPS: Lat 42.741446 Lon -112.899545 • Total sites: 8 • RV sites: 8 • Max RV Length: 17 • RV fee: Free • No water • Vault toilets • Activities: Fishing, non-power boating • Elevation: 4268

**Snake River Vista** • Agency: Bureau of Land Management • Tel: 208-677-6600 • Location: 6 miles SW of American Falls • GPS: Lat 42.708672 Lon -112.945489 • Total sites: 2 • RV sites: 2 • RV fee: Free • No water • No toilets • Elevation: 4319

**Snake River Vista Access - IFG** • Agency: State • Location: 5 miles SW of American Falls • GPS: Lat 42.742132 Lon -112.920942 • Total sites: Dispersed • RV sites: Undefined • RV fee: Free • Vault toilets • Activities: Fishing, power boating, non-power boating • Elevation: 4272

**West Ramp Acess - IFG** • Agency: State • Location: 3 miles NW of American Falls • GPS: Lat 42.814858 Lon -112.894658 • Total sites: Dispersed • RV sites: Undefined • RV fee: Free • No toilets • Elevation: 4373

## Ashton

**Sand Creek Ponds Access - IFG** • Agency: State • Tel: 208-334-3700 • Location: 20 miles NW of Ashton • GPS: Lat 44.213842 Lon -111.617662 • Open: All year • Total sites: Dispersed • RV sites: Undefined • RV fee: Free • No water • Vault toilets • Activities: Fishing, non-power boating • Elevation: 5543

## Athol

**Granite Lake - IFG** • Agency: State • Tel: 208-334-3700 • Location: 5 miles N of Athol • GPS: Lat 48.006332 Lon -116.689041 • Open: All year • Total sites: Dispersed • RV sites: Undefined • RV fee: Free • No water • Vault toilets • Activities: Fishing, power boating, non-power boating • Elevation: 2160

## Atlanta

**Queens River Transfer Camp** (Boise NF) • Agency: US Forest Service • Tel: 208-392-6681 • Location: 7 miles NW of Atlanta (limited services), 55 miles E of Idaho City • GPS: Lat 43.843162 Lon -115.183984 • Total sites: 6 • RV sites: 6 • RV fee: Free • No water • Vault toilets • Elevation: 5250

## Avery

**Camp 3** (Idaho Panhandle NF) • Agency: US Forest Service • Location: 25 miles SW of Avery (limited services), 47 miles SE of St Maries • GPS: Lat 47.129986 Lon -116.103074 • Open: May-Sep • Total sites: 4 • RV sites: 4 • RV fee: Free • No water • Vault toilets • Activities: Hiking, fishing, motor sports • Elevation: 3222

**Conrad Crossing** (Idaho Panhandle NF) • Agency: US Forest Service • Location: 28 miles E of Avery (limited services), 30 miles SW of St Regis, MT • GPS: Lat 47.158448 Lon -115.416833 • Open: May-Sep • Total sites: 8 • RV sites: 8 • RV fee: Free • Central water • Vault toilets • Activities: Hiking, fishing, non-power boating • Elevation: 3432

**Donkey Creek** (Idaho Panhandle NF) • Agency: US Forest Service • Location: 20 miles W of Avery (limited services), 42 miles SE of St Maries • GPS: Lat 47.185119 Lon -116.080703 • Total sites: 5 • RV sites: 4 • RV fee: Free • No water • No toilets • Activities: Fishing • Elevation: 2930

**Fly Flat** (Idaho Panhandle NF) • Agency: US Forest Service • Location: 32 miles E of Avery (limited services), 32 miles SW of St Regis, MT • GPS: Lat 47.112793 Lon -115.390869 • Open: May-Oct • Total sites: 14 • RV sites: 14 • RV fee: Free • Central water • Vault toilets • Activities: Hiking, fishing • Elevation: 3507

**Line Creek Stock Camp** (Idaho Panhandle NF) • Agency: US Forest Service • Location: 39 miles SE of Avery (limited services), 43 miles SW of St Regis, MT • GPS: Lat 47.043923 Lon -115.349783 • Open: May-Sep • Total sites: 9 • RV sites: 9 • RV fee: Free • No water • Vault toilets • Activities: Hiking, fishing • Elevation: 3743

**Mammoth Springs** (Idaho Panhandle NF) • Agency: US Forest Service • Location: 33 miles SE of Avery (limited services), 48 miles SW of St Regis, MT • GPS: Lat 47.103929 Lon -115.629608 • Open: Jun-Oct • Total sites: 8 • RV sites: 8 • RV fee: Free • Central water • Vault toilets • Activities: Hiking, motor sports • Elevation: 5633

**Spruce Tree** (Idaho Panhandle NF) • Agency: US Forest Service • Location: 40 miles SE of Avery (limited services), 41 miles SW of St Regis, MT • GPS: Lat 47.037994 Lon -115.347921 • Open: May-Oct • Total sites: 9 • RV sites: 9 • RV fee: Free • Central water • Vault toilets • Activities: Hiking, fishing • Elevation: 3786

## Bellevue

**Magic Reservoir - Lava Cove** • Agency: Bureau of Land Management • Location: 29 miles S of Bellevue • GPS: Lat 43.289604 Lon -114.397215 • Total sites: Dispersed • RV sites: Undefined • RV fee: Free • No water • Elevation: 4807

**Magic Reservoir - Lava Point** • Agency: Bureau of Land Management • Tel: 208-732-7200 • Location: 30 miles S of Bellevue • GPS: Lat 43.290437 Lon -114.389114 • Total sites: 9 • RV sites: 9 • RV fee: Free • No water • Vault toilets • Activities: Fishing, power boating, non-power boating • Elevation: 4808

**Magic Reservoir - Magic Dam** • Agency: Bureau of Land Management • Location: 19 miles S of Bellevue • GPS: Lat 43.256588 Lon -114.353426 • Total sites: Dispersed • RV sites: Undefined • RV fee: Free • No water • Elevation: 4808

**Magic Reservoir - Moonstone Access** • Agency: Bureau of Land Management • Tel: 208-334-3700 • Location: 16 miles SW of Bellevue • GPS: Lat 43.335703 Lon -114.432869 • Open: All year • Total sites: Dispersed • RV sites: Undefined • RV fee: Free • No water • Vault toilets • Activities: Fishing, power boating, non-power boating • Elevation: 4816

**Magic Reservoir - Myrtle Point** • Agency: Bureau of Land Management • Tel: 208-732-7200 • Location: 27 miles S of Bellevue • GPS: Lat 43.266233 Lon -114.377155 • Total sites: 1 • RV sites: 1 • RV fee: Free • No water • Vault toilets • Activities: Fishing, power boating, non-power boating • Elevation: 4784

**Magic Reservoir - Richfield Diversion** • Agency: Bureau of Land Management • Location: 20 miles S of Bellevue • GPS: Lat 43.220653 Lon -114.357019 • Total sites: Dispersed • RV sites: Undefined • RV fee: Free • No water • Elevation: 4690

**Stanton Crossing Access - IFG** • Agency: State • Location: 11 miles S of Bellevue • GPS: Lat 43.329264 Lon -114.320152 • Total sites: Dispersed • RV sites: Undefined • RV fee: Free • No toilets • Activities: Fishing • Elevation: 4839

## Blackfoot

**Cutthroat Creek** • Agency: Bureau of Land Management • Tel: 208-478-6340 • Location: 32 miles SE of Blackfoot • GPS: Lat 43.039654 Lon -111.856104 • Total sites: 3 • RV sites: 3 • RV fee: Free • No water • Vault toilets • Activities: Fishing, power boating, non-power boating • Elevation: 5876

**Graves Creek** • Agency: Bureau of Land Management • Tel: 208-478-6340 • Location: 29 miles SE of Blackfoot • GPS: Lat 43.043836 Lon -111.911149 • Total sites: 5 • RV sites: 5 • RV fee: Free • No water • Vault toilets • Activities: Fishing, power boating • Elevation: 5833

**Morgans Bridge** (Blackfoot River) • Agency: Bureau of Land Management • Tel: 208-478-6340 • Location: 28 miles SE of Blackfoot • GPS: Lat 43.058103 Lon -111.923338 • Open: May-Oct • Total sites: 5 • RV sites: 5 • RV fee: Free • No water • Vault toilets • Activities: Fishing, power boating • Elevation: 5820

**Sage Hen Flats** • Agency: Bureau of Land Management • Tel: 208-478-6340 • Location: 34 miles SE of Blackfoot • GPS: Lat 43.020141 Lon -111.826438 • Total sites: 5 • RV sites: 5 • Max RV Length: 15 • RV fee: Free • No water • Vault toilets • Activities: Fishing, power boating • Elevation: 5909

## Bloomington

**Harrys Hollow** (Caribou-Targhee NF) • Agency: US Forest Service • Location: 6 miles W of Bloomington (limited services), 18 miles SW of Montpelier • GPS: Lat 42.190296 Lon -111.508191 • Total sites: 3 • RV sites: 3 • RV fee: Free • No water • Vault toilets • Elevation: 6742

## Boise

**Cottonwood** (Boise NF) • Agency: US Forest Service • Tel: 208-587-7961 • Location: 29 miles E of Boise • GPS: Lat 43.632278 Lon -115.825072 • Open: May-Sep • Total sites: 3 • RV sites: 3 • RV fee: Free • No water • Vault toilets • Activities: Hiking, fishing, swimming • Elevation: 3300

**Willow Creek** (Arrowrock, Boise NF) • Agency: US Forest Service • Tel: 208-587-7961 • Location: 32 miles E of Boise • GPS: Lat 43.644043 Lon -115.752686 • Open: Apr-Oct • Total sites: 9 • RV sites: 9 • RV fee: Free • Central water • Vault toilets • Activities: Fishing • Elevation: 3307

## Bonners Ferry

**Brush Lake - IFG** • Agency: State • Location: 21 miles S of Bonners Ferry • GPS: Lat 48.887156 Lon -116.329662 • Total sites: Dispersed • RV sites: Undefined • RV fee: Free • No water • No toilets • Activities: Fishing • Elevation: 3032

**Moyie River Access - IFG** • Agency: State • Location: 28 miles NE of Bonners Ferry • GPS: Lat 48.971144 Lon -116.170364 • Total sites: Dispersed • RV sites: Undefined • RV fee: Free • No water • Vault toilets • Activities: Fishing • Elevation: 2597

**Smith Lake** (Idaho Panhandle NF) • Agency: US Forest Service • Location: 7 miles N of Bonners Ferry • GPS: Lat 48.778823 Lon -116.263806 • Open: May-Sep • Total sites: 7 • RV sites: 7 • Max RV Length: 16 • RV fee: Free • Central water • Vault toilets • Activities: Fishing, swimming • Elevation: 3032

**Dawson Lake Access Area - IFG** • Agency: State • Location: 9 miles NE of Bonners Ferry • GPS: Lat 48.781162 Lon -116.237783 • Total sites: Dispersed • RV sites: Undefined • RV fee: Free • No water • Vault toilets • Activities: Fishing, power boating (electric motors only), non-power boating • Elevation: 2963

## Bovill

**Blue Lagoon Ponds Access - IFG** • Agency: State • Location: 1 mile W of Bovill (limited services), 30 miles NE of Moscow • GPS: Lat 46.851547 Lon -116.420478 • Total sites: Dispersed • RV sites: Undefined • RV fee: Free • No water • No toilets • Activities: Fishing • Elevation: 3002

## Bruneau

**Cove Arm Lake - IFG** • Agency: State • Location: 10 miles NW of Bruneau (limited services), 25 miles SW of Mountain Home • GPS: Lat 42.96529 Lon -115.86125 • Total sites: Dispersed • RV sites: Undefined • RV fee: Free • No water • Vault toilets • Activities: Fishing, power boating • Elevation: 2474

**Crane Falls - Access - IFG** • Agency: State • Location: 8 miles N of Bruneau (limited services), 23 miles SW of Mountain Home • GPS: Lat 42.965857 Lon -115.838559 • Total sites: Dispersed • RV sites: Undefined • RV fee: Free • No water • Vault toilets • Activities: Fishing • Elevation: 2461

**Crane Falls East - IP** • Agency: Utility Company • Tel: 541-785-7209 • Location: 8 miles N of Bruneau (limited services), 23 miles SW of Mountain Home • GPS: Lat 42.970526 Lon -115.834074 • Stay limit: 14 days • Total sites: Dispersed • RV sites: Undefined • RV fee: Free • No water • Vault toilets • Activities: Fishing, power boating • Elevation: 2466

**Grasmere Reservoir Public Access - IFG** • Agency: State • Location: 44 miles S of Bruneau (limited services), 65 miles S of Mountain Home • GPS: Lat 42.363233 Lon -115.909261 • Total sites: Dispersed • RV sites: Undefined • RV fee: Free • No toilets • Elevation: 5210

**Jacks Creek - IP** • Agency: Utility Company • Tel: 541-785-7209 • Location: 5 miles NW of Bruneau (limited services), 24 miles SW of Mountain Home • GPS: Lat 42.902877 Lon -115.864269 • Stay limit: 14 days • Total sites: Dispersed • RV sites: Undefined • RV fee: Free • No water • Vault toilets • Activities: Fishing, power boating • Elevation: 2460

## Buhl

**Niagara Springs WMA - Cedar Draw - IFG** • Agency: State • Tel: 208-324-4359 • Location: 10 miles NE of Buhl • GPS: Lat 42.659632 Lon -114.670685 • Open: All year • Total sites: Dispersed • RV sites: Undefined • RV fee: Free • No water • Vault toilets • Activities: Fishing, power boating, non-power boating • Elevation: 2985

## Calder

**Big Creek** (Marble Creek) (Idaho Panhandle NF) • Agency: US Forest Service • Location: 8 miles NE of Calder (limited services), 32 miles E of St Maries • GPS: Lat 47.303456 Lon -116.120193 • Open: May-Sep • Total sites: 9 • RV sites: 9 • RV fee: Free • Central water • Vault toilets • Activities: Hiking, fishing, swimming, motor sports • Elevation: 2444

## Cambridge

**Brownlee Creek Access - IFG** • Agency: State • Tel: 208-334-3700 • Location: 23 miles NW of Cambridge (limited services), 52 miles S of Weiser • GPS: Lat 44.786792 Lon -116.911876 • Open: All year • Total sites: Dispersed • RV sites: Undefined • RV fee: Free • No water • Vault toilets • Activities: Fishing, power boating, non-power boating • Elevation: 2091

## Carey

**Copper Creek** (Sawtooth NF) • Agency: US Forest Service • Tel: 208-622-5371 • Location: 27 miles N of Carey (limited services), 50 miles NE of Bellevue • GPS: Lat 43.607146 Lon -113.929486 • Open: May-Oct • Total sites: 8 • RV sites: 8 • RV fee: Free • No water • Vault toilets • Activities: Fishing • Elevation: 6604

**Fish Creek Reservoir** • Agency: Bureau of Land Management • Tel: 208-732-7200 • Location: 14 miles NE of Carey (limited services), 37 miles E of Bellevue • GPS: Lat 43.432048 Lon -113.824136 • Total sites: 1 • RV sites: 1 • RV fee: Free • No water • Vault toilets • Activities: Fishing, power boating, non-power boating • Elevation: 5338

**Little Wood River Reservoir** • Agency: US Bureau of Reclamation • Tel: 208-678-0461 • Location: 11 miles NW of Carey (limited services), 33 miles E of Bellevue • GPS: Lat 43.435106 Lon -114.029215 • Open: All year • Total sites: 16 • RV sites: 16 • RV fee: Free • Central water • Vault toilets • Activities: Fishing, swimming, power boating, hunting, non-power boating • Elevation: 5279

**Preacher (Pangari) Bridge** - IFG • Agency: State • Tel: 208-334-3700 • Location: 10 miles SW of Carey (limited services), 32 miles SE of Bellevue • GPS: Lat 43.190288 Lon -114.019173 • Open: All year • Total sites: Dispersed • RV sites: Undefined • RV fee: Free • No water • No toilets • Activities: Fishing • Elevation: 4631

**Silver Creek North** • Agency: Bureau of Land Management • Tel: 208-732-7200 • Location: 8 miles SW of Carey (limited services), 20 miles SE of Bellevue • GPS: Lat 43.250552 Lon -113.996463 • Open: Apr-Nov • Total sites: 1 • RV sites: 1 • RV fee: Free • No water • Vault toilets • Elevation: 4722

**Silver Creek South** • Agency: Bureau of Land Management • Tel: 208-732-7200 • Location: 7 miles SW of Carey (limited services), 21 miles SE of Bellevue • GPS: Lat 43.245947 Lon -113.995983 • Open: Apr-Nov • Total sites: 2 • RV sites: 2 • RV fee: Free • No water • Vault toilets • Elevation: 4706

## Cascade

**Buck Mountain** (Boise NF) • Agency: US Forest Service • Tel: 208-382-7400 • Location: 37 miles NE of Cascade • GPS: Lat 44.681788 Lon -115.539819 • Open: May-Sep • Total sites: 4 • RV sites: 4 • RV fee: Free • No water • Vault toilets • Activities: Hiking, fishing, motor sports • Elevation: 6686

**Deer Flat** (Boise NF) • Agency: US Forest Service • Tel: 208-259-3361 • Location: 57 miles SE of Cascade • GPS: Lat 44.408713 Lon -115.553703 • Open: Jun-Sep • Total sites: 5 • RV sites: 5 • Max RV Length: 22 • RV fee: Free • No water • Vault toilets • Elevation: 6283

**Herrick Reservoir Access - IFG** • Agency: State • Location: 10 miles S of Cascade • GPS: Lat 44.376968 Lon -115.982959 • Total sites: Dispersed • RV sites: Undefined • RV fee: Free • No toilets • Elevation: 4875

**Highway 55** • Agency: State • Location: 22 miles S of Cascade • GPS: Lat 44.242776 Lon -116.102822 • Total sites: Dispersed • RV sites: Undefined • RV fee: Free • No water • No toilets • Elevation: 4197

**Penn Basin** (Boise NF) • Agency: US Forest Service • Tel: 208-382-7400 • Location: 38 miles NE of Cascade • GPS: Lat 44.624417 Lon -115.524476 • Open: May-Sep • Total sites: 6 • RV sites: 6 • RV fee: Free • No water • Vault toilets • Activities: Hiking, fishing, motor sports • Elevation: 6683

**Summit Lake** (Boise NF) • Agency: US Forest Service • Tel: 208-382-7400 • Location: 32 miles NE of Cascade • GPS: Lat 44.644943 Lon -115.585514 • Open: May-Sep • Total sites: 3 • RV sites: 3 • RV fee: Free • No water • Vault toilets • Activities: Hiking, fishing • Elevation: 7313

**Tripod Reservoir Access - IFG** • Agency: State • Location: 18 miles S of Cascade • GPS: Lat 44.290058 Lon -116.099464 • Total sites: Dispersed • RV sites: Undefined • RV fee: Free • No water • Vault toilets • Activities: Fishing • Elevation: 5056

**Trout Creek** (Boise NF) • Agency: US Forest Service • Tel: 208-382-7400 • Location: 36 miles NE of Cascade • GPS: Lat 44.747081 Lon -115.555146 • Open: May-Sep • Total sites: 8 • RV sites: 8 • RV fee: Free • No water • Vault toilets • Activities: Hiking, fishing, motor sports • Elevation: 6348

**Wellington Sno-Park** • Agency: State • Location: 17 miles S of Cascade • GPS: Lat 44.297534 Lon -116.088821 • Total sites: Dispersed • RV sites: Undefined • RV fee: Free • No water • Vault toilets • Elevation: 4528

## Castleford

**Balanced Rock** • Agency: County • Tel: 208-734-9491 • Location: 5 miles E of Castleford (limited services), 14 miles SW of Buhl • GPS: Lat 42.542542 Lon -114.949807 • Total sites: 15 • RV sites: 7 (tight turn-around) • RV fee: Free • No water • Vault toilets • Activities: Hiking • Elevation: 3437

## Challis

**93 Bridge - IFG** • Agency: State • Location: 2 miles S of Challis • GPS: Lat 44.469496 Lon -114.201288 • Total sites: Dispersed • RV sites: Undefined • RV fee: Free • No toilets • Elevation: 4997

**Big Creek** (Big Creek Peak, Salmon-Challis NF) • Agency: US Forest Service • Tel: 208-879-4100 • Location: 50 miles E of Challis • GPS: Lat 44.441716 Lon -113.598972 • Open: May-Sep • Total sites: 3 • RV sites: 3 • Max RV Length: 16 • RV fee: Free • No water • Vault toilets • Activities: Hiking, motor sports • Elevation: 6657

**Boulder White Clouds** • Agency: Bureau of Land Management • Tel: 208-879-6200 • Location: 43 miles SW of Challis • GPS: Lat 44.027199 Lon -114.465425 • Total sites: Dispersed • RV sites: Undefined • RV fee: Free • No water • No toilets • Activities: Hiking, fishing, hunting, equestrian area • Elevation: 6425

**Colston Creek Access - IFG** • Agency: State • Tel: 208-334-3700 • Location: 23 miles NE of Challis • GPS: Lat 44.753062 Lon -113.995672 • Open: All year • Total sites: 6 • RV sites: 6 • RV fee: Free • No water • Vault toilets • Activities: Fishing, power boating, non-power boating • Elevation: 4556

**Deadman Hole** • Agency: Bureau of Land Management • Tel: 208-879-6200 • Location: 12 miles S of Challis • GPS: Lat 44.344377 Lon -114.269932 • Open: All year • Total sites: 5 • RV sites: 5 • RV fee: Free • Central water • Vault toilets • Activities: Fishing • Elevation: 5233

**Deer Gulch Access - IFG** • Agency: State • Tel: 208-334-3700 • Location: 18 miles NE of Challis • GPS: Lat 44.703684 Lon -114.042945 • Open: All year • Total sites: Dispersed • RV sites: Undefined • RV fee: Free • No water • Vault toilets • Activities: Fishing, power boating, non-power boating • Elevation: 4632

**Eightmile** (Salmon-Challis NF) • Agency: US Forest Service • Tel: 208-879-4100 • Location: 28 miles W of Challis • GPS: Lat 44.426304 Lon -114.621188 • Open: May-Sep • Total sites: 4 • RV sites: 4 • Max RV Length: 16 • RV fee: Free • No water • Vault toilets • Notes: Meadow across the road can accomodate larger camp trailers • Activities: Fishing • Elevation: 6850

**Ellis North - IFG** • Agency: State • Location: 17 miles NE of Challis • GPS: Lat 44.691283 Lon -114.049686 • Total sites: Dispersed • RV sites: Undefined • RV fee: Free • No water • Vault toilets • Activities: Fishing • Elevation: 4652

**Ellis South Access - IFG** • Agency: State • Tel: 208-334-3700 • Location: 16 miles NE of Challis • GPS: Lat 44.687035 Lon -114.055725 • Open: All year • Total sites: Dispersed • RV sites: Undefined • RV fee: Free • No water • Vault toilets • Activities: Fishing • Elevation: 4658

**Little Boulder** • Agency: Bureau of Land Management • Tel: 208-879-6200 • Location: 39 miles SW of Challis • GPS: Lat 44.088561 Lon -114.445017 • Open: All year • Total sites: 3 • RV sites: 3 • RV fee: Free • Central water • Vault toilets • Activities: Hiking, fishing, swimming, equestrian area • Elevation: 6177

**Little West Fork** (Salmon-Challis NF) • Agency: US Forest Service • Tel: 208-879-4100 • Location: 22 miles N of Challis • GPS: Lat 44.684726 Lon -114.342465 • Total sites: 1 • RV sites: 1 • RV fee: Free • No water • No toilets • Elevation: 7592

**Lost Spring** (Salmon-Challis NF) • Agency: US Forest Service • Tel: 208-756-5200 • Location: 47 miles NW of Challis • GPS: Lat 44.842999 Lon -114.466441 • Open: Jul-Oct • Total sites: 6 • RV sites: 6 • RV fee: Free • No water • Vault toilets • Elevation: 5344

**Lower Herd Creek Trailhead** • Agency: Bureau of Land Management • Location: 29 miles S of Challis • GPS: Lat 44.150721 Lon -114.296288 • Total sites: Dispersed • RV sites: Undefined • RV fee: Free • No water • No toilets • Activities: Hiking • Elevation: 5795

**Lower McKim Creek Access - IFG** • Agency: State • Tel: 208-334-3700 • Location: 28 miles N of Challis • GPS: Lat 44.810353 Lon -114.009592 • Open: All year • Total sites: Dispersed • RV sites: Undefined • RV fee: Free • No water • No toilets • Activities: Fishing • Elevation: 4486

**Middle Fork Peak** (Salmon-Challis NF) • Agency: US Forest Service • Tel: 208-756-5200 • Location: 67 miles NW of Challis • GPS: Lat 44.961855 Lon -114.643602 • Open: Jul-Oct • Total sites: 3 • RV sites: 3 • RV fee: Free • No water • Vault toilets • Activities: Hiking • Elevation: 7812

**Morgan Creek** • Agency: Bureau of Land Management • Tel: 208-879-6200 • Location: 13 miles N of Challis • GPS: Lat 44.667956 Lon -114.229757 • Open: May-Oct • Total sites: 4 • RV sites: 4 • RV fee: Free • Central water • Vault toilets • Activities: Hiking, mountain biking, fishing, swimming, equestrian area • Elevation: 5545

**Mosquito Flat** (Salmon-Challis NF) • Agency: US Forest Service • Tel: 208-879-4100 • Location: 17 miles W of Challis • GPS: Lat 44.519616 Lon -114.433212 • Open: May-Oct • Total sites: 11 • RV sites: 11 • Max RV Length: 32 • RV fee: Free • Central water • Vault toilets • Activities: Fishing, power boating, non-power boating • Elevation: 7024

**Pennal Gulch Access - IFG** • Agency: State • Tel: 208-334-3700 • Location: 3 miles N of Challis • GPS: Lat 44.545105 Lon -114.179145 • Open: All year • Total sites: Dispersed • RV sites: Undefined • RV fee: Free • No water • No toilets • Activities: Fishing, power boating, non-power boating • Elevation: 4879

**Upper McKim Creek Access - IFG** • Agency: State • Tel: 208-334-3700 • Location: 27 miles N of Challis • GPS: Lat 44.797346 Lon -114.003815 • Open: All year • Total sites: Dispersed • RV sites: Undefined • RV fee: Free • No water • No toilets • Activities: Fishing, power boating, non-power boating • Elevation: 4495

**Watts Bridge Access - IFG** • Agency: State • Location: 10 miles N of Challis • GPS: Lat 44.631888 Lon -114.146669 • Open: All year • Total sites: 12 • RV sites: 12 • RV fee: Free • No water • Vault toilets • Activities: Fishing • Elevation: 4757

**West Fork Morgan Creek** (Salmon-Challis NF) • Agency: US Forest Service • Tel: 208-879-4100 • Location: 19 miles N of Challis • GPS: Lat 44.702738 Lon -114.315662 • Open: Jul-Oct • Total sites: 1 • RV sites: 1 • RV fee: Free • No water • Vault toilets • Elevation: 6453

## Clark Fork

**Pend Oreille WMA - Clark Fork Drift Yard - IFG** • Agency: State • Location: 4 miles NW of Clark Fork (limited services), 20 miles SE of Ponderay • GPS: Lat 48.173664 Lon -116.231998 • Open: All year • Total sites: Dispersed • RV sites: Undefined • RV fee: Free • No water • Vault toilets • Activities: Fishing, power boating, non-power boating • Elevation: 2071

**Pend Oreille WMA - Johnson Creek - IFG** • Agency: State • Location: 4 miles W of Clark Fork (limited services), 27 miles SE of Ponderay • GPS: Lat 48.13894 Lon -116.228644 • Total sites: Dispersed • RV sites: Undefined • RV fee: Free • No water • Vault toilets • Activities: Fishing, power boating, non-power boating • Elevation: 2070

**Whiskey Rock Bay** (Idaho Panhandle NF) • Agency: US Forest Service • Location: 27 miles SW of Clark Fork (limited services), 34 miles SW of Athol • GPS: Lat 48.050677 Lon -116.452781 • Open: May-Sep • Total sites: 9 • RV sites: 9 • RV fee: Free • Central water • Vault toilets • Activities: Fishing, swimming, power boating, non-power boating • Elevation: 2123

## Clarkia

**Cedar Creek** (Idaho Panhandle NF) • Agency: US Forest Service • Location: 3 miles N of Clarkia (limited services), 27 miles SE of St Maries • GPS: Lat 47.050956 Lon -116.289101 • Open: May-Sep • Total sites: 3 • RV sites: 3 • RV fee: Free • No water • Vault toilets • Activities: Fishing, swimming • Elevation: 2779

**Orphan Point Saddle** • Agency: Bureau of Land Management • Tel: 208-769-5000 • Location: 20 miles E of Clarkia (limited services), 51 miles SE of St Maries • GPS: Lat 47.044825 Lon -115.944908 • Open: Jul-Sep • Total sites: Dispersed • RV sites: Undefined • RV fee: Free • No water • Vault toilets • Activities: Hiking, fishing, hunting, equestrian area • Elevation: 5954

## Clayton

**South Butte Access - IFG** • Agency: State • Tel: 208-334-3700 • Location: 3 miles W of Clayton (limited services), 26 miles SW of Challis • GPS: Lat 44.249196 Lon -114.453732 • Open: All year • Total sites: Dispersed • RV sites: Undefined • RV fee: Free • No water • Vault toilets • Activities: Fishing, power boating, non-power boating • Elevation: 5507

## Clifton

**Twin Lakes Reservoir Access - IFG** • Agency: State • Location: 3 miles E of Clifton (limited services), 15 miles NW of Preston • GPS: Lat 42.202499 Lon -111.974939 • Total sites: 57 • RV sites: 57 • RV fee: Free • No water • Vault toilets • Activities: Fishing, power boating • Elevation: 4842

## Coolin

**Chase Lake - IFG** • Agency: State • Tel: 208-334-3700 • Location: 2 miles S of Coolin (limited services), 27 miles N of Priest River • GPS: Lat 48.457547 Lon -116.828653 • Open: All year • Total sites: Dispersed • RV sites: Undefined • RV fee: Free • Activities: Fishing, power boating, non-power boating • Elevation: 2507

## Council

**Sheep Rock** (Payette NF) • Agency: US Forest Service • Tel: 208-253-0100 • Location: 48 miles NW of Council (limited services), 94 miles N of Weiser • GPS: Lat 45.191573 Lon -116.669156 • Total sites: 2 • RV sites: Undefined • RV fee: Free • No water • Vault toilets • Activities: Hiking, equestrian area • Elevation: 6598

## Dixie

**Sam's Creek** (Nez Perce-Clearwater NF) • Agency: US Forest Service • Tel: 208-842-2245 • Location: 3 miles NE of Dixie (limited services), 81 miles SE of Grangeville • GPS: Lat 45.536287 Lon -115.495845 • Open: All year (limited winter access) • Total sites: 3 • RV sites: 3 • Max RV Length: 22 • RV fee: Free • No water • Vault toilets • Activities: Hiking, motor sports • Elevation: 5423

## Donnelly

**Paddy Flat** (Payette NF) • Agency: US Forest Service • Tel: 208-634-0400 • Location: 12 miles NE of Donnelly • GPS: Lat 44.776345 Lon -115.943037 • Open: May-Sep • Total sites: 2 • RV sites: 2 • RV fee: Free • No water • Vault toilets • Activities: Hiking, equestrian area • Elevation: 5338

**Rapid Creek** (Payette NF) • Agency: US Forest Service • Tel: 208-634-0400 • Location: 13 miles NE of Donnelly • GPS: Lat 44.790105 Lon -115.931773 • Open: Jul-Sep • Total sites: 2 • RV sites: 2 • RV fee: Free • No water • Vault toilets • Activities: Motor sports • Elevation: 5548

## Downey

**Cherry Creek** (Caribou-Targhee NF) • Agency: US Forest Service • Location: 10 miles S of Downey (limited services), 22 miles NE of Malad City • GPS: Lat 42.304568 Lon -112.135844 • Total sites: 5 • RV sites: 5 • RV fee: Free • No water • No toilets • Activities: Hiking • Elevation: 5830

**Hawkins Reservoir** • Agency: Bureau of Land Management • Tel: 208-373-4000 • Location: 14 miles NW of Downey (limited services), 37 miles S of Pocatello • GPS: Lat 42.512699 Lon -112.332738 • Open: May-Oct • Total sites: 10 • RV sites: 10 • RV fee: Free • No water • Vault toilets • Activities: Fishing, swimming, power boating, non-power boating • Elevation: 5223

**Heart Mountain Spring** • Agency: Bureau of Land Management • Tel: 208-478-6340 • Location: 16 miles SE of Downey (limited services), 19 miles N of Preston • GPS: Lat 42.322448 Lon -111.946742 • Total sites: 4 • RV sites: 4 • RV fee: Free • No water • No toilets • Activities: Hunting • Elevation: 5279

## Driggs

**Rainey Bridge Access - IFG** • Agency: State • Location: 7 miles NW of Driggs • GPS: Lat 43.751447 Lon -111.204087 • Total sites: Dispersed • RV sites: Undefined • RV fee: Free • No toilets • Activities: Fishing • Elevation: 5989

**Teton Creek Access - IFG** • Agency: State • Tel: 208-334-3700 • Location: 4 miles SW of Driggs • GPS: Lat 43.696131 Lon -111.165877 • Open: All year • Total sites: Dispersed • RV sites: Undefined • RV fee: Free • No water • Vault toilets • Activities: Fishing, power boating, non-power boating • Elevation: 6011

## Elk City

**14 Mile Trailhead** (Nez Perce-Clearwater NF) • Agency: US Forest Service • Location: 27 miles SE of Elk City (limited services), 76 miles SE of Grangeville • GPS: Lat 45.688711 Lon -115.168916 • Open: May-Oct • Total sites: 2 • RV sites: 2 • RV fee: Free • No water • Vault toilets • Activities: Hiking, hunting, motor sports, equestrian area • Elevation: 6982

**Bridge Creek** (Nez Perce-Clearwater NF) • Agency: US Forest Service • Tel: 208-842-2245 • Location: 23 miles E of Elk City (limited services), 71 miles E of Grangeville • GPS: Lat 45.783055 Lon -115.206529 • Open: All year (limited winter access) • Total sites: 5 • RV sites: 5 • Max RV Length: 20 • RV fee: Free • No water • Vault toilets • Activities: Hiking, motor sports • Elevation: 4847

**Crooked River #3** (Nez Perce-Clearwater NF) • Agency: US Forest Service • Tel: 208-842-2245 • Location: 9 miles SW of Elk City (limited services), 46 miles E of Grangeville • GPS: Lat 45.798037 Lon -115.530274 • Open: All year (limited winter access) • Total sites: 1 • RV sites: 1 • RV fee: Free • No water • Vault toilets • Activities: Fishing • Elevation: 3976

**Deep Creek** (Bitterroot NF) • Agency: US Forest Service • Tel: 406-821-3269 • Location: 76 miles E of Elk City (limited services), 49 miles SW of Darby, MT • GPS: Lat 45.714061 Lon -114.709281 • Stay limit: 16 days • Total sites: 3 • RV sites: 3 • Max RV Length: 30 • RV fee: Free • No water • Vault toilets • Activities: Fishing, equestrian area • Elevation: 4337

**French Gulch** (Nez Perce-Clearwater NF) • Agency: US Forest Service • Tel: 208-842-2245 • Location: 7 miles SE of Elk City (limited services), 55 miles E of Grangeville • GPS: Lat 45.775518 Lon -115.385792 • Open: All year (limited winter access) • Total sites: 2 • RV sites:

2 • RV fee: Free • No water • Vault toilets • Activities: Hiking, fishing • Elevation: 4265

**Granite Springs** (Nez Perce-Clearwater NF) • Agency: US Forest Service • Tel: 208-842-2245 • Location: 30 miles SE of Elk City (limited services), 79 miles SE of Grangeville • GPS: Lat 45.725046 Lon -115.129192 • Open: All year • Total sites: 4 • RV sites: 4 • RV fee: Free • Central water • Vault toilets • Notes: Spring water, high-clearance vehicles recommended. Limited winter access • Activities: Hiking, motor sports, equestrian area • Elevation: 6683

**Indian Creek** (Spot Mt, Bitterroot NF) • Agency: US Forest Service • Tel: 406-821-3269 • Location: 77 miles E of Elk City (limited services), 59 miles SW of Darby, MT • GPS: Lat 45.789032 Lon -114.763769 • Total sites: 2 • RV sites: 2 • Max RV Length: 25 • RV fee: Free • No water • Vault toilets • Activities: Hiking, fishing, equestrian area • Elevation: 3406

**Leggett Creek** (Nez Perce-Clearwater NF) • Agency: US Forest Service • Tel: 208-842-2245 • Location: 14 miles W of Elk City (limited services), 37 miles SE of Grangeville • GPS: Lat 45.827803 Lon -115.628908 • Open: All year (limited winter access) • Total sites: 5 • RV sites: 5 • RV fee: Free • No water • Vault toilets • Activities: Fishing • Elevation: 3730

**Limber Luke** (Nez Perce-Clearwater NF) • Agency: US Forest Service • Tel: 208-842-2245 • Location: 13 miles N of Elk City (limited services), 58 miles E of Kooskia • GPS: Lat 45.963589 Lon -115.424007 • Total sites: 5 • RV sites: 5 • RV fee: Free • No water • Vault toilets • Activities: Hunting, equestrian area • Elevation: 5389

**Magruder Crossing** (Bitterroot NF) • Agency: US Forest Service • Tel: 406-821-3269 • Location: 72 miles E of Elk City (limited services), 53 miles SW of Darby, MT • GPS: Lat 45.736291 Lon -114.759174 • Stay limit: 16 days • Total sites: 6 • RV sites: 6 • Max RV Length: 30 • RV fee: Free • No water • Vault toilets • Activities: Fishing, equestrian area • Elevation: 3832

**Mallad Creek** (Nez Perce-Clearwater NF) • Agency: US Forest Service • Tel: 208-842-2245 • Location: 26 miles S of Elk City (limited services), 75 miles SE of Grangeville • GPS: Lat 45.579256 Lon -115.308627 • Open: All year (limited winter access) • Total sites: 5 • RV sites: 5 • RV fee: Free • No water • Vault toilets • Activities: Hiking, fishing, motor sports, equestrian area • Elevation: 5108

**O'Hara Saddle** (Nez Perce-Clearwater NF) • Agency: US Forest Service • Tel: 208-842-2245 • Location: 13 miles N of Elk City (limited services), 63 miles E of Grangeville • GPS: Lat 45.952271 Lon -115.517223 • Open: All year (limited winter access) • Total sites: 2 • RV sites: 2 • RV fee: Free • No water • No toilets • Activities: Hunting, motor sports • Elevation: 5184

**Observation Point** (Bitterroot NF) • Agency: US Forest Service • Tel: 406-821-3269 • Location: 61 miles SE of Elk City (limited services), 65 miles SW of Darby, MT • GPS: Lat 45.665376 Lon -114.809505 • Total sites: 4 • RV sites: 4 • RV fee: Free • No water • Vault toilets • Elevation: 7598

**Orogrande #1 and #2** (Nez Perce-Clearwater NF) • Agency: US Forest Service • Tel: 208-842-2245 • Location: 12 miles S of Elk City (limited services), 56 miles SE of Grangeville • GPS: Lat 45.702093 Lon -115.544483 • Open: All year (limited winter access) • Total sites: 3 • RV sites: 3 • RV fee: Free • No water • Vault toilets • Activities: Fishing, motor sports • Elevation: 4603

**Orogrande #3 and #4** (Nez Perce-Clearwater NF) • Agency: US Forest Service • Tel: 208-842-2245 • Location: 12 miles S of Elk City (limited services), 56 miles SE of Grangeville • GPS: Lat 45.698336 Lon -115.546177 • Open: All year (limited winter access) • Total sites: 6 • RV sites: 6 • RV fee: Free • No water • Vault toilets • Activities: Fishing, motor sports • Elevation: 4646

**Oxbow** (Nez Perce-Clearwater NF) • Agency: US Forest Service • Tel: 208-842-2245 • Location: 15 miles W of Elk City (limited services), 41 miles E of Grangeville • GPS: Lat 45.856541 Lon -115.618058 • Open: All year • Total sites: 1 • RV sites: 1 • RV fee: Free • No water • Vault toilets • Activities: Fishing • Elevation: 3878

**Race Creek** (Nez Perce-Clearwater NF) • Agency: US Forest Service • Tel: 208-926-4258 • Location: 31 miles NE of Elk City (limited services), 41 miles E of Kooskia • GPS: Lat 46.044038 Lon -115.284032 • Open: All year (limited winter access) • Total sites: 3 • RV sites: 3 • RV fee: Free • No water • Vault toilets • Activities: Hiking, mountain biking, fishing • Elevation: 1893

**Raven Creek** • Agency: US Forest Service • Tel: 406-821-3269 • Location: 75 miles E of Elk City (limited services), 56 miles SW of Darby, MT • GPS: Lat 45.761995 Lon -114.783556 • Total sites: 2 • RV sites: 2 • Max RV Length: 25 • RV fee: Free • No water • Vault toilets • Activities: Fishing, hunting • Elevation: 3711

**Red River WMA** • Agency: State • Tel: 208-799-5010 • Location: 9 miles S of Elk City (limited services), 57 miles E of Grangeville • GPS: Lat 45.752877 Lon -115.391329 • Total sites: Dispersed • RV sites: Undefined • RV fee: Free • No toilets • Activities: Hiking, fishing, hunting, motor sports, equestrian area • Elevation: 4252

**Sing Lee** (Nez Perce-Clearwater NF) • Agency: US Forest Service • Tel: 208-842-2245 • Location: 17 miles NW of Elk City (limited services), 43 miles E of Grangeville • GPS: Lat 45.885108 Lon -115.625228 • Open: All year (limited winter access) • Total sites: 4 • RV sites: 4 • RV fee: Free • Central water • Vault toilets • Activities: Hiking, fishing, motor sports • Elevation: 3996

**Slims Camp** (Nez Perce-Clearwater NF) • Agency: US Forest Service • Tel: 208-926-4258 • Location: 29 miles NE of Elk City (limited services), 42 miles E of Kooskia • GPS: Lat 46.030311 Lon -115.289988 • Open: All year • Total sites: 2 • RV sites: 2 • RV fee: Free • No water • Vault toilets • Activities: Hiking, mountain biking, fishing • Elevation: 1796

**Sourdough Saddle** (Nez Perce-Clearwater NF) • Agency: US Forest Service • Tel: 208-842-2245 • Location: 39 miles SW of Elk City (limited services), 61 miles SE of Grangeville • GPS: Lat 45.722563 Lon -115.805756 • Total sites: 4 • RV sites: 4 • RV fee: Free • No water • Vault toilets • Activities: Hiking, equestrian area • Elevation: 6095

**Table Meadows** (Nez Perce-Clearwater NF) • Agency: US Forest Service • Tel: 208-842-2245 • Location: 11 miles NW of Elk City (limited services), 61 miles E of Grangeville • GPS: Lat 45.934253 Lon -115.511608 • Open: All year (limited winter access) • Total sites: 6 • RV sites: 6 • RV fee: Free • No water • Vault toilets • Activities: Hiking, hunting, equestrian area • Elevation: 4895

**Ten Mile** (Nez Perce-Clearwater NF) • Agency: US Forest Service • Tel: 208-842-2245 • Location: 26 miles SE of Elk City (limited services), 48 miles SE of Grangeville • GPS: Lat 45.761216 Lon -115.658993 • Open: All year (limited winter access) • Total sites: 2 • RV sites: 2 • RV fee: Free • No water • No toilets • Elevation: 4094

**Trapper Creek** (Nez Perce-Clearwater NF) • Agency: US Forest Service • Tel: 208-842-2245 • Location: 16 miles S of Elk City (limited services), 65 miles SE of Grangeville • GPS: Lat 45.674178 Lon -115.344016 • Open: All year (limited winter access) • Total sites: 1 • RV sites: 1 • RV fee: Free • No water • Vault toilets • Activities: Hunting • Elevation: 4680

**Windy Saddle** (Nez Perce-Clearwater NF) • Agency: US Forest Service • Location: 46 miles E of Elk City (limited services), 95 miles E of Grangeville • GPS: Lat 45.882187 Lon -115.042773 • Total sites: 6 • RV sites: 3 • RV fee: Free • No water • Vault toilets • Activities: Hiking, equestrian area • Elevation: 6549

## Elk River

**Partridge Creek** (Nez Perce-Clearwater NF) • Agency: US Forest Service • Tel: 208-875-1131 • Location: 2 miles E of Elk River (limited services), 51 miles E of Moscow • GPS: Lat 46.784317 Lon -116.148461 • Open: May-Oct • Total sites: 10 • RV sites: 10 • RV fee: Free • No water • Vault toilets • Activities: Motor sports • Elevation: 3022

## Emmett

**Little Gem Cycle Park** • Agency: Bureau of Land Management • Tel: 208-384-3300 • Location: 2 miles E of Emmett • GPS: Lat 43.855286 Lon -116.442303 • Open: All year • Total sites: Dispersed • RV sites: Undefined • RV fee: Free • No water • No toilets • Activities: Hiking, mountain biking, motor sports, equestrian area • Elevation: 2776

## Fairfield

**Bear Creek Transfer Camp** (Sawtooth NF) • Agency: US Forest Service • Location: 34 miles N of Fairfield (limited services), 70 miles NW of Bellevue • GPS: Lat 43.726289 Lon -114.904914 • Open: May-Oct • Total sites: 6 • RV sites: 6 • RV fee: Free • No water • Vault toilets • Activities: Hiking, fishing, hunting, equestrian area • Elevation: 6083

**Camas Creek Access - IFG** • Agency: State • Tel: 208-334-3700 • Location: 10 miles E of Fairfield (limited services), 25 miles SW of Bellevue • GPS: Lat 43.337139 Lon -114.598292 • Open: All year • Total sites: Dispersed • RV sites: Undefined • RV fee: Free • No water • No toilets • Activities: Fishing • Elevation: 4966

**Camas Prairie Centennial Marsh WMA - IFG** • Agency: State • Location: 15 miles SW of Fairfield (limited services), 50 miles SW of Bellevue • GPS: Lat 43.264477 Lon -114.999793 • Total sites: Dispersed • RV sites: Undefined • RV fee: Free • No water • Vault toilets • Activities: Fishing • Elevation: 5056

**Five Points** (Sawtooth NF) • Agency: US Forest Service • Tel: 208-764-3202 • Location: 18 miles N of Fairfield (limited services), 53 miles NW of Bellevue • GPS: Lat 43.542478 Lon -114.818662 • Total sites: 5 • RV sites: 5 • RV fee: Free • No water • Vault toilets • Elevation: 5892

**Hunter Creek Transfer Camp** (Sawtooth NF) • Agency: US Forest Service • Tel: 208-764-3202 • Location: 22 miles NW of Fairfield (limited services), 45 miles NE of Mountain Home • GPS: Lat 43.424222 Lon -115.132442 • Open: May-Oct • Total sites: 4 • RV sites: 4 • RV fee: Free • No water • Vault toilets • Activities: Hiking, equestrian area • Elevation: 5455

**Pioneer** (Sawtooth NF) • Agency: US Forest Service • Tel: 208-764-3202 • Location: 11 miles N of Fairfield (limited services), 46 miles W of Bellevue • GPS: Lat 43.489571 Lon -114.831383 • Open: May-Sep • Total sites: 5 • RV sites: 5 • RV fee: Free • Central water • Vault toilets • Activities: Hiking, mountain biking, fishing, equestrian area • Elevation: 5846

**Skeleton** • Agency: US Forest Service • Location: 34 miles NW of Fairfield (limited services), 70 miles NW of Bellevue • GPS: Lat 43.590082 Lon -115.018428 • Total sites: 5 • RV sites: 5 • RV fee: Free • No water • Vault toilets • Activities: Hiking • Elevation: 5095

## Featherville

**Little Roaring River Lake** (Boise NF) • Agency: US Forest Service • Tel: 208-587-7961 • Location: 19 miles W of Featherville (limited services), 77 miles NE of Mountain Home • GPS: Lat 43.629575 Lon -115.443523 • Open: Jul-Sep • Total sites: 4 • RV sites: 4 • RV fee: Free • No water • Vault toilets • Activities: Hiking, fishing, motor sports, non-power boating • Elevation: 7858

**Willow Creek Transfer Camp** (Sawtooth NF) • Agency: US Forest Service • Tel: 208-764-3202 • Location: 9 miles E of Featherville (limited services), 69 miles NE of Mountain Home • GPS: Lat 43.626408 Lon -115.134416 • Open: May-Oct • Total sites: 3 • RV sites: 3 • RV fee: Free (donation appreciated) • No water • Vault toilets • Activities: Hiking, fishing, motor sports • Elevation: 5118

## Firth

**Firth City Park Access Area - IFG** • Agency: State • Location: 1 mile W of Firth (limited services), 12 miles SW of Idaho Falls • GPS: Lat 43.308529 Lon -112.192183 • Total sites: Dispersed • RV sites: Undefined • RV fee: Free • No toilets • Activities: Fishing • Elevation: 4574

## Glenns Ferry

**King Hill Access - IFG** • Agency: State • Tel: 208-334-3700 • Location: 6 miles NE of Glenns Ferry (limited services), 32 miles SE of Mountain Home • GPS: Lat 43.000253 Lon -115.214446 • Open: All year • Total sites: Dispersed • RV sites: Undefined • RV fee: Free • No water • Vault toilets • Activities: Fishing, power boating, non-power boating • Elevation: 2511

## Gooding

**Dog Creek Reservoir - IFG** • Agency: State • Tel: 208-334-3700 • Location: 7 miles N of Gooding • GPS: Lat 43.024436 Lon -114.742556 • Open: All year • Total sites: Dispersed • RV sites: Undefined • RV fee: Free • No water • Vault toilets • Activities: Fishing, power boating, non-power boating • Elevation: 3627

## Grand View

**Poison Creek** • Agency: Bureau of Land Management • Tel: 208-384-3300 • Location: 22 miles SW of Grand View (limited services), 46 miles SW of Mountain Home • GPS: Lat 42.757332 Lon -116.297255 • Total sites: 4 • RV sites: 1 • RV fee: Free • No water • Vault toilets • Activities: Hiking • Elevation: 4483

## Grangeville

**Meadow Creek** (Hungry Ridge, Nez Perce-Clearwater NF) • Agency: US Forest Service • Tel: 208-839-2211 • Location: 18 miles SE of Grangeville • GPS: Lat 45.828974 Lon -115.928205 • Open: All year (limited winter access) • Total sites: 3 • RV sites: 3 • RV fee: Free • No water • Vault toilets • Activities: Hiking, fishing • Elevation: 2464

## Hagerman

**Bell Rapids Sportsman's Access - IFG** • Agency: State • Location: 3 miles SW of Hagerman • GPS: Lat 42.793058 Lon -114.936639 • Total sites: Dispersed • RV sites: Undefined • RV fee: Free • No water • Vault toilets • Activities: Fishing, power boating, non-power boating • Elevation: 2808

## Hailey

**Deer Creek** (Sawtooth NF) • Agency: US Forest Service • Tel: 208-622-5371 • Location: 12 miles W of Hailey • GPS: Lat 43.528683 Lon -114.504669 • Open: May-Sep • Stay limit: 16 days • Total sites: 3 • RV sites: 3 (numerous other sites along creek) • Max RV Length: 16 • RV fee: Free • No water • Vault toilets • Activities: Mountain biking, hunting • Elevation: 6112

## Hansen

**FS Flats** (Sawtooth NF) • Agency: US Forest Service • Tel: 208-678-0430 • Location: 30 miles S of Hansen (limited services), 37 miles S of Twin Falls • GPS: Lat 42.154118 Lon -114.258898 • Stay limit: 14 days • Total sites: 19 • RV sites: 19 • RV fee: Free • No water • Vault toilets • Activities: Motor sports • Elevation: 6971

## Harrison

**Coeur d'Alene River WMA - Thompson Lake Outlet - IFG** • Agency: State • Location: 4 miles SW of Harrison (limited services), 28 miles S of Coeur d'Alene • GPS: Lat 47.485672 Lon -116.724325 • Open: All year • Total sites: Dispersed • RV sites: Undefined • RV fee: Free • No water • No toilets • Activities: Fishing, power boating, non-power boating • Elevation: 2137

## Hollister

**Bear Gulch** (Hopper Gulch, Sawtooth NF) • Agency: US Forest Service • Tel: 208-678-0439 • Location: 17 miles SE of Hollister (limited services), 30 miles S of Twin Falls • GPS: Lat 42.227454 Lon -114.378672 • Open: May-Oct • Stay limit: 14 days • Total sites: 8 • RV sites: 8 • RV fee: Free • No water • Vault toilets • Activities: Hiking, fishing • Elevation: 6017

## Howe

**Little Lost River - IFG** • Agency: State • Location: 26 miles N of Howe (limited services), 48 miles N of Arco • GPS: Lat

44.103213 Lon -113.238744 • Total sites: Dispersed • RV sites: Undefined • RV fee: Free • No water • No toilets • Activities: Fishing • Elevation: 5777

## Idaho City

**Bald Mountain** (Boise NF) • Agency: US Forest Service • Tel: 208-392-6681 • Location: 11 miles SE of Idaho City (limited services), 44 miles E of Boise • GPS: Lat 43.749168 Lon -115.737703 • Open: Jul-Sep • Total sites: 4 • RV sites: 4 • RV fee: Free • No water • Vault toilets • Activities: Hiking, mountain biking, motor sports • Elevation: 6794

**Graham Bridge** (Boise NF) • Agency: US Forest Service • Tel: 208-392-6681 • Location: 46 miles NE of Idaho City (limited services), 79 miles NE of Boise • GPS: Lat 43.963886 Lon -115.274778 • Total sites: 3 • RV sites: 3 • RV fee: Free • No water • Vault toilets • Elevation: 5695

**Ninemeyer** (Boise NF) • Agency: US Forest Service • Tel: 208-392-6681 • Location: 32 miles E of Idaho City • GPS: Lat 43.755774 Lon -115.567925 • Open: Jun-Oct • Total sites: 8 • RV sites: 8 • RV fee: Free • No water • Vault toilets • Activities: Fishing • Elevation: 3855

**Robert E Lee** (Boise NF) • Agency: US Forest Service • Location: 35 miles NE of Idaho City • GPS: Lat 43.905798 Lon -115.434609 • Total sites: 8 • RV sites: 4 (no large RV's) • RV fee: Free • No water • No toilets • Activities: Fishing • Elevation: 4705

**Troutdale** (Boise NF) • Agency: US Forest Service • Tel: 208-587-7961 • Location: 37 miles SE of Idaho City • GPS: Lat 43.716272 Lon -115.625111 • Open: Apr-Oct • Total sites: 5 • RV sites: 5 • RV fee: Free • No water • Vault toilets • Activities: Fishing • Elevation: 3566

**Willow Creek** (Idaho City, Boise NF) • Agency: US Forest Service • Tel: 208-392-6681 • Location: 23 miles NE of Idaho City (limited services), 56 miles NE of Boise • GPS: Lat 43.959142 Lon -115.532166 • Total sites: 4 • RV sites: 4 • RV fee: Free • No water • Vault toilets • Activities: Fishing • Elevation: 5426

## Idaho Falls

**Tex Creek WMA - Clowards Crossing** • Agency: State • Tel: 208-525-7290 • Location: 14 miles E of Idaho Falls • GPS: Lat 43.443723 Lon -111.786538 • Open: All year • Total sites: Dispersed • RV sites: Undefined • RV fee: Free • No water • No toilets • Activities: Fishing, power boating, non-power boating • Elevation: 5301

**Tex Creek WMA - Kepps Crossing** • Agency: State • Tel: 208-525-7290 • Location: 13 miles E of Idaho Falls • GPS: Lat 43.408094 Lon -111.783947 • Open: All year • Total sites: Dispersed • RV sites: Undefined • RV fee: Free • No toilets • Activities: Fishing, power boating, non-power boating • Elevation: 5420

## Irwin

**Palisades Creek - IFG** • Agency: State • Location: 4 miles SE of Irwin (limited services), 28 miles SW of Victor • GPS: Lat 43.365789 Lon -111.237179 • Total sites: Dispersed • RV sites: Undefined • RV fee: Free • No water • Vault toilets • Elevation: 5371

## Island Park

**Bill Frome** • Agency: County • Location: 16 miles NW of Island Park (limited services), 20 miles W of West Yellowstone, MT • GPS: Lat 44.649902 Lon -111.438268 • Total sites: 35 • RV sites: 35 • RV fee: Free • No water • Vault toilets • Activities: Fishing, power boating, non-power boating • Elevation: 6486

**Henrys Lake South Shore Access - IFG** • Agency: State • Location: 10 miles NW of Island Park (limited services), 23 miles W of West Yellowstone, MT • GPS: Lat 44.615644 Lon -111.417305 • Total sites: Dispersed • RV sites: Undefined • RV fee: Free • No water • Vault toilets • Elevation: 6492

**Mill Creek Access - IFG** • Agency: State • Tel: 208-334-3700 • Location: 9 miles SW of Island Park (limited services), 31 miles W of West Yellowstone, MT • GPS: Lat 44.448069 Lon -111.426426 • Total sites: Dispersed • RV sites: Undefined • RV fee: Free • Vault toilets • Activities: Fishing, power boating, non-power boating • Elevation: 6312

## Kamiah

**Lolo Creek** (Nez Perce-Clearwater NF) • Agency: US Forest Service • Tel: 208-926-4274 • Location: 23 miles NE of Kamiah • GPS: Lat 46.293437 Lon -115.752283 • Open: May-Oct • Total sites: 8 • RV sites: 6 • RV fee: Free • No toilets • Elevation: 2878

**Longcamp - IFG** • Agency: State • Tel: 208-799-5010 • Location: 5 miles NW of Kamiah • GPS: Lat 46.276126 Lon -116.097529 • Open: All year • Total sites: Dispersed • RV sites: Undefined • RV fee: Free • No water • Vault toilets • Activities: Fishing, power boating, non-power boating • Elevation: 1143

**Rocky Ridge Lake** (Nez Perce-Clearwater NF) • Agency: US Forest Service • Tel: 208-926-4274 • Location: 47 miles NE of Kamiah • GPS: Lat 46.441078 Lon -115.491879 • Open: Jun-Sep • Total sites: 6 • RV sites: 6 • RV fee: Free • No water • No toilets • Activities: Hiking, fishing • Elevation: 5671

## Kellogg

**Lake Elsie** (Idaho Panhandle NF) • Agency: US Forest Service • Tel: 208-783-2363 • Location: 14 miles SE of Kellogg • GPS: Lat 47.428208 Lon -116.022835 • Total sites: 7 • RV sites: 3 • RV fee: Free • No water • Vault toilets • Activities: Fishing • Elevation: 5138

## Ketchum

**East Fork Baker Creek** (Sawtooth NF) • Agency: US Forest Service • Tel: 208-622-5371 • Location: 17 miles NW of Ketchum • GPS: Lat 43.744618 Lon -114.565129 • Open: Jun-Nov • Total sites: 7 • RV sites: 7 • RV fee: Free • No water • Vault toilets • Activities: Hiking, mountain biking, fishing • Elevation: 6926

**Federal Gulch** (Sawtooth NF) • Agency: US Forest Service • Tel: 208-622-5371 • Location: 17 miles E of Ketchum • GPS: Lat 43.668589 Lon -114.153456 • Open: Jun-Sep • Stay limit: 16 days • Total sites: 3 • RV sites: 3 • Max RV Length: 18 • RV fee: Free • No water • Vault toilets • Activities: Hiking, fishing, hunting • Elevation: 6801

**Garden Creek** • Agency: Bureau of Land Management • Tel: 208-879-6200 • Location: 27 miles NE of Ketchum • GPS: Lat 43.976459 Lon -114.064557 • Open: May-Oct • Total sites: 5 • RV sites: 5 • RV fee: Free • No water • Vault toilets • Activities: Hiking, fishing • Elevation: 6795

**Rooks Creek** (Sawtooth NF) • Agency: US Forest Service • Location: 12 miles SW of Ketchum • GPS: Lat 43.649749 Lon -114.522937 • Total sites: 5 • RV sites: 5 • RV fee: Free • No water • Vault toilets • Elevation: 6460

**Sawmill** (Sawtooth NF) • Agency: US Forest Service • Tel: 208-622-5371 • Location: 16 miles E of Ketchum • GPS: Lat 43.666556 Lon -114.163628 • Open: May-Sep • Stay limit: 16 days • Total sites: 3 • RV sites: 3 • Max RV Length: 16 • RV fee: Free • No water • Vault toilets • Elevation: 6762

## Kimberly

**Third Fork** (Sawtooth NF) • Agency: US Forest Service • Tel: 208-678-0439 • Location: 24 miles S of Kimberly • GPS: Lat 42.252024 Lon -114.248199 • Open: May-Sep • Stay limit: 14 days • Total sites: 5 • RV sites: 5 • RV fee: Free • No water • Vault toilets • Activities: Hiking • Elevation: 5197

## Kooskia

**Button Beach - IFG** • Agency: State • Tel: 208-334-3700 • Location: 2 miles SE of Kooskia • GPS: Lat 46.166567 Lon -115.995587 • Open: All year • Total sites: Dispersed • RV sites: Undefined • RV fee: Free • No water • Vault toilets • Activities: Fishing, power boating, non-power boating • Elevation: 1225

**CCC** (Nez Perce-Clearwater NF) • Agency: US Forest Service • Tel: 208-926-4258 • Location: 28 miles E of Kooskia • GPS: Lat 46.090691 Lon -115.520092 • Open: All year (limited winter access) • Total sites: 3 • RV sites: 1 • RV fee: Free • No water • Vault toilets • Activities: Hiking, mountain biking, fishing • Elevation: 1576

**Elk Summit** (Nez Perce-Clearwater NF) • Agency: US Forest Service • Tel: 208-942-3113 • Location: 37 miles S of Lolo Hot Springs (limited services), 69 miles SW of Missoula, MT • GPS: Lat 46.327986 Lon -114.647344 • Open: All year (limited winter access) • Total sites: 16 • RV sites: 16 • RV fee: Free • No water • Vault toilets • Activities: Motor sports • Elevation: 5781

**Knife Edge** (Nez Perce-Clearwater NF) • Agency: US Forest Service • Tel: 208-926-4274 • Location: 33 miles NE of Kooskia • GPS: Lat 46.227242 Lon -115.474474 • Open: All year (limited winter access) • Total sites: 5 • RV sites: 5 • RV fee: Free • No water • Vault toilets • Activities: Hiking, mountain biking, fishing, hunting, motor sports, non-power boating, equestrian area • Elevation: 1788

**Kooskia Access - IFG** • Agency: State • Location: 1 mile SE of Kooskia • GPS: Lat 46.136098 Lon -115.956306 • Total sites: Dispersed • RV sites: Undefined • RV fee: Free • No water • No toilets • Activities: Fishing • Elevation: 1279

**Slide Creek** (Nez Perce-Clearwater NF) • Agency: US Forest Service • Tel: 208-926-4258 • Location: 32 miles E of Kooskia • GPS: Lat 46.084831 Lon -115.452568 • Open: All year (limited winter access) • Total sites: 3 • RV sites: 3 • RV fee: Free • No water • Vault toilets • Activities: Hiking, mountain biking, fishing, swimming, non-power boating • Elevation: 1906

**Twenty Mile Bar** (Nez Perce-Clearwater NF) • Agency: US Forest Service • Tel: 208-926-4258 • Location: 36 miles E of Kooskia • GPS: Lat 46.073011 Lon -115.376516 • Open: All year (limited winter access) • Total sites: 2 • RV sites: 2 • RV fee: Free • No water • Vault toilets • Activities: Hiking, mountain biking, fishing, swimming, power boating, non-power boating • Elevation: 1886

**Twenty-five Mile Bar** (Nez Perce-Clearwater NF) • Agency: US Forest Service • Tel: 208-926-4258 • Location: 34 miles E of Kooskia • GPS: Lat 46.076114 Lon -115.412178 • Open: All year • Total sites: 3 • RV sites: 3 • RV fee: Free • No water • Vault toilets • Activities: Hiking, mountain biking, fishing, swimming • Elevation: 1745

## Lava Hot Springs

**Portenuf River Lower Access - IFG** • Agency: State • Location: 2 miles N of Lava Hot Springs • GPS: Lat 42.64194 Lon -112.003759 • Total sites: Dispersed • RV sites: Undefined • RV fee: Free • No water • Vault toilets • Activities: Fishing • Elevation: 5138

**Twenty-four Mile Reservoir Access - IFG** • Agency: State • Location: 27 miles N of Lava Hot Springs • GPS: Lat 42.905451 Lon -111.885542 • Total sites: Dispersed • RV sites: Undefined • RV fee: Free • No water • No toilets • Activities: Fishing • Elevation: 5923

## Leadore

**Bear Valley Horse Camp** (Salmon-Challis NF) • Agency: US Forest Service • Tel: 208-768-2500 • Location: 31 miles NW of Leadore (limited services), 38 miles S of Salmon • GPS: Lat 44.785566 Lon -113.766192 • Open: May-Sep • Total sites: 6 • RV sites: 6 • RV fee: Free • No water • Vault toilets • Activities: Hiking, equestrian area • Elevation: 6676

**Bear Valley Trailhead Upper CG** (Salmon-Challis NF) • Agency: US Forest Service • Location: 32 miles NW of Leadore (limited services), 39 miles S of Salmon • GPS: Lat 44.792799 Lon -113.779858 • Open: May-Oct • Total sites: 6 • RV sites: 6 • RV fee: Free • No water • Vault toilets • Activities: Hiking • Elevation: 6845

**Big Eightmile** (Salmon-Challis NF) • Agency: US Forest Service • Tel: 208-768-2500 • Location: 14 miles SW of Leadore (limited services), 57 miles S of Salmon • GPS: Lat 44.608583 Lon -113.577099 • Open: May-Sep • Total sites: 10 • RV sites: 10 • RV fee: Free • Central water • Vault toilets • Activities: Motor sports • Elevation: 7546

**Hawley Creek - Lower** (Salmon-Challis NF) • Agency: US Forest Service • Tel: 208-768-2500 • Location: 9 miles E of Leadore (limited services), 54 miles SE of Salmon • GPS: Lat 44.667474 Lon -113.190627 • Open: May-Sep • Total sites: 4 • RV sites: 4 • RV fee: Free • No water • Vault toilets • Activities: Fishing • Elevation: 6722

**Hawley Creek - Upper** (Salmon-Challis NF) • Agency: US Forest Service • Tel: 208-768-2500 • Location: 10 miles E of Leadore (limited services), 55 miles SE of Salmon • GPS: Lat 44.67181 Lon -113.181507 • Open: May-Sep • Total sites: 6 • RV sites: 6 • RV fee: Free • No water • Vault toilets • Activities: Fishing • Elevation: 6791

**Hayden Creek Access - IFG** • Agency: State • Tel: 208-334-3700 • Location: 19 miles NW of Leadore (limited services), 26 miles SE of Salmon • GPS: Lat 44.867733 Lon -113.624437 • Open: All year • Total sites: 8 • RV sites: 8 • RV fee: Free • No water • Vault toilets • Activities: Fishing, power boating, non-power boating • Elevation: 5156

**Hayden Pond - IFG** • Agency: State • Tel: 208-334-3700 • Location: 22 miles NW of Leadore (limited services), 29 miles S of Salmon • GPS: Lat 44.838271 Lon -113.663401 • Open: All year • Total sites: Dispersed • RV sites: Undefined • RV fee: Free • No water • Vault toilets • Activities: Fishing • Elevation: 5411

**Reservoir Creek Trailhead** (Salmon-Challis NF) • Agency: US Forest Service • Tel: 208-768-2500 • Location: 11 miles E of Leadore (limited services), 56 miles SE of Salmon • GPS: Lat 44.676682 Lon -113.158234 • Open: May-Sep • Total sites: 2 • RV sites: 2 • RV fee: Free • No water • Vault toilets • Activities: Hiking • Elevation: 6903

**Smokey Cubs** • Agency: Bureau of Land Management • Tel: 208-756-5400 • Location: 4 miles NE of Leadore (limited services), 49 miles SE of Salmon • GPS: Lat 44.703085 Lon -113.293962 • Open: May-Oct • Total sites: 8 • RV sites: 8 • RV fee: Free • No water • Vault toilets • Activities: Hiking, mountain biking, fishing, swimming, hunting, equestrian area • Elevation: 6273

**Timber Creek Reservoir - Lower** (Salmon-Challis NF) • Agency: US Forest Service • Tel: 208-768-2500 • Location: 10 miles SW of Leadore (limited services), 53 miles SE of Salmon • GPS: Lat 44.581076 Lon -113.466366 • Open: May-Sep • Total sites: 2 • RV sites: 2 • RV fee: Free • No water • Vault toilets • Activities: Fishing, non-power boating • Elevation: 7589

**Timber Creek Reservoir - Upper** (Salmon-Challis NF) • Agency: US Forest Service • Tel: 208-768-2500 • Location: 10 miles SW of Leadore (limited services), 54 miles SE of Salmon • GPS: Lat 44.576867 Lon -113.470996 • Open: May-Sep • Total sites: 5 • RV sites: 5 • RV fee: Free • No water • Vault toilets • Activities: Fishing, non-power boating • Elevation: 7592

## Lenore

**Lenore Access - IFG** • Agency: State • Location: In Lenore (limited services), 16 miles E of Orofino • GPS: Lat 46.506587 Lon -116.549005 • Total sites: Dispersed • RV sites: Undefined • RV fee: Free • No toilets • Elevation: 904

## Lewiston

**Beardy Gulch - IFG** • Agency: State • Tel: 208-334-3700 • Location: 9 miles E of Lewiston • GPS: Lat 46.444229 Lon -116.847596 • Open: Sep-Jun • Total sites: Dispersed • RV sites: Undefined • RV fee: Free • No water • Vault toilets • Activities: Fishing, non-power boating • Elevation: 785

**Gibbs Eddy Access Area - IFG** • Agency: State • Location: 13 miles NE of Lewiston • GPS: Lat 46.480311 Lon -116.753112 • Total sites: Dispersed • RV sites: Undefined • RV fee: Free • No water • Vault toilets • Activities: Fishing, power boating • Elevation: 819

**Mann Lake - IFG** • Agency: State • Location: 6 miles E of Lewiston • GPS: Lat 46.368972 Lon -116.849557 • Total sites: Dispersed • RV sites: Undefined • RV fee: Free • No water • Vault toilets • Activities: Fishing • Elevation: 1819

## Lone Pine

**Birch Creek** • Agency: Bureau of Land Management • Tel: 208-524-7500 • Location: 4 miles SE of Lone Pine (limited services), 67 miles NW of Idaho Falls • GPS: Lat 44.139206 Lon -112.899933 • Open: May-Nov • Total sites: 25 • RV sites: 25 • RV fee: Free (donation appreciated) • Central water • Vault toilets • Activities: Fishing • Elevation: 6023

**Kaufman Access - IFG** • Agency: State • Tel: 208-334-3700 • Location: 4 miles NE of Lone Pine (limited services), 75 miles NW of Idaho Falls • GPS: Lat 44.230864 Lon -112.975492 • Open: All year • Total sites: Dispersed • RV sites: Undefined • RV fee: Free • No water • Vault toilets • Activities: Fishing, power boating, non-power boating • Elevation: 6394

## Lucile

**Long Gulch - IFG** • Agency: State • Tel: 208-334-3700 • Location: 6 miles N of Lucile (limited services), 15 miles N of Riggins • GPS: Lat 45.614292 Lon -116.276489 • Open: All year • Total sites: Dispersed • RV sites: Undefined • RV fee: Free • No water • Vault toilets • Activities: Fishing, non-power boating • Elevation: 1620

## Mackay

**Big Lost River Lower Access - IFG** • Agency: State • Tel: 208-334-3700 • Location: 3 miles NW of Mackay • GPS: Lat 43.940247 Lon -113.650725 • Open: All year • Total sites: Dispersed • RV sites: Undefined • RV fee: Free • No water • Vault toilets • Activities: Fishing, power boating, non-power boating • Elevation: 5966

**Big Lost River Upper Access - IFG** • Agency: State • Tel: 208-334-3700 • Location: 24 miles NW of Mackay • GPS: Lat 44.018991 Lon -113.988768 • Open: All year • Total sites: Dispersed • RV sites: Undefined • RV fee: Free • No water • Vault toilets • Activities: Fishing, power boating, non-power boating • Elevation: 6584

**Broad Canyon** (Salmon-Challis NF) • Agency: US Forest Service • Location: 39 miles SW of Mackay • GPS: Lat 43.768363 Lon -113.943128 • Open: Jul-Sep • Total sites: 8 • RV sites: 8 • Max RV Length: 35 • RV fee: Free • No water • Vault toilets • Activities: Hiking, equestrian area • Elevation: 7825

**Mackay Dam - IFG** • Agency: State • Tel: 208-334-3700 • Location: 4 miles NW of Mackay • GPS: Lat 43.951805 Lon -113.670923 • Open: All year • Total sites: Dispersed • RV sites: Undefined • RV fee: Free • No water • Vault toilets • Activities: Fishing, power boating, non-power boating • Elevation: 6022

**Mackay Reservoir Lower Access - IFG** • Agency: State • Tel: 208-334-3700 • Location: 6 miles NW of Mackay • GPS: Lat 43.964115 Lon -113.702751 • Open: All year • Total sites: Dispersed • RV sites: Undefined • RV fee: Free • No water • Vault toilets • Activities: Fishing, power boating, non-power boating • Elevation: 6090

**Mackay Reservoir Upper Access - IFG** • Agency: State • Tel: 208-334-3700 • Location: 6 miles NW of Mackay • GPS: Lat 43.967742 Lon -113.710763 • Open: All year • Total sites: Dispersed • RV sites: Undefined • RV fee: Free • No water • Vault toilets • Activities: Fishing, power boating, non-power boating • Elevation: 6087

**Mackay Tourist Park** • Agency: Municipal • Tel: 208-588-2274 • Location: In Mackay • GPS: Lat 43.911468 Lon -113.621556 • Total sites: 40 • RV sites: 40 • RV fee: Free • Central water • Flush toilets • Notes: 2 nights free, reservations available if paying • Elevation: 5904

**Pass Creek** • Agency: Bureau of Land Management • Location: 23 miles NE of Mackay • GPS: Lat 44.066308 Lon -113.421645 • Total sites: Dispersed • RV sites: Undefined • RV fee: Free • No water • No toilets • Elevation: 6869

**Pass Creek Narrows** (Salmon-Challis NF) • Agency: US Forest Service • Location: 13 miles NE of Mackay • GPS: Lat 43.950649 Lon -113.444765 • Open: May-Sep • Total sites: 7 • RV sites: 7 • RV fee: Free • No water • Vault toilets • Activities: Hiking, fishing, rock climbing, motor sports • Elevation: 6376

**Rothwell Acess - IFG** • Agency: State • Tel: 208-334-3700 • Location: 10 miles SE of Mackay • GPS: Lat 43.847227 Lon -113.442278 • Open: All year • Total sites: Dispersed • RV sites: Undefined • RV fee: Free • No water • No toilets • Activities: Fishing • Elevation: 5660

## Malad City

**Crowther Reservoir - IFG** • Agency: State • Tel: 208-334-3700 • Location: In Malad City • GPS: Lat 42.204529 Lon -112.255001 • Open: All year • Total sites: Dispersed • RV sites: Undefined • RV fee: Free • No water • Vault toilets • Activities: Fishing, non-power boating • Elevation: 4722

**Deep Creek Reservoir Access - IFG** • Agency: State • Location: 8 miles NE of Malad City • GPS: Lat 42.208301 Lon -112.174061 • Total sites: Dispersed • RV sites:

Undefined • RV fee: Free • No toilets • Activities: Fishing • Elevation: 5201

**Daniels Reservoir Access - IFG** • Agency: State • Tel: 208-232-4703 • Location: 17 miles NW of Malad City • GPS: Lat 42.351411 Lon -112.437335 • Total sites: Dispersed • RV sites: Undefined • RV fee: Free • No water • Vault toilets • Activities: Fishing, power boating, non-power boating • Elevation: 5187

## Malta

**McClenden Springs** • Agency: Bureau of Land Management • Tel: 208-677-6600 • Location: 5 miles NW of Malta (limited services), 33 miles SE of Heyburn • GPS: Lat 42.335987 Lon -113.407394 • Total sites: Dispersed • RV sites: Undefined • RV fee: Free • No water • Vault toilets • Activities: Hiking, mountain biking, fishing, motor sports • Elevation: 4839

**Sublett Reservoir - IFG** • Agency: State • Tel: 208-334-3700 • Location: 18 miles E of Malta (limited services), 45 miles SE of Heyburn • GPS: Lat 42.323909 Lon -113.046442 • Open: All year • Total sites: Dispersed • RV sites: Undefined • RV fee: Free • No water • Vault toilets • Activities: Fishing, non-power boating • Elevation: 5351

## Marsing

**North Fork Owyhee River** • Agency: Bureau of Land Management • Tel: 208-384-3300 • Location: 78 miles S of Marsing, 32 miles S of Jordan Valley, OR • GPS: Lat 42.59256 Lon -116.98166 • Total sites: 5 • RV sites: 5 • Max RV Length: 16 • RV fee: Free • No toilets • Elevation: 4836

**Trappers Flat Access - IFG** • Agency: State • Location: 9 miles S of Marsing • GPS: Lat 43.453733 Lon -116.742036 • Total sites: Dispersed • RV sites: Undefined • RV fee: Free • No water • Vault toilets • Elevation: 2251

## May

**Morse Creek** (Salmon-Challis NF) • Agency: US Forest Service • Tel: 208-879-4100 • Location: 7 miles NE of May (limited services), 34 miles NE of Challis • GPS: Lat 44.630867 Lon -113.790528 • Open: May-Sep • Total sites: 3 • RV sites: 3 • Max RV Length: 16 • RV fee: Free • No water • Vault toilets • Activities: Hiking, fishing • Elevation: 6332

**Pahsimeroi RiverAccess - IFG** • Agency: State • Tel: 208-334-3700 • Location: 6 miles NW of May (limited services), 24 miles NE of Challis • GPS: Lat 44.620381 Lon -113.974501 • Open: All year • Total sites: Dispersed • RV sites: Undefined • RV fee: Free • No water • Vault toilets • Activities: Fishing • Elevation: 4859

**Summit Creek** • Agency: Bureau of Land Management • Tel: 208-879-6200 • Location: 36 miles SE of May (limited services), 64 miles SE of Challis • GPS: Lat 44.272368 Lon -113.449167 • Open: May-Oct • Total sites: 7 • RV sites: 7 • RV fee: Free • No water • Vault toilets • Activities: Hiking, mountain biking, fishing, hunting, equestrian area • Elevation: 6414

## McCall

**Corduroy Meadows** (Payette NF) • Agency: US Forest Service • Location: 35 miles N of McCall • GPS: Lat 45.343204 Lon -115.946772 • Total sites: 1 • RV sites: 1 • RV fee: Free • No water • No toilets • Elevation: 6406

**Fish Lake Access - IFG** • Agency: State • Tel: 208-334-3700 • Location: 8 miles W of McCall • GPS: Lat 44.903941 Lon -116.216601 • Open: All year • Total sites: Dispersed • RV sites: Undefined • RV fee: Free • No water • No toilets • Activities: Fishing, power boating, non-power boating • Elevation: 4671

**Pete Creek** (Payette NF) • Agency: US Forest Service • Location: 32 miles N of McCall • GPS: Lat 45.305872 Lon -115.931774 • Total sites: 11 • RV sites: 11 • RV fee: Free • No water • Vault toilets • Activities: Hiking, mountain biking, equestrian area • Elevation: 6288

**Pond Camp** (Payette NF) • Agency: US Forest Service • Location: 35 miles N of McCall • GPS: Lat 45.339552 Lon -115.945335 • Total sites: 9 • RV sites: 9 • RV fee: Free • No water • Vault toilets • Activities: Hiking • Elevation: 6423

## McCammon

**Goodenough Creek** • Agency: Bureau of Land Management • Tel: 208-478-6340 • Location: 5 miles W of McCammon (limited services), 17 miles W of Lava Hot Springs • GPS: Lat 42.654382 Lon -112.285813 • Open: May-Nov • Total sites: 13 • RV sites: 13 • RV fee: Free • No water • Vault toilets • Activities: Hiking, mountain biking, motor sports • Elevation: 5517

**Indian Rocks** • Agency: State • Location: 2 miles NW of McCammon (limited services), 14 miles NW of Lava Hot Springs • GPS: Lat 42.678302 Lon -112.220313 • Total sites: Dispersed • RV sites: Undefined • RV fee: Free • No water • No toilets • Notes: Former state park • Elevation: 4710

## Melba

**Map Rock Access - IFG** • Agency: State • Location: 11 miles W of Melba (limited services), 16 miles SW of Nampa • GPS: Lat 43.405588 Lon -116.682217 • Total sites:

Dispersed • RV sites: Undefined • RV fee: Free • No water • Vault toilets • Activities: Fishing • Elevation: 2246

**Swan Falls Dam RA - IP** • Agency: Utility Company • Tel: 208-388-2231 • Location: 18 miles SE of Melba (limited services), 30 miles S of Bosie • GPS: Lat 43.235409 Lon -116.374346 • Stay limit: 14 days • Total sites: 5 • RV sites: 5 • Max RV Length: 25 • RV fee: Free • No water • Vault toilets • Activities: Hiking, fishing, power boating, non-power boating • Elevation: 2334

**Swan Falls River Access - IP** • Agency: Utility Company • Tel: 208-388-2231 • Location: 19 miles SE of Melba (limited services), 30 miles S of Nampa • GPS: Lat 43.259477 Lon -116.398289 • Total sites: 15 • RV sites: 15 (camping areas above and below the dam) • RV fee: Free • No water • Vault toilets • Activities: Hiking, mountain biking, fishing, swimming, power boating, non-power boating, equestrian area • Elevation: 2305

## Menan

**Menan Buttes Access - IFG** • Agency: State • Tel: 208-525-7290 • Location: 2 miles N of Menan (limited services), 15 miles SW of Rexburg • GPS: Lat 43.751467 Lon -111.978953 • Open: All year • Total sites: Dispersed • RV sites: Undefined • RV fee: Free • No water • Vault toilets • Activities: Fishing, power boating, non-power boating • Elevation: 4809

## Montpelier

**Dingle Pond - IFG** • Agency: State • Location: 5 miles S of Montpelier • GPS: Lat 42.247879 Lon -111.271315 • Total sites: Dispersed • RV sites: Undefined • RV fee: Free • No water • No toilets • Activities: Fishing • Elevation: 5948

## Mountain Home

**Little Camas Reservoir- IFG** • Agency: State • Tel: 208-334-3700 • Location: 27 miles NE of Mountain Home • GPS: Lat 43.347792 Lon -115.391307 • Open: All year • Total sites: Dispersed • RV sites: Undefined • RV fee: Free • No water • Vault toilets • Activities: Fishing, power boating, non-power boating • Elevation: 4934

## Moyie Springs

**Perkins Lake -IFG** • Agency: State • Tel: 208-678-0439 • Location: 7 miles NE of Moyie Springs (limited services), 15 miles NE of Bonners Ferry • GPS: Lat 48.759584 Lon -116.093375 • Total sites: Dispersed • RV sites: Undefined • RV fee: Free • No water • Vault toilets • Activities: Fishing • Elevation: 2700

## Murphy Hot Springs

**Big Cottonwood** • Agency: Bureau of Land Management • Tel: 208-735-2060 • Location: 1 mile N of Murphy Hot Springs (limited services), 76 miles SW of Twin Falls • GPS: Lat 42.031336 Lon -115.367297 • Total sites: 2 • RV sites: 2 • RV fee: Free • No water • Vault toilets • Activities: Fishing, swimming • Elevation: 5138

**Juniper Grove** • Agency: Bureau of Land Management • Tel: 208-735-2060 • Location: 1 mile N of Murphy Hot Springs (limited services), 76 miles SW of Twin Falls • GPS: Lat 42.035844 Lon -115.372798 • Total sites: 3 • RV sites: 3 • RV fee: Free • No water • Vault toilets • Activities: Hiking, fishing, swimming, non-power boating • Elevation: 5102

**The Forks** • Agency: Bureau of Land Management • Tel: 208-735-2060 • Location: 2 miles N of Murphy Hot Springs (limited services), 78 miles SW of Twin Falls • GPS: Lat 42.049133 Lon -115.390358 • Total sites: 4 • RV sites: 4 • RV fee: Free • No water • No toilets • Activities: Power boating, non-power boating • Elevation: 5997

## New Meadows

**Trail Creek Access - IFG** • Agency: State • Tel: 208-334-3700 • Location: 16 miles N of New Meadows (limited services), 26 miles NW of McCall • GPS: Lat 45.185973 Lon -116.302391 • Open: All year • Total sites: Dispersed • RV sites: Undefined • RV fee: Free • No water • Vault toilets • Activities: Fishing • Elevation: 3161

## North Fork

**Bobcat Gulch - IFG** • Agency: State • Location: 4 miles SE of North Fork (limited services), 17 miles N of Salmon • GPS: Lat 45.365392 Lon -113.964303 • Total sites: 12 • RV sites: 12 • RV fee: Free • No water • Vault toilets • Activities: Fishing • Elevation: 3684

**Fourth of July Acess - IFG** • Agency: State • Tel: 208-334-3700 • Location: 5 miles SE of North Fork (limited services), 14 miles N of Salmon • GPS: Lat 45.359256 Lon -113.945149 • Open: All year • Total sites: Dispersed • RV sites: Undefined • RV fee: Free • No water • Vault toilets • Activities: Fishing, power boating, non-power boating • Elevation: 3688

**Horse Creek Hot Springs** (Salmon-Challis NF) • Agency: US Forest Service • Tel: 208-865-2700 • Location: 44 miles NW of North Fork (limited services), 50 miles SW of Darby, MT • GPS: Lat 45.504021 Lon -114.459792 • Open: Jun-Oct • Total sites: 9 • RV sites: 9 • RV fee: Free • No water • Vault toilets • Activities: Fishing • Elevation: 6072

**Red Rock Access - IFG** • Agency: State • Tel: 208-334-3700 • Location: 7 miles SE of North Fork (limited services), 13 miles N of Salmon • GPS: Lat 45.347661 Lon -113.920605 • Open: All year • Total sites: Dispersed • RV sites: Undefined • RV fee: Free • No water • Vault toilets • Activities: Fishing, power boating, non-power boating • Elevation: 3725

## Oakley

**Independence Lakes** (Sawtooth NF) • Agency: US Forest Service • Tel: 208-678-0439 • Location: 15 miles E of Oakley (limited services), 29 miles S of Burley • GPS: Lat 42.218924 Lon -113.673615 • Open: Jul-Oct • Stay limit: 14 days • Total sites: 9 • RV sites: 9 • RV fee: Free • No water • Vault toilets • Elevation: 7707

## Oldtown

**Pend Oreille WMA - Freeman Lake - IFG** • Agency: State • Location: 4 miles S of Oldtown • GPS: Lat 48.222846 Lon -117.032975 • Total sites: Dispersed • RV sites: Undefined • RV fee: Free • No water • Vault toilets • Activities: Fishing, power boating, non-power boating • Elevation: 2461

## Orofino

**Canyon Creek** (Dworshak Reservoir) • Agency: Corps of Engineers • Tel: 208-476-1255 • Location: 10 miles N of Orofino • GPS: Lat 46.555343 Lon -116.233796 • Open: May-Sep • Total sites: 17 • RV sites: 17 • Max RV Length: 10 • RV fee: Free • No water • Vault toilets • Activities: Fishing, swimming, power boating, non-power boating • Elevation: 1654

**Dam View** (Dworshak Reservoir) • Agency: Corps of Engineers • Tel: 208-476-1255 • Location: 7 miles NW of Orofino • GPS: Lat 46.516212 Lon -116.305119 • Open: Apr-Nov • Total sites: 6 • RV sites: 6 • RV fee: Free • Water available • Vault toilets • Activities: Hiking, fishing, swimming, hunting, motor sports, non-power boating, equestrian area • Elevation: 1627

**Five-Mile Creek - IFG** • Agency: State • Tel: 208-799-5010 • Location: 10 miles SE of Orofino • GPS: Lat 46.354873 Lon -116.163315 • Open: All year • Total sites: Dispersed • RV sites: Undefined • RV fee: Free • No water • Vault toilets • Activities: Fishing, power boating, non-power boating • Elevation: 1075

**Greer Access - IFG** • Agency: State • Location: 7 miles SE of Orofino • GPS: Lat 46.392515 Lon -116.177167 • Total sites: Dispersed • RV sites: Undefined • RV fee: Free • No toilets • Elevation: 1119

**Zans Access - IFG** • Agency: State • Tel: 208-334-3700 • Location: 6 miles SE of Orofino • GPS: Lat 46.418213 Lon -116.205673 • Open: All year • Total sites: Dispersed • RV sites: Undefined • RV fee: Free • No water • Vault toilets • Activities: Fishing, power boating, non-power boating • Elevation: 1034

## Payette

**Paddock Valley Reservoir - IFG** • Agency: State • Location: 25 miles NE of Payette • GPS: Lat 44.203856 Lon -116.595052 • Total sites: Dispersed • RV sites: Undefined • RV fee: Free • No water • Vault toilets • Activities: Fishing, power boating, non-power boating • Elevation: 3232

## Picabo

**Hayspur Hatchery - IFG** • Agency: State • Tel: 208-324-4359 • Location: 5 miles NW of Picabo (limited services), 13 miles SE of Bellevue • GPS: Lat 43.337956 Lon -114.146503 • Open: May-Oct • Total sites: Dispersed • RV sites: Undefined (large open area) • RV fee: Free • Central water • Vault toilets • Activities: Fishing • Elevation: 4875

**Silver Creek East - IFG** • Agency: State • Tel: 208-334-3700 • Location: 4 miles NW of Picabo (limited services), 13 miles SE of Bellevue • GPS: Lat 43.330464 Lon -114.091504 • Open: All year • Total sites: Dispersed • RV sites: Undefined • RV fee: Free • No water • Vault toilets • Activities: Fishing • Elevation: 4846

**Silver Creek West - IFG** • Agency: State • Tel: 208-334-3700 • Location: 3 miles NW of Picabo (limited services), 13 miles SE of Bellevue • GPS: Lat 43.325438 Lon -114.104363 • Open: All year • Total sites: Dispersed • RV sites: Undefined • RV fee: Free • No water • Vault toilets • Activities: Fishing • Elevation: 4848

## Pierce

**Campbell's Pond Access Area - IFG** • Agency: State • Tel: 208-476-4541 • Location: 8 miles NW of Pierce (limited services), 23 miles E of Orofino • GPS: Lat 46.543253 Lon -115.871456 • Total sites: Dispersed • RV sites: Undefined • Max RV Length: 16 • RV fee: Free • No water • Vault toilets • Activities: Hiking, fishing, power boating • Elevation: 3325

**Flat Creek** (Nez Perce-Clearwater NF) • Agency: US Forest Service • Location: 46 miles NE of Pierce (limited services), 69 miles NE of Orofino • GPS: Lat 46.721051 Lon -115.292398 • Total sites: 11 • RV sites: 11 • RV fee: Free • No water • Vault toilets • Elevation: 2708

**Grandad Creek** (Dworshak Reservoir) • Agency: Corps of Engineers • Tel: 208-476-1255 • Location: 38 miles N of Pierce (limited services), 57 miles NE of Orofino • GPS: Lat 46.824301 Lon -115.913068 • Open: May-Sep • Total sites: 10 • RV sites: 10 • Max RV Length: 20 • RV fee: Free • Central water • Vault toilets • Activities: Hiking, mountain biking, fishing, swimming, power boating, motor sports, non-power boating • Elevation: 1552

**Little Meadow Creek** (Dworshak Reservoir) • Agency: Corps of Engineers • Tel: 208-476-1255 • Location: 37 miles N of Pierce (limited services), 56 miles NE of Orofino • GPS: Lat 46.791284 Lon -115.953797 • Open: May-Sep • Total sites: 6 • RV sites: 6 • RV fee: Free • No water • Vault toilets • Activities: Fishing, power boating, non-power boating • Elevation: 1626

**Sousie Creek** • Agency: Miscellaneous • Location: 33 miles N of Pierce (limited services), 52 miles NE of Orofino • GPS: Lat 46.799994 Lon -115.656125 • Total sites: 10 • RV sites: 10 • RV fee: Free • No water • Vault toilets • Notes: Just outside Nez Perce-Clearwater NF • Elevation: 2395

## Pine

**Castle Creek** (Boise NF) • Agency: US Forest Service • Tel: 208-587-7961 • Location: 11 miles SW of Pine (limited services), 34 miles NE of Mountain Home • GPS: Lat 43.410805 Lon -115.395014 • Open: May-Sep • Total sites: 2 • RV sites: 2 • Max RV Length: 25 • RV fee: Free • No water • Vault toilets • Activities: Fishing, power boating, non-power boating • Elevation: 4268

**Evans Creek** (Boise NF) • Agency: US Forest Service • Tel: 208-587-7961 • Location: 14 miles SW of Pine (limited services), 31 miles NE of Mountain Home • GPS: Lat 43.400146 Lon -115.414244 • Open: May-Sep • Total sites: 10 • RV sites: 10 • RV fee: Free • No water • Vault toilets • Activities: Fishing, power boating, non-power boating • Elevation: 4222

**Ice Springs** (Boise NF) • Agency: US Forest Service • Tel: 208-587-7961 • Location: 12 miles W of Pine (limited services), 62 miles NE of Mountain Home • GPS: Lat 43.482909 Lon -115.396997 • Open: May-Sep • Total sites: 4 • RV sites: 4 • RV fee: Free • No water • Vault toilets • Activities: Hiking, fishing • Elevation: 4993

**Little Wilson Creek** (Boise NF) • Agency: US Forest Service • Tel: 208-587-7961 • Location: 17 miles SW of Pine (limited services), 29 miles NE of Mountain Home • GPS: Lat 43.377474 Lon -115.434413 • Open: May-Oct • Total sites: 2 • RV sites: 2 • RV fee: Free • No water • Vault toilets • Activities: Fishing, swimming, power boating, non-power boating • Elevation: 4255

**Spillway** (Boise NF) • Agency: US Forest Service • Tel: 208-587-7961 • Location: 19 miles SW of Pine (limited services), 26 miles NE of Mountain Home • GPS: Lat 43.357214 Lon -115.447505 • Open: May-Sep • Total sites: 3 • RV sites: 3 • RV fee: Free • No water • Vault toilets • Activities: Fishing, power boating, non-power boating • Elevation: 4203

**Tailwaters** (Boise NF) • Agency: US Forest Service • Tel: 208-587-7961 • Location: 19 miles SW of Pine (limited services), 26 miles NE of Mountain Home • GPS: Lat 43.355917 Lon -115.455304 • Total sites: 3 • RV sites: 3 • RV fee: Free • No water • Vault toilets • Activities: Fishing • Elevation: 3983

## Pingree

**McTucker Creek Access Area - IFG** • Agency: State • Location: 8 miles SW of Pingree (limited services), 23 miles SW of Blackfoot • GPS: Lat 43.028231 Lon -112.661613 • Total sites: Dispersed • RV sites: Undefined • RV fee: Free • No toilets • Activities: Fishing, power boating • Elevation: 4350

**McTucker Ponds Access Area - IFG** • Agency: State • Location: 7 miles SW of Pingree (limited services), 22 miles SW of Blackfoot • GPS: Lat 43.036092 Lon -112.649178 • Total sites: Dispersed • RV sites: Undefined • RV fee: Free • No toilets • Elevation: 4367

## Preston

**Condie Reservoir - IFG** • Agency: State • Tel: 208-334-3700 • Location: 10 miles N of Preston • GPS: Lat 42.210209 Lon -111.863453 • Open: All year • Total sites: Dispersed • RV sites: Undefined • RV fee: Free • No water • Vault toilets • Activities: Fishing, power boating, non-power boating • Elevation: 4907

**Glendale Reservoir Access - IFG** • Agency: State • Tel: 208-334-3700 • Location: 5 miles NE of Preston • GPS: Lat 42.128236 Lon -111.808124 • Total sites: Dispersed • RV sites: Undefined • RV fee: Free • No water • Vault toilets • Activities: Fishing, power boating • Elevation: 4961

**Johnson Reservoir - IFG** • Agency: State • Tel: 208-334-3700 • Location: 5 miles E of Preston • GPS: Lat 42.110152 Lon -111.807599 • Open: All year • Total sites: Dispersed • RV sites: Undefined • RV fee: Free • No water • Vault toilets • Activities: Fishing, power boating, non-power boating • Elevation: 4891

**Oneida Narrows Reservoir Access - IFG** • Agency: State • Location: 16 miles NE of Preston • GPS: Lat 42.273667 Lon -111.743907 • Total sites: Dispersed • RV sites: Undefined • RV fee: Free • No water • Vault toilets • Activities: Fishing • Elevation: 4902

**Riverdale Campground - IFG** • Agency: State • Location: 9 miles NE of Preston • GPS: Lat 42.195496 Lon -111.783295 • Total sites: Dispersed • RV sites: Undefined • RV fee: Free • No toilets • Activities: Fishing • Elevation: 4656

## Rexburg

**Warm Slough Access - IFG** • Agency: State • Location: 8 miles NW of Rexburg • GPS: Lat 43.871327 Lon

-111.867707 • Total sites: Dispersed • RV sites: Undefined • RV fee: Free • No water • Vault toilets • Elevation: 4829

## Riggins

**Hazzard Creek Access - IFG** • Agency: State • Location: 18 miles S of Riggins • GPS: Lat 45.180644 Lon -116.300999 • Total sites: Dispersed • RV sites: Undefined • RV fee: Free • No toilets • Activities: Fishing • Elevation: 3202

**Iron Phone Junction** (Nez Perce-Clearwater NF) • Agency: US Forest Service • Tel: 208-839-2211 • Location: 13 miles NW of Riggins • GPS: Lat 45.533566 Lon -116.420873 • Open: All year (limited winter access) • Total sites: 4 • RV sites: 4 • RV fee: Free • No water • Vault toilets • Elevation: 5340

**Island Bar** • Agency: Bureau of Land Management • Tel: 208-962-3245 • Location: 4 miles E of Riggins • GPS: Lat 45.41795 Lon -116.261151 • Open: All year • Total sites: Dispersed • RV sites: Undefined • RV fee: Free • No water • Vault toilets • Activities: Fishing, swimming, power boating, non-power boating • Elevation: 1818

**Lightning Creek Access - IFG** • Agency: State • Tel: 208-799-5010 • Location: 3 miles N of Riggins • GPS: Lat 45.465488 Lon -116.307219 • Total sites: Dispersed • RV sites: Undefined • RV fee: Free • No water • Vault toilets • Activities: Fishing, power boating • Elevation: 1676

**Rattlesnake Access - IFG** • Agency: State • Location: 12 miles S of Riggins • GPS: Lat 45.267333 Lon -116.342009 • Total sites: Dispersed • RV sites: Undefined • RV fee: Free • No water • No toilets • Activities: Fishing • Elevation: 2614

**Shorts Bar** • Agency: Bureau of Land Management • Tel: 208-962-3245 • Location: 2 miles E of Riggins • GPS: Lat 45.414227 Lon -116.301712 • Open: All year • Total sites: Dispersed • RV sites: Undefined • RV fee: Free • No water • Vault toilets • Activities: Fishing, swimming, power boating, non-power boating • Elevation: 1749

**Upper Bluff - Milepost 190 - IFG** • Agency: State • Tel: 208-334-3700 • Location: 4 miles S of Riggins • GPS: Lat 45.363322 Lon -116.359111 • Open: All year • Total sites: Dispersed • RV sites: Undefined • RV fee: Free • No water • Vault toilets • Activities: Fishing • Elevation: 2030

## Ririe

**Wolf Flats** • Agency: Bureau of Land Management • Tel: 208-524-7500 • Location: 12 miles E of Ririe (limited services), 26 miles E of Idaho Falls • GPS: Lat 43.598867 Lon -111.610709 • Total sites: Dispersed • RV sites: Undefined • RV fee: Free • No water • Vault toilets • Activities: Fishing, power boating • Elevation: 5065

## Roberts

**Jim Moore Pond Access - IFG** • Agency: State • Location: 3 miles N of Roberts (limited services), 13 miles N of Idaho Falls • GPS: Lat 43.683947 Lon -112.115892 • Total sites: Dispersed • RV sites: Undefined • RV fee: Free • No water • Vault toilets • Activities: Fishing • Elevation: 4770

## Rockland

**East Fork Rock Creek - IFG** • Agency: State • Location: 5 miles W of Rockland (limited services), 20 miles S of American Falls • GPS: Lat 42.563068 Lon -112.790482 • Total sites: Dispersed • RV sites: Undefined • RV fee: Free • No water • No toilets • Activities: Fishing • Elevation: 5047

**Mill Flat** (Sawtooth NF) • Agency: US Forest Service • Tel: 208-678-0439 • Location: 16 miles SW of Rockland (limited services), 34 miles SW of American Falls • GPS: Lat 42.432009 Lon -113.015975 • Open: Jun-Oct • Stay limit: 14 days • Total sites: 7 • RV sites: 7 • RV fee: Free • No water • Vault toilets • Activities: Hiking, fishing, motor sports • Elevation: 5938

**Sublett** (Sawtooth NF) • Agency: US Forest Service • Tel: 208-678-0439 • Location: 25 miles SW of Rockland (limited services), 40 miles S of American Falls • GPS: Lat 42.327704 Lon -113.003233 • Open: Jun-Nov • Stay limit: 14 days • Total sites: 9 • RV sites: 9 • RV fee: Free • No water • Vault toilets • Activities: Hiking • Elevation: 5430

## Rose Lake

**Coeur d'Alene River WMA - Bull Run Lake - IFG** • Agency: State • Location: 1 mile S of Rose Lake (limited services), 15 miles W of Pinehurst • GPS: Lat 47.531175 Lon -116.481066 • Total sites: Dispersed • RV sites: Undefined • RV fee: Free • No water • No toilets • Activities: Fishing • Elevation: 2138

**Coeur d'Alene River WMA - Rose Lake - IFG** • Agency: State • Location: 1 mile N of Rose Lake (limited services), 15 miles W of Pinehurst • GPS: Lat 47.553332 Lon -116.457359 • Total sites: Dispersed • RV sites: Undefined • RV fee: Free • No water • Vault toilets • Activities: Fishing, power boating, non-power boating • Elevation: 2175

**Medicine Lake - IFG** • Agency: State • Location: 9 miles S of Rose Lake (limited services), 21 miles N of St Maries • GPS: Lat 47.473866 Lon -116.588102 • Total sites: Dispersed • RV sites: Undefined • RV fee: Free • No water • Vault toilets • Activities: Fishing, power boating • Elevation: 2169

## Sagle

**Morton Slough - IFG** • Agency: State • Tel: 208-334-3700 • Location: 9 miles W of Sagle (limited services), 14 miles SW of Sandpoint • GPS: Lat 48.180682 Lon -116.713821 • Open: All year • Total sites: Dispersed • RV sites: Undefined • RV fee: Free • No water • Vault toilets • Activities: Fishing, power boating, non-power boating • Elevation: 2075

**Shepherd Lake East - IFG** • Agency: State • Location: 3 miles SE of Sagle (limited services), 8 miles S of Sandpoint • GPS: Lat 48.185738 Lon -116.524201 • Total sites: Dispersed • RV sites: Undefined • RV fee: Free • No water • Vault toilets • Activities: Fishing • Elevation: 2300

**Shepherd Lake West - IFG** • Agency: State • Location: 3 miles SE of Sagle (limited services), 8 miles S of Sandpoint • GPS: Lat 48.187921 Lon -116.530013 • Total sites: Dispersed • RV sites: Undefined • RV fee: Free • No water • Vault toilets • Activities: Fishing • Elevation: 2305

## Salmon

**Carmen Bridge Access - IFG** • Agency: State • Tel: 208-334-3700 • Location: 3 miles N of Salmon • GPS: Lat 45.229393 Lon -113.891534 • Open: All year • Total sites: Dispersed • RV sites: Undefined • RV fee: Free • No water • Vault toilets • Activities: Fishing, power boating, non-power boating • Elevation: 3873

**Cougar Point** (Salmon-Challis NF) • Agency: US Forest Service • Tel: 208-756-5200 • Location: 15 miles SW of Salmon • GPS: Lat 45.082567 Lon -114.054335 • Open: May-Oct • Total sites: 18 • RV sites: 18 • RV fee: Free • No water • Vault toilets • Activities: Hiking • Elevation: 6581

**Lemhi Hole Access - IFG** • Agency: State • Tel: 208-334-3700 • Location: In Salmon • GPS: Lat 45.187184 Lon -113.893111 • Open: All year • Total sites: Dispersed • RV sites: Undefined • RV fee: Free • No water • Vault toilets • Activities: Fishing, power boating, non-power boating • Elevation: 3923

**Lime Creek Access Area - IFG** • Agency: State • Location: 19 miles S of Salmon • GPS: Lat 44.922691 Lon -113.962732 • Total sites: Dispersed • RV sites: Undefined • RV fee: Free • No toilets • Elevation: 4331

## Shelley

**Trail Creek Bridge** • Agency: Bureau of Land Management • Tel: 208-478-6340 • Location: 27 miles SE of Shelley • GPS: Lat 43.131645 Lon -111.912332 • Total sites: 6 • RV sites: 6 • RV fee: Free • No water • Vault toilets • Activities: Fishing, power boating • Elevation: 5568

## Soda Springs

**Blackfoot Reservoir Access 1 - IFG** • Agency: State • Location: 19 miles N of Soda Springs • GPS: Lat 42.922168 Lon -111.522397 • Total sites: Dispersed • RV sites: Undefined • RV fee: Free • No water • No toilets • Activities: Fishing • Elevation: 6147

**Cold Springs** (Banks, Caribou-Targhee NF) • Agency: US Forest Service • Tel: 208-847-0375 • Location: 12 miles S of Soda Springs • GPS: Lat 42.510625 Lon -111.582985 • Open: May-Sep • Total sites: 6 • RV sites: 6 • RV fee: Free • No water • Vault toilets • Activities: Fishing • Elevation: 6371

**Eightmile** (Caribou-Targhee NF) • Agency: US Forest Service • Tel: 208-847-0375 • Location: 14 miles S of Soda Springs • GPS: Lat 42.487631 Lon -111.584482 • Open: May-Sep • Total sites: 5 • RV sites: 5 • RV fee: Free • No water • Vault toilets • Activities: Hiking, fishing • Elevation: 6749

**Oregon Trail City Park** • Agency: Municipal • Tel: 208-547-4964 • Location: 2 miles W of Soda Springs • GPS: Lat 42.657539 Lon -111.653491 • Total sites: Dispersed • RV sites: Undefined • RV fee: Free • No water • Vault toilets • Activities: Mountain biking, fishing, swimming, power boating, non-power boating • Elevation: 5735

**Pebble Beach - IFG** • Agency: State • Tel: 208-334-3700 • Location: 28 miles N of Soda Springs • GPS: Lat 42.954902 Lon -111.639836 • Open: All year • Total sites: Dispersed • RV sites: Undefined • RV fee: Free • No water • Vault toilets • Activities: Fishing, power boating, non-power boating • Elevation: 6133

**Pine Bar** (Caribou-Targhee NF) • Agency: US Forest Service • Tel: 208-547-4356 • Location: 44 miles NE of Soda Springs, 23 miles SW of Alpine, WY • GPS: Lat 42.972455 Lon -111.210285 • Total sites: 6 • RV sites: 6 • RV fee: Free • No water • Vault toilets • Activities: Hiking, fishing • Elevation: 6424

**Poison Creek Access - IFG** • Agency: State • Location: 33 miles N of Soda Springs • GPS: Lat 43.024381 Lon -111.711157 • Total sites: Dispersed • RV sites: Undefined • RV fee: Free • No water • No toilets • Activities: Fishing • Elevation: 6122

**Tin Cup** (Caribou-Targhee NF) • Agency: US Forest Service • Tel: 208-547-4356 • Location: 51 miles NE of Soda Springs, 17 miles S of Alpine, WY • GPS: Lat 43.004643 Lon -111.102652 • Open: May-Sep • Total sites: 5 • RV sites: 5 • RV fee: Free • No water • Vault toilets • Activities: Fishing • Elevation: 5863

## St Anthony

**St Anthony Dunes - Red Road** • Agency: Bureau of Land Management • Tel: 208-524-7500 • Location: 8 miles NW of St Anthony • GPS: Lat 44.015367 Lon -111.788165 • Total sites: Dispersed • RV sites: Undefined • RV fee: Free • No water • Vault toilets • Activities: Motor sports, equestrian area • Elevation: 5015

**Sand Creek WMA - IFG** • Agency: State • Tel: 208-624-7065 • Location: 6 miles NE of St. Anthony • GPS: Lat 44.016939 Lon -111.598353 • Open: All year • Total sites: Dispersed • RV sites: Undefined • RV fee: Free • No water • Vault toilets • Activities: Fishing • Elevation: 5059

## St. Charles

**Bear Lake (North Jetty) Access Area - IFG** • Agency: State • Location: 5 miles W of St. Charles (limited services), 17 miles S of Montpelier • GPS: Lat 42.120254 Lon -111.297278 • Total sites: Dispersed • RV sites: Undefined • RV fee: Free • No water • Vault toilets • Elevation: 5928

## St. Maries

**St. Maries WMA - IFG** • Agency: State • Tel: 208-769-1414 • Location: 1 mile SE of St. Maries • GPS: Lat 47.307263 Lon -116.542037 • Total sites: Dispersed • RV sites: Undefined • RV fee: Free • No toilets • Activities: Fishing, power boating, non-power boating • Elevation: 2143

## Stanley

**Bear Valley** (Boise NF) • Agency: US Forest Service • Tel: 208-259-3361 • Location: 33 miles NW of Stanley • GPS: Lat 44.410971 Lon -115.369787 • Open: Jun-Sep • Total sites: 6 • RV sites: 6 • RV fee: Free • No water • Vault toilets • Activities: Hiking, fishing • Elevation: 6414

**Gold Creek Access - IFG** • Agency: State • Tel: 208-334-3700 • Location: 9 miles S of Stanley • GPS: Lat 44.111821 Lon -114.862369 • Open: All year • Total sites: Dispersed • RV sites: Undefined • RV fee: Free • No water • No toilets • Activities: Fishing • Elevation: 6553

**Josephus Lake** (Salmon-Challis NF) • Agency: US Forest Service • Tel: 208-879-4101 • Location: 38 miles NW of Stanley • GPS: Lat 44.548894 Lon -115.143553 • Open: Jul-Oct • Total sites: 3 • RV sites: 3 • RV fee: Free • No water • Vault toilets • Activities: Hiking • Elevation: 7072

**Marsh Creek** (Sawtooth NF) • Agency: US Forest Service • Location: 20 miles NW of Stanley • GPS: Lat 44.410575 Lon -115.184298 • Total sites: 3 • RV sites: 3 • RV fee: Free • No water • Vault toilets • Activities: Hiking • Elevation: 6486

## Swan Valley

**Snake River - Lufkin Bottoms** • Agency: US Forest Service • Location: 18 miles NW of Swan Valley (limited services), 32 miles E of Idaho Falls • GPS: Lat 43.581197 Lon -111.464968 • Total sites: 7 • RV sites: 7 • RV fee: Free • No water • No toilets • Activities: Power boating, non-power boating • Elevation: 5139

## Tendoy

**Agency Creek** • Agency: Bureau of Land Management • Tel: 208-756-5400 • Location: 6 miles E of Tendoy (limited services), 25 miles SE of Salmon • GPS: Lat 44.961238 Lon -113.542103 • Total sites: 4 • RV sites: 4 • RV fee: Free • No toilets • Elevation: 5430

## Terreton

**Mud Lake WMA South Ramp - IFG** • Agency: State • Tel: 208-334-3700 • Location: 3 miles S of Terreton (limited services), 32 miles W of Rexburg • GPS: Lat 43.872015 Lon -112.408929 • Open: All year • Total sites: Dispersed • RV sites: Undefined • RV fee: Free • No water • Vault toilets • Activities: Fishing, power boating, non-power boating • Elevation: 4789

## Troy

**Spring Valley Reservoir Access Area - IFG** • Agency: State • Tel: 208-799-5010 • Location: 5 miles N of Troy (limited services), 16 miles NE of Moscow • GPS: Lat 46.786817 Lon -116.755714 • Total sites: Dispersed • RV sites: Undefined • RV fee: Free • No water • Vault toilets • Activities: Fishing, power boating, non-power boating • Elevation: 2795

## Victor

**Fox Creek East Access Area - IFG** • Agency: State • Location: 6 miles NW of Victor • GPS: Lat 43.650484 Lon -111.166591 • Total sites: Dispersed • RV sites: Undefined • RV fee: Free • No toilets • Activities: Fishing • Elevation: 6001

**Fox Creek West Access - IFG** • Agency: State • Tel: 208-334-3700 • Location: 8 miles NW of Victor • GPS: Lat 43.655598 Lon -111.178345 • Open: All year • Total sites: Dispersed • RV sites: Undefined • RV fee: Free • No water • Vault toilets • Activities: Fishing, power boating, non-power boating • Elevation: 6013

## Warren

**Shiefer** (Payette NF) • Agency: US Forest Service • Tel: 208-634-0400 • Location: 13 miles SE of Warren (limited services), 57 miles NE of McCall • GPS: Lat 45.173472 Lon -115.579919 • Total sites: 5 • RV sites: 5 • RV fee:

Free • No water • Vault toilets • Activities: Swimming • Elevation: 2979

## Weiser

**Justrite** (Payette NF) • Agency: US Forest Service • Tel: 208-549-4200 • Location: 24 miles N of Weiser • GPS: Lat 44.540918 Lon -116.953046 • Total sites: 4 • RV sites: 4 • RV fee: Free • No water • Vault toilets • Activities: Hiking, mountain biking, fishing • Elevation: 4341

**Kiwanis** (Payette NF) • Agency: US Forest Service • Tel: 208-549-4200 • Location: 22 miles N of Weiser • GPS: Lat 44.512715 Lon -116.953094 • Total sites: 1 • RV sites: 1 • RV fee: Free • No water • Vault toilets • Notes: Can be dusty and noisy • Activities: Motor sports • Elevation: 3881

**Paradise** (Payette NF) • Agency: US Forest Service • Tel: 208-549-4200 • Location: 24 miles N of Weiser • GPS: Lat 44.543602 Lon -116.952505 • Total sites: 2 • RV sites: 2 • Max RV Length: 15 • RV fee: Free • Central water • Vault toilets • Activities: Hiking, mountain biking • Elevation: 4357

**Weiser Sand Dunes OHV** • Agency: Bureau of Land Management • Tel: 208-384-3300 • Location: 15 miles W of Weiser • GPS: Lat 44.297578 Lon -117.208388 • Total sites: Dispersed • RV sites: Undefined • RV fee: Free • No water • Vault toilets • Activities: Motor sports • Elevation: 2167

## Westmond

**Pend Oreille WMA - Cocolalla Lake - IFG** • Agency: State • Location: In Westmond (limited services), 10 miles S of Sandpoint • GPS: Lat 48.139237 Lon -116.602556 • Total sites: Dispersed • RV sites: Undefined • RV fee: Free • No water • Vault toilets • Activities: Fishing, power boating, non-power boating • Elevation: 2241

## Weston

**Dry Canyon** (Caribou-Targhee NF) • Agency: US Forest Service • Tel: 208-236-7500 • Location: 10 miles W of Weston (limited services), 16 miles S of Malad City • GPS: Lat 42.057849 Lon -112.143917 • Open: May-Sep • Total sites: 3 • RV sites: 3 • RV fee: Free • No water • Vault toilets • Activities: Hiking, fishing, hunting • Elevation: 6355

## White Bird

**North Fork** (Slate Creek, Nez Perce-Clearwater NF) • Agency: US Forest Service • Tel: 208-839-2211 • Location: 18 miles SE of White Bird (limited services), 28 miles NE of Riggins • GPS: Lat 45.639956 Lon -116.119606 • Open: All year (limited winter access) • Total sites: 5 • RV sites: 5 • Max RV Length: 22 • RV fee: Free • No water • Vault toilets • Activities: Fishing • Elevation: 2986

**Rocky Bluff** (Nez Perce-Clearwater NF) • Agency: US Forest Service • Tel: 208-839-2211 • Location: 27 miles SE of White Bird (limited services), 30 miles S of Grangeville • GPS: Lat 45.632316 Lon -116.010984 • Open: All year (limited winter access) • Total sites: 5 • RV sites: 3 • Max RV Length: 15 • RV fee: Free • No water • No toilets • Activities: Fishing • Elevation: 5253

**Twin Bridges Access - IFG** • Agency: State • Location: 8 miles S of White Bird (limited services), 20 miles N of Riggins • GPS: Lat 45.660604 Lon -116.291912 • Total sites: Dispersed • RV sites: Undefined • RV fee: Free • No water • Vault toilets • Activities: Fishing • Elevation: 1533

**White Bird Gravel Pit** • Agency: Bureau of Land Management • Tel: 208-962-3245 • Location: 2 miles SW of White Bird (limited services), 18 miles SW of Grangeville • GPS: Lat 45.743659 Lon -116.324746 • Open: All year • Total sites: Dispersed • RV sites: Undefined • RV fee: Free • No water • Vault toilets • Activities: Fishing, swimming, power boating, non-power boating • Elevation: 1493

## Winchester

**Soldier Meadows Reservoir - IFG** • Agency: State • Location: 11 miles SW of Winchester (limited services), 23 miles SE of Lewiston • GPS: Lat 46.167326 Lon -116.735082 • Total sites: Dispersed • RV sites: Undefined • RV fee: Free • No water • Vault toilets • Activities: Fishing, power boating • Elevation: 4531

## Yellow Pine

**Golden Gate** (Boise NF) • Agency: US Forest Service • Tel: 208-382-7400 • Location: 2 miles S of Yellow Pine (limited services), 51 miles NE of Cascade • GPS: Lat 44.935345 Lon -115.485407 • Open: May-Sep • Total sites: 9 • RV sites: 9 • RV fee: Free • No water • Vault toilets • Activities: Hiking, fishing, motor sports • Elevation: 4875

**Ice Hole** (Boise NF) • Agency: US Forest Service • Tel: 208-382-7400 • Location: 6 miles S of Yellow Pine (limited services), 48 miles NE of Cascade • GPS: Lat 44.887939 Lon -115.499512 • Open: May-Oct • Total sites: 10 • RV sites: 10 • RV fee: Free • Central water • Vault toilets • Activities: Hiking, mountain biking, fishing, motor sports • Elevation: 5092

**Yellow Pine** (Boise NF) • Agency: US Forest Service • Tel: 208-382-7400 • Location: 1 mile S of Yellow Pine (limited services), 53 miles NE of Cascade • GPS: Lat 44.95459 Lon -115.496582 • Open: May-Sep • Total sites: 14 • RV sites: 14 • RV fee: Free • Central water • Vault toilets • Activities: Fishing, motor sports • Elevation: 4734

# Montana

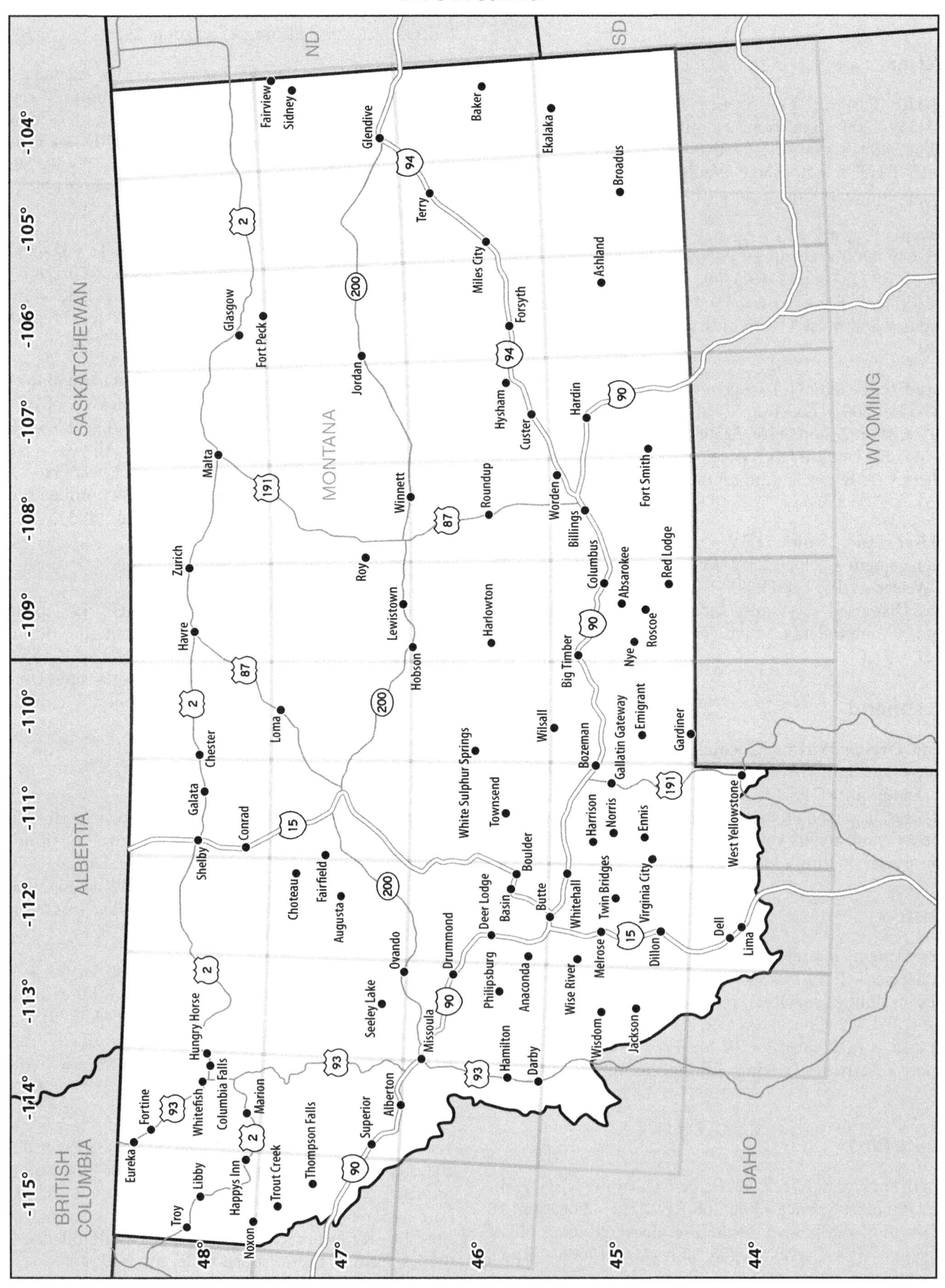
SASKATCHEWAN
ALBERTA
BRITISH COLUMBIA
ND
SD
WYOMING
IDAHO
MONTANA
-104°
-105°
-106°
-107°
-108°
-109°
-110°
-111°
-112°
-113°
-114°
-115°
48°
47°
46°
45°
44°
Fairview
Sidney
Baker
Ekalaka
Glendive
Broadus
Terry
Miles City
Ashland
Glasgow
Fort Peck
Forsyth
Jordan
Hysham
Custer
Hardin
Malta
Winnett
Roundup
Worden
Fort Smith
Billings
Zurich
Roy
Columbus
Absarokee
Red Lodge
Lewistown
Harlowton
Roscoe
Nye
Havre
Big Timber
Hobson
Loma
Wilsall
Emigrant
Gallatin Gateway
Gardiner
Chester
White Sulphur Springs
Bozeman
Galata
Townsend
Harrison
Norris
Ennis
West Yellowstone
Conrad
Shelby
Boulder
Twin Bridges
Virginia City
Choteau
Fairfield
Augusta
Basin
Butte
Whitehall
Deer Lodge
Dillon
Dell
Lima
Melrose
Drummond
Ovando
Philipsburg
Anaconda
Wise River
Seeley Lake
Hungry Horse
Missoula
Wisdom
Jackson
Hamilton
Darby
Columbia Falls
Whitefish
Fortine
Marion
Superior
Alberton
Eureka
Libby
Happys Inn
Trout Creek
Thompson Falls
Troy
Noxon
2
15
87
90
93
94
191
200

# Montana — Camping Areas

| Abbreviation | Description |
|---|---|
| FAS | Fishing Access Site |
| NF | National Forest |
| NM | National Monument |
| NRA | National Recreation Area |
| NWR | National Wildlife Refuge |
| OHV | Off-Highway Vehicle |
| RA | Recreation Area |
| TMA | Travel Management Area |
| WMA | Wildlife Management Area |

## Absarokee

**Buffalo Jump FAS** • Agency: State • Tel: 406-247-2940 • Location: 22 miles SW of Absarokee (limited services), 36 miles SW of Columbus • GPS: Lat 45.436082 Lon -109.797351 • Open: All year • Stay limit: 7 days • Total sites: 3 • RV sites: 3 • RV fee: Free • No water • Vault toilets • Activities: Fishing, non-power boating • Elevation: 4800

**Cliff Swallow FAS** • Agency: State • Tel: 406-247-2940 • Location: 9 miles W of Absarokee (limited services), 23 miles SW of Columbus • GPS: Lat 45.515034 Lon -109.632333 • Open: All year • Stay limit: 7 days • Total sites: 8 • RV sites: 8 • RV fee: Free • No water • Vault toilets • Activities: Fishing • Elevation: 4416

**Moraine FAS** • Agency: State • Tel: 406-247-2940 • Location: 18 miles W of Absarokee (limited services), 31 miles SW of Columbus • GPS: Lat 45.461006 Lon -109.757785 • Open: All year • Stay limit: 7 days • Total sites: 2 • RV sites: 2 • RV fee: Free • No water • Vault toilets • Activities: Fishing • Elevation: 4718

## Alberton

**Clearwater Crossing** (Lolo NF) • Agency: US Forest Service • Tel: 406-626-5201 • Location: 25 miles SW of Alberton (limited services), 52 miles W of Missoula • GPS: Lat 46.908889 Lon -114.803115 • Total sites: 3 • RV sites: 3 • RV fee: Free • Central water • Vault toilets • Activities: Hiking, equestrian area • Elevation: 3493

**Kreis Pond** (Lolo NF) • Agency: US Forest Service • Tel: 406-626-5201 • Location: 12 miles N of Alberton (limited services), 28 miles NW of Missoula • GPS: Lat 47.09982 Lon -114.42633 • Total sites: 7 • RV sites: 7 • RV fee: Free • No water • Vault toilets • Elevation: 3711

## Anaconda

**Racetrack** (Beaverhead-Deerlodge NF) • Agency: US Forest Service • Tel: 406-859-3211 • Location: 17 miles N of Anaconda • GPS: Lat 46.280272 Lon -112.938662 • Open: May-Sep • Total sites: 13 • RV sites: 13 • Max RV Length: 22 • RV fee: Free • Central water • Vault toilets • Activities: Hiking, fishing • Elevation: 5381

## Ashland

**Blacks Pond** (Custer Gallatin NF) • Agency: US Forest Service • Tel: 406-784-2344 • Location: 20 miles S of Ashland (limited services), 107 miles SW of Miles City • GPS: Lat 45.346975 Lon -106.286373 • Open: All year • Total sites: 2 • RV sites: 2 • RV fee: Free • No water • No toilets • Activities: Fishing • Elevation: 3678

**Cow Creek** (Custer Gallatin NF) • Agency: US Forest Service • Tel: 406-784-2344 • Location: 28 miles S of Ashland (limited services), 115 miles SW of Miles City • GPS: Lat 45.310201 Lon -106.244534 • Open: All year • Stay limit: 10 days • Total sites: 4 • RV sites: 4 • Max RV Length: 32 • RV fee: Free • No water • Vault toilets • Activities: Fishing • Elevation: 3888

**Holiday Spring** (Custer Gallatin NF) • Agency: US Forest Service • Tel: 406-784-2344 • Location: 17 miles NE of Ashland (limited services), 70 miles S of Miles City • GPS: Lat 45.638499 Lon -105.974276 • Open: Apr-Nov • Stay limit: 10 days • Total sites: 6 • RV sites: 6 • RV fee: Free • No water • Vault toilets • Activities: Hunting • Elevation: 4009

**Red Shale** (Custer Gallatin NF) • Agency: US Forest Service • Tel: 406-784-2344 • Location: 6 miles E of Ashland (limited services), 76 miles S of Miles City • GPS: Lat 45.568933 Lon -106.146433 • Open: Apr-Dec • Stay limit: 10 days • Total sites: 14 • RV sites: 14 • Max RV Length: 32 • RV fee: Free • No water • Vault toilets • Activities: Hunting • Elevation: 3209

## Augusta

**Double Falls** (Helena-Lewis & Clark NF) • Agency: US Forest Service • Tel: 406-466-5341 • Location: 19 miles W of Augusta (limited services), 45 miles SW of Choteau • GPS: Lat 47.407334 Lon -112.722084 • Total sites: 4 • RV sites: 4 • RV fee: Free • No water • Vault toilets • Notes: Mandatory food storage • Elevation: 5282

## Baker

**South Sandstone FAS** • Agency: State • Tel: 406-234-0900 • Location: 11 miles SW of Baker • GPS: Lat 46.333179 Lon -104.471795 • Open: All year • Total sites: 11 • RV sites: 11 • RV fee: Free • No water • Vault toilets • Activities: Fishing, swimming, power boating • Elevation: 2861

## Basin

**Mormon Gulch** (Beaverhead-Deerlodge NF) • Agency: US Forest Service • Tel: 406-287-3223 • Location: 6 miles W of Basin (limited services), 14 miles W of Boulder • GPS: Lat 46.256792 Lon -112.362653 • Open: May-Nov • Total sites: 16 • RV sites: 16 • Max RV Length: 16 • RV fee: Free • No water • Vault toilets • Elevation: 5824

**Whitehouse** (Beaverhead-Deerlodge NF) • Agency: US Forest Service • Tel: 406-494-2147 • Location: 11 miles W of Basin (limited services), 20 miles W of Boulder • GPS: Lat 46.258166 Lon -112.478539 • Open: May-Nov • Stay limit: 16 days • Total sites: 5 • RV sites: 5 • Max RV Length: 22 • RV fee: Free • Central water • Vault toilets • Activities: Hiking, fishing • Elevation: 6086

## Big Timber

**Big Beaver** (Custer Gallatin NF) • Agency: US Forest Service • Tel: 406-932-5155 • Location: 32 miles SW of Big Timber • GPS: Lat 45.463875 Lon -110.199043 • Open: All year (limited winter access) • Total sites: 5 • RV sites: 5 • Max RV Length: 32 • RV fee: Free • No water • Vault toilets • Activities: Fishing • Elevation: 5348

**Big Rock FAS** • Agency: State • Tel: 406-444-2535 • Location: 5 miles S of Big Timber • GPS: Lat 45.791905 Lon -109.965242 • Open: All year • Stay limit: 7 days • Total sites: 5 • RV sites: 5 • RV fee: Free • No water • Vault toilets • Activities: Fishing, swimming • Elevation: 4226

**Boulder Forks FAS** • Agency: State • Tel: 406-444-2535 • Location: 16 miles SW of Big Timber • GPS: Lat 45.657927 Lon -110.108652 • Open: All year • Stay limit: 7 days • Total sites: 5 • RV sites: 5 • RV fee: Free • No water • Vault toilets • Activities: Fishing, swimming • Elevation: 4780

**Hells Canyon** (Custer Gallatin NF) • Agency: US Forest Service • Tel: 406-932-5155 • Location: 40 miles SW of Big Timber • GPS: Lat 45.361892 Lon -110.215052 • Open: All year (limited winter access) • Total sites: 11 • RV sites: 11 • Max RV Length: 20 • RV fee: Free • No water • Vault toilets • Activities: Hiking, fishing • Elevation: 6132

**Otter Creek FAS** • Agency: State • Tel: 406-247-2940 • Location: 2 miles NE of Big Timber • GPS: Lat 45.854439 Lon -109.914245 • Open: All year • Stay limit: 7 days • Total sites: 3 • RV sites: 3 • RV fee: Free • No water • Vault toilets • Activities: Fishing, swimming, power boating, non-power boating • Elevation: 4003

**Pelican FAS** • Agency: State • Tel: 406-247-2940 • Location: 11 miles SE of Big Timber • GPS: Lat 45.758081 Lon -109.770693 • Open: All year • Stay limit: 7 days • Total sites: 3 • RV sites: 3 • RV fee: Free • No water • Vault toilets • Elevation: 3891

## Billings

**Acton** • Agency: Bureau of Land Management • Tel: 406-896-5013 • Location: 23 miles N of Billings • GPS: Lat 46.044301 Lon -108.663791 • Open: All year • Total sites: Dispersed • RV sites: Undefined • RV fee: Free • No water • No toilets • Activities: Hiking, mountain biking, hunting, equestrian area • Elevation: 3949

## Boulder

**Galena Gulch** • Agency: Bureau of Land Management • Tel: 406-533-7600 • Location: 6 miles W of Boulder • GPS: Lat 46.254304 Lon -112.183717 • Open: All year • Total sites: 9 • RV sites: 9 • RV fee: Free • Central water • Vault toilets • Activities: Fishing • Elevation: 5062

## Bozeman

**Battle Ridge** (Custer Gallatin NF) • Agency: US Forest Service • Tel: 406-522-2520 • Location: 19 miles NE of Bozeman • GPS: Lat 45.882487 Lon -110.879923 • Open: May-Sep • Total sites: 13 • RV sites: 13 • RV fee: Free • Central water • Vault toilets • Elevation: 6390

**Hyalite Below Dam** (Custer Gallatin NF) • Agency: US Forest Service • Location: 17 miles S of Bozeman • GPS: Lat 45.488645 Lon -110.981294 • Total sites: 11 • RV sites: 11 • RV fee: Free • No water (water at nearby day-use area) • Vault toilets • Elevation: 6670

## Broadus

**Broadus City Park** • Agency: Municipal • Location: In Broadus • GPS: Lat 45.439303 Lon -105.409654 • Total sites: 6 • RV sites: 6 • RV fee: Free • Central water • Flush toilets • Elevation: 3034

**Moorhead Recreation Site** (Powder River) • Agency: Bureau of Land Management • Tel: 406-233-2800 • Location: 37 miles SW of Broadus • GPS: Lat 45.055143 Lon -105.878317 • Total sites: 8 • RV sites: 8 • RV fee: Free • No water • Vault toilets • Activities: Hiking, fishing, equestrian area • Elevation: 3362

## Butte

**Basin Canyon** (Beaverhead-Deerlodge NF) • Agency: US Forest Service • Tel: 406-287-3223 • Location: 8 miles S of Butte • GPS: Lat 45.855608 Lon -112.546106 • Total sites: 2 • RV sites: 2 • Max RV Length: 16 • RV fee: Free • No water • Vault toilets • Elevation: 5828

**Toll Mountain** (Beaverhead-Deerlodge NF) • Agency: US Forest Service • Tel: 406-287-3223 • Location: 15 miles SE of Butte • GPS: Lat 45.847955 Lon -112.366663 • Open: May-Sep • Stay limit: 16 days • Total sites: 5 • RV sites:

5 • Max RV Length: 22 • RV fee: Free • No water • Vault toilets • Activities: Hiking • Elevation: 5909

## Chester

**Lake Elwell - Island Area** • Agency: US Bureau of Reclamation • Tel: 406-456-3228 • Location: 19 miles SW of Chester (limited services), 51 miles SE of Shelby • GPS: Lat 48.327167 Lon -111.148428 • Open: All year • Total sites: Dispersed • RV sites: Undefined • RV fee: Free • Central water • Flush toilets • Activities: Hiking, mountain biking, fishing, swimming, power boating, non-power boating • Elevation: 3007

**Lake Elwell - Sanford Park** • Agency: US Bureau of Reclamation • Tel: 406-759-5077 • Location: 19 miles SW of Chester (limited services), 51 miles SE of Shelby • GPS: Lat 48.310961 Lon -111.088957 • Total sites: 15 • RV sites: 15 • RV fee: Free • No water • Vault toilets • Activities: Power boating, non-power boating • Elevation: 2838

**Lake Elwell - South Bootlegger** • Agency: US Bureau of Reclamation • Tel: 406-456-3228 • Location: 32 miles SW of Chester (limited services), 39 NE of Conrad • GPS: Lat 48.331112 Lon -111.308435 • Total sites: Dispersed • RV sites: Undefined • RV fee: Free • Central water • Vault toilets • Activities: Fishing, power boating, non-power boating • Elevation: 2999

**Lake Elwell - Tiber Marina** • Agency: US Bureau of Reclamation • Tel: 406-456-3228 • Location: 19 miles SW of Chester (limited services), 51 miles SE of Shelby • GPS: Lat 48.332535 Lon -111.128555 • Total sites: 12 • RV sites: 9 • RV fee: Free • No water • Vault toilets • Activities: Fishing, power boating, non-power boating • Elevation: 3039

**Lake Elwell - Turners Point** • Agency: US Bureau of Reclamation • Tel: 406-456-3228 • Location: 32 miles SW of Chester (limited services), 39 NE of Conrad • GPS: Lat 48.347036 Lon -111.296709 • Total sites: Dispersed • RV sites: Undefined • RV fee: Free • No water • Vault toilets • Activities: Fishing, power boating, non-power boating • Elevation: 3018

**Lake Elwell - VFW** • Agency: US Bureau of Reclamation • Tel: 406-456-3228 • Location: 19 miles SW of Chester (limited services), 51 miles SE of Shelby • GPS: Lat 48.317454 Lon -111.106536 • Total sites: 13 • RV sites: 8 • RV fee: Free • No water • Vault toilets • Activities: Fishing, power boating, non-power boating • Elevation: 3023

**Lake Elwell - Willow Creek** • Agency: US Bureau of Reclamation • Tel: 406-456-3228 • Location: 16 miles SW of Chester (limited services), 32 miles SE of Shelby • GPS: Lat 48.396396 Lon -111.221571 • Total sites: Dispersed • RV sites: Undefined • RV fee: Free • No water • Vault toilets • Activities: Fishing, power boating, non-power boating • Elevation: 3041

**Moffat Bridge RA** • Agency: Bureau of Land Management • Tel: 406-262-2820 • Location: 17 miles S of Chester (limited services), 41 miles NW of Fort Benton • GPS: Lat 48.265736 Lon -110.993152 • Open: Apr-Aug • Total sites: Dispersed • RV sites: Undefined • RV fee: Free • No water • Vault toilets • Notes: 3-night limit • Activities: Power boating • Elevation: 2791

## Choteau

**Elko** (Helena-Lewis & Clark NF) • Agency: US Forest Service • Tel: 406-466-5341 • Location: 30 miles NW of Choteau • GPS: Lat 47.924348 Lon -112.763595 • Total sites: 3 • RV sites: 3 • RV fee: Free • No water • Vault toilets • Notes: Mandatory food storage • Activities: Hiking, fishing • Elevation: 5349

**Mill Falls** (Helena-Lewis & Clark NF) • Agency: US Forest Service • Location: 30 miles W of Choteau • GPS: Lat 47.859049 Lon -112.772458 • Total sites: 4 • RV sites: 4 • RV fee: Free • No water • Vault toilets • Notes: Mandatory food storage • Activities: Fishing • Elevation: 5682

## Columbia Falls

**Moose Lake** (Flathead NF) • Agency: US Forest Service • Tel: 406-387-3800 • Location: 45 miles NW of Columbia Falls • GPS: Lat 48.628775 Lon -114.388784 • Stay limit: 14 days • Total sites: 3 • RV sites: 3 • RV fee: Free • No water • Vault toilets • Activities: Fishing • Elevation: 5728

## Columbus

**Fireman's Point FAS** • Agency: State • Tel: 406-444-2535 • Location: 3 miles SW of Columbus • GPS: Lat 45.623231 Lon -109.289824 • Open: All year • Stay limit: 7 days • Total sites: Dispersed • RV sites: Undefined • RV fee: Free • No water • Vault toilets • Activities: Fishing, swimming • Elevation: 3625

**Itch-Kep-Pe City Park** • Agency: Municipal • Tel: 406-322-5313 • Location: 1 mile S of Columbus • GPS: Lat 45.627698 Lon -109.250097 • Open: Apr-Oct • Stay limit: 14 days • Total sites: 30 • RV sites: 30 • RV fee: Free • Central water • Vault toilets • Activities: Fishing, swimming, power boating • Elevation: 3570

**Swinging Bridge FAS** • Agency: State • Tel: 406-444-2535 • Location: 7 miles SW of Columbus • GPS: Lat 45.583837 Lon -109.332078 • Open: All year • Stay limit: 7 days • Total sites: 5 • RV sites: 5 • RV fee: Free • No water • Vault toilets • Activities: Fishing, swimming • Elevation: 3753

## Conrad

**Arod Lake FAS** • Agency: State • Tel: 406-444-2535 • Location: 19 miles SW of Conrad • GPS: Lat 47.995441 Lon -112.028263 • Open: All year • Stay limit: 7 days • Total sites: 1 • RV sites: 1 • RV fee: Free • No water • Vault toilets • Activities: Fishing, swimming, power boating • Elevation: 3740

## Custer

**Captain Clark FAS** • Agency: State • Tel: 406-444-2535 • Location: 10 miles E of Custer (limited services), 41 miles NW of Billings • GPS: Lat 46.075108 Lon -107.722048 • Open: All year • Stay limit: 7 days • Total sites: 5 • RV sites: 5 • RV fee: Free • No water • Vault toilets • Activities: Fishing, swimming, power boating • Elevation: 2785

**Manuel Lisa FAS** • Agency: State • Tel: 406-247-2940 • Location: 5 miles E of Custer (limited services), 31 miles N of Hardin • GPS: Lat 46.144324 Lon -107.464934 • Open: All year • Stay limit: 7 days • Total sites: 5 • RV sites: 5 • RV fee: Free • No water • Vault toilets • Activities: Fishing, swimming, power boating • Elevation: 2694

## Darby

**Crazy Creek Horse Camp** (Bitterroot NF) • Agency: US Forest Service • Tel: 406-821-3201 • Location: 19 miles SE of Darby • GPS: Lat 45.813428 Lon -114.069631 • Open: Jun-Nov • Total sites: 5 • RV sites: 5 • RV fee: Free • No water • Vault toilets • Activities: Equestrian area • Elevation: 4832

**Jennings Camp** (Bitterroot NF) • Agency: US Forest Service • Tel: 406-821-3201 • Location: 27 miles SE of Darby • GPS: Lat 45.896241 Lon -113.819515 • Open: May-Nov • Total sites: 4 • RV sites: 4 • Max RV Length: 20 • RV fee: Free • No water • Vault toilets • Activities: Fishing • Elevation: 4895

**Sam Billings Memorial** (Bitterroot NF) • Agency: US Forest Service • Tel: 406-821-3269 • Location: 18 miles SE of Darby • GPS: Lat 45.825741 Lon -114.250667 • Open: May-Nov • Total sites: 11 • RV sites: 11 • Max RV Length: 30 • RV fee: Free • No water • Vault toilets • Activities: Hiking, fishing • Elevation: 4524

**Schumaker** (Bitterroot NF) • Agency: US Forest Service • Tel: 406-821-3913 • Location: 27 miles NW of Darby • GPS: Lat 46.151268 Lon -114.496812 • Open: Jul-Sep • Total sites: 14 • RV sites: 14 • RV fee: Free • No water • Vault toilets • Activities: Hiking, fishing, power boating • Elevation: 6549

**Slate Creek** (Bitterroot NF) • Agency: US Forest Service • Tel: 406-821-3269 • Location: 28 miles S of Darby • GPS: Lat 45.697908 Lon -114.281373 • Open: May-Nov • Total sites: 4 • RV sites: 4 • Max RV Length: 25 • RV fee: Free • No water • Vault toilets • Activities: Fishing, swimming, power boating • Elevation: 4820

## Deer Lodge

**Orofino** (Beaverhead-Deerlodge NF) • Agency: US Forest Service • Tel: 406-859-3211 • Location: 12 miles SE of Deer Lodge • GPS: Lat 46.259372 Lon -112.608902 • Open: May-Sep • Stay limit: 16 days • Total sites: 10 • RV sites: 10 • Max RV Length: 22 • RV fee: Free • Central water • Vault toilets • Elevation: 6463

## Dell

**Big Sheep Creek** • Agency: Bureau of Land Management • Tel: 406-683-8000 • Location: 7 miles SW of Dell (limited services), 46 miles S of Dillon • GPS: Lat 44.663825 Lon -112.761742 • Open: May-Oct • Total sites: 6 • RV sites: 6 • RV fee: Free • No water • Vault toilets • Activities: Fishing • Elevation: 6312

## Dillon

**Barretts Station Park** • Agency: US Bureau of Reclamation • Tel: 406-683-6472 • Location: 7 miles SW of Dillon • GPS: Lat 45.129149 Lon -112.741586 • Open: All year • Total sites: Dispersed • RV sites: Undefined • RV fee: Free • Central water • Vault toilets • Notes: Near RR tracks • Activities: Fishing, power boating, non-power boating • Elevation: 5262

**Clark Canyon Reservoir - Beaverhead** • Agency: US Bureau of Reclamation • Tel: 406-683-6472 • Location: 18 miles SW of Dillon • GPS: Lat 44.997125 Lon -112.856057 • Open: All year • Total sites: 8 • RV sites: 8 • RV fee: Free • Central water • Vault toilets • Activities: Fishing, power boating • Elevation: 5571

**Clark Canyon Reservoir - Beaverhead River** • Agency: US Bureau of Reclamation • Tel: 406-683-6472 • Location: 19 miles SW of Dillon • GPS: Lat 45.001559 Lon -112.856029 • Open: All year • Total sites: Dispersed • RV sites: Undefined • RV fee: Free • Central water • Vault toilets • Activities: Fishing, power boating • Elevation: 5482

**Clark Canyon Reservoir - Cameahwait** • Agency: US Bureau of Reclamation • Tel: 406-683-6472 • Location: 22 miles SW of Dillon • GPS: Lat 44.985425 Lon -112.898529 • Open: All year • Total sites: 11 • RV sites: 11 • RV fee: Free • Central water • Vault toilets • Activities: Fishing • Elevation: 5591

**Clark Canyon Reservoir - Hap Hawkins** • Agency: US Bureau of Reclamation • Tel: 406-683-6472 • Location: 28 miles SW of Dillon • GPS: Lat 44.967572 Lon -112.902145 • Open: All year • Total sites: Dispersed • RV sites: Undefined • RV fee: Free • Central water • Vault toilets • Activities: Fishing • Elevation: 5554

**Clark Canyon Reservoir - Horse Prairie** • Agency: US Bureau of Reclamation • Tel: 406-683-6472 • Location: 21 miles SW of Dillon • GPS: Lat 44.988058 Lon -112.888566 • Total sites: 10 • RV sites: 10 • RV fee: Free • Central water • Vault toilets • Activities: Fishing • Elevation: 5571

**Clark Canyon Reservoir - Lonetree** • Agency: US Bureau of Reclamation • Tel: 406-683-6472 • Location: 30 miles SW of Dillon • GPS: Lat 44.947202 Lon -112.870277 • Open: All year • Total sites: 10 • RV sites: 10 • RV fee: Free • Central water • Vault toilets • Activities: Fishing, power boating • Elevation: 5545

**Glen FAS** • Agency: State • Tel: 406-444-2535 • Location: 19 miles N of Dillon • GPS: Lat 45.467209 Lon -112.666837 • Stay limit: 7 days • Total sites: 7 • RV sites: 7 • Max RV Length: 30 • RV fee: Free • No water • Vault toilets • Activities: Fishing, power boating, non-power boating • Elevation: 4961

## Drummond

**Garnet Ghost Town** • Agency: Bureau of Land Management • Tel: 406-329-3914 • Location: 20 miles NW of Drummond (limited services), 35 miles E of Missoula • GPS: Lat 46.824674 Lon -113.335168 • Total sites: Dispersed • RV sites: Undefined • RV fee: Free • Central water • Vault toilets • Activities: Hiking, mountain biking, fishing, motor sports • Elevation: 6040

## Ekalaka

**Lantis Spring** (Custer Gallatin NF) • Agency: US Forest Service • Tel: 605-797-4432 • Location: 31 miles SE of Ekalaka (limited services), 65 miles S of Baker • GPS: Lat 45.630606 Lon -104.177136 • Open: May-Nov • Stay limit: 14 days • Total sites: 4 • RV sites: 4 • Max RV Length: 16 • RV fee: Free • Central water • Vault toilets • Elevation: 3914

**Wickham Gulch** (Custer Gallatin NF) • Agency: US Forest Service • Tel: 605-797-4432 • Location: 45 miles SE of Ekalaka (limited services), 78 miles S of Baker • GPS: Lat 45.580109 Lon -104.070973 • Open: All year • Stay limit: 14 days • Total sites: 2 • RV sites: 2 • Max RV Length: 16 • RV fee: Free • Central water • Vault toilets • Elevation: 3520

**Ekalaka Park** (Custer Gallatin NF) • Agency: US Forest Service • Tel: 605-797-4432 • Location: 8 miles S of Ekalaka (limited services), 43 miles S of Baker • GPS: Lat 45.798633 Lon -104.511426 • Open: May-Nov • Stay limit: 14 days • Total sites: 8 • RV sites: 8 • Max RV Length: 30 • RV fee: Free • Central water • Vault toilets • Elevation: 3780

**Macnab Pond** (Custer Gallatin NF) • Agency: US Forest Service • Tel: 605-797-4432 • Location: 8 miles SE of Ekalaka (limited services), 43 miles S of Baker • GPS: Lat 45.835842 Lon -104.432014 • Open: May-Nov • Total sites: 2 • RV sites: 2 • Max RV Length: 30 • RV fee: Free • No water • Vault toilets • Activities: Fishing • Elevation: 3474

## Emigrant

**Dan Bailey FAS** • Agency: State • Tel: 406-444-2535 • Location: 7 miles NE of Emigrant (limited services), 15 miles S of Livingston • GPS: Lat 45.420417 Lon -110.636693 • Open: All year • Stay limit: 7 days • Total sites: 3 • RV sites: 3 • Max RV Length: 20 • RV fee: Free • No water • Vault toilets • Activities: Fishing, swimming, power boating • Elevation: 4806

## Ennis

**Bear Creek** (Beaverhead-Deerlodge NF) • Agency: US Forest Service • Tel: 406-682-4253 • Location: 19 miles SE of Ennis • GPS: Lat 45.156557 Lon -111.553688 • Open: Jun-Oct • Stay limit: 16 days • Total sites: 12 • RV sites: 12 • Max RV Length: 28 • RV fee: Free • Central water • Vault toilets • Activities: Fishing, power boating • Elevation: 6365

**Meadow Lake FAS** • Agency: State • Tel: 406-444-2535 • Location: 8 miles N of Ennis • GPS: Lat 45.442861 Lon -111.708399 • Open: All year • Stay limit: 7 days • Total sites: 9 • RV sites: 9 • Max RV Length: 25 • RV fee: Free • No water • Vault toilets • Activities: Fishing, swimming, power boating • Elevation: 4836

## Eureka

**Camp 32** (Kootenai NF) • Agency: US Forest Service • Tel: 406-296-2536 • Location: 9 miles SW of Eureka • GPS: Lat 48.837 Lon -115.19 • Open: All year • Stay limit: 14 days • Total sites: 8 • RV sites: 8 • Max RV Length: 20 • RV fee: Free • Central water • Vault toilets • Activities: Hiking, fishing • Elevation: 2779

**Caribou** (Kootenai NF) • Agency: US Forest Service • Tel: 406-295-4693 • Location: 38 miles W of Eureka • GPS: Lat 48.948806 Lon -115.503202 • Open: All year • Stay limit: 14 days • Total sites: 3 • RV sites: 3 • Max RV Length: 32 • RV fee: Free • No water • Vault toilets • Activities: Hiking, fishing • Elevation: 3770

**Little Therriault Horse Camp** (Kootenai NF) • Agency: US Forest Service • Tel: 406-882-4451 • Location: 37 miles NE of Eureka • GPS: Lat 48.944102 Lon -114.892285 • Open: All year • Stay limit: 16 days • Total sites: 2 • RV sites:

2 • Max RV Length: 32 • RV fee: Free • Central water • Vault toilets • Activities: Equestrian area • Elevation: 5518

**Rock Lake** (Kootenai NF) • Agency: US Forest Service • Tel: 406-882-4451 • Location: 5 miles S of Eureka • GPS: Lat 48.823787 Lon -115.010269 • Stay limit: 14 days • Total sites: 5 • RV sites: 5 • Max RV Length: 20 • RV fee: Free • No water • Vault toilets • Activities: Fishing, non-power boating • Elevation: 2890

**Tobacco River** (Kootenai NF) • Agency: US Forest Service • Tel: 406-296-2536 • Location: 4 miles W of Eureka • GPS: Lat 48.894411 Lon -115.134981 • Open: All year • Stay limit: 14 days • Total sites: 6 • RV sites: 6 • Max RV Length: 20 • RV fee: Free • No water • Vault toilets • Activities: Hiking, fishing • Elevation: 2457

**Tuchuck** (Flathead NF) • Agency: US Forest Service • Tel: 406-387-3800 • Location: 30 miles E of Eureka • GPS: Lat 48.922626 Lon -114.599057 • Open: Jun-Sep • Stay limit: 14 days • Total sites: 7 • RV sites: 7 • Max RV Length: 22 • RV fee: Free • No water • Vault toilets • Activities: Fishing, equestrian area • Elevation: 4629

## Fairfield

**Freezeout Lake WMA** • Agency: State • Tel: 406-467-2488 • Location: 6 miles NW of Fairfield (limited services), 11 miles SE of Choteau • GPS: Lat 47.677245 Lon -112.043934 • Open: Jan-Sep • Total sites: Dispersed • RV sites: Undefined • RV fee: Free • No water • No toilets • Activities: Fishing, power boating, non-power boating • Elevation: 3763

**Lowry Bridge** (Sun River) • Agency: Bureau of Land Management • Tel: 406-538-1900 • Location: 10 miles S of Fairfield (limited services), 26 miles SE of Choteau • GPS: Lat 47.513135 Lon -112.007986 • Total sites: 5 • RV sites: 5 • RV fee: Free • No water • Vault toilets • Activities: Fishing, power boating, non-power boating • Elevation: 3628

## Fairview

**Snowden Bridge FAS** • Agency: State • Tel: 406-444-2535 • Location: 12 miles NW of Fairview (limited services), 24 miles N of Sidney • GPS: Lat 48.006267 Lon -104.102884 • Open: All year • Stay limit: 7 days • Total sites: 3 • RV sites: 3 • RV fee: Free • No water • Vault toilets • Activities: Fishing, power boating, non-power boating • Elevation: 1850

## Forsyth

**Far West FAS** • Agency: State • Tel: 406-444-2535 • Location: 11 miles E of Forsyth • GPS: Lat 46.280175 Lon -106.485131 • Open: All year • Stay limit: 7 days • Total sites: 5 • RV sites: 5 • RV fee: Free • No water • Vault toilets • Activities: Fishing, swimming, power boating • Elevation: 2480

## Fort Peck

**Bear Creek** • Agency: Corps of Engineers • Tel: 406-526-3411 • Location: 10 miles SE of Fort Peck (limited services), 29 miles SE of Glasgow • GPS: Lat 47.947777 Lon -106.301073 • Open: All year • Total sites: Dispersed • RV sites: Undefined • RV fee: Free • No water • Vault toilets • Activities: Hiking, mountain biking, fishing, swimming, power boating, non-power boating • Elevation: 2260

**Bone Trail** • Agency: Corps of Engineers • Tel: 406-526-3411 • Location: 52 miles SW of Fort Peck (limited services), 59 miles SE of Glasgow • GPS: Lat 47.689641 Lon -107.176118 • Open: All year • Total sites: 6 • RV sites: 6 • RV fee: Free • No water • Vault toilets • Activities: Fishing, power boating • Elevation: 2306

**Duck Creek** (Fort Peck Lake) • Agency: Corps of Engineers • Tel: 406-526-3411 • Location: 7 miles SW of Fort Peck (limited services), 20 miles S of Glasgow • GPS: Lat 47.970014 Lon -106.540356 • Open: All year • Total sites: 15 • RV sites: 15 • RV fee: Free • No water • Vault toilets • Activities: Fishing, power boating, non-power boating • Elevation: 2241

**Flat Lake** (Fort Peck Lake) • Agency: Corps of Engineers • Tel: 406-526-3411 • Location: 5 miles E of Fort Peck (limited services), 23 miles SE of Glasgow • GPS: Lat 48.017373 Lon -106.372261 • Open: All year • Total sites: 3 • RV sites: 3 • RV fee: Free • No water • Vault toilets • Activities: Fishing, power boating • Elevation: 2231

**Floodplain** (Fort Peck Lake) • Agency: Corps of Engineers • Tel: 406-526-3224 • Location: 2 miles NE of Fort Peck (limited services), 23 miles SE of Glasgow • GPS: Lat 48.033816 Lon -106.428542 • Open: All year • Total sites: 5 • RV sites: 5 • Max RV Length: 50 • RV fee: Free • Central water • Vault toilets • Activities: Fishing, power boating, non-power boating • Elevation: 2034

**Fort Peck West** (Fort Peck Project) • Agency: Corps of Engineers • Tel: 406-526-3493 • Location: 2 miles W of Fort Peck (limited services), 16 miles SE of Glasgow • GPS: Lat 47.996509 Lon -106.484597 • Total sites: 3 • RV sites: 3 • RV fee: Free • No toilets • Elevation: 2259

**McGuire Creek** (Fort Peck Lake) • Agency: Corps of Engineers • Tel: 406-526-3411 • Location: 46 miles S of Fort Peck (limited services), 64 miles SE of Glasgow • GPS: Lat 47.627081 Lon -106.230709 • Open: All year • Total sites: 12 • RV sites: 12 • RV fee: Free • No water • Vault toilets • Activities: Fishing, power boating, non-power boating • Elevation: 2234

**Nelson Creek** (Fort Peck Lake) • Agency: Corps of Engineers • Tel: 406-526-3411 • Location: 46 miles S of Fort Peck (limited services), 64 miles SE of Glasgow • GPS: Lat 47.562681 Lon -106.223866 • Open: All year • Total sites: 25 • RV sites: 25 • Max RV Length: 40 • RV fee: Free • No water • Vault toilets • Activities: Fishing, power boating • Elevation: 2298

**Rock Creek FAS** • Agency: State • Tel: 406-228-3700 • Location: 34 miles SE of Fort Peck (limited services), 52 miles SE of Glasgow • GPS: Lat 47.765586 Lon -106.289989 • Open: All year • Stay limit: 7 days • Total sites: 4 • RV sites: 4 • RV fee: Free • No water • Vault toilets • Activities: Fishing, swimming, power boating • Elevation: 2313

**Roundhouse Point** (Fort Peck Project) • Agency: Corps of Engineers • Tel: 406-526-3493 • Location: 1 mile N of Fort Peck (limited services), 22 miles SE of Glasgow • GPS: Lat 48.024691 Lon -106.443038 • Total sites: Dispersed • RV sites: Undefined • RV fee: Free • No water • Elevation: 2060

**The Pines** (Fort Peck Lake) • Agency: Corps of Engineers • Tel: 406-526-3411 • Location: 28 miles SW of Fort Peck (limited services), 34 miles S of Glasgow • GPS: Lat 47.839275 Lon -106.632371 • Open: All year • Total sites: 30 • RV sites: 30 • Max RV Length: 30 • RV fee: Free • Central water • Vault toilets • Activities: Fishing, power boating • Elevation: 2251

**Troika Reservoir** • Agency: Bureau of Land Management • Tel: 406-228-3750 • Location: 37 miles SW of Fort Peck (limited services), 44 miles SW of Glasgow • GPS: Lat 47.811969 Lon -107.123725 • Open: All year • Total sites: Dispersed • RV sites: Undefined • RV fee: Free • No water • Vault toilets • Activities: Fishing, hunting • Elevation: 2545

## Fort Smith

**Bighorn Canyon NRA - Afterbay North** • Agency: National Park Service • Tel: 406-666-2412 • Location: In Fort Smith (limited services), 42 miles SW of Hardin • GPS: Lat 45.318441 Lon -107.940864 • Open: All year • Total sites: 14 • RV sites: 8 • RV fee: Free • Central water • Vault toilets • Activities: Hiking, fishing, swimming, non-power boating • Elevation: 3204

**Bighorn Canyon NRA - Afterbay South** • Agency: National Park Service • Tel: 307-548-5406 • Location: In Fort Smith (limited services), 42 miles SW of Hardin • GPS: Lat 45.315277 Lon -107.941664 • Open: All year • Total sites: 28 • RV sites: 28 • RV fee: Free • Central water • Vault toilets • Activities: Hiking, fishing, swimming, non-power boating • Elevation: 3192

## Fortine

**Grave Creek** (Kootenai NF) • Agency: US Forest Service • Tel: 406-882-4451 • Location: 6 miles N of Fortine (limited services), 12 miles SE of Eureka • GPS: Lat 48.819282 Lon -114.886547 • Open: All year (access may be limited in winter) • Stay limit: 14 days • Total sites: 4 • RV sites: 4 • Max RV Length: 20 • RV fee: Free • No water • Vault toilets • Activities: Fishing • Elevation: 3030

## Galata

**Lake Elwell - North Bootlegger** • Agency: US Bureau of Reclamation • Tel: 406-456-3228 • Location: 9 miles S of Galata (limited services), 32 miles SE of Shelby • GPS: Lat 48.359763 Lon -111.328517 • Total sites: Dispersed • RV sites: Undefined • RV fee: Free • No water • Vault toilets • Activities: Fishing, power boating, non-power boating • Elevation: 3002

## Gallatin Gateway

**Spanish Creek** • Agency: US Forest Service • Location: 17 miles SW of Gallatin Gateway (limited services), 26 miles SW of Bozeman • GPS: Lat 45.447388 Lon -111.377289 • Open: May-Sep • Total sites: 5 • RV sites: Undefined • RV fee: Free • Central water • Vault toilets • Activities: Hiking, mountain biking • Elevation: 6109

## Gardiner

**Carbella** • Agency: Bureau of Land Management • Tel: 406-533-7600 • Location: 16 miles NW of Gardiner • GPS: Lat 45.212653 Lon -110.900373 • Open: All year • Total sites: 10 • RV sites: 10 • Max RV Length: 50 • RV fee: Free • No water • Vault toilets • Activities: Fishing, power boating • Elevation: 4987

## Glasgow

**Glasgow Base Pond FAS** • Agency: State • Tel: 406-444-2535 • Location: 20 miles N of Glasgow • GPS: Lat 48.448253 Lon -106.577277 • Open: All year • Stay limit: 7 days • Total sites: 4 • RV sites: 4 • RV fee: Free • No water • Vault toilets • Activities: Fishing, power boating, non-power boating • Elevation: 2733

**Paulo Reservoir** • Agency: Bureau of Land Management • Tel: 406-228-3750 • Location: 11 miles W of Glasgow • GPS: Lat 48.171759 Lon -106.870985 • Open: All year • Total sites: Dispersed • RV sites: Undefined • RV fee: Free • No water • Vault toilets • Activities: Fishing • Elevation: 2240

## Glendive

**Short Pine OHV Area** • Agency: Bureau of Land Management • Tel: 406-233-2831 • Location: 6 miles S of Glendive • GPS: Lat 47.017726 Lon -104.726687 • Open: All year • Total sites: Dispersed • RV sites: Undefined • RV fee: Free • No water • No toilets • Activities: Motor sports • Elevation: 2146

## Hamilton

**Black Bear** (Bitterroot NF) • Agency: US Forest Service • Tel: 406-821-3913 • Location: 15 miles SE of Hamilton • GPS: Lat 46.166026 Lon -113.924677 • Open: Jun-Sep • Stay limit: 16 days • Total sites: 6 • RV sites: 6 • Max RV Length: 50 • RV fee: Free • No water • Vault toilets • Activities: Hiking, swimming • Elevation: 4626

**Crystal Creek** (Beaverhead-Deerlodge NF) • Agency: US Forest Service • Tel: 406-859-3211 • Location: 30 miles E of Hamilton • GPS: Lat 46.232615 Lon -113.745901 • Open: Jul-Sep • Total sites: 3 • RV sites: 3 • Max RV Length: 16 • RV fee: Free • No water • Vault toilets • Activities: Hiking • Elevation: 6972

## Happys Inn

**Island Lake FAS** • Agency: State • Tel: 406-444-2535 • Location: 17 miles NE of Happys Inn (limited services), 50 miles W of Kalispell • GPS: Lat 48.235818 Lon -114.974829 • Stay limit: 7 days • Total sites: 1 • RV sites: 1 • RV fee: Free • No water • No toilets • Activities: Fishing • Elevation: 3517

**Lake Creek** (Kootenai NF) • Agency: US Forest Service • Tel: 406-293-7773 • Location: 22 miles W of Happys Inn (limited services), 30 miles S of Libby • GPS: Lat 48.038909 Lon -115.489955 • Open: All year (limited winter access) • Stay limit: 14 days • Total sites: 4 • RV sites: 4 • Max RV Length: 32 • RV fee: Free • Central water • Vault toilets • Activities: Hiking, fishing, hunting • Elevation: 3412

**Pleasant Valley** (Kootenai NF) • Agency: US Forest Service • Location: 9 miles W of Happys Inn (limited services), 30 miles SE of Libby • GPS: Lat 48.042314 Lon -115.290626 • Open: All year (limited winter access) • Stay limit: 14 days • Total sites: 7 • RV sites: 7 • Max RV Length: 32 • RV fee: Free • No water • Vault toilets • Elevation: 3067

**Sylvan Lake** (Kootenai NF) • Agency: US Forest Service • Tel: 406-293-7773 • Location: 23 miles SW of Happys Inn (limited services), 45 miles SE of Libby • GPS: Lat 47.916343 Lon -115.278677 • Open: All year (limited winter access) • Stay limit: 16 days • Total sites: 5 • RV sites: 5 • RV fee: Free • No water • Vault toilets • Activities: Hiking, motor sports • Elevation: 3627

## Hardin

**General Custer FAS** • Agency: State • Tel: 406-444-2535 • Location: 13 miles N of Hardin • GPS: Lat 45.927357 Lon -107.575357 • Open: All year • Stay limit: 7 days • Total sites: 1 • RV sites: 1 • RV fee: Free • No water • Vault toilets • Activities: Fishing, swimming, power boating • Elevation: 2802

**Grant Marsh FAS** • Agency: State • Tel: 406-444-2535 • Location: 8 miles N of Hardin • GPS: Lat 45.843895 Lon -107.583879 • Open: All year • Stay limit: 7 days • Total sites: 1 • RV sites: 1 • RV fee: Free • No water • Vault toilets • Activities: Fishing, swimming, power boating • Elevation: 2838

**Mallards Landing FAS** • Agency: State • Tel: 406-247-2940 • Location: 19 miles S of Hardin • GPS: Lat 45.521299 Lon -107.725505 • Open: All year • Stay limit: 7 days • Total sites: 1 • RV sites: 1 • RV fee: Free • No water • Vault toilets • Activities: Fishing, swimming, power boating • Elevation: 2992

**Two Leggins FAS** • Agency: State • Location: 7 miles S of Hardin • GPS: Lat 45.644995 Lon -107.658652 • Open: All year • Stay limit: 7 days • Total sites: 1 • RV sites: 1 • Max RV Length: 20 • RV fee: Free • No water • Vault toilets • Activities: Fishing, power boating, non-power boating • Elevation: 2953

## Harlowton

**Daisy Dean** (Helena-Lewis & Clark NF) • Agency: US Forest Service • Location: 34 miles NW of Harlowton • GPS: Lat 46.623207 Lon -110.358729 • Total sites: 10 • RV sites: 10 • RV fee: Free • No water • Vault toilets • Activities: Equestrian area • Elevation: 6099

**Jellison Place** (Helena-Lewis & Clark NF) • Agency: US Forest Service • Tel: 406-632-4391 • Location: 25 miles NW of Harlowton • GPS: Lat 46.673281 Lon -110.072132 • Total sites: 10 • RV sites: 10 • RV fee: Free • No water • Vault toilets • Notes: Mandatory food storage • Activities: Hiking, equestrian area • Elevation: 5853

**Selkirk FAS** • Agency: State • Tel: 406-247-2940 • Location: 20 miles W of Harlowton (limited services), 38 miles E of White Sulphur Springs • GPS: Lat 46.465462 Lon -110.225596 • Open: All year • Stay limit: 7 days • Total sites: 5 • RV sites: 5 • RV fee: Free • No water • Vault toilets • Activities: Fishing, power boating • Elevation: 4672

## Harrison

**Potosi** (Beaverhead-Deerlodge NF) • Agency: US Forest Service • Tel: 406-682-4253 • Location: 13 miles SW of Harrison (limited services), 36 miles NW of Ennis • GPS: Lat 45.572359 Lon -111.913602 • Open: Jun-Sep • Total sites: 15 • RV sites: 15 • Max RV Length: 22 • RV fee: Free • Central water • Vault toilets • Activities: Hiking, fishing • Elevation: 6240

## Havre

**Fresno Reservoir - Fresno Beach Dispersed 1** • Agency: US Bureau of Reclamation • Tel: 406-759-5077 • Location: 11 miles NW of Havre • GPS: Lat 48.597857 Lon -109.960332 • Open: All year • Total sites: Dispersed • RV sites: Undefined • RV fee: Free • No water • Vault toilets • Activities: Fishing, swimming, power boating • Elevation: 2572

**Fresno Reservoir - Fresno Beach Dispersed 2** • Agency: US Bureau of Reclamation • Tel: 406-759-5077 • Location: 13 miles NW of Havre • GPS: Lat 48.595101 Lon -109.955918 • Open: All year • Total sites: Dispersed • RV sites: Undefined • RV fee: Free • No water • Vault toilets • Activities: Fishing, swimming, power boating • Elevation: 2640

**Fresno Reservoir - Fresno Beach Dispersed 3** • Agency: US Bureau of Reclamation • Tel: 406-759-5077 • Location: 11 miles NW of Havre • GPS: Lat 48.595717 Lon -109.951824 • Open: All year • Total sites: Dispersed • RV sites: Undefined • RV fee: Free • No water • Vault toilets • Activities: Fishing, swimming, power boating • Elevation: 2626

**Fresno Reservoir - Kiehns Bay** • Agency: US Bureau of Reclamation • Tel: 406-759-5077 • Location: 13 miles NW of Havre • GPS: Lat 48.611785 Lon -109.942593 • Open: All year • Total sites: Dispersed • RV sites: Undefined • RV fee: Free • No water • Vault toilets • Activities: Fishing • Elevation: 2601

**Fresno Reservoir - River Run** • Agency: US Bureau of Reclamation • Tel: 406-759-5077 • Location: 11 miles NW of Havre • GPS: Lat 48.599979 Lon -109.940116 • Open: All year • Total sites: Dispersed • RV sites: Undefined • RV fee: Free • Vault toilets • Activities: Fishing • Elevation: 2511

**Fresno Tailwater FAS** • Agency: State • Tel: 406-444-2535 • Location: 12 miles NW of Havre • GPS: Lat 48.599719 Lon -109.942951 • Open: All year • Stay limit: 7 days • Total sites: 3 • RV sites: 3 • RV fee: Free • No water • Vault toilets • Activities: Fishing, swimming, power boating • Elevation: 2525

## Hobson

**Hay Canyon** (Helena-Lewis & Clark NF) • Agency: US Forest Service • Location: 28 miles SW of Hobson (limited services), 50 miles SW of Lewistown • GPS: Lat 46.798738 Lon -110.300043 • Total sites: 9 • RV sites: 9 • Max RV Length: 30 • RV fee: Free • No water • Vault toilets • Notes: Mandatory food storage • Activities: Hiking, fishing • Elevation: 5178

**Judith River State WMA** • Agency: State • Tel: 406-547-2585 • Location: 24 miles SW of Hobson (limited services), 46 miles SW of Lewistown • GPS: Lat 46.887654 Lon -110.313779 • Open: May-Nov • Total sites: Dispersed • RV sites: Undefined • RV fee: Free • No water • No toilets • Activities: Hiking, mountain biking, hunting, motor sports • Elevation: 5197

## Hungry Horse

**Beaver Creek** (Flathead NF) • Agency: US Forest Service • Tel: 406-758-5376 • Location: 62 miles SE of Hungry Horse • GPS: Lat 47.923596 Lon -113.373361 • Open: May-Nov • Stay limit: 14 days • Total sites: 4 • RV sites: 4 • Max RV Length: 32 • RV fee: Free • No water • Vault toilets • Activities: Fishing, hunting, motor sports, equestrian area • Elevation: 4150

**Devils Corkscrew** (Flathead NF) • Agency: US Forest Service • Tel: 406-387-3800 • Location: 37 miles SE of Hungry Horse • GPS: Lat 48.110029 Lon -113.696335 • Stay limit: 16 days • Total sites: 4 • RV sites: 4 • Max RV Length: 32 • RV fee: Free • No water • Vault toilets • Elevation: 3648

**Graves Bay** (Flathead NF) • Agency: US Forest Service • Location: 34 miles SE of Hungry Horse • GPS: Lat 48.126689 Lon -113.809421 • Total sites: 10 • RV sites: 10 • RV fee: Free • Elevation: 3547

**Lakeview** (Flathead NF) • Agency: US Forest Service • Tel: 406-387-3800 • Location: 24 miles SE of Hungry Horse • GPS: Lat 48.219127 Lon -113.805384 • Total sites: 5 • RV sites: 5 • RV fee: Free • No water • Vault toilets • Activities: Fishing • Elevation: 3530

**Peters Creek** (Flathead NF) • Agency: US Forest Service • Tel: 406-758-5376 • Location: 42 miles SE of Hungry Horse • GPS: Lat 48.057377 Lon -113.644569 • Open: May-Sep • Stay limit: 14 days • Total sites: 6 • RV sites: 6 • Max RV Length: 30 • RV fee: Free • No water • Vault toilets • Notes: Mandatory food storage • Activities: Fishing, hunting • Elevation: 3691

## Hysham

**Myers Bridge FAS** • Agency: State • Tel: 406-233-2800 • Location: 6 miles SW of Hysham (limited services), 32 miles W of Forsyth • GPS: Lat 46.254517 Lon -107.342234 • Open: All year • Stay limit: 7 days • Total sites: 5 • RV sites: 5 • RV fee: Free • No water • Vault toilets • Activities: Hiking, fishing • Elevation: 2658

## Jackson

**North Van Houten** (Beaverhead-Deerlodge NF) • Agency: US Forest Service • Tel: 406-689-3243 • Location: 12 miles SW of Jackson (limited services), 86 miles SE of Darby • GPS: Lat 45.246561 Lon -113.478182 • Open: Jun-Sep • Stay limit: 16 days • Total sites: 3 • RV sites: 3 • Max RV Length: 20 • RV fee: Free • Central water • Vault toilets • Activities: Fishing, power boating • Elevation: 7057

**South Van Houten** (Beaverhead-Deerlodge NF) • Agency: US Forest Service • Tel: 406-689-3243 • Location: 12 miles SW of Jackson (limited services), 86 miles SE of Darby • GPS: Lat 45.243839 Lon -113.478157 • Open: Jun-Sep • Stay limit: 16 days • Total sites: 3 • RV sites: 3 • Max RV Length: 30 • RV fee: Free • Central water • Vault toilets • Activities: Fishing • Elevation: 7024

## Jordan

**Jimmy Kariotis City Park** • Agency: Municipal • Tel: 406-557-2692 • Location: In Jordan (limited services), 82 miles NW of Miles City • GPS: Lat 47.318195 Lon -106.910456 • Open: All year • Stay limit: 2 days • Total sites: 5 • RV sites: 1 • Max RV Length: 30 • RV fee: Free • Central water • Vault toilets • Elevation: 2592

## Lewistown

**Kiwanis Park** • Agency: Municipal • Location: 1 mile W of Lewistown • GPS: Lat 47.055186 Lon -109.460483 • Total sites: 18 • RV sites: 14 • RV fee: Free (donation appreciated) • Central water • Flush toilets • Notes: Right beside runway • Elevation: 4108

## Libby

**Alexander Creek** (Kootenai NF) • Agency: Corps of Engineers • Tel: 406-293-5577 • Location: 16 miles E of Libby • GPS: Lat 48.392478 Lon -115.328601 • Open: May-Oct • Total sites: 2 • RV sites: 2 • RV fee: Free • No water • Vault toilets • Elevation: 2162

**Barron Creek** (Kootenai NF) • Agency: US Forest Service • Tel: 406-293-7773 • Location: 26 miles NE of Libby • GPS: Lat 48.516 Lon -115.291 • Open: May-Oct • Total sites: 7 • RV sites: 7 • Max RV Length: 40 • RV fee: Free • No water • Vault toilets • Activities: Golf • Elevation: 2549

**Blackwell Flats** (Lake Koocanusa) • Agency: Corps of Engineers • Tel: 406-293-5577 • Location: 13 miles E of Libby • GPS: Lat 48.369101 Lon -115.321618 • Open: All year • Total sites: 7 • RV sites: 7 • RV fee: Free • No water • Vault toilets • Elevation: 2129

**Dunn Creek Flats** (Lake Koocanusa) • Agency: Corps of Engineers • Tel: 406-293-5577 • Location: 14 miles E of Libby • GPS: Lat 48.380386 Lon -115.319961 • Open: May-Oct • Total sites: 13 • RV sites: 13 • RV fee: Free • Central water • Vault toilets • Activities: Fishing, power boating, non-power boating • Elevation: 2136

**Loon Lake** (Kootenai NF) • Agency: US Forest Service • Tel: 406-293-7773 • Location: 20 miles N of Libby • GPS: Lat 48.597851 Lon -115.671557 • Open: All year • Stay limit: 14 days • Total sites: 4 • RV sites: 4 • Max RV Length: 20 • RV fee: Free • No water • Vault toilets • Activities: Fishing • Elevation: 3698

## Lima

**East Creek** (Beaverhead-Deerlodge NF) • Agency: US Forest Service • Tel: 406-683-3900 • Location: 9 miles SW of Lima (limited services), 56 miles S of Dillon • GPS: Lat 44.564 Lon -112.661 • Open: May-Sep • Stay limit: 16 days • Total sites: 4 • RV sites: 4 • Max RV Length: 16 • RV fee: Free • Central water • Vault toilets • Elevation: 7031

## Loma

**Upper Missouri River Breaks NM - Wood Bottom** • Agency: Bureau of Land Management • Tel: 406-622-4000 • Location: 2 miles S of Loma (limited services), 10 miles NE of Fort Benton • GPS: Lat 47.911308 Lon -110.493271 • Open: All year • Total sites: 4 • RV sites: 4 • RV fee: Free • No water • Vault toilets • Activities: Fishing, power boating • Elevation: 2562

## Malta

**Cottonwood RA** • Agency: Bureau of Land Management • Tel: 406-654-5100 • Location: 19 miles N of Malta • GPS: Lat 48.584176 Lon -107.718963 • Open: All year • Total sites: Dispersed • RV sites: Undefined • RV fee: Free • No water • Vault toilets • Activities: Fishing, hunting • Elevation: 2205

**Fourchette Creek** • Agency: Corps of Engineers • Tel: 406-526-3224 • Location: 57 miles S of Malta • GPS: Lat 47.668995 Lon -107.669112 • Open: All year • Total sites: 44 • RV sites: 44 • Max RV Length: 25 • RV fee: Free • No water • Vault toilets • Activities: Hiking, mountain biking, fishing, swimming, power boating, hunting, non-power boating • Elevation: 2247

## Marion

**Ashley Lake North** (Flathead NF) • Agency: US Forest Service • Tel: 406-758-5208 • Location: 18 miles N of Marion (limited services), 27 miles W of Kalispell • GPS: Lat 48.213724 Lon -114.616946 • Open: May-Sep • Stay limit: 5 days • Total sites: 5 • RV sites: 5 • Max RV Length: 12 • RV fee: Free • No water • Vault toilets • Activities: Power boating, non-power boating • Elevation: 4032

**Sylvia Lake** (Flathead NF) • Agency: US Forest Service • Tel: 406-758-5208 • Location: 22 miles N of Marion (limited services), 42 miles NW of Kalispell • GPS: Lat 48.344423 Lon -114.818601 • Open: May-Nov • Total sites: 3 • RV sites: 3 • Max RV Length: 12 • RV fee: Free • No water • Vault toilets • Activities: Fishing, non-power boating • Elevation: 5056

## Melrose

**Brownes Bridge FAS** • Agency: State • Tel: 406-444-2535 • Location: 6 miles S of Melrose (limited services), 38 miles S of Butte • GPS: Lat 45.546736 Lon -112.692613 • Stay limit: 7 days • Total sites: 5 • RV sites: 5 • Max RV Length: 20 • RV fee: Free • No water • Vault toilets • Activities: Fishing • Elevation: 5066

**Canyon Creek** (Vipond Park, Beaverhead-Deerlodge NF) • Agency: US Forest Service • Tel: 406-832-3178 • Location: 17 miles W of Melrose (limited services), 49 miles SW of Butte • GPS: Lat 45.62611 Lon -112.94139 • Total sites: 3 • RV sites: 3 • Max RV Length: 18 • RV fee: Free • No water • Vault toilets • Activities: Hiking, fishing • Elevation: 7323

## Miles City

**Mathews RA** • Agency: Bureau of Land Management • Tel: 406-233-2800 • Location: 7 miles NE of Miles City • GPS: Lat 46.501486 Lon -105.734547 • Open: All year • Total sites: Dispersed • RV sites: Undefined • RV fee: Free • No water • Vault toilets • Notes: Near RR tracks • Activities: Hiking, fishing, swimming • Elevation: 2322

**Twelve Mile Dam FAS** • Agency: State • Tel: 406-444-2535 • Location: 11 miles S of Miles City • GPS: Lat 46.249662 Lon -105.751922 • Open: All year • Stay limit: 7 days • Total sites: 8 • RV sites: 8 • RV fee: Free • No water • Vault toilets • Activities: Fishing, swimming, power boating • Elevation: 2434

## Missoula

**Garnet Rd** • Agency: Bureau of Land Management • Location: 24 miles E of Missoula • GPS: Lat 46.885031 Lon -113.463337 • Total sites: Dispersed • RV sites: Undefined • RV fee: Free • No water • No toilets • Elevation: 4166

## Norris

**Revenue Flats** • Agency: Bureau of Land Management • Tel: 406-683-8000 • Location: 6 miles SW of Norris (limited services), 16 miles N of Ennis • GPS: Lat 45.544456 Lon -111.770983 • Open: All year • Total sites: Dispersed • RV sites: Undefined • RV fee: Free • No water • Vault toilets • Activities: Hiking, mountain biking, rock climbing • Elevation: 5592

## Noxon

**Big Eddy** (Kootenai NF) • Agency: US Forest Service • Tel: 406-827-3533 • Location: 10 miles NW of Noxon (limited services), 44 miles NW of Tompson Falls • GPS: Lat 48.067 Lon -115.923 • Open: All year (limited winter access) • Stay limit: 16 days • Total sites: 5 • RV sites: 5 • Max RV Length: 30 • RV fee: Free • No water • Vault toilets • Activities: Hiking, fishing, swimming, power boating • Elevation: 2297

## Nye

**Initial Creek** (Custer Gallatin NF) • Agency: US Forest Service • Tel: 406-446-2103 • Location: 13 miles SW of Nye (limited services), 50 miles SW of Columbus • GPS: Lat 45.404 Lon -109.954 • Open: All year (no services in winter) • Stay limit: 16 days • Total sites: 6 • RV sites: 6 • Max RV Length: 20 • RV fee: Free • No water • No toilets • Elevation: 6214

## Ovando

**Monture Creek** (Lolo NF) • Agency: US Forest Service • Tel: 406-677-2233 • Location: 8 miles N of Ovando (limited services), 31 miles E of Seeley Lake • GPS: Lat 47.123893 Lon -113.145456 • Open: May-Sep • Total sites: 5 • RV sites: 5 • RV fee: Free • No water • Vault toilets • Activities: Hiking, fishing • Elevation: 4203

## Philipsburg

**Copper Creek** (Moose Lake, Beaverhead-Deerlodge NF) • Agency: US Forest Service • Tel: 406-859-3211 • Location: 26 miles SW of Philipsburg • GPS: Lat 46.066272 Lon -113.543706 • Open: May-Nov • Stay limit: 16 days • Total sites: 7 • RV sites: 7 • RV fee: Free • Central water • Vault toilets • Activities: Hiking, fishing • Elevation: 5981

**Flint Creek** (Beaverhead-Deerlodge NF) • Agency: US Forest Service • Tel: 406-859-3211 • Location: 8 miles S of Philipsburg • GPS: Lat 46.233448 Lon -113.300439 • Open: May-Oct • Total sites: 16 • RV sites: 16 • Max RV Length: 22 • RV fee: Free • No water • Vault toilets • Activities: Fishing • Elevation: 5620

**Spillway** (Beaverhead-Deerlodge NF) • Agency: US Forest Service • Tel: 406-859-3211 • Location: 19 miles S of Philipsburg • GPS: Lat 46.127441 Lon -113.383301 • Open: May-Nov • Total sites: 13 • RV sites: 13 • Max RV Length: 22 • RV fee: Free • Central water • Vault toilets • Activities: Hiking, fishing • Elevation: 6056

**Stony** (Beaverhead-Deerlodge NF) • Agency: US Forest Service • Tel: 406-859-3211 • Location: 19 miles W of Philipsburg • GPS: Lat 46.348739 Lon -113.607499 • Open: Apr-Oct • Total sites: 10 • RV sites: 10 • Max RV Length: 32 • RV fee: Free • Central water • Vault toilets • Activities: Fishing • Elevation: 4806

**East Fork** (Beaverhead-Deerlodge NF) • Agency: US Forest Service • Tel: 406-859-3211 • Location: 18 miles S of Philipsburg (limited services), 25 miles W of Anaconda • GPS: Lat 46.134885 Lon -113.387323 • Open: May-Nov • Stay limit: 16 days • Total sites: 7 • RV sites: 7 • Max RV Length: 22 • RV fee: Free • Central water • Vault toilets • Activities: Fishing • Elevation: 6096

## Red Lodge

**Beaver Lodge FAS** • Agency: State • Tel: 406-444-2535 • Location: 5 miles N of Red Lodge • GPS: Lat 45.263801 Lon -109.217978 • Open: All year • Stay limit: 7 days • Total sites: Dispersed • RV sites: Undefined • RV fee: Free • No water • Vault toilets • Activities: Fishing • Elevation: 5090

**Bull Springs FAS** • Agency: State • Tel: 406-444-2535 • Location: 6 miles N of Red Lodge • GPS: Lat 45.277681 Lon -109.209744 • Open: All year • Stay limit: 7 days • Total sites: 1 • RV sites: 1 • RV fee: Free • No water • Vault toilets • Elevation: 4997

**Horsethief Station FAS** • Agency: State • Tel: 406-444-2535 • Location: 3 miles N of Red Lodge • GPS: Lat 45.235094 Lon -109.229467 • Open: All year • Stay limit: 7 days • Total sites: 2 • RV sites: 2 • RV fee: Free • No water • Vault toilets • Activities: Fishing, swimming • Elevation: 5266

**M-K Campground** (Custer Gallatin NF) • Agency: US Forest Service • Tel: 406-446-2103 • Location: 14 miles SW of Red Lodge • GPS: Lat 45.038323 Lon -109.429648 • Open: May-Sep • Stay limit: 16 days • Total sites: 10 • RV sites: 7 • Max RV Length: 20 • RV fee: Free • No water • Vault toilets • Activities: Hiking, fishing • Elevation: 7408

**Palisades** (Custer Gallatin NF) • Agency: US Forest Service • Tel: 406-446-2103 • Location: 3 miles W of Red Lodge • GPS: Lat 45.171578 Lon -109.308995 • Open: May-Sep • Total sites: 6 • RV sites: 6 • Max RV Length: 16 • RV fee: Free • No water • Vault toilets • Elevation: 6378

## Roscoe

**Jimmy Joe** (Custer Gallatin NF) • Agency: US Forest Service • Tel: 406-446-2103 • Location: 11 miles SW of Roscoe (limited services), 30 miles NW of Red Lodge • GPS: Lat 45.232034 Lon -109.603149 • Open: May-Sep • Stay limit: 16 days • Total sites: 12 • RV sites: 12 • Max RV Length: 30 • RV fee: Free • No water • Vault toilets • Activities: Fishing • Elevation: 5597

## Roundup

**Cowbelles Corral** • Agency: Municipal • Tel: 406-323-1966 • Location: In Roundup • GPS: Lat 46.439697 Lon -108.531738 • Open: All year • Total sites: 34 • RV sites: 35 • Max RV Length: 40 • RV fee: Free (donation appreciated) • Central water • Vault toilets • Activities: Fishing, swimming • Elevation: 3179

## Roy

**Charles M. Russell NWR - Slippery Ann** • Agency: US Fish & Wildlife • Tel: 406-538-8706 • Location: 34 miles NE of Roy (limited services), 69 miles NE of Lewistown • GPS: Lat 47.617289 Lon -108.583021 • Total sites: Dispersed • RV sites: Undefined • RV fee: Free • No water • Vault toilets • Elevation: 2269

**Charles M. Russell NWR Dispersed** • Agency: US Fish & Wildlife • Tel: 406-538-8706 • Location: 44 miles NE of Roy (limited services), 67 miles SW of Malta • GPS: Lat 47.596356 Lon -108.405151 • Total sites: Dispersed • RV sites: Undefined • Max RV Length: 16 • RV fee: Free • No water • Vault toilets • Activities: Fishing • Elevation: 2258

**Charles M. Russell NWR Dispersed** • Agency: US Fish & Wildlife • Tel: 406-538-8706 • Location: 41 miles NE of Roy (limited services), 65 miles SW of Malta • GPS: Lat 47.616113 Lon -108.459771 • Total sites: Dispersed • RV sites: Undefined • RV fee: Free • No water • Vault toilets • Elevation: 2265

**Charles M. Russell NWR Dispersed** • Agency: US Fish & Wildlife • Tel: 406-538-8706 • Location: 37 miles NE of Roy (limited services), 72 miles NE of Lewistown • GPS: Lat 47.621541 Lon -108.530194 • Total sites: Dispersed • RV sites: Undefined • RV fee: Free • No water • Vault toilets • Elevation: 2271

**Charles M. Russell NWR Dispersed** • Agency: US Fish & Wildlife • Tel: 406-538-8706 • Location: 35 miles NE of Roy (limited services), 70 miles NE of Lewistown • GPS: Lat 47.617024 Lon -108.570274 • Total sites: Dispersed • RV sites: Undefined • RV fee: Free • No water • No toilets • Activities: Fishing • Elevation: 2306

**Charles M. Russell NWR Dispersed - Dry Lake Reservoir** • Agency: US Fish & Wildlife • Tel: 406-538-8706 • Location: 48 miles NE of Roy (limited services), 71 miles SW of Malta • GPS: Lat 47.662064 Lon -108.187916 • Total sites: Dispersed • RV sites: Undefined (several sites in this area) • RV fee: Free • No water • No toilets • Elevation: 2825

## Seeley Lake

**Lake Inez** (Lolo NF) • Agency: US Forest Service • Tel: 406-677-2233 • Location: 10 miles N of Seeley Lake • GPS: Lat 47.294099 Lon -113.567813 • Open: All year • Total sites: 5 • RV sites: 5 • RV fee: Free • No water • Vault toilets • Activities: Fishing, swimming, power boating, non-power boating • Elevation: 4209

**Lindberg Lake** (Flathead NF) • Agency: US Forest Service • Tel: 406-837-7500 • Location: 23 miles NW of Seeley Lake • GPS: Lat 47.407645 Lon -113.721879 • Stay limit: 16 days • Total sites: 11 • RV sites: 11 • Max RV Length: 20 • RV fee: Free • No water • Vault toilets • Activities: Fishing, swimming, power boating, non-power boating • Elevation: 4393

**Rainy Lake** (Lolo NF) • Agency: US Forest Service • Tel: 406-677-2233 • Location: 13 miles N of Seeley Lake • GPS: Lat 47.336831 Lon -113.593337 • Total sites: 5 • RV sites: 2 • RV fee: Free • No water • Vault toilets • Elevation: 4157

## Shelby

**Lake Elwell - Devon** • Agency: US Bureau of Reclamation • Tel: 406-456-3228 • Location: 27 miles SE of Shelby • GPS: Lat 48.338615 Lon -111.518359 • Total sites: Dispersed • RV sites: Undefined • RV fee: Free • No water • Vault toilets • Activities: Fishing, power boating, non-power boating • Elevation: 3005

## Sidney

**Seven Sisters FAS** • Agency: State • Tel: 406-234-0900 • Location: 11 miles S of Sidney • GPS: Lat 47.576149 Lon -104.231661 • Open: All year • Stay limit: 7 days • Total sites: 1 • RV sites: 1 • RV fee: Free • No water • Vault toilets • Activities: Fishing, non-power boating • Elevation: 1923

## Superior

**Missoula Lake** (Bitterroot NF) • Agency: US Forest Service • Location: 25 miles SW of Superior • GPS: Lat 47.060302 Lon -115.116204 • Total sites: 5 • RV sites: 5 • RV fee: Free • No water • Vault toilets • Elevation: 6319

## Terry

**Bonfield FAS** • Agency: State • Tel: 406-444-2535 • Location: 16 miles SW of Terry (limited services), 20 miles NE of Miles City • GPS: Lat 46.631822 Lon -105.566951 • Open: All year • Stay limit: 7 days • Total sites: 2 • RV sites: 2 • RV fee: Free • No water • Vault toilets • Activities: Fishing, swimming, power boating • Elevation: 2238

**Fallon Bridge FAS** • Agency: State • Tel: 406-444-2535 • Location: 11 miles NE of Terry (limited services), 28 miles SW of Glendive • GPS: Lat 46.856755 Lon -105.114249 • Stay limit: 7 days • Total sites: 1 • RV sites: 1 • RV fee: Free • No water • No toilets • Activities: Fishing, power boating, non-power boating • Elevation: 2172

**Powder River Depot FAS** • Agency: State • Tel: 406-444-2535 • Location: 6 miles SW of Terry (limited services), 31 miles NE of Miles City • GPS: Lat 46.743183 Lon -105.433116 • Total sites: 1 • RV sites: 1 • RV fee: Free • No water • No toilets • Activities: Fishing, power boating • Elevation: 2211

## Thompson Falls

**Gold Rush** (Lolo NF) • Agency: US Forest Service • Tel: 406-826-3821 • Location: 10 miles S of Thompson Falls • GPS: Lat 47.52282 Lon -115.31147 • Open: Jun-Oct • Total sites: 7 • RV sites: 7 • RV fee: Free • Central water • Vault toilets • Activities: Fishing • Elevation: 3573

**West Fork Fishtrap Creek** (Lolo NF) • Agency: US Forest Service • Tel: 406-826-3821 • Location: 28 miles NE of Thompson Falls • GPS: Lat 47.8166 Lon -115.14922 • Open: All year • Total sites: 4 • RV sites: 4 • RV fee: Free • Central water (no water Oct-May) • Vault toilets • Activities: Fishing • Elevation: 3596

## Townsend

**Canyon Ferry - Confederate** • Agency: US Bureau of Reclamation • Tel: 406-475-3921 • Location: 18 miles N of Townsend • GPS: Lat 46.481585 Lon -111.516718 • Open: All year • Total sites: Dispersed • RV sites: Undefined • RV fee: Free • No water • Vault toilets • Activities: Fishing, swimming • Elevation: 3806

**Canyon Ferry - Cottonwood** • Agency: US Bureau of Reclamation • Tel: 406-475-3921 • Location: 4 miles N of Townsend • GPS: Lat 46.373528 Lon -111.556551 • Open: All year • Total sites: 4 • RV sites: 4 • RV fee: Free • No water • Vault toilets • Activities: Fishing • Elevation: 3796

**Canyon Ferry - Indian Road** • Agency: US Bureau of Reclamation • Tel: 406-475-3921 • Location: 3 miles N of Townsend • GPS: Lat 46.358294 Lon -111.540204 • Open: All year • Total sites: 12 • RV sites: 12 • RV fee: Free • No water • Vault toilets • Activities: Fishing, power boating • Elevation: 3793

**Crow Creek** • Agency: Bureau of Land Management • Tel: 406-533-7600 • Location: 25 miles SW of Townsend • GPS: Lat 46.250852 Lon -111.673494 • Open: All year • Total sites: 8 • RV sites: 8 • RV fee: Free • No water • Vault toilets • Activities: Hiking, mountain biking, motor sports • Elevation: 4741

**Toston Dam Lower** • Agency: Bureau of Land Management • Tel: 406-533-7600 • Location: 16 miles S of Townsend • GPS: Lat 46.121894 Lon -111.398164 • Open: All year • Total sites: 2 • RV sites: 2 • Max RV Length: 24 • RV fee: Free • No water • Vault toilets • Activities: Power boating • Elevation: 3934

**Toston Dam Upper** • Agency: Bureau of Land Management • Tel: 406-533-7600 • Location: 17 miles S of Townsend • GPS: Lat 46.121805 Lon -111.409029 • Open: All year • Total sites: 6 • RV sites: 6 • Max RV Length: 24 • RV fee: Free • No water • Vault toilets • Activities: Fishing, power boating • Elevation: 3999

## Trout Creek

**Fishtrap Lake** (Lolo NF) • Agency: US Forest Service • Tel: 406-329-3750 • Location: 30 miles E of Trout Creek (limited services), 44 miles N of Thompson Falls • GPS: Lat 47.861395 Lon -115.202918 • Open: All year • Total sites: 13 • RV sites: 4 • Max RV Length: 28 • RV fee: Free • Central water (no water Oct-May) • Vault toilets • Activities: Hiking, fishing, non-power boating • Elevation: 4131

**Marten Creek** (Kootenai NF) • Agency: US Forest Service • Tel: 406-827-3533 • Location: 9 miles NW of Trout Creek (limited services), 30 miles NW of Thompson Falls • GPS: Lat 47.882121 Lon -115.747711 • Open: All year • Stay limit: 14 days • Total sites: 6 • RV sites: 6 • Max RV Length: 32 • RV fee: Free • No water • Vault toilets • Activities: Hiking, fishing, swimming, power boating • Elevation: 2418

## Troy

**Kilbrennan Lake** (Kootenai NF) • Agency: US Forest Service • Location: 12 miles N of Troy (limited services), 30 miles NW of Libby • GPS: Lat 48.596611 Lon -115.888234 • Open: All year • Stay limit: 14 days • Total sites: 7 • RV sites: 7 • Max RV Length: 24 • RV fee: Free • No water • Vault toilets • Activities: Fishing, power boating • Elevation: 2946

**Red Top** (Kootenai NF) • Agency: US Forest Service • Tel: 406-295-4693 • Location: 26 miles N of Troy (limited services), 42 miles NW of Libby • GPS: Lat 48.760935 Lon -115.918299 • Open: All year (limited winter access) • Stay limit: 14 days • Total sites: 3 • RV sites: 3 • RV fee: Free • No water • Vault toilets • Elevation: 2825

**Yaak Falls** (Kootenai NF) • Agency: US Forest Service • Tel: 406-295-4693 • Location: 16 miles N of Troy (limited services), 33 miles NW of Libby • GPS: Lat 48.645021 Lon -115.885458 • Open: All year (limited winter access) • Stay limit: 14 days • Total sites: 7 • RV sites: 7 • Max RV Length: 24 • RV fee: Free • No water • Vault toilets • Activities: Hiking, fishing • Elevation: 2444

## Twin Bridges

**Notch Bottom FAS** • Agency: State • Tel: 406-994-4042 • Location: 16 miles SW of Twin Bridges (limited services), 24 miles N of Dillon • GPS: Lat 45.437452 Lon -112.564958 • Stay limit: 7 days • Total sites: 3 • RV sites: 3 • Max RV Length: 20 • RV fee: Free • No water • Vault toilets • Activities: Fishing, power boating, non-power boating • Elevation: 4849

## Virginia City

**Cottonwood** (Beaverhead-Deerlodge NF) • Agency: US Forest Service • Tel: 406-682-4253 • Location: 38 miles S of Virginia City (limited services), 50 miles SW of Ennis • GPS: Lat 44.973933 Lon -111.976399 • Stay limit: 16 days • Total sites: 10 • RV sites: 10 • Max RV Length: 28 • RV fee: Free • No toilets • Activities: Fishing, hunting • Elevation: 6335

**Ruby Reservoir** • Agency: Bureau of Land Management • Tel: 406-683-8000 • Location: 15 miles SW of Virginia City (limited services), 69 miles S of Butte • GPS: Lat 45.225556 Lon -112.119413 • Open: All year • Total sites: Dispersed • RV sites: Undefined • RV fee: Free • No water • Vault toilets • Activities: Fishing, power boating, non-power boating • Elevation: 5407

## West Yellowstone

**Cherry Creek** (Custer Gallatin NF) • Agency: US Forest Service • Tel: 406-823-6961 • Location: 12 miles NW of West Yellowstone • GPS: Lat 44.751044 Lon -111.263946 • Open: May-Oct • Total sites: 7 • RV sites: 7 • RV fee: Free • No water • Vault toilets • Activities: Fishing, swimming • Elevation: 6545

**Raynold's Pass FAS** • Agency: State • Tel: 406-444-2535 • Location: 30 miles NW of West Yellowstone • GPS: Lat 44.826768 Lon -111.486821 • Open: All year • Stay limit: 7 days • Total sites: 6 • RV sites: 6 • Max RV Length: 25 • RV fee: Free • No water • Vault toilets • Activities: Fishing, swimming, power boating • Elevation: 6142

## White Sulphur Springs

**Bair Reservoir** • Agency: Bureau of Land Management • Location: 19 miles E of White Sulphur Springs • GPS: Lat 46.581875 Lon -110.569018 • Total sites: Dispersed • RV sites: Undefined • RV fee: Free • No water • Vault toilets • Elevation: 5338

**Basin Creek** (Helena-Lewis & Clark NF) • Agency: US Forest Service • Location: 35 miles NE of White Sulphur Springs • GPS: Lat 46.642202 Lon -110.430243 • Total sites: 4 • RV sites: 4 • RV fee: Free • No water • Vault toilets • Elevation: 5669

**Lion Creek Lower** (Helena-Lewis & Clark NF) • Agency: US Forest Service • Location: 21 miles NE of White Sulphur Springs • GPS: Lat 46.665849 Lon -110.573302 • Total sites: 1 • RV sites: 1 • RV fee: Free • No water • Vault toilets • Notes: Mandatory food storage • Elevation: 5869

**Russian Flat** (Helena-Lewis & Clark NF) • Agency: US Forest Service • Location: 48 miles NE of White Sulphur Springs • GPS: Lat 46.725368 Lon -110.423697 • Total sites: 2 • RV sites: 2 • RV fee: Free • No water • Vault toilets • Notes: Mandatory food storage • Elevation: 6346

**Whitetail Camp** (Helena-Lewis & Clark NF) • Agency: US Forest Service • Location: 38 miles NE of White Sulphur Springs • GPS: Lat 46.682363 Lon -110.502753 • Total sites: 12 • RV sites: 12 • RV fee: Free • No water • Vault toilets • Notes: Mandatory food storage • Elevation: 6375

## Whitefish

**Red Meadow Lake** (Flathead NF) • Agency: US Forest Service • Tel: 406-387-3800 • Location: 36 miles N of Whitefish • GPS: Lat 48.753736 Lon -114.563547 • Stay limit: 14 days • Total sites: 6 • RV sites: 6 • RV fee: Free • No water • Vault toilets • Elevation: 5562

**Upper Stillwater Lake** (Flathead NF) • Agency: US Forest Service • Tel: 406-758-5208 • Location: 24 miles NW of Whitefish • GPS: Lat 48.603516 Lon -114.656307 • Open: May-Nov • Total sites: 5 • RV sites: 5 • RV fee: Free • No water • Vault toilets • Activities: Hiking, fishing, non-power boating • Elevation: 3205

## Whitehall

**Pipestone TMA** • Agency: Bureau of Land Management • Tel: 406-533-7600 • Location: 10 miles W of Whitehall (limited services), 18 miles SE of Butte • GPS: Lat 45.923158 Lon -112.269821 • Open: All year • Total sites: Dispersed • RV sites: Undefined • RV fee: Free • No water • No toilets • Activities: Hiking, mountain biking, motor sports • Elevation: 5064

## Wilsall

**Shields River** (Custer Gallatin NF) • Agency: US Forest Service • Tel: 406-222-1892 • Location: 23 miles NE of Wilsall (limited services), 50 miles N of Livingston • GPS: Lat 46.184327 Lon -110.405053 • Open: Jun-Nov • Total sites: 6 • RV sites: 6 • Max RV Length: 22 • RV fee: Free • No water • Vault toilets • Elevation: 6417

## Winnett

**Crooked Creek** (Fort Peck Lake) • Agency: Corps of Engineers • Tel: 406-429-2999 • Location: 50 miles NE of Winnett (limited services), 93 miles NE of Lewistown • GPS: Lat 47.431933 Lon -107.937325 • Open: All year • Total sites: 20 • RV sites: 20 • Max RV Length: 25 • RV fee: Free • Central water • Vault toilets • Activities: Fishing, swimming, power boating, non-power boating • Elevation: 2254

## Wisdom

**American Legion Park** • Agency: Municipal • Location: 1 mile W of Wisdom (limited services), 53 miles SW of Anaconda • GPS: Lat 45.618819 Lon -113.458833 • Open: All year • Total sites: 15 • RV sites: 15 • RV fee: Free (donation appreciated) • Central water • Vault toilets • Elevation: 6052

**Pintler** (Beaverhead-Deerlodge NF) • Agency: US Forest Service • Tel: 406-832-3178 • Location: 25 miles N of Wisdom (limited services), 47 miles SW of Anaconda • GPS: Lat 45.838743 Lon -113.436441 • Stay limit: 16 days • Total sites: 2 • RV sites: 2 • Max RV Length: 18 • RV fee: Free • Central water • Vault toilets • Activities: Fishing • Elevation: 6365

## Wise River

**Anaconda Sportsman's Park** • Agency: Non-Profit Organization • Location: 13 miles NW of Wise River (limited services), 27 miles SW of Anaconda • GPS: Lat 45.885293 Lon -113.167687 • Open: Apr-Oct • Total sites: 40 • RV sites: 40 • Max RV Length: 45 • RV fee: Free (donation appreciated) • Central water • Vault toilets • Activities: Fishing • Elevation: 5807

**Bryant Creek** • Agency: Bureau of Land Management • Tel: 406-533-7600 • Location: 8 miles NW of Wise River (limited services), 30 miles S of Anaconda • GPS: Lat 45.858436 Lon -113.085386 • Total sites: Dispersed • RV sites: Undefined • RV fee: Free • No water • No toilets • Activities: Fishing • Elevation: 5759

**Dickie Bridge** • Agency: Bureau of Land Management • Tel: 406-533-7600 • Location: 7 miles NW of Wise River (limited services), 42 miles SW of Butte • GPS: Lat 45.849751 Lon -113.068533 • Open: All year • Total sites: 10 • RV sites: 10 • Max RV Length: 24 • RV fee: Free • No water • Vault toilets • Activities: Fishing • Elevation: 5722

**East Bank** • Agency: Bureau of Land Management • Tel: 406-533-7600 • Location: 8 miles NW of Wise River (limited services), 30 miles S of Anaconda • GPS: Lat 45.856963 Lon -113.083996 • Open: All year • Total sites: 9 • RV sites: 9 • Max RV Length: 24 • RV fee: Free • No water • Vault toilets • Activities: Hiking, fishing, power boating, non-power boating • Elevation: 5751

**Seymour Creek** (Beaverhead-Deerlodge NF) • Agency: US Forest Service • Tel: 406-832-3178 • Location: 20 miles NW of Wise River (limited services), 28 miles SW of Anaconda • GPS: Lat 45.988162 Lon -113.184851 • Open: May-Sep • Stay limit: 16 days • Total sites: 17 • RV sites: 17 • Max RV Length: 18 • RV fee: Free • Central water • Vault toilets • Activities: Hiking, fishing • Elevation: 6824

## Worden

**Bundy Bridge FAS** • Agency: State • Tel: 406-444-2535 • Location: 8 miles NE of Worden (limited services), 25 miles NE of Billings • GPS: Lat 45.995804 Lon -108.010542 • Open: All year • Stay limit: 7 days • Total sites: Dispersed • RV sites: Undefined • RV fee: Free • No water • Vault toilets • Activities: Fishing • Elevation: 2883

## Zurich

**BR-12 Prairie Marsh** • Agency: Bureau of Land Management • Tel: 406-262-2820 • Location: 9 miles N of Zurich (limited services), 16 miles NE of Chinook • GPS: Lat 48.701212 Lon -109.039178 • Total sites: Dispersed • RV sites: Undefined • RV fee: Free • No water • No toilets • Activities: Hunting • Elevation: 2727

# Nevada

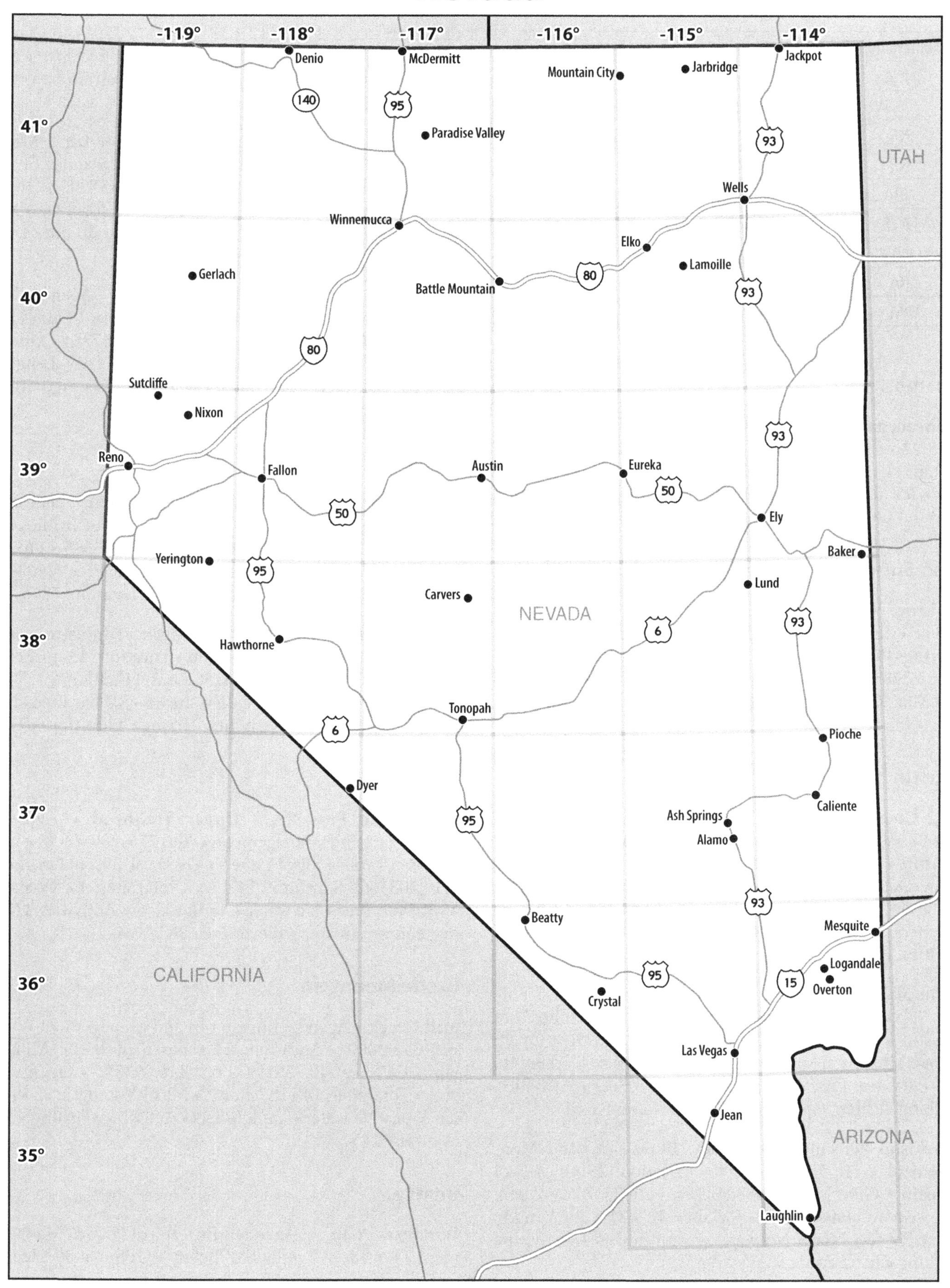
-119°
-118°
-117°
-116°
-115°
-114°
41°
40°
39°
38°
37°
36°
35°
Denio
McDermitt
Mountain City
Jarbridge
Jackpot
140
95
Paradise Valley
93
UTAH
Wells
Winnemucca
Elko
Lamoille
Gerlach
Battle Mountain
80
Sutcliffe
Nixon
Reno
Fallon
Austin
Eureka
50
Ely
Baker
Yerington
Lund
Carvers
NEVADA
6
Hawthorne
Tonopah
Pioche
Dyer
Ash Springs
Caliente
Alamo
Beatty
Mesquite
Logandale
Overton
15
CALIFORNIA
Crystal
Las Vegas
Jean
ARIZONA
Laughlin

# Nevada — Camping Areas

| Abbreviation | Description |
|---|---|
| NCA | National Conservation Area |
| NDOW | Neveada Dept of Wildlife |
| NF | National Forest |
| NP | National Park |
| NRA | National Recreation Area |
| NWR | National Wildlife Refuge |
| OHVA | Off-Highway Vehicle Area |
| RA | Recreation Area |
| WMA | Wildlife Management Area |

## Alamo

**Pahranagat NWR** • Agency: US Fish & Wildlife • Tel: 775-725-3417 • Location: 5 miles S of Alamo • GPS: Lat 37.303115 Lon -115.124954 • Total sites: 14 • RV sites: 10 • RV fee: Free • No water • Vault toilets • Notes: No ground fires • Elevation: 3406

## Ash Springs

**Pahroc Wash** • Agency: Bureau of Land Management • Tel: 775-289-1800 • Location: 28 miles N of Ash Springs (limited services), 65 miles NW of Caliente • GPS: Lat 37.783858 Lon -115.059336 • Total sites: 1 • RV sites: 1 • Max RV Length: 18 • RV fee: Free • No water • No toilets • Elevation: 4648

## Austin

**Big Creek** (Humboldt-Toiyabe NF) • Agency: US Forest Service • Tel: 775-964-2671 • Location: 15 miles S of Austin • GPS: Lat 39.345493 Lon -117.136112 • Open: May-Oct • Total sites: 5 • RV sites: 5 • Max RV Length: 35 • RV fee: Free • Central water • Vault toilets • Notes: Trailers prohibited from crossing the top of FSR 002 • Activities: Fishing, hunting • Elevation: 6942

**Columbine** (Humboldt-Toiyabe NF) • Agency: US Forest Service • Tel: 775-964-2671 • Location: 54 miles S of Austin • GPS: Lat 38.900342 Lon -117.376796 • Open: May-Oct • Total sites: 5 • RV sites: 5 • Max RV Length: 35 • RV fee: Free • No water • Vault toilets • Activities: Hiking, fishing, equestrian area • Elevation: 8661

**Hickison Petroglyph** • Agency: Bureau of Land Management • Tel: 775-635-4000 • Location: 25 miles E of Austin • GPS: Lat 39.448804 Lon -116.751702 • Open: All year • Total sites: 16 • RV sites: 16 • Max RV Length: 25 • RV fee: Free • No water • Vault toilets • Activities: Hiking • Elevation: 6581

**San Juan Creek** (Humboldt-Toiyabe NF) • Agency: US Forest Service • Tel: 775-964-2671 • Location: 34 miles S of Austin • GPS: Lat 39.121823 Lon -117.275517 • Open: May-Oct • Total sites: 10 • RV sites: 10 • RV fee: Free • No water • Vault toilets • Activities: Hiking, equestrian area • Elevation: 7282

**Spencer Hot Springs** • Agency: Bureau of Land Management • Tel: 775-635-4000 • Location: 19 miles SE of Austin • GPS: Lat 39.326879 Lon -116.857595 • Total sites: Dispersed • RV sites: Undefined • RV fee: Free • No water • No toilets • Notes: Be courteous and do not camp right on the springs • Elevation: 5685

**Toquima Caves** (Humboldt-Toiyabe NF) • Agency: US Forest Service • Tel: 775-482-6286 • Location: 29 miles SE of Austin • GPS: Lat 39.187411 Lon -116.787364 • Open: May-Oct • Total sites: 5 • RV sites: 1 • Max RV Length: 25 • RV fee: Free • No water • Vault toilets • Activities: Hiking • Elevation: 7972

## Baker

**Great Basin NP - Strawberry Creek** • Agency: National Park Service • Tel: 775-234-7331 • Location: 11 miles SE of Baker • GPS: Lat 39.060905 Lon -114.273515 • Open: All year • Total sites: 8 • RV sites: 6 • RV fee: Free • No water • Vault toilets • Activities: Hiking • Elevation: 7276

**Sacramento Pass RA - The Pond** • Agency: Bureau of Land Management • Tel: 775-289-1800 • Location: 13 miles SE of Baker • GPS: Lat 39.121475 Lon -114.304978 • Stay limit: 14 days • Total sites: 6 • RV sites: 6 • RV fee: Free • No water • Vault toilets • Activities: Hiking • Elevation: 6728

## Baker

**Sacramento Pass RA - Upper Trailhead** • Agency: Bureau of Land Management • Tel: 775-289-1800 • Location: 14 miles SE of Baker • GPS: Lat 39.114226 Lon -114.303366 • Stay limit: 14 days • Total sites: 4 • RV sites: 4 • RV fee: Free • No water • Vault toilets • Activities: Hiking, equestrian area • Elevation: 6867

## Battle Mountain

**Mill Creek** • Agency: Bureau of Land Management • Tel: 775-635-4000 • Location: 24 miles S of Battle Mountain • GPS: Lat 40.356199 Lon -116.993876 • Open: All year • Total sites: 14 • RV sites: 3 • Max RV Length: 28 • RV fee: Free • No water • Vault toilets • Activities: Fishing • Elevation: 5243

## Beatty

**Bombo's Pond** • Agency: Bureau of Land Management • Location: 2 miles S of Beatty • GPS: Lat 36.882328

Lon -116.754357 • Total sites: Dispersed • RV sites: Undefined • RV fee: Free • No water • No toilets • Notes: Good bird watching • Activities: Hiking, mountain biking • Elevation: 3194

**Bull Frog** • Agency: Bureau of Land Management • Tel: 775-482-7800 • Location: 2 miles W of Beatty • GPS: Lat 36.906879 Lon -116.792472 • Open: All year • Total sites: Dispersed • RV sites: Undefined • RV fee: Free • No water • No toilets • Elevation: 3627

## Caliente

**Chief Mountain South** • Agency: Bureau of Land Management • Tel: 775-289-1800 • Location: 9 miles E of Caliente • GPS: Lat 37.604482 Lon -114.659276 • Total sites: 6 • RV sites: 6 • RV fee: Free • No water • Vault toilets • Activities: Motor sports • Elevation: 6082

**Chief Mountain West** • Agency: Bureau of Land Management • Tel: 775-289-1800 • Location: 20 miles E of Caliente • GPS: Lat 37.66456 Lon -114.754072 • Total sites: 4 • RV sites: 3 • RV fee: Free • No water • Vault toilets • Activities: Motor sports • Elevation: 4883

## Carvers

**Pine Creek** (Humboldt-Toiyabe NF) • Agency: US Forest Service • Tel: 775-482-6286 • Location: 36 miles NE of Carvers (limited services), 65 miles N of Tonopah • GPS: Lat 38.795619 Lon -116.850387 • Open: May-Oct • Total sites: 21 • RV sites: 21 • RV fee: Free • No water • Vault toilets • Activities: Fishing, equestrian area • Elevation: 7493

## Crystal

**Valley of Fire Highway** • Agency: Bureau of Land Management • Location: 7 miles SW of Crystal (limited services), 32 miles NE of Las Vegas • GPS: Lat 36.444389 Lon -114.675385 • Total sites: Dispersed • RV sites: Undefined • RV fee: Free • No water • No toilets • Elevation: 2280

## Denio

**Bilk Creek Reservoir - NDOW** • Agency: State • Location: 33 miles S of Denio (limited services), 72 miles NW of Winnemucca • GPS: Lat 41.631159 Lon -118.391554 • Open: All year • Total sites: Dispersed • RV sites: Undefined • RV fee: Free • Notes: On private property but open to public, please be respectful • Activities: Fishing, non-power boating • Elevation: 4308

**Black Rock Desert NCA - Jackson Creek** • Agency: Bureau of Land Management • Tel: 775-623-1500 • Location: 53 miles S of Denio (limited services), 87 miles NW of Winnemucca • GPS: Lat 41.321047 Lon -118.532806 • Total sites: Dispersed • RV sites: Undefined • RV fee: Free • No water • No toilets • Activities: Motor sports • Elevation: 4345

**Sheldon NWR - Big Spring Reservoir** • Agency: US Fish & Wildlife • Tel: 541-947-3315 • Location: 39 miles W of Denio (limited services), 83 miles SE of Lakeview, OR • GPS: Lat 41.928984 Lon -119.172723 • Total sites: Dispersed • RV sites: Undefined • RV fee: Free • No water • Vault toilets • Activities: Hiking, fishing, non-power boating • Elevation: 5515

**Sheldon NWR - Catnip Reservoir** • Agency: US Fish & Wildlife • Tel: 541-947-3315 • Location: 53 miles W of Denio (limited services), 82 miles SE of Lakeview, OR • GPS: Lat 41.912883 Lon -119.459793 • Total sites: Dispersed • RV sites: Undefined • RV fee: Free • No water • No toilets • Activities: Hiking, fishing • Elevation: 5791

**Sheldon NWR - East Rock Spring** • Agency: US Fish & Wildlife • Tel: 541-947-3315 • Location: 45 miles SW of Denio (limited services), 139 miles NW of Winnemucca • GPS: Lat 41.674344 Lon -119.048742 • Total sites: Dispersed • RV sites: Undefined • RV fee: Free • No water • No toilets • Activities: Hiking • Elevation: 6099

**Sheldon NWR - Fish Spring** • Agency: US Fish & Wildlife • Tel: 541-947-3315 • Location: 53 miles W of Denio (limited services), 54 miles E of Cedarville, CA • GPS: Lat 41.762607 Lon -119.368911 • Total sites: Dispersed • RV sites: Undefined • RV fee: Free • No water • Vault toilets • Activities: Hiking • Elevation: 6004

**Sheldon NWR - Virgin Valley** • Agency: US Fish & Wildlife • Tel: 541-947-3315 • Location: 30 miles W of Denio (limited services), 92 miles SE of Lakeview, OR • GPS: Lat 41.853569 Lon -119.001962 • Open: All year • Total sites: Dispersed • RV sites: Undefined • RV fee: Free • Central water • Flush toilets • Activities: Hiking, swimming • Elevation: 4842

## Dyer

**Fish Lake Valley Hot Springs** • Agency: County • Location: 19 miles N of Dyer (limited services), 58 miles W of Tonopah • GPS: Lat 37.859391 Lon -117.982649 • Open: All year • Total sites: Dispersed • RV sites: Undefined • Max RV Length: 40+ • RV fee: Free • No water • Vault toilets • Activities: Motor sports • Elevation: 4735

## Elko

**Dorsey Reservoir - NDOW** • Agency: State • Location: 22 miles N of Elko • GPS: Lat 41.062782 Lon -115.812343 • Total sites: Dispersed • RV sites: Undefined • RV fee: Free • No water • No toilets • Activities: Fishing • Elevation: 6224

## Ely

**Cleve Creek** • Agency: Bureau of Land Management • Tel: 775-289-1800 • Location: 42 miles E of Ely • GPS: Lat 39.213832 Lon -114.543477 • Open: May-Sep • Total sites: 12 • RV sites: 12 • Max RV Length: 24 • RV fee: Free • No water • Vault toilets • Activities: Fishing • Elevation: 6278

**Garnet Hill** • Agency: Bureau of Land Management • Tel: 775-289-1800 • Location: 2 miles NW of Ely • GPS: Lat 39.262792 Lon -114.927429 • Open: All year • Total sites: Dispersed • RV sites: Undefined • Max RV Length: 20 • RV fee: Free • No water • Vault toilets • Notes: Rockhound site • Activities: Hiking, mountain biking • Elevation: 6867

**Illipah Reservoir** • Agency: Bureau of Land Management • Tel: 775-289-1800 • Location: 37 miles W of Ely • GPS: Lat 39.334498 Lon -115.389695 • Open: All year • Total sites: 14 • RV sites: 14 • RV fee: Free • No water • Vault toilets • Activities: Fishing • Elevation: 6837

**Kalamazoo** (Humboldt-Toiyabe NF) • Agency: US Forest Service • Tel: 775-289-3031 • Location: 32 miles NE of Ely • GPS: Lat 39.565337 Lon -114.597821 • Open: Jun-Sep • Total sites: 5 • RV sites: 5 • RV fee: Free • No water • No toilets • Activities: Hiking, mountain biking, fishing, hunting • Elevation: 7032

## Eureka

**Cold Creek Reservoir - NDOW** • Agency: State • Location: 48 miles N of Eureka • GPS: Lat 39.842786 Lon -115.749258 • Total sites: Dispersed • RV sites: Undefined • RV fee: Free • Activities: Fishing, power boating, non-power boating • Elevation: 6001

## Fallon

**Lee Hot Springs** • Agency: Bureau of Land Management • Location: 18 miles S of Fallon • GPS: Lat 39.208828 Lon -118.724601 • Total sites: Dispersed • RV sites: Undefined • RV fee: Free • No water • No toilets • Elevation: 4035

## Gerlach

**Black Rock Desert NCA** • Agency: Bureau of Land Management • Tel: 775-623-1500 • Location: 12 miles NE of Gerlach • GPS: Lat 40.756479 Lon -119.243193 • Open: All year • Total sites: Dispersed • RV sites: Undefined • RV fee: Free • Notes: Home of Burning Man • Activities: Hiking, motor sports • Elevation: 3904

**Black Rock Desert NCA - Black Rock Hot Springs** • Agency: Bureau of Land Management • Tel: 775-623-1500 • Location: 80 miles N of Gerlach (limited services), 157 miles N of Fernley • GPS: Lat 40.973479 Lon -119.008026 • Total sites: Dispersed • RV sites: Undefined • RV fee: Free • No water • No toilets • Activities: Hiking • Elevation: 3965

**Black Rock Desert NCA - Cassidy Mine** • Agency: Bureau of Land Management • Tel: 775-623-1500 • Location: 17 miles NE of Gerlach • GPS: Lat 40.830395 Lon -119.232012 • Total sites: Dispersed • RV sites: Undefined • RV fee: Free • No water • No toilets • Activities: Hiking • Elevation: 4146

**Black Rock Desert NCA - Double Hot Springs** • Agency: Bureau of Land Management • Tel: 775-623-1500 • Location: 37 miles N of Gerlach • GPS: Lat 41.080119 Lon -119.106001 • Total sites: Dispersed • RV sites: Undefined • RV fee: Free • No water • No toilets • Elevation: 3920

**Black Rock Desert NCA - Stevens Camp** • Agency: Bureau of Land Management • Tel: 530-279-6101 • Location: 76 miles N of Gerlach (limited services), 45 miles E of Cedarville, CA • GPS: Lat 41.490349 Lon -119.491389 • Open: All year • Total sites: 4 • RV sites: 4 • Max RV Length: 27 • RV fee: Free • No water • Vault toilets • Activities: Hiking, hunting, motor sports • Elevation: 5780

**Black Rock NCA - Trego Hot Springs** • Agency: Bureau of Land Management • Tel: 775-623-1500 • Location: 20 miles NE of Gerlach (limited services), 90 miles N of Fernley • GPS: Lat 40.771217 Lon -119.116607 • Total sites: Dispersed • RV sites: Undefined • RV fee: Free • No water • No toilets • Notes: Near RR tracks • Elevation: 3941

**Boulder Reservoir - NDOW** • Agency: State • Location: 71 miles N of Gerlach (limited services), 40 miles SE of Cedarville, CA • GPS: Lat 41.348359 Lon -119.747428 • Total sites: 7 • RV sites: 7 • RV fee: Free • No water • No toilets • Activities: Fishing, non-power boating • Elevation: 5768

**Divine Springs** • Agency: Bureau of Land Management • Tel: 530-233-4666 • Location: 82 miles NW of Gerlach (limited services), 30 miles SE of Cedarville, CA • GPS: Lat 41.329541 Lon -119.873254 • Open: All year • Total sites: 5 • RV sites: 5 • Max RV Length: 24 • RV fee: Free • No water • No toilets • Activities: Hiking, mountain biking, hunting • Elevation: 6506

**Massacre Ranch** • Agency: Bureau of Land Management • Tel: 530-279-6101 • Location: 80 miles N of Gerlach (limited services), 35 miles E of Cedarville, CA • GPS: Lat 41.561051 Lon -119.587369 • Total sites: 4 • RV sites: 4 • Max RV Length: 24 • RV fee: Free • No water • Vault toilets • Activities: Hiking, mountain biking, hunting, equestrian area • Elevation: 5901

**Soldier Meadow** • Agency: Bureau of Land Management • Tel: 775-623-1500 • Location: 64 miles N of Gerlach (limited services), 83 miles E of Cedarville, CA • GPS: Lat 41.360607 Lon -119.222902 • Total sites: 7 • RV sites:

7 • RV fee: Free • No water • Vault toilets • Elevation: 4564

**Squaw Valley Reservoir - NDOW** • Agency: State • Location: 17 miles S of Gerlach (limited services), 66 miles SE of Cedarville, CA • GPS: Lat 40.829109 Lon -119.536988 • Total sites: Dispersed • RV sites: Undefined • RV fee: Free • No water • No toilets • Notes: On private property but open to public, please be respectful • Activities: Fishing • Elevation: 4451

## Hawthorne

**Walker Lake - Tamarack** • Agency: Bureau of Land Management • Tel: 775-885-6000 • Location: 18 miles N of Hawthorne • GPS: Lat 38.736558 Lon -118.768079 • Stay limit: 14 days • Total sites: 12 • RV sites: 12 • RV fee: Free • No water • Vault toilets • Activities: Fishing, power boating, non-power boating • Elevation: 4042

## Jackpot

**Jakes Creek (Boies) Reservoir - NDOW** • Agency: State • Location: 31 miles S of Jackpot • GPS: Lat 41.605141 Lon -114.896985 • Total sites: Dispersed • RV sites: Undefined • RV fee: Free • No water • No toilets • Activities: Fishing • Elevation: 5781

**Salmon Falls Creek RA** • Agency: Bureau of Land Management • Tel: 775-753-0200 • Location: 4 miles S of Jackpot • GPS: Lat 41.946451 Lon -114.692868 • Open: All year • Total sites: Dispersed • RV sites: Undefined • RV fee: Free • No water • No toilets • Activities: Hiking, fishing, hunting, rock climbing, non-power boating • Elevation: 5226

## Jarbridge

**Lower Bluster** (Humboldt-Toiyabe NF) • Agency: US Forest Service • Tel: 775-331-6444 • Location: 3 miles S of Jarbridge (limited services), 102 miles N of Elko • GPS: Lat 41.838215 Lon -115.426697 • Open: Jun-Sep • Stay limit: 14 days • Total sites: 2 • RV sites: 2 • Max RV Length: 25 • RV fee: Free • No water • Vault toilets • Activities: Hiking, fishing • Elevation: 6696

**Pine Creek** (Jarbridge, Humboldt-Toiyabe NF) • Agency: US Forest Service • Tel: 775-331-6444 • Location: 3 miles S of Jarbridge (limited services), 102 miles N of Elko • GPS: Lat 41.835688 Lon -115.426141 • Open: All year (may be inaccessible in winter) • Stay limit: 14 days • Total sites: 5 • RV sites: 5 • Max RV Length: 25 • RV fee: Free • No water • Vault toilets • Activities: Hiking, fishing, hunting • Elevation: 6782

**Sawmill** (Humboldt-Toiyabe NF) • Agency: US Forest Service • Tel: 775-752-3357 • Location: Just N of Jarbridge (limited services), 105 miles N of Elko • GPS: Lat 41.885462 Lon -115.429515 • Open: All year (may be inaccessible in winter) • Total sites: 5 • RV sites: 5 • RV fee: Free • No water • Vault toilets • Activities: Hiking, fishing, hunting, motor sports • Elevation: 6116

## Jean

**Jean/Roach Dry Lakes** • Agency: Bureau of Land Management • Tel: 702-515-5000 • Location: 7 miles E of Jean (limited services), 19 miles S of Las Vegas • GPS: Lat 35.781504 Lon -115.278875 • Total sites: Dispersed • RV sites: Undefined • RV fee: Free • No water • No toilets • Activities: Motor sports • Elevation: 2803

## Lamoille

**Lamoille Creek - NDOW** • Agency: State • Location: 6 miles S of Lamoille (limited services), 23 miles SE of Elko • GPS: Lat 40.661389 Lon -115.441435 • Total sites: Dispersed • RV sites: Undefined • RV fee: Free • No water • No toilets • Activities: Fishing • Elevation: 7123

## Las Vegas

**Lake Mead NRA - Boxcar Canyon** • Agency: National Park Service • Tel: 702-293-8990 • Location: 19 miles E of Las Vegas • GPS: Lat 36.120912 Lon -114.783143 • Total sites: Dispersed • RV sites: Undefined • RV fee: Free • No water • No toilets • Elevation: 1243

**Lake Mead NRA - Government Wash** • Agency: National Park Service • Location: 18 miles E of Las Vegas • GPS: Lat 36.128723 Lon -114.783684 • Total sites: Dispersed • RV sites: Undefined • RV fee: Free • No water • No toilets • Elevation: 1207

## Laughlin

**Lake Mead NRA - Telephone Cove** • Agency: National Park Service • Location: 9 miles N of Laughlin • GPS: Lat 35.2305 Lon -114.594 • Open: All year • Total sites: Dispersed • RV sites: Undefined • RV fee: Free • No water • Vault toilets • Activities: Hiking, fishing, swimming, power boating, non-power boating • Elevation: 649

## Logandale

**Logan Trail Dispersed 1** • Agency: Bureau of Land Management • Tel: 702-515-5371 • Location: 4 miles W of Logandale • GPS: Lat 36.587679 Lon -114.528121 • Total sites: Dispersed • RV sites: Undefined • RV fee: Free • No water • No toilets • Activities: Hiking • Elevation: 1690

**Logan Trail Dispersed 2** • Agency: Bureau of Land Management • Tel: 702-515-5371 • Location: 4 miles W of Logandale • GPS: Lat 36.584563 Lon -114.534615 • Total sites: Dispersed • RV sites: Undefined • RV fee: Free • No water • No toilets • Activities: Hiking • Elevation: 1726

**Logan Trail Dispersed 3 and 4** • Agency: Bureau of Land Management • Tel: 702-515-5371 • Location: 6 miles W of Logandale • GPS: Lat 36.577214 Lon -114.539489 • Total sites: Dispersed • RV sites: Undefined • RV fee: Free • No water • No toilets • Activities: Hiking • Elevation: 1764

**Logan Trail Dispersed 5** • Agency: Bureau of Land Management • Tel: 702-515-5371 • Location: 6 miles W of Logandale • GPS: Lat 36.573604 Lon -114.544418 • Total sites: Dispersed • RV sites: Undefined • RV fee: Free • No water • No toilets • Activities: Hiking • Elevation: 1798

**Logan Trail Dispersed 7** (Bassett) • Agency: Bureau of Land Management • Tel: 702-515-5371 • Location: 6 miles W of Logandale • GPS: Lat 36.559706 Lon -114.550203 • Total sites: Dispersed • RV sites: Undefined • RV fee: Free • No water • Vault toilets • Activities: Hiking • Elevation: 1869

**Logan Trail Dispersed 8** • Agency: Bureau of Land Management • Tel: 702-515-5371 • Location: 9 miles W of Logandale • GPS: Lat 36.549389 Lon -114.550186 • Total sites: Dispersed • RV sites: Undefined • RV fee: Free • No water • No toilets • Activities: Hiking • Elevation: 1919

## Lund

**Cherry Creek** (Humboldt-Toiyabe NF) • Agency: US Forest Service • Tel: 775-289-3031 • Location: 39 miles S of Lund (limited services), 103 miles S of Ely • GPS: Lat 38.153799 Lon -115.624325 • Open: May-Sep • Total sites: 4 • RV sites: 4 • Max RV Length: 20 • RV fee: Free • No water • Vault toilets • Activities: Hiking • Elevation: 6932

**Gap Mountain** • Agency: Bureau of Land Management • Tel: 775-289-1800 • Location: 38 miles S of Lund (limited services), 74 miles S of Ely • GPS: Lat 38.328054 Lon -115.050939 • Open: All year • Total sites: 6 • RV sites: 6 • RV fee: Free • No water • No toilets • Elevation: 5482

**Wayne E. Kirch WMA - Dave Deacon/Hot Creek** • Agency: State • Location: 39 miles S of Lund (limited services), 74 miles S of Ely • GPS: Lat 38.388588 Lon -115.133993 • Total sites: 15 • RV sites: 15 • RV fee: Free • Central water • Vault toilets • Activities: Fishing, power boating, non-power boating • Elevation: 5213

## Mesquite

**Whitney Pocket** • Agency: Bureau of Land Management • Location: 32 miles S of Mesquite • GPS: Lat 36.522978 Lon -114.140562 • Open: All year • Total sites: Dispersed • RV sites: Undefined • RV fee: Free • No water • No toilets • Activities: Hiking, rock climbing, motor sports • Elevation: 3018

## Mountain City

**Jack Creek** (Humboldt-Toiyabe NF) • Agency: US Forest Service • Tel: 775-738-5171 • Location: 44 miles S of Mountain City (limited services), 61 miles N of Elko • GPS: Lat 41.513491 Lon -116.063984 • Open: All year (may be inaccessible in winter) • Total sites: 3 • RV sites: 3 • Max RV Length: 30 • RV fee: Free • No water • Vault toilets • Activities: Fishing, hunting • Elevation: 6519

**Wildhorse** • Agency: Indian Reservation • Location: 17 miles SE of Mountain City (limited services), 65 miles N of Elko • GPS: Lat 41.685457 Lon -115.814075 • Total sites: Dispersed • RV sites: Undefined • RV fee: Free • Elevation: 6240

## Nixon

**The Mugwumps** • Agency: Bureau of Land Management • Location: 9 miles N of Nixon (limited services), 27 miles N of Fernley • GPS: Lat 39.943436 Lon -119.381019 • Total sites: Dispersed • RV sites: Undefined • RV fee: Free • No water • No toilets • Activities: Hiking, motor sports • Elevation: 3977

## Overton

**Lake Mead NRA - Stewarts Point** • Agency: National Park Service • Location: 15 miles S of Overton • GPS: Lat 36.377354 Lon -114.396517 • Total sites: Dispersed • RV sites: Undefined • RV fee: Free • No water • Vault toilets • Elevation: 1199

**Overton WMA** • Agency: State • Location: 1 mile S of Overton • GPS: Lat 36.515638 Lon -114.423294 • Open: All year • Total sites: 6 • RV sites: 6 • RV fee: Free • No water • No toilets • Notes: Near RR tracks • Activities: Hiking • Elevation: 1240

**Snowbird Mesa/Poverty Flats** • Agency: Bureau of Land Management • Location: 4 miles S of Overton • GPS: Lat 36.483488 Lon -114.450948 • Total sites: Dispersed • RV sites: Undefined • RV fee: Free • No water • No toilets • Activities: Hiking • Elevation: 1640

## Paradise Valley

**Martin Creek - NDOW** • Agency: State • Location: 7 miles NE of Paradise Valley (limited services), 46 miles N of Winnemucca • GPS: Lat 41.530287 Lon -117.421986 • Total sites: Dispersed • RV sites: Undefined • RV fee: Free • No water • No toilets • Activities: Fishing • Elevation: 4649

## Pioche

**Meadow Valley** • Agency: Bureau of Land Management • Tel: 775-289-1800 • Location: 17 miles E of

Pioche • GPS: Lat 38.008223 Lon -114.206913 • Total sites: Dispersed • RV sites: Undefined • RV fee: Free • No water • No toilets • Activities: Hiking, fishing, swimming, hunting • Elevation: 5745

**Patterson Pass** • Agency: Bureau of Land Management • Tel: 775-289-1800 • Location: 48 miles N of Pioche • GPS: Lat 38.591928 Lon -114.667508 • Open: All year • Total sites: 10 • RV sites: 10 • RV fee: Free • No water • Vault toilets • Activities: Fishing, hunting, motor sports • Elevation: 6175

**Stampede** • Agency: Bureau of Land Management • Tel: 775-289-1800 • Location: 7 miles N of Pioche • GPS: Lat 37.977477 Lon -114.537203 • Total sites: 4 • RV sites: 4 • RV fee: Free • No water • Vault toilets • Activities: Motor sports • Elevation: 6187

## Reno

**Whites Creek - NDOW** • Agency: State • Location: 7 miles S of Reno • GPS: Lat 39.378153 Lon -119.847913 • Total sites: Dispersed • RV sites: Undefined • RV fee: Free • No water • No toilets • Activities: Fishing • Elevation: 6233

## Sutcliffe

**Dry Lake OHVA** • Agency: Bureau of Land Management • Tel: 530-257-0456 • Location: 27 miles NW of Sutcliffe (limited services), 52 miles N of Spanish Springs (north of Reno) • GPS: Lat 40.237923 Lon -119.854985 • Total sites: Dispersed • RV sites: Undefined • RV fee: Free • No water • Vault toilets • Activities: Motor sports • Elevation: 4263

## Tonopah

**Highway 95 Tonopah** • Agency: Bureau of Land Management • Location: 1 mile S of Tonopah • GPS: Lat 38.049657 Lon -117.218042 • Open: All year • Total sites: Dispersed • RV sites: Undefined • RV fee: Free • No water • No toilets • Elevation: 6297

**Peavine** (Humboldt-Toiyabe NF) • Agency: US Forest Service • Tel: 775-482-6286 • Location: 48 miles N of Tonopah • GPS: Lat 38.616291 Lon -117.302569 • Open: May-Oct • Total sites: 15 • RV sites: 15 • Max RV Length: 35 • RV fee: Free • No water • Vault toilets • Activities: Fishing • Elevation: 6391

## Wells

**I-80 Dispersed** • Agency: Bureau of Land Management • Location: 24 miles E of Wells • GPS: Lat 41.064252 Lon -114.521733 • Total sites: Dispersed • RV sites: Undefined • RV fee: Free • No water • No toilets • Elevation: 6312

## Winnemucca

**Sonoma Canyon** • Agency: Bureau of Land Management • Tel: 775-623-1500 • Location: 14 miles S of Winnemucca • GPS: Lat 40.817678 Lon -117.692705 • Open: All year • Total sites: Dispersed • RV sites: Undefined • RV fee: Free • No water • No toilets • Activities: Hiking • Elevation: 5079

**Water Canyon** • Agency: Bureau of Land Management • Tel: 775-623-1500 • Location: 4 miles SE of Winnemucca • GPS: Lat 40.929559 Lon -117.673613 • Open: All year • Total sites: Dispersed • RV sites: Undefined • Max RV Length: 30 • RV fee: Free • No water • Vault toilets • Activities: Hiking, mountain biking, rock climbing, motor sports • Elevation: 5453

## Yerington

**Mason Valley WMA - Lux Lane** • Agency: State • Tel: 775-423-3171 • Location: 10 miles N of Yerington • GPS: Lat 39.087601 Lon -119.119305 • Open: All year • Total sites: Dispersed • RV sites: Undefined • RV fee: Free • No water • Vault toilets • Activities: Hiking, fishing, power boating, non-power boating, equestrian area • Elevation: 4336

**Mason Valley WMA - North Pond 1** • Agency: State • Tel: 775-423-3171 • Location: 13 miles N of Yerington • GPS: Lat 39.122951 Lon -119.108062 • Open: All year • Total sites: Dispersed • RV sites: Undefined • RV fee: Free • No water • Vault toilets • Activities: Hiking, fishing, power boating, non-power boating, equestrian area • Elevation: 4314

**Mason Valley WMA - North Pond 2** • Agency: State • Tel: 775-423-3171 • Location: 13 miles N of Yerington • GPS: Lat 39.122794 Lon -119.101202 • Open: All year • Total sites: Dispersed • RV sites: Undefined • RV fee: Free • No water • No toilets • Activities: Hiking, fishing, power boating, non-power boating, equestrian area • Elevation: 4317

**Wilson Canyon** • Agency: Bureau of Land Management • Tel: 775-885-6000 • Location: 14 miles S of Yerington • GPS: Lat 38.808786 Lon -119.232903 • Open: All year • Total sites: Dispersed • RV sites: Undefined • RV fee: Free • No water • Vault toilets • Activities: Hiking, fishing • Elevation: 4701

**Yerington City Park** • Agency: Municipal • Tel: 775-463-7733 • Location: In Yerington • GPS: Lat 38.989602 Lon -119.181892 • Total sites: Dispersed • RV sites: Undefined • RV fee: Free • No water • No toilets • Elevation: 4403

# New Mexico

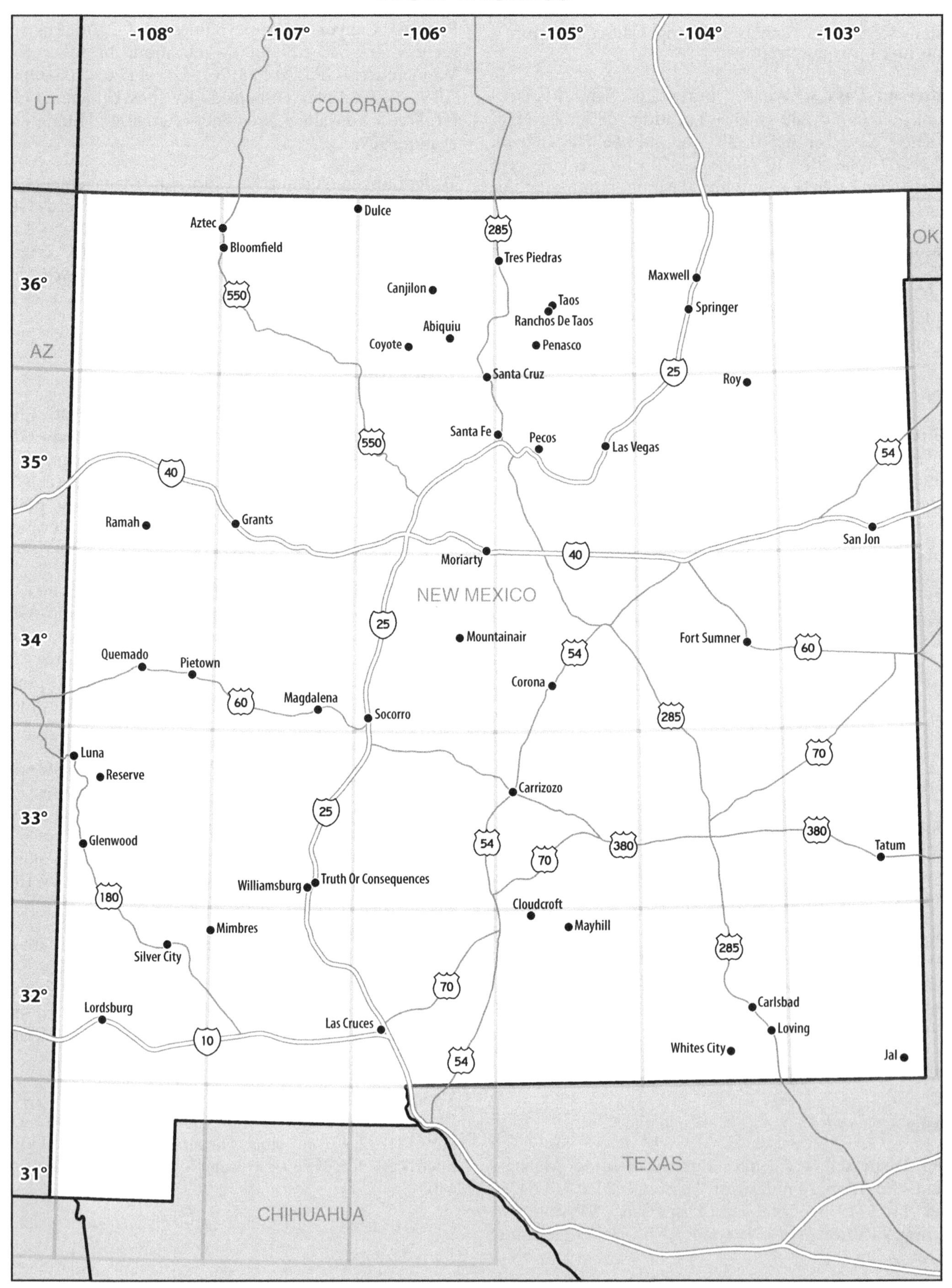

-108°
-107°
-106°
-105°
-104°
-103°
36°
35°
34°
33°
32°
31°
UT
COLORADO
OK
AZ
NEW MEXICO
TEXAS
CHIHUAHUA
Dulce
Aztec
Bloomfield
Tres Piedras
Maxwell
Canjilon
Taos
Ranchos De Taos
Springer
Abiquiu
Coyote
Penasco
Santa Cruz
Roy
Santa Fe
Pecos
Las Vegas
Ramah
Grants
San Jon
Moriarty
Mountainair
Fort Sumner
Quemado
Pietown
Corona
Magdalena
Socorro
Luna
Reserve
Carrizozo
Glenwood
Tatum
Williamsburg
Truth Or Consequences
Cloudcroft
Mayhill
Mimbres
Silver City
Carlsbad
Lordsburg
Las Cruces
Loving
Whites City
Jal
285
550
25
54
40
60
70
380
180
10

# New Mexico — Camping Areas

| Abbreviation | Description |
|---|---|
| NCA | National Conservation Area |
| NF | National Forest |
| NM | National Monument |
| NMGF | New Mexico Department of Game & Fish |
| NMSLO | New Mexico State Land Office |
| NWR | National Wildlife Refuge |
| OHV | Off-Highway Vehicle |
| RA | Recreation Area |
| SWFA | State Wildlife and Fishing Area |

## Abiquiu

**Rio Chama** (Santa Fe NF) • Agency: US Forest Service • Tel: 575-638-5526 • Location: 27 miles NW of Abiquiu (limited services), 54 miles S of Chama • GPS: Lat 36.355248 Lon -106.673673 • Open: Apr-Oct • Total sites: 18 • RV sites: 18 • Max RV Length: 20 • RV fee: Free • No water • Vault toilets • Activities: Fishing • Elevation: 6427

## Aztec

**Simon Canyon RA** • Agency: Bureau of Land Management • Tel: 505 599-8900 • Location: 20 miles E of Aztec • GPS: Lat 36.823354 Lon -107.660314 • Total sites: Dispersed • RV sites: Undefined • RV fee: Free • No water • No toilets • Elevation: 5725

## Bloomfield

**Angel Peak** • Agency: Bureau of Land Management • Tel: 505-564-7600 • Location: 21 miles S of Bloomfield • GPS: Lat 36.548202 Lon -107.860305 • Open: All year • Total sites: 9 • RV sites: 4 • RV fee: Free • No water • Vault toilets • Activities: Hiking • Elevation: 6697

## Canjilon

**Canjilon Creek** (Carson NF) • Agency: US Forest Service • Location: 10 miles NE of Canjilon (limited services), 42 miles SE of Chama • GPS: Lat 36.543352 Lon -106.317422 • Open: Jun-Sep • Total sites: 4 • RV sites: 4 • Max RV Length: 16 • RV fee: Free • No water • Vault toilets • Activities: Fishing • Elevation: 9452

## Carlsbad

**Alkali Lake OHV** • Agency: Bureau of Land Management • Location: 5 miles N of Carlsbad • GPS: Lat 32.498919 Lon -104.211436 • Open: All year • Total sites: Dispersed • RV sites: Undefined • RV fee: Free • No water • No toilets • Activities: Motor sports • Elevation: 3281

**Avalon Reservoir** • Agency: Municipal • Tel: 505-885-3203 • Location: 4 miles N of Carlsbad • GPS: Lat 32.493081 Lon -104.247742 • Total sites: Dispersed • RV sites: Undefined • RV fee: Free • No toilets • Elevation: 3173

**Hackberry Lake OHV** • Agency: Bureau of Land Management • Tel: 575-234-5972 • Location: 20 miles NE of Carlsbad • GPS: Lat 32.570251 Lon -103.968716 • Open: All year • Total sites: Dispersed • RV sites: Undefined • RV fee: Free • No water • No toilets • Activities: Motor sports • Elevation: 3196

**Hess - NMSLO** • Agency: State • Tel: 505-827-5851 • Location: 32 miles SW of Carlsbad • GPS: Lat 32.244552 Lon -104.601451 • Total sites: Dispersed • RV sites: Undefined • RV fee: Free • No water • No toilets • Activities: Hiking, hunting • Elevation: 4419

## Carrizozo

**Gallancher Ranch Road - NMSLO** • Agency: State • Tel: 505-827-5851 • Location: 37 miles NW of Carrizozo • GPS: Lat 33.879852 Lon -106.218012 • Total sites: Dispersed • RV sites: Undefined • RV fee: Free • No water • No toilets • Activities: Hunting • Elevation: 6850

## Cloudcroft

**Karr Canyon Upper** (Lincoln NF) • Agency: US Forest Service • Tel: 575-434-7200 • Location: 7 miles S of Cloudcroft • GPS: Lat 32.880557 Lon -105.780365 • Open: All year • Total sites: 6 • RV sites: 6 • Max RV Length: 16 • RV fee: Free • No water • Vault toilets • Elevation: 9400

**Upper Karr** (Lincoln NF) • Agency: US Forest Service • Tel: 575-682-2551 • Location: 7 miles S of Cloudcroft • GPS: Lat 32.880363 Lon -105.780001 • Open: All year • Total sites: 6 • RV sites: 6 • Max RV Length: 16 • RV fee: Free • No water • Vault toilets • Elevation: 9341

## Corona

**Red Cloud** (Cibola NF) • Agency: US Forest Service • Location: 12 miles SW of Corona • GPS: Lat 34.190267 Lon -105.725883 • Total sites: 5 • RV sites: 5 • RV fee: Free • No water • Vault toilets • Elevation: 7264

## Coyote

**Resumidero** (Santa Fe NF) • Agency: US Forest Service • Tel: 575-638-5526 • Location: 12 miles SW of Coyote (limited services), 35 miles NE of Cuba • GPS: Lat 36.113076 Lon -106.745846 • Open: May-Sep • Total sites:

15 • RV sites: 6 • Max RV Length: 16 • RV fee: Free • No water • Vault toilets • Activities: Fishing • Elevation: 8976

**Rio Puerco** (Santa Fe NF) • Agency: US Forest Service • Tel: 575-638-5526 • Location: 13 miles SW of Coyote (limited services), 41 miles NE of Cuba • GPS: Lat 36.100641 Lon -106.723683 • Open: May-Sep • Total sites: 5 • RV sites: 5 • Max RV Length: 20 • RV fee: Free • No water • Vault toilets • Activities: Hiking, fishing • Elevation: 8271

## Dulce

**Buzzard Park** (Carson NF) • Agency: US Forest Service • Tel: 505-632-2956 • Location: 18 miles W of Dulce (limited services), 44 miles W of Chama • GPS: Lat 36.881061 Lon -107.216887 • Open: May-Nov • Total sites: 4 • RV sites: 4 • RV fee: Free • No water • No toilets • Elevation: 6975

**Cedar Springs** (Carson NF) • Agency: US Forest Service • Tel: 505-632-2956 • Location: 33 miles SW of Dulce (limited services), 58 miles W of Chama • GPS: Lat 36.671958 Lon -107.253189 • Open: May-Nov • Total sites: 4 • RV sites: 4 • RV fee: Free • No water • No toilets • Elevation: 7461

## Fort Sumner

**Bosque Redondo Lake - NMGF** • Agency: State • Location: 4 miles S of Fort Sumner • GPS: Lat 34.431279 Lon -104.212698 • Open: All year • Total sites: Dispersed • RV sites: Undefined • RV fee: Free • No water • No toilets • Activities: Fishing • Elevation: 3983

## Glenwood

**Bighorn** • Agency: US Forest Service • Tel: 575-539-2481 • Location: In Glenwood (limited services), 60 miles NW of Silver City • GPS: Lat 33.324129 Lon -108.882746 • Open: All year • Stay limit: 14 days • Total sites: 6 • RV sites: 6 • Max RV Length: 30 • RV fee: Free • No water • Vault toilets • Notes: Can walk to town • Elevation: 4833

**Cosmic** (Gila NF) • Agency: US Forest Service • Tel: 575-539-2481 • Location: 13 miles N of Glenwood (limited services), 72 miles NW of Silver City • GPS: Lat 33.480066 Lon -108.922918 • Total sites: 4 • RV sites: 4 • RV fee: Free • No water • Vault toilets • Notes: First International Dark Sky Sanctuary in North America • Elevation: 5363

## Grants

**El Malpais NCA - Joe Skeen** • Agency: Bureau of Land Management • Tel: 505-240-0300 • Location: 17 miles S of Grants • GPS: Lat 34.943585 Lon -107.820616 • Open: All year • Total sites: 11 • RV sites: 10 • RV fee: Free • No water • Vault toilets • Activities: Hiking • Elevation: 6959

**Ojo Redondo** (Cibola NF) • Agency: US Forest Service • Tel: 505-287-8833 • Location: 20 miles W of Grants • GPS: Lat 35.158849 Lon -108.107332 • Open: Jun-Oct • Total sites: 15 • RV sites: 15 • Max RV Length: 22 • RV fee: Free • No water • Vault toilets • Activities: Hiking, mountain biking • Elevation: 8835

## Jal

**Jal City Park** • Agency: Municipal • Tel: 575-395-2620 • Location: In Jal • GPS: Lat 32.101259 Lon -103.191322 • Total sites: 5 • RV sites: 5 • RV fee: Free • Electric sites: 5 • Water available • Flush toilets • Elevation: 3018

## Las Cruces

**Baylor Canyon** • Agency: Bureau of Land Management • Location: 9 miles E of Las Cruces • GPS: Lat 32.346346 Lon -106.609177 • Total sites: Dispersed • RV sites: Undefined • RV fee: Free • No water • No toilets • Activities: Hiking • Elevation: 5183

## Las Vegas

**Johnson Mesa** (Santa Fe NF) • Agency: US Forest Service • Tel: 505-757-6121 • Location: 22 miles NW of Las Vegas • GPS: Lat 35.703394 Lon -105.468662 • Open: Apr-Nov • Total sites: 17 • RV sites: 17 • Max RV Length: 30 • RV fee: Free • No water • Vault toilets • Elevation: 9465

## Lordsburg

**Lordsburg Veterans Park** • Agency: Municipal • Location: 1 mile S of Lordsburg • GPS: Lat 32.332479 Lon -108.721285 • Total sites: 20 • RV sites: 20 • RV fee: Free • Central water • No toilets • Elevation: 4370

## Loving

**Red Road - NMSLO** • Agency: State • Tel: 505-827-5851 • Location: 32 miles E of Loving (limited services), 40 miles E of Carlsbad • GPS: Lat 32.346812 Lon -103.738623 • Total sites: Dispersed • RV sites: Undefined • RV fee: Free • No water • No toilets • Activities: Hunting • Elevation: 3462

## Luna

**Head Of the Ditch** (Apache NF) • Agency: US Forest Service • Tel: 505-547-2612 • Location: 2 miles W of Luna (limited services), 12 miles W of Alpine, AZ • GPS: Lat 33.818745 Lon -108.990777 • Open: All year • Total sites:

12 • RV sites: 4 • Max RV Length: 40 • RV fee: Free • No water • Vault toilets • Elevation: 7244

## Magdalena

**Bear Trap** (Cibola NF) • Agency: US Forest Service • Tel: 505-854-2281 • Location: 27 miles SW of Magdalena (limited services), 53 miles SW of Socorro on I-25 • GPS: Lat 33.883174 Lon -107.514862 • Open: May-Sep • Total sites: 4 • RV sites: 4 • Max RV Length: 20 • RV fee: Free • No water • Vault toilets • Elevation: 8606

**Hughes Mill** (Cibola NF) • Agency: US Forest Service • Tel: 575-854-2281 • Location: 30 miles SW of Magdalena (limited services), 56 miles SW of Socorro on I-25 • GPS: Lat 33.857247 Lon -107.540276 • Open: May-Oct • Total sites: 2 • RV sites: 2 (also dispersed sites) • Max RV Length: 20 • RV fee: Free • No water • Vault toilets • Elevation: 8274

**Water Canyon** (Cibola NF) • Agency: US Forest Service • Tel: 505-854-2381 • Location: 16 miles SE of Magdalena (limited services), 20 miles W of Socorro on I-25 • GPS: Lat 34.024619 Lon -107.133125 • Open: Mar-Nov • Total sites: 16 • RV sites: 16 • Max RV Length: 20 • RV fee: Free • No water • Vault toilets • Elevation: 6870

## Maxwell

**Maxwell NWR - #13 Lake** • Agency: US Fish & Wildlife • Tel: 575-375-2331 • Location: 5 miles NW of Maxwell (limited services), 24 miles S of Raton on I-25 • GPS: Lat 36.581259 Lon -104.589449 • Open: Mar-Oct • Total sites: Dispersed • RV sites: Undefined • RV fee: Free • No water • Vault toilets • Notes: 3-day limit • Activities: Fishing, non-power boating • Elevation: 6053

## Mayhill

**James Canyon** (Lincoln NF) • Agency: US Forest Service • Location: 2 miles NW of Mayhill (limited services), 16 miles W of Cloudcroft • GPS: Lat 32.904536 Lon -105.504667 • Open: All year • Total sites: 5 • RV sites: 5 • Max RV Length: 16 • RV fee: Free • No water • Vault toilets • Elevation: 6801

## Mimbres

**Black Canyon Lower** (Gila NF) • Agency: US Forest Service • Tel: 575-536-2250 • Location: 30 miles N of Mimbres (limited services), 50 miles N of Bayard & Santa Clara • GPS: Lat 33.184064 Lon -108.035107 • Open: Apr-Nov • Stay limit: 14 days • Total sites: 3 • RV sites: 3 • RV fee: Free • No water • Vault toilets • Elevation: 6765

**Forks** (Gila NF) • Agency: US Forest Service • Tel: 575-536-2250 • Location: 35 miles N of Mimbres (limited services), 38 miles N of Silver City • GPS: Lat 33.183819 Lon -108.205823 • Total sites: 7 • RV sites: 7 • RV fee: Free • No water • Vault toilets • Elevation: 5571

**Gallinas Upper** (Gila NF) • Agency: US Forest Service • Tel: 575-388-8201 • Location: 18 miles E of Mimbres (limited services), 26 miles NE of Bayard & Santa Clara • GPS: Lat 32.898743 Lon -107.823695 • Open: All year • Stay limit: 14 days • Total sites: 10 • RV sites: 10 • RV fee: Free • No water • Vault toilets • Activities: Hiking, mountain biking, equestrian area • Elevation: 7024

**Iron Creek** (Gila NF) • Agency: US Forest Service • Tel: 505-536-2250 • Location: 20 miles E of Mimbres (limited services), 28 miles NE of Bayard & Santa Clara • GPS: Lat 32.909123 Lon -107.805018 • Open: Mar-Oct • Stay limit: 14 days • Total sites: 15 • RV sites: 15 • Max RV Length: 17 • RV fee: Free • No water • Vault toilets • Activities: Hiking, mountain biking, equestrian area • Elevation: 7260

**Lower Scorpion** (Gila NF) • Agency: US Forest Service • Tel: 575-536-2250 • Location: 40 miles NW of Mimbres (limited services), 43 miles N of Silver City • GPS: Lat 33.230254 Lon -108.257616 • Total sites: 7 • RV sites: 7 • Max RV Length: 17 • RV fee: Free • No water • Vault toilets • Activities: Fishing, equestrian area • Elevation: 5764

**Railroad Canyon** (Gila NF) • Agency: US Forest Service • Tel: 575-388-8201 • Location: 19 miles W of Mimbres (limited services), 27 miles NE of Bayard & Santa Clara • GPS: Lat 32.908974 Lon -107.816725 • Open: All year • Total sites: 6 • RV sites: 6 • RV fee: Free • No water • Vault toilets • Activities: Hiking • Elevation: 7149

**Rocky Canyon** (Gila NF) • Agency: US Forest Service • Tel: 575-536-2250 • Location: 23 miles N of Mimbres (limited services), 41 miles N of Bayard & Santa Clara • GPS: Lat 33.100174 Lon -108.013248 • Open: Apr-Nov • Total sites: 2 • RV sites: 2 • Max RV Length: 17 • RV fee: Free • No water • Vault toilets • Activities: Hiking, equestrian area • Elevation: 7484

**Upper Scorpion** (Gila NF) • Agency: US Forest Service • Tel: 575-536-2250 • Location: 40 miles N of Mimbres (limited services), 43 miles N of Silver City • GPS: Lat 33.230679 Lon -108.260772 • Total sites: 10 • RV sites: 10 • Max RV Length: 17 • RV fee: Free • Central water (at Visitor Center) • Vault toilets • Activities: Hiking • Elevation: 5840

## Moriarty

**Martinez Road - NMSLO** • Agency: State • Tel: 505-827-5851 • Location: 14 miles E of Moriarty • GPS: Lat 34.997555 Lon -105.786234 • Total sites: Dispersed • RV sites: Undefined • RV fee: Free • No water • No toilets • Activities: Hunting • Elevation: 6746

## Mountainair

**New Canyon** (Cibola NF) • Agency: US Forest Service • Location: 19 miles NW of Mountainair • GPS: Lat 34.671133 Lon -106.410193 • Open: All year • Total sites: 3 • RV sites: 3 • Max RV Length: 18 • RV fee: Free • No water • Vault toilets • Activities: Hiking • Elevation: 7904

## Pecos

**Davis Willow** (Santa Fe NF) • Agency: US Forest Service • Tel: 505-757-6121 • Location: 15 miles N of Pecos • GPS: Lat 35.757409 Lon -105.663266 • Open: Apr-Nov • Total sites: 15 • RV sites: 15 • RV fee: Free • No water • Vault toilets • Elevation: 8114

**Links Tract** (Santa Fe NF) • Agency: US Forest Service • Location: 15 miles N of Pecos • GPS: Lat 35.757152 Lon -105.662069 • Total sites: 12 • RV sites: 12 • Max RV Length: 32 • RV fee: Free • No water • Vault toilets • Elevation: 8176

## Penasco

**Hodges** (Carson NF) • Agency: US Forest Service • Tel: 575-587-2255 • Location: 5 miles S of Penasco (limited services), 24 miles S of Ranchos De Taos • GPS: Lat 36.114022 Lon -105.639376 • Open: May-Oct • Total sites: 8 • RV sites: 8 • RV fee: Free • No water • Vault toilets • Activities: Hiking, mountain biking, fishing • Elevation: 8478

**Trampas Trailhead** (Carson NF) • Agency: US Forest Service • Location: 13 miles S of Penasco (limited services), 46 miles NE of Santa Fe • GPS: Lat 36.044556 Lon -105.673089 • Open: All year • Total sites: 4 • RV sites: 4 • RV fee: Free • No water • Vault toilets • Elevation: 9035

## Pietown

**Jackson City Park** • Agency: Municipal • Location: In Pietown (limited services), 82 miles W of Sccorro on I-25 • GPS: Lat 34.298759 Lon -108.131391 • Open: All year • Stay limit: 3 days • Total sites: 20 • RV sites: 20 • Max RV Length: 25 • RV fee: Free • No water • Vault toilets • Elevation: 7795

## Quemado

**Armijo Springs** (Gila NF) • Agency: US Forest Service • Tel: 575-773-4678 • Location: 20 miles S of Quemado (limited services), 66 miles E of Springville, AZ • GPS: Lat 34.096528 Lon -108.569956 • Open: All year • Stay limit: 14 days • Total sites: 5 • RV sites: 5 • Max RV Length: 40 • RV fee: Free • No water • Vault toilets • Elevation: 7959

**El Caso** (Gila NF) • Agency: US Forest Service • Tel: 505-773-4678 • Location: 20 miles S of Quemado (limited services), 66 miles E of Springville, AZ • GPS: Lat 34.137404 Lon -108.471583 • Open: All year • Stay limit: 14 days • Total sites: 22 • RV sites: 22 • Max RV Length: 20 • RV fee: Free • No water • Vault toilets • Activities: Hiking, mountain biking, fishing, non-power boating, equestrian area • Elevation: 7695

**Valle Tio Vinces** (Gila NF) • Agency: US Forest Service • Tel: 575-773-4678 • Location: 31 miles S of Quemado • GPS: Lat 34.029903 Lon -108.350778 • Open: All year • Stay limit: 14 days • Total sites: 4 • RV sites: 4 • Max RV Length: 40 • RV fee: Free • No water • Vault toilets • Activities: Hiking, mountain biking • Elevation: 8120

## Ramah

**El Morro NM** • Agency: National Park Service • Tel: 505-783-4226 • Location: 12 miles SE of Ramah (limited services), 41 miles W of Grants on I-40 • GPS: Lat 35.036897 Lon -108.336817 • Open: All year • Total sites: 9 • RV sites: 9 • Max RV Length: 27 • RV fee: Free • Central water (no water in winter) • Vault toilets • Activities: Hiking • Elevation: 7209

## Ranchos De Taos

Hwy 518 Scenic Overlook • Agency: State • Location: 11 miles S of Ranchos De Taos • GPS: Lat 36.214456 Lon -105.593185 • Total sites: Dispersed • RV sites: Undefined • RV fee: Free • No water • No toilets • Elevation: 8530

## Reserve

**Aeroplane Mesa** (Gila NF) • Agency: US Forest Service • Tel: 575-533-6231 • Location: 46 miles SE of Reserve (limited services), 103 miles N of Silver City • GPS: Lat 33.417495 Lon -108.441222 • Open: All year • Total sites: 6 • RV sites: 6 • RV fee: Free • No water • Vault toilets • Elevation: 8022

**Apache Creek** (Gila NF) • Agency: US Forest Service • Tel: 575-533-6231 • Location: 13 miles NE of Reserve (limited services), 72 miles E of Springerville, AZ • GPS: Lat 33.828564 Lon -108.627903 • Open: May-Nov • Stay limit: 14 days • Total sites: 20 • RV sites: 20 • RV fee: Free • No water • Vault toilets • Elevation: 6460

**Cottonwood** (Gila NF) • Agency: US Forest Service • Tel: 575-539-2481 • Location: 13 miles NE of Reserve (limited services), 83 miles NW of Silver City • GPS: Lat 33.618849 Lon -108.894143 • Open: Apr-Nov • Stay limit: 14

days • Total sites: 4 • RV sites: 4 • Max RV Length: 22 • RV fee: Free • No water • Vault toilets • Elevation: 5813

## Roy

**Mills Canyon Rim** (Cibola NF) • Agency: US Forest Service • Tel: 505-374-9652 • Location: 16 miles NW of Roy (limited services), 40 miles SE of Springer on I-25 • GPS: Lat 36.071977 Lon -104.350478 • Total sites: 6 • RV sites: 6 • RV fee: Free • No water • Vault toilets • Activities: Equestrian area • Elevation: 5738

## San Jon

**San Jon Municipal Park** • Agency: Municipal • Location: In San Jon (limited services), 22 miles E of Tucumcari on I-40 • GPS: Lat 35.107286 Lon -103.331701 • Open: All year • Total sites: 10 • RV sites: 10 • Max RV Length: 30 • RV fee: Free • Flush toilets • Elevation: 4034

## Santa Cruz

**Borrego Mesa** (Santa Fe NF) • Agency: US Forest Service • Tel: 505-753-7331 • Location: 17 miles E of Santa Cruz • GPS: Lat 35.979192 Lon -105.772525 • Open: All year • Total sites: 8 • RV sites: 8 • Max RV Length: 14 • RV fee: Free • No water • No toilets • Activities: Hiking, equestrian area • Elevation: 8802

## Santa Fe

**Aspen Basin** (Santa Fe NF) • Agency: US Forest Service • Tel: 505-753-7331 • Location: 14 miles NE of Santa Fe • GPS: Lat 35.795966 Lon -105.805287 • Open: All year • Total sites: 10 • RV sites: 10 • RV fee: Free • No water • Vault toilets • Elevation: 10358

## Silver City

**Cherry Creek** (Gila NF) • Agency: US Forest Service • Tel: 575-388-8201 • Location: 12 miles N of Silver City • GPS: Lat 32.914239 Lon -108.224214 • Open: All year • Stay limit: 14 days • Total sites: 12 • RV sites: 12 • Max RV Length: 17 • RV fee: Free • No water • Vault toilets • Elevation: 6864

**McMillan** (Gila NF) • Agency: US Forest Service • Tel: 575-388-8201 • Location: 12 miles N of Silver City • GPS: Lat 32.924001 Lon -108.213686 • Open: Apr-Oct • Stay limit: 14 days • Total sites: 3 • RV sites: 3 • Max RV Length: 17 • RV fee: Free • No water • Vault toilets • Elevation: 7034

## Socorro

**The Box** • Agency: Bureau of Land Management • Tel: 505-835-0412 • Location: 7 miles SW of Socorro • GPS: Lat 34.001755 Lon -106.992534 • Open: All year • Total sites: Dispersed • RV sites: Undefined • RV fee: Free • No water • Vault toilets • Activities: Rock climbing • Elevation: 5464

## Springer

**Springer Lake Wildlife Area - NMGF** • Agency: State • Tel: 575-445-2311 • Location: 4 miles NW of Springer • GPS: Lat 36.407424 Lon -104.649986 • Total sites: Dispersed • RV sites: Undefined • RV fee: Free • No water • Vault toilets • Activities: Hiking, fishing • Elevation: 5922

## Taos

**Cuchilla del Medio** (Carson NF) • Agency: US Forest Service • Tel: 575-586-0520 • Location: 11 miles N of Taos • GPS: Lat 36.559253 Lon -105.535424 • Open: May-Sep • Total sites: 3 • RV sites: 3 • Max RV Length: 16 • RV fee: Free • No water • Vault toilets • Activities: Hiking, fishing • Elevation: 8064

**Lower Hondo** (Carson NF) • Agency: US Forest Service • Tel: 575-586-0520 • Location: 10 miles N of Taos • GPS: Lat 36.548528 Lon -105.549558 • Open: May-Oct • Total sites: 4 • RV sites: 4 • Max RV Length: 16 • RV fee: Free • No water • Vault toilets • Activities: Hiking, fishing • Elevation: 7861

## Tatum

**Randolph Rampy Park** • Agency: Municipal • Tel: 575-398-4633 • Location: In Tatum • GPS: Lat 33.258939 Lon -103.311799 • Open: All year • Total sites: 5 • RV sites: 5 • RV fee: Free • Electric sites: 5 • Water at site • No toilets • Notes: 3-day limit • Elevation: 4001

## Tres Piedras

**El Rito Creek** (Carson NF) • Agency: US Forest Service • Tel: 575-581-4554 • Location: 19 miles W of Tres Piedras (limited services), 50 miles S of Antonito, CO • GPS: Lat 36.579414 Lon -106.168605 • Open: Apr-Nov • Total sites: 12 • RV sites: 12 • RV fee: Free • No water • Vault toilets • Activities: Fishing • Elevation: 8091

**Laguna Larga** (Carson NF) • Agency: US Forest Service • Tel: 575-758-8678 • Location: 24 miles N of Tres Piedras (limited services), 33 miles S of Antonito, CO • GPS: Lat 36.884181 Lon -106.108633 • Open: May-Oct • Total sites: 4 • RV sites: 4 • RV fee: Free • No water • No toilets • Activities: Fishing, non-power boating • Elevation: 9003

**Rio de Los Pinos** (Carson NF) • Agency: US Forest Service • Tel: 575-758-8678 • Location: 40 miles NW of Tres Piedras (limited services), 16 miles SW of Antonito, CO • GPS: Lat 36.955753 Lon -106.178232 • Open: Jun-Sep • Total sites: 4 • RV sites: 4 • Max RV Length: 16 • RV fee: Free • No water • Vault toilets • Activities: Hiking, mountain biking, fishing • Elevation: 8290

**Rio de los Pinos SWFA** • Agency: State • Location: 36 miles N of Tres Piedras (limited services), 12 miles SW from Antonito, CO • GPS: Lat 36.952986 Lon -106.120086 • Total sites: Dispersed • RV sites: Undefined • RV fee: Free • No water • Vault toilets • Elevation: 8189

## Truth or Consequences

**Luna Park** (Cibola NF) • Agency: US Forest Service • Tel: 575-854-2281 • Location: 31 miles N of Truth or Consequences • GPS: Lat 33.495904 Lon -107.415317 • Open: Mar-Nov • Total sites: 3 • RV sites: 3 • Max RV Length: 20 • RV fee: Free • No water • Vault toilets • Elevation: 6873

## Whites City

**Chosa** • Agency: Bureau of Land Management • Location: 7 miles S of Whites City (limited services), 21 miles SW of Carlsbad • GPS: Lat 32.088528 Lon -104.432161 • Stay limit: 14 days • Total sites: Dispersed • RV sites: Undefined (room for 25 RV's) • RV fee: Free • No water • No toilets • Elevation: 3744

## Williamsburg

**Old Ladder Ranch Road** • Agency: Bureau of Land Management • Location: 2 miles S of Williamsburg • GPS: Lat 33.100689 Lon -107.285217 • Total sites: Dispersed • RV sites: Undefined • RV fee: Free • No water • No toilets • Elevation: 4227

# Oregon

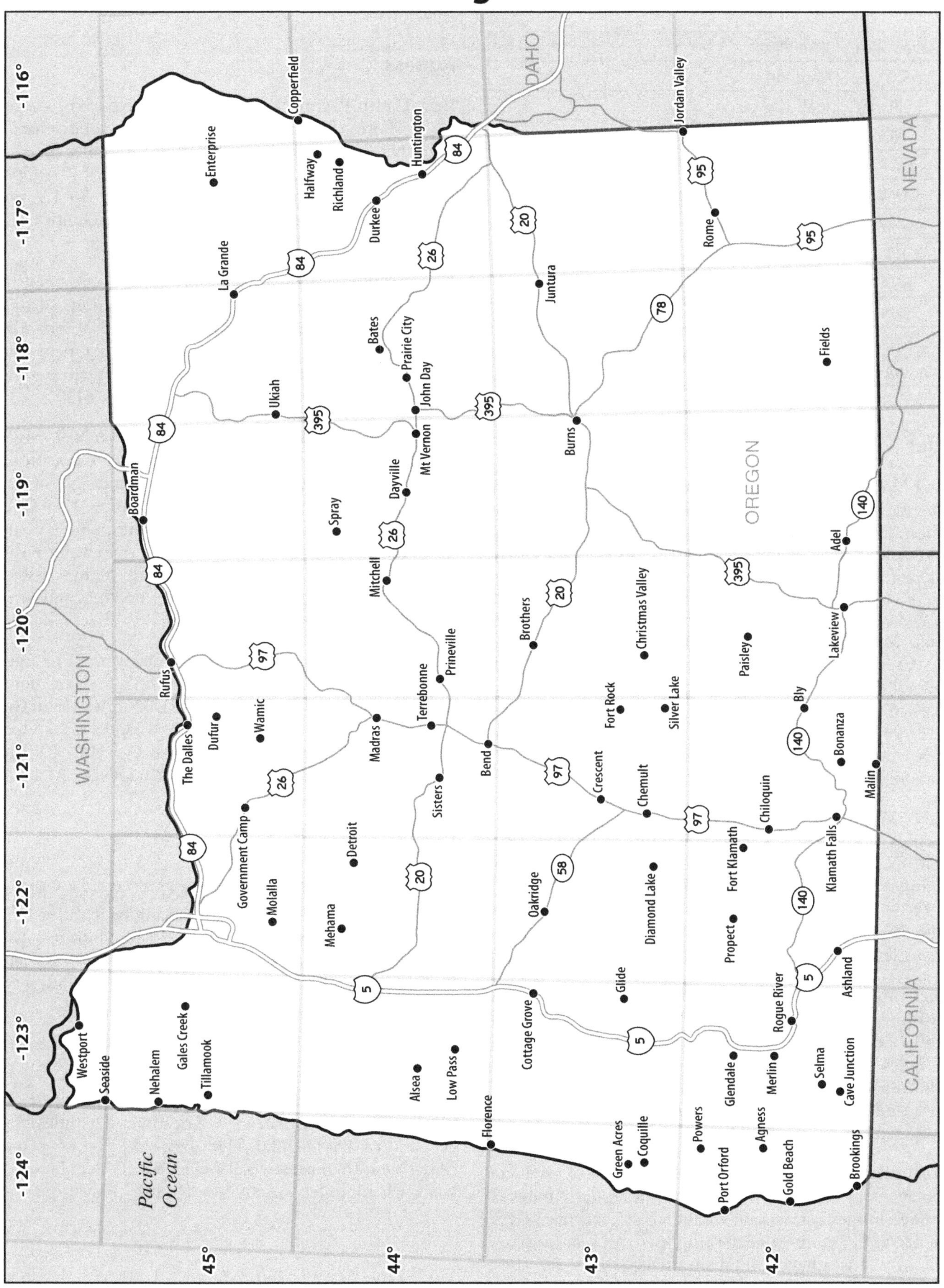
WASHINGTON
NEVADA
CALIFORNIA
OREGON
Pacific Ocean
-116°
-117°
-118°
-119°
-120°
-121°
-122°
-123°
-124°
45°
44°
43°
42°
Copperfield
Enterprise
Halfway
Richland
Huntington
Durkee
La Grande
Jordan Valley
Rome
Juntura
Bates
Prairie City
John Day
Ukiah
Mt Vernon
Dayville
Spray
Mitchell
Burns
Fields
Adel
Boardman
Rufus
The Dalles
Dufur
Wamic
Madras
Terrebonne
Prineville
Brothers
Christmas Valley
Paisley
Lakeview
Fort Rock
Silver Lake
Bly
Bonanza
Malin
Bend
Crescent
Chemult
Chiloquin
Klamath Falls
Fort Klamath
Sisters
Government Camp
Detroit
Molalla
Mehama
Oakridge
Diamond Lake
Propect
Glide
Ashland
Rogue River
Cottage Grove
Westport
Seaside
Nehalem
Gales Creek
Tillamook
Alsea
Low Pass
Florence
Green Acres
Coquille
Powers
Port Orford
Glendale
Merlin
Agness
Gold Beach
Selma
Cave Junction
Brookings
84
26
20
95
78
395
97
140
58
5

# Oregon — Camping Areas

| Abbreviation | Description |
|---|---|
| CG | Campground |
| IP | Idaho Power |
| NF | National Forest |
| ODF | Oregon Department of Forestry |
| ODFW | Oregon Department of Fish and Wildlife |
| OHV | Off-Highway Vehicle |
| RA | Recreation Area |
| RNA | Research Natural Area |
| SNA | State Natural Area |
| SWA | State Wildlife Area |
| WA | Wildlife Area |

## Adel

**Hart Mountain National Antelope Refuge - Camp Hart Mt** • Agency: US Fish & Wildlife • Tel: 509-488-3140 • Location: 33 miles N of Adel (limited services), 52 miles NE of Lakeview • GPS: Lat 42.542762 Lon -119.773364 • Open: All year • Total sites: 9 • RV sites: 9 • RV fee: Free • No water • Vault toilets • Elevation: 4594

**Hart Mountain National Antelope Refuge - Guano Creek** • Agency: US Fish & Wildlife • Tel: 509-488-3140 • Location: 36 miles N of Adel (limited services), 67 miles NE of Lakeview • GPS: Lat 42.432032 Lon -119.729728 • Open: All year • Total sites: Dispersed • RV sites: Undefined • RV fee: Free • No water • No toilets • Elevation: 6228

**Hart Mountain National Antelope Refuge - Hot Springs** • Agency: US Fish & Wildlife • Tel: 509-488-3140 • Location: 46 miles NE of Adel (limited services), 67 miles NE of Lakeview • GPS: Lat 42.502463 Lon -119.689771 • Open: All year • Total sites: Dispersed • RV sites: Undefined • RV fee: Free • No water • Vault toilets • Elevation: 5947

**Hart Mountain National Antelope Refuge - Post Meadows** • Agency: US Fish & Wildlife • Tel: 509-488-3140 • Location: 36 miles NE of Adel (limited services), 68 miles NE of Lakeview • GPS: Lat 42.412683 Lon -119.718516 • Open: All year • Total sites: Dispersed • RV sites: Undefined • RV fee: Free • No water • No toilets • Elevation: 5970

**Sunstone Collection Area** • Agency: Bureau of Land Management • Tel: 541-947-2177 • Location: 42 miles N of Adel (limited services), 65 miles NE of Lakeview • GPS: Lat 42.723815 Lon -119.860471 • Open: All year (impassable in wet weather) • Total sites: Dispersed • RV sites: Undefined • RV fee: Free • No water • Vault toilets • Elevation: 4632

## Agness

**Bear Camp Pasture** (Rogue River-Siskiyou NF) • Agency: US Forest Service • Tel: 541-471 6514 • Location: 20 miles NE of Agness (limited services), 48 miles NE Gold Beach • GPS: Lat 42.627158 Lon -123.830147 • Open: May-Sep • Stay limit: 14 days • Total sites: 1 • RV sites: 1 • RV fee: Free • No water • Vault toilets • Activities: Hiking • Elevation: 4806

**Grassy Flats** (Rogue River-Siskiyou NF) • Agency: US Forest Service • Tel: 541-471 6514 • Location: 14 miles E of Agness (limited services), 41 miles NE of Gold Beach • GPS: Lat 42.553 Lon -123.919 • Open: May-Oct • Stay limit: 14 days • Total sites: 5 • RV sites: 5 • RV fee: Free • No water • No toilets • Elevation: 4429

**Oak Flat/Gravel Bar** (Rogue River-Siskiyou NF) • Agency: US Forest Service • Tel: 541-247-3600 • Location: 4 miles S of Agness (limited services), 30 miles NE of Gold Beach • GPS: Lat 42.517147 Lon -124.039712 • Open: All year • Stay limit: 14 days • Total sites: 15 • RV sites: 15 • Max RV Length: 18 • RV fee: Free • No water • Vault toilets • Activities: Hiking, mountain biking, fishing, swimming, motor sports, non-power boating, equestrian area • Elevation: 364

**Rogue River - Illahe** (Rogue River-Siskiyou NF) • Agency: US Forest Service • Tel: 541-479-3735 • Location: 6 miles N of Agness (limited services), 33 miles NE of Gold Beach • GPS: Lat 42.626199 Lon -124.057353 • Open: May-Sep • Stay limit: 14 days • Total sites: 14 • RV sites: 9 • RV fee: Free • Central water • Flush toilets • Activities: Hiking • Elevation: 341

## Alsea

**Hubert K McBee Memorial CG** • Agency: Miscellaneous • Tel: 541-424-3112 • Location: 9 miles SE of Alsea (limited services), 16 miles W of Monroe • GPS: Lat 44.331538 Lon -123.501264 • Total sites: 9 • RV sites: 9 • RV fee: Free • No water • Vault toilets • Notes: Reservation required • Activities: Hiking • Elevation: 781

## Ashland

**Mt Ashland** (Klamath NF) • Agency: US Forest Service • Tel: 530-493-2243 • Location: 22 miles S of Ashland • GPS: Lat 42.075548 Lon -122.714284 • Open: May-Oct • Total sites: 9 • RV sites: 9 • RV fee: Free • No water • Vault toilets • Activities: Hiking • Elevation: 6795

## Bates

**Head O Boulder Forest Camp** (Malheur NF) • Agency: US Forest Service • Tel: 541-575-3000 • Location: 28 miles NW of Bates (limited services), 40 miles N of Prairie City • GPS: Lat 44.755 Lon -118.692 • Stay limit: 14 days • Total sites: 3 • RV sites: 3 • RV fee: Free • No water • Vault toilets • Elevation: 7182

## Bend

**China Hat** (Deschutes NF) • Agency: US Forest Service • Tel: 541-383-5300 • Location: 35 miles SE of Bend • GPS: Lat 43.657625 Lon -121.036915 • Open: Apr-Oct • Total sites: 13 • RV sites: 13 • Max RV Length: 30 • RV fee: Free • No water • Vault toilets • Activities: Hiking, motor sports • Elevation: 5079

**Mayfield Pond** • Agency: Bureau of Land Management • Tel: 541-416-6700 • Location: 8 miles E of Bend • GPS: Lat 44.083311 Lon -121.130578 • Total sites: Dispersed • RV sites: Undefined • RV fee: Free • No water • No toilets • Notes: Lots of shooting here • Elevation: 3304

**North Millican OHV - Cinder Pit** • Agency: Bureau of Land Management • Tel: 541-416-6700 • Location: 30 miles SE of Bend • GPS: Lat 43.931147 Lon -120.934254 • Open: All year • Total sites: Dispersed • RV sites: Undefined • RV fee: Free • No water • No toilets • Activities: Hiking, motor sports • Elevation: 4220

**North Millican OHV - North Horse Camp** • Agency: Bureau of Land Management • Tel: 541-416-6700 • Location: 21 miles SE of Bend • GPS: Lat 43.899473 Lon -120.928866 • Open: All year • Total sites: Dispersed • RV sites: Undefined • RV fee: Free • No water • No toilets • Activities: Hiking, motor sports • Elevation: 4427

**North Millican OHV - ODOT Pit** • Agency: Bureau of Land Management • Tel: 541-416-6700 • Location: 23 miles SE of Bend • GPS: Lat 43.876213 Lon -120.895928 • Open: All year • Total sites: Dispersed • RV sites: Undefined • RV fee: Free • No water • No toilets • Activities: Hiking, motor sports • Elevation: 4406

**Road 25 Trailhead** (Deschutes NF) • Agency: US Forest Service • Location: 26 miles SE of Bend • GPS: Lat 43.789517 Lon -121.027483 • Total sites: 19 • RV sites: 19 • RV fee: Free • No water • Vault toilets • Activities: Hiking, motor sports • Elevation: 4790

**South Millican OHV - Evan Wells** • Agency: Bureau of Land Management • Tel: 541-416-6700 • Location: 26 miles SE of Bend • GPS: Lat 43.832128 Lon -121.016717 • Open: All year • Total sites: Dispersed • RV sites: Undefined • RV fee: Free • No water • No toilets • Activities: Hiking, motor sports • Elevation: 4357

**South Millican OHV - Ford Road** • Agency: Bureau of Land Management • Tel: 541-416-6700 • Location: 25 miles SE of Bend • GPS: Lat 43.874044 Lon -120.987088 • Open: All year • Total sites: Dispersed • RV sites: Undefined • RV fee: Free • No water • No toilets • Activities: Hiking, motor sports • Elevation: 4229

**South Millican OHV - South Horse Camp** • Agency: Bureau of Land Management • Tel: 541-416-6700 • Location: 18 miles SE of Bend • GPS: Lat 43.905068 Lon -121.011998 • Open: All year • Total sites: Dispersed • RV sites: Undefined • RV fee: Free • No water • No toilets • Activities: Hiking, motor sports • Elevation: 4358

## Bly

**Corral Creek** (Fremont-Winema NF) • Agency: US Forest Service • Tel: 541-943-3114 • Location: 17 miles NE of Bly (limited services), 44 miles NW of Lakeview • GPS: Lat 42.457116 Lon -120.784746 • Open: All year (reduced services Oct-May) • Total sites: 6 • RV sites: 6 • RV fee: Free • No water • Vault toilets • Activities: Hiking, fishing • Elevation: 5955

**Gerber RA - Barnes Valley** • Agency: Bureau of Land Management • Tel: 541-947-2177 • Location: 23 miles S of Bly (limited services), 47 miles W of Lakeview • GPS: Lat 42.176164 Lon -121.060695 • Open: All year • Total sites: Dispersed • RV sites: Undefined • RV fee: Free • No water • Vault toilets • Elevation: 4851

**Gerber RA - Basin** • Agency: Bureau of Land Management • Tel: 541-947-2177 • Location: 28 miles S of Bly (limited services), 45 miles W of Lakeview • GPS: Lat 42.119429 Lon -121.007431 • Open: All year • Total sites: Dispersed • RV sites: Undefined • RV fee: Free • No water • Vault toilets • Elevation: 5258

**Gerber RA - Pitch Log Creek** • Agency: Bureau of Land Management • Tel: 541-947-2177 • Location: 22 miles S of Bly (limited services), 42 miles W of Lakeview • GPS: Lat 42.159267 Lon -121.007028 • Open: All year • Total sites: Dispersed • RV sites: Undefined • RV fee: Free • No water • No toilets • Elevation: 5138

**Gerber RA - Stan H Spring** • Agency: Bureau of Land Management • Tel: 541-947-2177 • Location: 18 miles SW of Bly (limited services), 41 miles E of Klamath Falls • GPS: Lat 42.229975 Lon -121.139046 • Open: All year • Total sites: Dispersed • RV sites: Undefined • RV fee: Free • No water • Vault toilets • Elevation: 4855

**Gerber RA - The Potholes** • Agency: Bureau of Land Management • Tel: 541-947-2177 • Location: 20 miles SW of Bly (limited services), 42 miles E of Klamath Falls • GPS: Lat 42.218683 Lon -121.150489 • Open: All year • Total sites: Dispersed • RV sites: Undefined • RV fee: Free • No water • Vault toilets • Elevation: 4942

**Gerber RA - Upper Midway** • Agency: Bureau of Land Management • Tel: 541-947-2177 • Location: 28 miles S of Bly (limited services), 46 miles W of Lakeview • GPS: Lat 42.113348 Lon -121.024898 • Open: All year • Total sites: Dispersed • RV sites: Undefined • RV fee: Free • No water • Vault toilets • Elevation: 5194

**Gerber RA - Wildhorse** • Agency: Bureau of Land Management • Tel: 541-947-2177 • Location: 27 miles S of Bly (limited services), 45 miles W of Lakeview • GPS: Lat 42.125849 Lon -121.012685 • Total sites: Dispersed • RV sites: Undefined • RV fee: Free • No water • Vault toilets • Elevation: 5214

**Holbrook Reservoir** (Fremont-Winema NF) • Agency: US Forest Service • Tel: 541-353-2427 • Location: 20 miles SE of Bly (limited services), 36 miles NW of Lakeview • GPS: Lat 42.265477 Lon -120.853135 • Open: All year (reduced services Oct-May) • Total sites: 1 • RV sites: 1 • RV fee: Free • No water • Vault toilets • Activities: Fishing, swimming, power boating, non-power boating • Elevation: 5439

## Boardman

**Threemile Canyon/Quesnel** • Agency: Corps of Engineers • Tel: 541-506-7819 • Location: 13 miles W of Boardman • GPS: Lat 45.811293 Lon -119.970087 • Total sites: Dispersed • RV sites: Undefined • RV fee: Free • No water • Vault toilets • Activities: Fishing, power boating • Elevation: 275

## Bonanza

**Gerber RA - Miller Creek** • Agency: Bureau of Land Management • Tel: 541-947-2177 • Location: 20 miles E of Bonanza (limited services), 40 miles E of Klamath Falls • GPS: Lat 42.184356 Lon -121.130149 • Open: All year • Total sites: Dispersed • RV sites: Undefined • RV fee: Free • No water • Vault toilets • Elevation: 4844

## Brookings

**Little Redwood** (Rogue River-Siskiyou NF) • Agency: US Forest Service • Tel: 541-247-3600 • Location: 13 miles NE of Brookings • GPS: Lat 42.154053 Lon -124.145752 • Open: May-Sep • Stay limit: 14 days • Total sites: 12 • RV sites: 12 • Max RV Length: 25 • RV fee: Free • Central water • Vault toilets • Elevation: 190

## Brothers

**Double Cabin** (Ochoco NF) • Agency: US Forest Service • Tel: 541-416-6500 • Location: 26 miles NE of Brothers (limited services), 44 miles SE of Prineville • GPS: Lat 44.029298 Lon -120.320336 • Open: All year • Stay limit: 14 days • Total sites: 5 • RV sites: 5 • RV fee: Free • No water • Vault toilets • Elevation: 5246

## Burns

**Alder Springs Camp** (Malheur NF) • Agency: US Forest Service • Tel: 541-575-3000 • Location: 41 miles NW of Burns • GPS: Lat 43.877429 Lon -119.505422 • Open: May-Sep • Stay limit: 14 days • Total sites: 3 • RV sites: 3 • RV fee: Free • No water • Vault toilets • Elevation: 5489

## Cave Junction

**Josephine** (Rogue River-Siskiyou NF) • Agency: US Forest Service • Tel: 541-592-4000 • Location: 7 miles NW of Cave Junction • GPS: Lat 42.242434 Lon -123.686041 • Open: All year • Stay limit: 14 days • Total sites: 6 • RV sites: 6 • RV fee: Free • No water • Vault toilets • Elevation: 1204

## Chemult

**Corral Springs** (Fremont-Winema NF) • Agency: US Forest Service • Tel: 541-365-7001 • Location: 5 miles NW of Chemult (limited services), 34 miles SW of LaPine • GPS: Lat 43.252518 Lon -121.822121 • Open: All year (reduced services Oct-May) • Total sites: 5 • RV sites: 5 • Max RV Length: 50 • RV fee: Free • No water • Vault toilets • Activities: Hiking, mountain biking, hunting • Elevation: 4878

## Chiloquin

**Scott Creek** (Fremont-Winema NF) • Agency: US Forest Service • Tel: 541-365-7001 • Location: 27 miles N of Chiloquin (limited services), 51 miles N of Klamath Falls • GPS: Lat 42.885341 Lon -121.924226 • Open: All year (reduced services Oct-May) • Total sites: 6 • RV sites: 6 • RV fee: Free • No water • Vault toilets • Activities: Motor sports • Elevation: 4710

## Christmas Valley

**Christmas Valley Sand Dunes - Junipers** • Agency: Bureau of Land Management • Tel: 541-947-2177 • Location: 20 miles NE of Christmas Valley (limited services), 78 miles SE of Bend • GPS: Lat 43.352751 Lon -120.45185 • Total sites: Dispersed • RV sites: Undefined • RV fee: Free • No water • No toilets • Activities: Motor sports • Elevation: 4301

**Lost Forest RNA - North Dunes 1** • Agency: Bureau of Land Management • Tel: 541-947-2177 • Location: 24 miles NE of Christmas Valley (limited services), 84 miles SE of Bend • GPS: Lat 43.345923 Lon -120.367678 • Total sites: Dispersed • RV sites: Undefined • RV fee: Free • No water • Activities: Hiking • Elevation: 4304

**Lost Forest RNA - North Dunes 2** • Agency: Bureau of Land Management • Tel: 541-947-2177 • Location: 23 miles NE of Christmas Valley (limited services), 82 miles SE of Bend • GPS: Lat 43.354543 Lon -120.385034 • Total sites: Dispersed • RV sites: Undefined • RV fee: Free • No water • Activities: Hiking • Elevation: 4301

**Lost Forest RNA - Road 6121** • Agency: Bureau of Land Management • Tel: 541-947-2177 • Location: 26 miles NE of Christmas Valley (limited services), 88 miles SE of Bend • GPS: Lat 43.342445 Lon -120.308821 • Total sites: Dispersed • RV sites: Undefined • RV fee: Free • No water • Activities: Hiking • Elevation: 4498

**Lost Forest RNA - Road 6121** • Agency: Bureau of Land Management • Tel: 541-947-2177 • Location: 33 miles NE of Christmas Valley (limited services), 77 miles SE of Bend • GPS: Lat 43.394291 Lon -120.260598 • Total sites: Dispersed • RV sites: Undefined • RV fee: Free • No water • Activities: Hiking • Elevation: 4603

**Lost Forest RNA - Road 6141** • Agency: Bureau of Land Management • Tel: 541-947-2177 • Location: 26 miles NE of Christmas Valley (limited services), 84 miles SE of Bend • GPS: Lat 43.380766 Lon -120.363897 • Total sites: Dispersed • RV sites: Undefined • RV fee: Free • No water • Activities: Hiking • Elevation: 4478

**Lost Forest RNA - Road 6141A** • Agency: Bureau of Land Management • Tel: 541-947-2177 • Location: 29 miles NE of Christmas Valley (limited services), 76 miles SE of Bend • GPS: Lat 43.393516 Lon -120.305474 • Total sites: Dispersed • RV sites: Undefined • RV fee: Free • No water • Activities: Hiking • Elevation: 4560

**Lost Forest RNA - Road 6151 East** • Agency: Bureau of Land Management • Tel: 541-947-2177 • Location: 28 miles NE of Christmas Valley (limited services), 87 miles SE of Bend • GPS: Lat 43.363108 Lon -120.281817 • Total sites: Dispersed • RV sites: Undefined • RV fee: Free • No water • Activities: Hiking • Elevation: 4626

**Lost Forest RNA - Road 6151 West** • Agency: Bureau of Land Management • Tel: 541-947-2177 • Location: 24 miles NE of Christmas Valley (limited services), 83 miles SE of Bend • GPS: Lat 43.359873 Lon -120.370591 • Total sites: Dispersed • RV sites: Undefined • RV fee: Free • No water • Activities: Hiking • Elevation: 4321

## Copperfield

**Copper Creek** (Snake River) • Agency: Bureau of Land Management • Tel: 541-523-1256 • Location: 9 miles NE of Copperfield (limited services), 26 miles NE of Halfway • GPS: Lat 45.079317 Lon -116.785996 • Open: All year • Total sites: 8 • RV sites: 2 • RV fee: Free • No water • Vault toilets • Activities: Hiking, fishing, power boating, non-power boating • Elevation: 1718

**Hells Canyon Reservoir - Airstrip** (Snake River) • Agency: Bureau of Land Management • Tel: 541-473-3144 • Location: 3 miles N of Copperfield (limited services), 20 miles NE of Halfway • GPS: Lat 45.010676 Lon -116.849156 • Total sites: 12 • RV sites: 12 • RV fee: Free • No water • Vault toilets • Elevation: 1705

**Hells Canyon Reservoir - Bob's Creek** (Snake River) • Agency: Bureau of Land Management • Tel: 541-473-3144 • Location: 2 miles N of Copperfield (limited services), 19 miles NE of Halfway • GPS: Lat 44.998042 Lon -116.849666 • Total sites: 13 • RV sites: 13 • RV fee: Free • No water • Vault toilets • Activities: Non-power boating • Elevation: 1706

**Hells Canyon Reservoir - Westfall** (Snake River) • Agency: Bureau of Land Management • Tel: 541-473-3144 • Location: 1 mile N of Copperfield (limited services), 18 miles NE of Halfway • GPS: Lat 44.990557 Lon -116.854616 • Total sites: 15 • RV sites: 15 • RV fee: Free • No water • Vault toilets • Elevation: 1718

## Coquille

**Park Creek Recreation Site** • Agency: Bureau of Land Management • Tel: 541-756-0100 • Location: 23 miles NE of Coquille • GPS: Lat 43.245609 Lon -123.895221 • Open: Jun-Sep • Total sites: 15 • RV sites: 15 • RV fee: Free • No water • Vault toilets • Activities: Hiking, fishing, swimming • Elevation: 732

## Cottage Grove

**Hobo Forest Camp** (Umpqua NF) • Agency: US Forest Service • Tel: 541-957-3200 • Location: 25 miles SE of Cottage Grove • GPS: Lat 43.647035 Lon -122.667811 • Open: All year (no services in winter) • Stay limit: 14 days • Total sites: 4 • RV sites: 4 • Max RV Length: 16 • RV fee: Free • No water • Vault toilets • Elevation: 2113

**Mineral Forest Camp** (Umpqua NF) • Agency: US Forest Service • Tel: 541-957-3200 • Location: 27 miles SE of Cottage Grove • GPS: Lat 43.582621 Lon -122.713668 • Open: All year (reduced services Sep-May) • Stay limit: 14 days • Total sites: 3 • RV sites: 3 • RV fee: Free • No water • Vault toilets • Elevation: 1913

## Crescent

**Lava Flow** (Deschutes-Ochoco NF) • Agency: US Forest Service • Location: 18 miles NW of Crescent (limited services), 36 miles W of LaPine • GPS: Lat 43.622943 Lon -121.820543 • Open: Apr-Oct • Total sites: 6 • RV sites: 6 • Max RV Length: 60 • RV fee: Free • No water • Vault toilets • Activities: Fishing, power boating, non-power boating • Elevation: 4475

## Dayville

**Frazier** (Ochoco NF) • Agency: US Forest Service • Tel: 541-416-6500 • Location: 33 miles S of Dayville (limited services), 63 miles SW of John Day • GPS: Lat 44.220865 Lon -119.576757 • Open: May-Sep • Stay limit: 14 days • Total sites: 10 • RV sites: 9 • RV fee: Free • No water • Vault toilets • Elevation: 4603

**Mud Springs Horse Camp** (Ochoco NF) • Agency: US Forest Service • Tel: 541-416-6500 • Location: 31 miles S of Dayville (limited services), 61 miles SW of John Day • GPS: Lat 44.302028 Lon -119.646881 • Stay limit: 14 days • Total sites: 6 • RV sites: 6 • RV fee: Free • No water • Vault toilets • Activities: Equestrian area (9 corrals) • Elevation: 4938

**Schneider Wilderness Area** • Agency: Bureau of Land Management • Tel: 541-987-2171 • Location: 5 miles S of Dayville (limited services), 35 miles W of John Day • GPS: Lat 44.411117 Lon -119.541756 • Total sites: Dispersed • RV sites: Undefined • RV fee: Free • No water • No toilets • Elevation: 2585

## Detroit

**Breitenbush Lake** (Mt Hood NF) • Agency: US Forest Service • Tel: 541-553-2001 • Location: 53 miles NE of Detroit (limited services), 72 miles NW of Madras • GPS: Lat 44.765107 Lon -121.785687 • Total sites: 20 • RV sites: 20 • RV fee: Free • No water • Vault toilets • Activities: Fishing, non-power boating • Elevation: 5541

## Diamond Lake

**Thielsen Forest Camp** (Umpqua NF) • Agency: US Forest Service • Tel: 541-498-2531 • Location: 5 miles N of Diamond Lake (limited services), 55 miles E of Glide • GPS: Lat 43.256028 Lon -122.164725 • Open: All year • Stay limit: 14 days • Total sites: 4 • RV sites: 4 • Max RV Length: 20 • RV fee: Free • No water • Vault toilets • Elevation: 4531

## Dufur

**Fifteenmile** (Mt Hood NF) • Agency: US Forest Service • Tel: 503-668 1700 • Location: 23 miles SW of Dufur (limited services), 36 miles SW of The Dalles • GPS: Lat 45.350278 Lon -121.472778 • Open: Jun-Sep • Total sites: 3 • RV sites: 3 • Max RV Length: 16 • RV fee: Free • No water • Vault toilets • Activities: Hiking • Elevation: 4610

## Durkee

**Burnt River Canyon #1 Dispersed** • Agency: Bureau of Land Management • Location: 6 miles W of Durkee (limited services), 26 miles SE of Baker City • GPS: Lat 44.575676 Lon -117.539316 • Total sites: Dispersed • RV sites: Undefined • RV fee: Free • No water • No toilets • Activities: Rock climbing • Elevation: 2793

**Burnt River Canyon #2 Dispersed** • Agency: Bureau of Land Management • Location: 13 miles W of Durkee (limited services), 34 miles SE of Baker City • GPS: Lat 44.549977 Lon -117.646749 • Total sites: Dispersed • RV sites: Undefined • RV fee: Free • No water • No toilets • Activities: Rock climbing • Elevation: 3153

**Burnt River Canyon #3 Dispersed** • Agency: Bureau of Land Management • Location: 14 miles W of Durkee (limited services), 35 miles SE of Baker City • GPS: Lat 44.551231 Lon -117.662511 • Total sites: Dispersed • RV sites: Undefined • RV fee: Free • No water • No toilets • Activities: Rock climbing • Elevation: 3189

## Enterprise

**Coyote** (Wallowa-Whitman NF) • Agency: US Forest Service • Tel: 541-523-6391 • Location: 41 miles N of Enterprise • GPS: Lat 45.842285 Lon -117.113281 • Open: Jun-Sep • Stay limit: 14 days • Total sites: 29 • RV sites: 8 • RV fee: Free • No water • Vault toilets • Elevation: 5085

**Dougherty Springs** (Wallowa-Whitman NF) • Agency: US Forest Service • Tel: 541-523-6391 • Location: 46 miles NE of Enterprise • GPS: Lat 45.852295 Lon -117.033203 • Open: Jun-Sep • Stay limit: 14 days • Total sites: 12 • RV sites: 4 • RV fee: Free • No water • Vault toilets • Elevation: 5154

## Fields

**Alvord Desert** • Agency: Bureau of Land Management • Tel: 541-573-4400 • Location: 20 miles N of Fields (limited services), 108 miles SE of Burns • GPS: Lat 42.508042 Lon -118.532443 • Total sites: Dispersed • RV sites: Undefined • RV fee: Free • No water • No toilets • Activities: Hiking, power boating, non-power boating • Elevation: 4044

**Little Cottonwood Creek Canyon** • Agency: Bureau of Land Management • Location: 8 miles S of Fields (limited services), 120 miles S of Burns • GPS: Lat 42.161832 Lon -118.609509 • Total sites: 8 • RV sites: Undefined (dispersed sites along the road) • RV fee: Free • No water • No toilets • Activities: Hiking • Elevation: 4314

**Mann Lake RA** • Agency: Bureau of Land Management • Tel: 541-573-4400 • Location: 40 miles NE of Fields (limited services), 88 miles SE of Burns • GPS: Lat 42.777916 Lon -118.438809 • Open: All year • Total sites: Dispersed • RV sites: Undefined • RV fee: Free • No water • Vault toilets • Activities: Hiking, mountain biking, fishing, swimming, power boating, non-power boating • Elevation: 4206

**Willow Creek Hot Springs** • Agency: Bureau of Land Management • Tel: 541-473-3144 • Location: 34 miles E of Fields (limited services), 138 miles SE of Burns • GPS: Lat 42.275257 Lon -118.265472 • Total sites: 4 • RV sites: 4 • RV fee: Free • No water • Vault toilets • Notes: Clothing optional • Activities: Fishing • Elevation: 4544

## Florence

**Dry Lake Horse Camp** (Siuslaw NF) • Agency: US Forest Service • Tel: 541-563-8400 • Location: 9 miles N of Florence • GPS: Lat 44.096473 Lon -124.070714 • Open: All year • Stay limit: 14 days • Total sites: 3 • RV sites: 3 • RV fee: Free • No water • Vault toilets • Activities: Equestrian area • Elevation: 1099

**North Fork Siuslaw** (Siuslaw NF) • Agency: US Forest Service • Tel: 541-563-8400 • Location: 15 miles NE of Florence • GPS: Lat 44.101526 Lon -123.936956 • Open: May-Sep • Stay limit: 14 days • Total sites: 7 • RV sites: 7 • RV fee: Free • No water • Vault toilets • Elevation: 240

## Fort Klamath

**Sevenmile Marsh Horse Camp** (Fremont-Winema NF) • Agency: US Forest Service • Tel: 541-883-6714 • Location: 8 miles W of Fort Klamath (limited services), 43 miles NW of Klamath Falls • GPS: Lat 42.714375 Lon -122.130955 • Open: Jun-Sep • Total sites: 8 • RV sites: 8 • RV fee: Free • No water • Vault toilets • Activities: Equestrian area • Elevation: 4833

## Fort Rock

**Cabin Lake** (Deschutes NF) • Agency: US Forest Service • Location: 10 miles N of Fort Rock (limited services), 30 miles SE of LaPine • GPS: Lat 43.495064 Lon -121.057634 • Total sites: 14 • RV sites: 14 • RV fee: Free • No water • No toilets • Elevation: 4554

## Gales Creek

**Tillamook State Forest - Lyda Camp** • Agency: State • Tel: 503-842-2545 • Location: 20 miles W of Gales Creek (limited services), 25 miles NW of Forest Grove • GPS: Lat 45.587816 Lon -123.441013 • Open: All year • Total sites: Dispersed • RV sites: Undefined • RV fee: Free • No water • Vault toilets • Activities: Motor sports • Elevation: 1142

## Glendale

**Skull Creek** • Agency: Bureau of Land Management • Tel: 541-618-2200 • Location: 11 miles NW of Glendale (limited services), 31 miles SW of Canyonville • GPS: Lat 42.771925 Lon -123.570627 • Open: All year • Total sites: 5 • RV sites: Undefined • RV fee: Free • No water • No toilets • Activities: Hiking • Elevation: 1198

## Glide

**Buckhead Mountain** (Umpqua NF) • Agency: US Forest Service • Tel: 541-825-3100 • Location: 37 miles SE of Glide (limited services), 50 miles E of Roseburg • GPS: Lat 43.177256 Lon -122.625617 • Stay limit: 14 days • Total sites: 3 • RV sites: 3 • Max RV Length: 18 • RV fee: Free • Vault toilets • Elevation: 5075

**Clearwater Forebay** (Umpqua NF) • Agency: US Forest Service • Tel: 541-498-2531 • Location: 45 miles E of Glide (limited services), 61 miles E of Roseburg • GPS: Lat 43.261991 Lon -122.404545 • Stay limit: 14 days • Total sites: 5 • RV sites: 5 • RV fee: Free • No water • Vault toilets • Activities: Hiking, fishing • Elevation: 3185

**Scaredman Recreation Site** • Agency: Bureau of Land Management • Tel: 541-464-3291 • Location: 25 miles NE of Glide (limited services), 41 miles NE of Roseburg • GPS: Lat 43.380398 Lon -122.760446 • Stay limit: 14 days • Total sites: 9 • RV sites: 9 • RV fee: Free • Central water • Vault toilets • Activities: Mountain biking, swimming • Elevation: 1552

## Gold Beach

**Game Lake** (Rogue River-Siskiyou NF) • Agency: US Forest Service • Tel: 541-247-3600 • Location: 36 miles E of Gold Beach • GPS: Lat 42.432765 Lon -124.087062 • Open: May-Nov • Stay limit: 14 days • Total sites: 3 • RV sites: 3 • RV fee: Free • No water • Vault toilets • Elevation: 3983

**Wildhorse** (Rogue River-Siskiyou NF) • Agency: US Forest Service • Tel: 541-247-3600 • Location: 29 miles E of Gold Beach • GPS: Lat 42.460766 Lon -124.162819 • Open: May-Nov • Stay limit: 14 days • Total sites: 3 • RV sites: 3 • RV fee: Free • No water • Vault toilets • Elevation: 3556

## Government Camp

**Devils Half Acre** (Mt Hood NF) • Agency: US Forest Service • Tel: 541-352-6002 • Location: 6 miles SE of Government Camp • GPS: Lat 45.273948 Lon -121.679715 • Open: May-Oct • Total sites: 2 • RV sites: 2 • RV fee: Free • No water • Vault toilets • Elevation: 3881

**Grindstone** (Mt Hood NF) • Agency: US Forest Service • Tel: 503-668 1700 • Location: 8 miles SE of Government Camp • GPS: Lat 45.247319 Lon -

121.658907 • Total sites: 3 • RV sites: 3 • RV fee: Free • No water • Vault toilets • Elevation: 3402

**Hood River Meadows** (Mt Hood NF) • Agency: US Forest Service • Tel: 503-668 1700 • Location: 12 miles E of Government Camp • GPS: Lat 45.320637 Lon -121.634325 • Total sites: 5 • RV sites: 5 • Max RV Length: 21 • RV fee: Free • No water • No toilets • Activities: Hiking • Elevation: 4520

## Green Acres

**East Shore** • Agency: Bureau of Land Management • Tel: 541-756-0100 • Location: 19 miles S of Green Acres (limited services), 31 miles SE of Reedsport • GPS: Lat 43.577356 Lon -123.818879 • Open: All year • Total sites: 6 • RV sites: 6 • Max RV Length: 40 • RV fee: Free • No water • Vault toilets • Activities: Fishing, swimming, power boating, non-power boating • Elevation: 508

**Fawn Creek** • Agency: Bureau of Land Management • Tel: 541-756-0100 • Location: 21 miles N of Green Acres (limited services), 26 miles NE of Reedsport • GPS: Lat 43.784104 Lon -123.829722 • Open: Jun-Sep • Total sites: Dispersed • RV sites: Undefined • RV fee: Free • No water • Vault toilets • Activities: Fishing, swimming • Elevation: 64

**Smith River Falls** • Agency: Bureau of Land Management • Tel: 541-756-0100 • Location: 20 miles N of Green Acres (limited services), 26 miles NE of Reedsport • GPS: Lat 43.784532 Lon -123.814232 • Open: May-Sep • Total sites: 10 • RV sites: 10 • Max RV Length: 20 • RV fee: Free • No water • Vault toilets • Activities: Fishing, power boating • Elevation: 89

**Vincent Creek** • Agency: Bureau of Land Management • Tel: 541-756-0100 • Location: 16 miles N of Green Acres (limited services), 30 miles NE of Reedsport • GPS: Lat 43.79275 Lon -123.77734 • Open: May-Sep • Total sites: 5 • RV sites: 5 • RV fee: Free • No water • Vault toilets • Activities: Mountain biking, fishing • Elevation: 213

## Halfway

**Boulder Park** (Wallowa-Whitman NF) • Agency: US Forest Service • Tel: 541-523-6391 • Location: 33 miles NW of Halfway (limited services), 43 miles NE of Baker City • GPS: Lat 45.068311 Lon -117.406406 • Open: May-Sep • Stay limit: 14 days • Total sites: 7 • RV sites: 7 • RV fee: Free • No water • Vault toilets • Elevation: 4954

**McBride** (Wallowa-Whitman NF) • Agency: US Forest Service • Tel: 541-523-6391 • Location: 9 miles NW of Halfway (limited services), 62 miles NE of Baker City • GPS: Lat 44.934672 Lon -117.222522 • Open: Jul-Sep • Stay limit: 14 days • Total sites: 7 • RV sites: 7 • Max RV Length: 30 • RV fee: Free • No water • Vault toilets • Activities: Hunting • Elevation: 4774

**Two Color** (Wallowa-Whitman NF) • Agency: US Forest Service • Tel: 541-523-6391 • Location: 30 miles NW of Halfway (limited services), 40 miles NE of Baker City • GPS: Lat 45.037354 Lon -117.445557 • Open: Jun-Sep • Stay limit: 14 days • Total sites: 11 • RV sites: 11 • RV fee: Free • No water • Vault toilets • Activities: Fishing • Elevation: 4806

## Huntington

**Snake River Road** • Agency: Bureau of Land Management • Location: 2 miles NE of Huntington (limited services), 30 miles NW of Ontario • GPS: Lat 44.364799 Lon -117.228376 • Total sites: Dispersed • RV sites: Undefined • RV fee: Free • No water • No toilets • Notes: Near RR tracks • Elevation: 2083

## John Day

**Canyon Meadows** (Malheur NF) • Agency: US Forest Service • Tel: 541-575-3000 • Location: 22 miles SE of John Day • GPS: Lat 44.238525 Lon -118.771973 • Open: May-Sep • Stay limit: 14 days • Total sites: 5 • RV sites: 5 • RV fee: Free • No water • Vault toilets • Activities: Hiking • Elevation: 5197

## Jordan Valley

**Antelope Reservoir** • Agency: Bureau of Land Management • Tel: 541-473-3144 • Location: 13 miles SW of Jordan Valley (limited services), 70 miles SW of Nampa, ID • GPS: Lat 42.908492 Lon -117.236901 • Open: All year • Total sites: 4 • RV sites: 4 • RV fee: Free • No water • Vault toilets • Activities: Fishing, power boating, non-power boating • Elevation: 4339

**Cow Lakes** • Agency: Bureau of Land Management • Tel: 541-473-3144 • Location: 19 miles NW of Jordan Valley (limited services), 66 miles SW of Nampa, ID • GPS: Lat 43.096335 Lon -117.328217 • Open: All year • Total sites: 10 • RV sites: 10 • RV fee: Free • No water • Vault toilets • Activities: Fishing, power boating, non-power boating • Elevation: 4362

## Juntura

**Beaulah Reservoir** • Agency: US Bureau of Reclamation • Location: 16 miles N of Juntura (limited services), 62 miles NE of Burns • GPS: Lat 43.923184 Lon -118.142679 • Total sites: Dispersed • RV sites: Undefined • RV fee: Free • No water • No toilets • Activities: Fishing, power boating, non-power boating • Elevation: 3372

**Warm Springs** • Agency: Bureau of Land Management • Tel: 406 821-3201 • Location: 32 miles SW of Juntura (limited services), 53 miles E of Burns • GPS: Lat 43.638843 Lon -118.256317 • Open: All year • Total sites: Dispersed • RV sites: Undefined • RV fee: Free • No water • Vault toilets • Activities: Hiking, mountain biking, fishing • Elevation: 3432

## Klamath Falls

**Eagle Ridge** • Agency: County • Tel: 541-883-5121 • Location: 20 miles NW of Klamath Falls • GPS: Lat 42.405488 Lon -121.952673 • Open: All year • Stay limit: 14 days • Total sites: 6 • RV sites: 5 • RV fee: Free • Central water • Vault toilets • Activities: Fishing, power boating, non-power boating • Elevation: 4327

**Odessa** (Fremont-Winema NF) • Agency: US Forest Service • Tel: 541-885-3400 • Location: 21 miles NW of Klamath Falls • GPS: Lat 42.429045 Lon -122.061419 • Open: All year • Total sites: 6 • RV sites: 6 • RV fee: Free • No water • No toilets • Activities: Fishing, hunting, non-power boating • Elevation: 4190

## La Grande

**Frog Heaven Forest Camp** (Wallowa-Whitman NF) • Agency: US Forest Service • Tel: 541-523-6391 • Location: 37 miles SW of La Grande • GPS: Lat 45.212624 Lon -118.601921 • Open: May-Sep • Stay limit: 14 days • Total sites: 6 • RV sites: 6 • RV fee: Free • No water • No toilets • Elevation: 4797

**Morgan Lake Park** • Agency: Municipal • Tel: 541-962-1352 • Location: 3 miles SW of La Grande • GPS: Lat 45.301419 Lon -118.139267 • Open: Apr-Oct • Stay limit: 3 days • Total sites: Dispersed • RV sites: Undefined • RV fee: Free • No water • Vault toilets • Activities: Fishing, power boating, non-power boating • Elevation: 4171

**Mount Emily RA - Fox Hill** • Agency: County • Tel: 541-963-1319 • Location: 2 miles N of La Grande • GPS: Lat 45.362244 Lon -118.121174 • Open: All year • Stay limit: 14 days • Total sites: Dispersed • RV sites: Undefined • RV fee: Free • No water • Vault toilets • Activities: Hiking, mountain biking, motor sports • Elevation: 3787

## Lakeview

**Deep Creek** (Fremont-Winema NF) • Agency: US Forest Service • Tel: 541-947-6300 • Location: 21 miles SE of Lakeview • GPS: Lat 42.057583 Lon -120.174339 • Open: All year (reduced services Oct-May) • Total sites: 4 • RV sites: 4 • RV fee: Free • No water • Vault toilets • Activities: Fishing • Elevation: 5876

**Dismal Creek** (Fremont-Winema NF) • Agency: US Forest Service • Location: 21 miles SE of Lakeview • GPS: Lat 42.062389 Lon -120.152574 • Open: Jun-Oct • Total sites: 3 • RV sites: 3 • RV fee: Free • No water • Vault toilets • Activities: Fishing • Elevation: 5760

**Drews Creek** (Fremont-Winema NF) • Agency: US Forest Service • Tel: 541-947-3334 • Location: 15 miles SW of Lakeview • GPS: Lat 42.119277 Lon -120.581392 • Open: All year (reduced services Oct-May) • Total sites: 3 • RV sites: 3 • RV fee: Free • Central water • Vault toilets • Activities: Hiking, mountain biking, swimming, power boating, non-power boating • Elevation: 4842

**Mud Creek** (Fremont-Winema NF) • Agency: US Forest Service • Tel: 541-947-6300 • Location: 19 miles NE of Lakeview • GPS: Lat 42.281714 Lon -120.204986 • Open: All year (reduced services Oct-May) • Total sites: 7 • RV sites: 7 • RV fee: Free • No water • Vault toilets • Activities: Fishing • Elevation: 6486

**Vee Lake** (Fremont-Winema NF) • Agency: US Forest Service • Tel: 541-947-6300 • Location: 30 miles NE of Lakeview • GPS: Lat 42.422085 Lon -120.161946 • Open: All year (reduced services Oct-May) • Total sites: 1 • RV sites: 1 • RV fee: Free • No water • Vault toilets • Activities: Hiking, mountain biking, motor sports • Elevation: 6132

**Willow Creek** (Fremont-Winema NF) • Agency: US Forest Service • Tel: 541-947-6300 • Location: 16 miles SE of Lakeview • GPS: Lat 42.093062 Lon -120.201818 • Open: All year (reduced services Oct-May) • Total sites: 8 • RV sites: 8 • RV fee: Free • No water • Vault toilets • Activities: Fishing • Elevation: 6129

## Low Pass

**Hult Pond** • Agency: Bureau of Land Management • Tel: 541-683-6600 • Location: 6 miles NW of Low Pass (limited services), 23 miles W of Junction City • GPS: Lat 44.240359 Lon -123.495455 • Total sites: Dispersed • RV sites: Undefined • RV fee: Free • Vault toilets • Activities: Hiking, fishing, non-power boating • Elevation: 820

**Upper Lake Creek** • Agency: Bureau of Land Management • Tel: 541-683-6600 • Location: 5 miles NW of Low Pass (limited services), 25 miles NW of Eugene • GPS: Lat 44.237569 Lon -123.499515 • Open: All year • Total sites: Dispersed • RV sites: Undefined • RV fee: Free • No water • Vault toilets • Activities: Hiking, mountain biking, fishing, swimming, power boating, motor sports, non-power boating • Elevation: 793

## Madras

**Deschutes River - Frog Springs** (Deschutes River) • Agency: Bureau of Land Management • Tel: 541-416-6700 • Location: 18 miles N of Madras • GPS: Lat 44.794962 Lon -121.123623 • Total sites: Dispersed • RV sites: Undefined • RV fee: Free • No water • Vault toilets • Activities: Whitewater rafting • Elevation: 1337

## Malin

**Gerber RA - Rock Creek** • Agency: Bureau of Land Management • Tel: 541-947-2177 • Location: 26 miles E of Malin (limited services), 36 miles E of Merrill • GPS: Lat 42.009966 Lon -120.962246 • Open: All year • Total sites: Dispersed • RV sites: Undefined • RV fee: Free • No water • Vault toilets • Elevation: 4939

**Willow Valley Reservoir** • Agency: Bureau of Land Management • Tel: 541-883-6916 • Location: 20 miles E of Malin (limited services), 30 miles E of Merrill • GPS: Lat 42.008756 Lon -121.116621 • Total sites: Dispersed • RV sites: Undefined • RV fee: Free • No water • Vault toilets • Activities: Fishing, power boating, non-power boating • Elevation: 4537

## McDermitt

**US 95** • Agency: Bureau of Land Management • Location: 5 miles N of McDermitt (limited services), 79 miles N of Winnemucca, NV • GPS: Lat 42.076278 Lon -117.733884 • Total sites: Dispersed • RV sites: Undefined • RV fee: Free • No water • No toilets • Elevation: 4658

## Mehama

**Santiam State Forest - Rhody Lake** • Agency: State • Tel: 503-859-2151 • Location: 24 miles NE of Mehama (limited services), 30 miles N of Mill City • GPS: Lat 44.892227 Lon -122.409657 • Open: May-Sep • Total sites: 3 • RV sites: 3 • RV fee: Free • No water • Vault toilets • Elevation: 3674

## Merlin

**Meyers Camp** (Rogue River-Siskiyou NF) • Agency: US Forest Service • Tel: 541-592-4000 • Location: 20 miles W of Merlin • GPS: Lat 42.472516 Lon -123.670827 • Open: May-Sep • Stay limit: 14 days • Total sites: 2 • RV sites: 2 • RV fee: Free • No water • Vault toilets • Elevation: 2497

**Rogue River - Argo Landing** (Rogue River) • Agency: Bureau of Land Management • Tel: 541-479-3735 • Location: 17 miles NW of Merlin • GPS: Lat 42.625185 Lon -123.597193 • Total sites: Dispersed • RV sites: Undefined • RV fee: Free • No water • Vault toilets • Notes: Use of fire pans mandatory • Activities: Non-power boating • Elevation: 625

## Mitchell

**Allen Creek Horse Camp** (Ochoco NF) • Agency: US Forest Service • Tel: 541-416-6500 • Location: 16 miles S of Mitchell (limited services), 43 miles E of Prineville • GPS: Lat 44.398276 Lon -120.171993 • Open: All year • Stay limit: 14 days • Total sites: 11 • RV sites: 11 • RV fee: Free • No water (water for stock) • Vault toilets • Activities: Equestrian area (16 stalls) • Elevation: 4846

**Barnhouse** (Ochoco NF) • Agency: US Forest Service • Tel: 541-416-6500 • Location: 17 miles SE of Mitchell (limited services), 60 miles W of John Day • GPS: Lat 44.473809 Lon -119.934569 • Open: All year • Stay limit: 14 days • Total sites: 6 • RV sites: 6 • Max RV Length: 25 • RV fee: Free • No water • Vault toilets • Activities: Hiking • Elevation: 5076

**Bear Creek Road** • Agency: Bureau of Land Management • Location: 13 miles NW of Mitchell (limited services), 52 miles NE of Prineville • GPS: Lat 44.629654 Lon -120.307737 • Total sites: Dispersed • RV sites: Undefined • RV fee: Free • No water • No toilets • Elevation: 2363

**Big Spring** (Ochoco NF) • Agency: US Forest Service • Tel: 541-416-6500 • Location: 33 miles SE of Mitchell (limited services), 52 miles E of Prineville • GPS: Lat 44.331874 Lon -119.991419 • Open: All year • Stay limit: 14 days • Total sites: 5 • RV sites: 5 • RV fee: Free • No water • Vault toilets • Elevation: 5052

**Biggs Springs** (Ochoco NF) • Agency: US Forest Service • Tel: 541-416-6500 • Location: 30 miles S of Mitchell (limited services), 41 miles E of Prineville • GPS: Lat 44.272121 Lon -120.259769 • Open: All year • Stay limit: 14 days • Total sites: 3 • RV sites: 3 • RV fee: Free • No water • Vault toilets • Activities: Hiking, fishing • Elevation: 4898

**Bingham Spring** (Ochoco NF) • Agency: US Forest Service • Tel: 541-416-6500 • Location: 26 miles W of Mitchell (limited services), 31 miles NE of Prineville • GPS: Lat 44.514082 Lon -120.529316 • Open: All year • Stay limit: 14 days • Total sites: 4 • RV sites: 1 • Max RV Length: 18 • RV fee: Free • No water • Vault toilets • Activities: Hiking • Elevation: 5495

**Burnt Ranch** • Agency: Bureau of Land Management • Tel: 541-416-6700 • Location: 19 miles NW of Mitchell (limited services), 58 miles NE of Prineville • GPS: Lat 44.746191 Lon -120.364384 • Total sites: Dispersed • RV sites: Undefined • RV fee: Free • No water • Vault toilets • Elevation: 1499

**Burnt Ranch Dispersed** • Agency: Bureau of Land Management • Tel: 541-416-6700 • Location: 19 miles NW of Mitchell (limited services), 57 miles NE of Prineville • GPS: Lat 44.742745 Lon -120.361204 • Total sites:

Dispersed • RV sites: Undefined • RV fee: Free • No water • No toilets • Elevation: 1459

**Cottonwood** (Antone, Ochoco NF) • Agency: US Forest Service • Tel: 541-416-6500 • Location: 26 miles SE of Mitchell (limited services), 69 miles W of John Day • GPS: Lat 44.387618 Lon -119.854969 • Open: All year • Stay limit: 14 days • Total sites: 6 • RV sites: 5 • RV fee: Free • No water • Vault toilets • Activities: Hiking, mountain biking • Elevation: 5745

**Cottonwood Pit** (Ochoco NF) • Agency: US Forest Service • Tel: 541-416-6500 • Location: 28 miles SE of Mitchell (limited services), 71 miles W of John Day • GPS: Lat 44.368809 Lon -119.869979 • Open: May-Sep • Stay limit: 14 days • Total sites: 3 • RV sites: 3 • RV fee: Free • No water • Vault toilets • Elevation: 5630

**Manning Pasture** • Agency: Bureau of Land Management • Location: 12 miles NW of Mitchell (limited services), 50 miles NE of Prineville • GPS: Lat 44.696335 Lon -120.284758 • Total sites: Dispersed • RV sites: Undefined • RV fee: Free • No water • No toilets • Elevation: 1749

**Old Logging Road** • Agency: Bureau of Land Management • Tel: 208-678-0439 • Location: 4 miles NW of Mitchell (limited services), 44 miles NE of Prineville • GPS: Lat 44.606215 Lon -120.185941 • Total sites: Dispersed • RV sites: Undefined • RV fee: Free • No water • No toilets • Activities: Hiking • Elevation: 2907

**Priest Hole** • Agency: Bureau of Land Management • Location: 18 miles NW of Mitchell (limited services), 56 miles NE of Prineville • GPS: Lat 44.741664 Lon -120.354182 • Total sites: Dispersed • RV sites: Undefined • RV fee: Free • No water • Vault toilets • Elevation: 1480

**Rocky Road** • Agency: Bureau of Land Management • Location: 12 miles NW of Mitchell (limited services), 50 miles NE of Prineville • GPS: Lat 44.691157 Lon -120.281767 • Total sites: Dispersed • RV sites: Undefined • RV fee: Free • No water • No toilets • Elevation: 1760

**Scotts Camp** (Ochoco NF) • Agency: US Forest Service • Tel: 541-416-6500 • Location: 14 miles S of Mitchell (limited services), 59 miles NE of Prineville • GPS: Lat 44.424523 Lon -120.145264 • Open: All year • Stay limit: 14 days • Total sites: 3 • RV sites: 3 • RV fee: Free • No water • Vault toilets • Elevation: 5423

**Stovepipe Springs** • Agency: Bureau of Land Management • Location: 13 miles NW of Mitchell (limited services), 52 miles NE of Prineville • GPS: Lat 44.708267 Lon -120.271621 • Total sites: Dispersed • RV sites: Undefined • RV fee: Free • No water • No toilets • Activities: Hiking • Elevation: 1950

**Wildwood** (Ochoco NF) • Agency: US Forest Service • Tel: 541-416-6500 • Location: 18 miles SW of Mitchell (limited services), 35 miles NE of Prineville • GPS: Lat 44.485 Lon -120.335 • Open: All year • Stay limit: 14 days • Total sites: 5 • RV sites: 5 • RV fee: Free • No water • Vault toilets • Activities: Hiking • Elevation: 4869

## Molalla

**Molalla River RA - Red Dog** • Agency: Bureau of Land Management • Tel: 503-375-5646 • Location: 22 miles SE of Molalla • GPS: Lat 44.980721 Lon -122.387494 • Total sites: Dispersed • RV sites: Undefined • RV fee: Free • No water • No toilets • Activities: Hiking, mountain biking, fishing, swimming, non-power boating • Elevation: 1604

**Molalla River RA - Shadow View** • Agency: Bureau of Land Management • Tel: 503-375-5646 • Location: 21 miles SE of Molalla • GPS: Lat 44.978639 Lon -122.390582 • Total sites: Dispersed • RV sites: Undefined • RV fee: Free • No water • No toilets • Activities: Hiking, mountain biking, fishing, swimming, non-power boating • Elevation: 1545

## Mt Vernon

**Billy Fields Forest Camp** (Malheur NF) • Agency: US Forest Service • Tel: 541-575-3000 • Location: 17 miles SW of Mt Vernon (limited services), 24 miles SW of John Day • GPS: Lat 44.346585 Lon -119.299542 • Open: Jun-Oct • Stay limit: 14 days • Total sites: 4 • RV sites: 3 • RV fee: Free • No water • Vault toilets • Activities: Hiking, fishing • Elevation: 4190

**Oregon Mine** (Malheur NF) • Agency: US Forest Service • Tel: 541-575-3000 • Location: 24 miles SW of Mt Vernon (limited services), 32 miles SW of John Day • GPS: Lat 44.276935 Lon -119.296968 • Open: All year • Stay limit: 14 days • Total sites: 1 • RV sites: 1 • RV fee: Free • No water • Vault toilets • Activities: Equestrian area • Elevation: 4409

## Nehalem

**Tillamook State Forest - Cook Creek 1** • Agency: State • Tel: 503-842-2545 • Location: 13 miles E of Nehalem • GPS: Lat 45.699573 Lon -123.744807 • Total sites: Dispersed • RV sites: Undefined • RV fee: Free • No water • Elevation: 96

**Tillamook State Forest - Cook Creek 2** • Agency: State • Tel: 503-842-2545 • Location: 13 miles E of Nehalem • GPS: Lat 45.696924 Lon -123.737649 • Total sites: Dispersed • RV sites: Undefined • RV fee: Free • No water • Elevation: 128

## Oakridge

**Everage Flat** (Willamette NF) • Agency: US Forest Service • Location: 18 miles S of Oakridge • GPS: Lat 43.524096 Lon -122.447401 • Stay limit: 14 days • Total sites: 8 • RV sites: 6 • RV fee: Free • No water • No toilets • Elevation: 1942

## Paisley

**Chewaucan Crossing Trailhead** (Fremont-Winema NF) • Agency: US Forest Service • Tel: 541-943-3114 • Location: 8 miles SW of Paisley (limited services), 44 miles NW of Lakeview • GPS: Lat 42.616626 Lon -120.606173 • Open: All year (reduced services Oct-May) • Total sites: 5 • RV sites: 5 • RV fee: Free • No water • Vault toilets • Activities: Hiking, fishing • Elevation: 4806

**Clear Springs** (Fremont-Winema NF) • Agency: US Forest Service • Tel: 541-943-3114 • Location: 25 miles SW of Paisley (limited services), 35 miles NW of Lakeview • GPS: Lat 42.471846 Lon -120.711657 • Open: All year (reduced services Oct-May) • Total sites: 2 • RV sites: 2 • RV fee: Free • Central water • Vault toilets • Activities: Fishing • Elevation: 5466

**Currier Horse Camp** (Fremont-Winema NF) • Agency: US Forest Service • Tel: 541-943-3114 • Location: 24 miles W of Paisley (limited services), 68 miles NW of Lakeview • GPS: Lat 42.729426 Lon -120.819381 • Open: Jun-Sep • Total sites: 4 • RV sites: 4 • RV fee: Free • No water • No toilets • Activities: Equestrian area • Elevation: 6900

**Dairy Point** (Fremont-Winema NF) • Agency: US Forest Service • Tel: 541-943-3114 • Location: 21 miles S of Paisley (limited services), 30 miles NW of Lakeview • GPS: Lat 42.467041 Lon -120.640637 • Open: All year (reduced services Oct-May) • Total sites: 5 • RV sites: 5 • RV fee: Free • Central water • Vault toilets • Activities: Fishing • Elevation: 5201

**Dead Horse Creek** (Fremont-Winema NF) • Agency: US Forest Service • Location: 24 miles SW of Paisley (limited services), 35 miles NW of Lakeview • GPS: Lat 42.474167 Lon -120.703889 • Open: Apr-Oct • Total sites: 4 • RV sites: 4 • RV fee: Free • No water • Vault toilets • Activities: Fishing • Elevation: 5390

**Happy Camp** (Fremont-Winema NF) • Agency: US Forest Service • Tel: 541-943-3114 • Location: 23 miles SW of Paisley (limited services), 33 miles NW of Lakeview • GPS: Lat 42.476078 Lon -120.684258 • Open: All year (reduced services Oct-May) • Total sites: 9 • RV sites: 9 • RV fee: Free • Central water • Vault toilets • Activities: Fishing • Elevation: 5325

**Jones Crossing Forest Camp** (Fremont-Winema NF) • Agency: US Forest Service • Tel: 541-943-3114 • Location: 9 miles SW of Paisley (limited services), 40 miles NW of Lakeview • GPS: Lat 42.605851 Lon -120.598874 • Open: All year (reduced services Oct-May) • Total sites: 8 • RV sites: 8 • RV fee: Free • No water • Vault toilets • Activities: Fishing • Elevation: 4829

**Lee Thomas** (Fremont-Winema NF) • Agency: US Forest Service • Tel: 541-943-3114 • Location: 26 miles SW of Paisley (limited services), 51 miles NW of Lakeview • GPS: Lat 42.590151 Lon -120.838902 • Open: All year (reduced services Oct-May) • Total sites: 7 • RV sites: 7 • RV fee: Free • Central water • Activities: Fishing • Elevation: 6253

**Moss Meadow Horse Camp** (Fremont-Winema NF) • Agency: US Forest Service • Tel: 541-943-3114 • Location: 18 miles S of Paisley (limited services), 39 miles N of Lakeview • GPS: Lat 42.478974 Lon -120.484527 • Open: All year (reduced services Sep-Jun) • Total sites: 3 • RV sites: 3 • RV fee: Free • No water • Vault toilets • Activities: Equestrian area • Elevation: 5961

**Pike's Crossing** (Fremont-Winema NF) • Agency: US Forest Service • Tel: 541-943-4479 • Location: 29 miles W of Paisley (limited services), 60 miles NW of Lakeview • GPS: Lat 42.697896 Lon -120.933069 • Open: May-Oct • Total sites: 6 • RV sites: 6 • RV fee: Free • No water • Vault toilets • Activities: Fishing • Elevation: 5712

**Sandhill Crossing** (Fremont-Winema NF) • Agency: US Forest Service • Tel: 541-943-4479 • Location: 29 miles W of Paisley (limited services), 52 miles NW of Lakeview • GPS: Lat 42.594055 Lon -120.879944 • Open: All year (reduced services Oct-May) • Total sites: 5 • RV sites: 5 • RV fee: Free • Central water • Vault toilets • Activities: Fishing • Elevation: 6119

**Upper Jones** (Fremont-Winema NF) • Agency: US Forest Service • Location: 9 miles W of Paisley (limited services), 50 miles NW of Lakeview • GPS: Lat 42.598642 Lon -120.599055 • Open: Apr-Oct • Total sites: 2 • RV sites: 2 • RV fee: Free • No water • No toilets • Activities: Fishing • Elevation: 4879

## Port Orford

**Butler Bar** (Rogue River-Siskiyou NF) • Agency: US Forest Service • Tel: 541-439-6200 • Location: 21 miles E of Port Orford • GPS: Lat 42.726161 Lon -124.271991 • Open: All year • Stay limit: 14 days • Total sites: 7 • RV sites: 7 • RV fee: Free • Central water • Vault toilets • Activities: Hiking, mountain biking, swimming • Elevation: 669

**Laird Lake** (Rogue River-Siskiyou NF) • Agency: US Forest Service • Tel: 541-439-6200 • Location: 27 miles SE of Port Orford • GPS: Lat 42.699259 Lon -124.203098 • Open:

All year • Stay limit: 14 days • Total sites: 4 • RV sites: 4 • RV fee: Free • No water • Vault toilets • Activities: Hiking, mountain biking, fishing, swimming, hunting, motor sports, non-power boating • Elevation: 1893

**Sunshine Bar** (Rogue River-Siskiyou NF) • Agency: US Forest Service • Tel: 541-439-6200 • Location: 18 miles SE of Port Orford • GPS: Lat 42.712405 Lon -124.311761 • Open: All year • Stay limit: 14 days • Total sites: 6 • RV sites: 6 • RV fee: Free • No water • Vault toilets • Activities: Hiking, swimming, hunting • Elevation: 594

## Powers

**Buck Creek** (Rogue River-Siskiyou NF) • Agency: US Forest Service • Tel: 541-439-6200 • Location: 25 miles SE of Powers (limited services), 45 miles SE of Myrtle Point • GPS: Lat 42.774739 Lon -123.952364 • Open: All year • Stay limit: 14 days • Total sites: 2 • RV sites: 2 • RV fee: Free • No water • Vault toilets • Activities: Hiking, mountain biking • Elevation: 2277

**China Flat** (Rogue River-Siskiyou NF) • Agency: US Forest Service • Tel: 541-439-6200 • Location: 11 miles S of Powers (limited services), 32 miles S of Myrtle Point • GPS: Lat 42.778692 Lon -124.065509 • Stay limit: 14 days • Total sites: 15 • RV sites: 15 • RV fee: Free • No water • Vault toilets • Elevation: 725

**Eden Valley** (Rogue River-Siskiyou NF) • Agency: US Forest Service • Tel: 541-439-6200 • Location: 21 miles SE of Powers (limited services), 40 miles SE of Myrtle Point • GPS: Lat 42.809014 Lon -123.890941 • Open: All year • Stay limit: 14 days • Total sites: 11 • RV sites: 11 • RV fee: Free • No water • Vault toilets • Activities: Hiking, mountain biking • Elevation: 2441

**Myrtle Grove** (Rogue River-Siskiyou NF) • Agency: US Forest Service • Tel: 541-439-6200 • Location: 8 miles S of Powers (limited services), 29 miles S of Myrtle Point • GPS: Lat 42.785651 Lon -124.024461 • Open: All year • Stay limit: 14 days • Total sites: 5 • RV sites: 5 • RV fee: Free • No water • Vault toilets • Elevation: 699

**Sru Lake** (Rogue River-Siskiyou NF) • Agency: US Forest Service • Tel: 541-439-6200 • Location: 21 miles S of Powers (limited services), 41 miles S of Myrtle Point • GPS: Lat 42.730834 Lon -124.006088 • Open: All year • Stay limit: 14 days • Total sites: 6 • RV sites: 6 • RV fee: Free • No water • Vault toilets • Activities: Fishing • Elevation: 2362

## Prairie City

**Crescent** (Malheur NF) • Agency: US Forest Service • Tel: 541-820-3800 • Location: 16 miles SE of Prairie City (limited services), 30 miles SE of John Day • GPS: Lat 44.281779 Lon -118.545261 • Open: May-Sep • Stay limit: 14 days • Total sites: 4 • RV sites: 4 • RV fee: Free • No water • Vault toilets • Activities: Fishing • Elevation: 5236

**Elk Creek** (Malheur NF) • Agency: US Forest Service • Tel: 541-820-3800 • Location: 26 miles SE of Prairie City (limited services), 39 miles SE of John Day • GPS: Lat 44.245921 Lon -118.398393 • Open: May-Sep • Stay limit: 14 days • Total sites: 5 • RV sites: 5 • RV fee: Free • No water • Vault toilets • Activities: Fishing • Elevation: 5062

**North Fork Malheur** (Malheur NF) • Agency: US Forest Service • Tel: 541-820-3800 • Location: 29 miles SE of Prairie City (limited services), 42 miles SE of John Day • GPS: Lat 44.208885 Lon -118.382434 • Open: May-Sep • Stay limit: 14 days • Total sites: 5 • RV sites: 5 • RV fee: Free • No water • Vault toilets • Activities: Hiking, fishing • Elevation: 4780

**Slide Creek** (Malheur NF) • Agency: US Forest Service • Tel: 541-820-3800 • Location: 9 miles S of Prairie City (limited services), 22 miles SE of John Day • GPS: Lat 44.342302 Lon -118.657366 • Open: May-Sep • Stay limit: 14 days • Total sites: 3 • RV sites: 3 • RV fee: Free • No water • Vault toilets • Activities: Hiking, fishing • Elevation: 4934

## Prineville

**Dry Creek Horse Camp** (Ochoco NF) • Agency: US Forest Service • Tel: 541-416-6500 • Location: 15 miles NE of Prineville • GPS: Lat 44.417768 Lon -120.669165 • Stay limit: 14 days • Total sites: 5 • RV sites: 5 • Max RV Length: 20 • RV fee: Free • No water • Vault toilets • Activities: Equestrian area • Elevation: 3963

**Elkhorn** (Ochoco NF) • Agency: US Forest Service • Tel: 541-416-6500 • Location: 38 miles SE of Prineville • GPS: Lat 44.080509 Lon -120.319147 • Open: All year • Stay limit: 14 days • Total sites: 4 • RV sites: 4 • RV fee: Free • No water • Vault toilets • Elevation: 4452

**Juniper Point** • Agency: US Bureau of Reclamation • Location: 42 miles SE of Prineville • GPS: Lat 44.118843 Lon -120.725493 • Total sites: Dispersed • RV sites: Undefined • RV fee: Free • No water • Vault toilets • Elevation: 3304

**Prineville Reservoir WA - Cattleguard - ODFW** • Agency: State • Tel: 541-447-5111 • Location: 19 miles SE of Prineville • GPS: Lat 44.155393 Lon -120.668196 • Open: Apr-Nov • Total sites: Dispersed • RV sites: Undefined • RV fee: Free • No water • Vault toilets • Activities: Hiking, fishing, power boating, hunting, non-power boating • Elevation: 3248

**Prineville Reservoir WA - Juniper Bass - ODFW** • Agency: State • Tel: 541-447-5111 • Location: 18 miles SE of Prineville • GPS: Lat 44.147743 Lon -120.678993 • Open:

Apr-Nov • Total sites: Dispersed • RV sites: Undefined • RV fee: Free • No water • Vault toilets • Activities: Hiking, fishing, power boating, hunting, non-power boating • Elevation: 3264

**Prineville Reservoir WA - Oldfield - ODFW** • Agency: State • Tel: 541-447-5111 • Location: 18 miles SE of Prineville • GPS: Lat 44.168433 Lon -120.652111 • Open: Apr-Nov • Total sites: Dispersed • RV sites: Undefined • RV fee: Free • No water • Vault toilets • Activities: Hiking, fishing, power boating, hunting, non-power boating • Elevation: 3264

**Prineville Reservoir WA - Owl Creek 1 - ODFW** • Agency: State • Tel: 541-447-5111 • Location: 17 miles SE of Prineville • GPS: Lat 44.146534 Lon -120.693706 • Open: Apr-Nov • Total sites: Dispersed • RV sites: Undefined • RV fee: Free • No water • No toilets • Activities: Hiking, fishing, power boating, hunting, non-power boating • Elevation: 3314

**Prineville Reservoir WA - Owl Creek 2 - ODFW** • Agency: State • Tel: 541-447-5111 • Location: 18 miles SE of Prineville • GPS: Lat 44.152381 Lon -120.684408 • Open: Apr-Nov • Total sites: Dispersed • RV sites: Undefined • RV fee: Free • No water • No toilets • Activities: Hiking, fishing, power boating, hunting, non-power boating • Elevation: 3310

**Roberts Bay East** • Agency: US Bureau of Reclamation • Location: 38 miles SE of Prineville • GPS: Lat 44.121245 Lon -120.703573 • Total sites: Dispersed • RV sites: Undefined • RV fee: Free • No water • Vault toilets • Activities: Fishing, power boating, non-power boating • Elevation: 3254

**Roberts Bay West** • Agency: US Bureau of Reclamation • Location: 40 miles SE of Prineville • GPS: Lat 44.123373 Lon -120.716436 • Total sites: Dispersed • RV sites: Undefined • RV fee: Free • No water • Vault toilets • Activities: Fishing, power boating, non-power boating • Elevation: 3258

**White Rock** (Ochoco NF) • Agency: US Forest Service • Tel: 541-416-6500 • Location: 28 miles NE of Prineville • GPS: Lat 44.423165 Lon -120.543703 • Open: All year • Stay limit: 14 days • Total sites: 3 • RV sites: 1 • RV fee: Free • No water • Vault toilets • Activities: Hiking • Elevation: 5479

**Wiley Flat** (Ochoco NF) • Agency: US Forest Service • Tel: 541-416-6500 • Location: 42 miles SE of Prineville • GPS: Lat 44.042271 Lon -120.297644 • Open: All year • Stay limit: 14 days • Total sites: 5 • RV sites: 5 • RV fee: Free • No water • Vault toilets • Elevation: 5364

## Prospect

**Huckleberry Mountain** (Rogue River-Siskiyou NF) • Agency: US Forest Service • Tel: 541-560-3400 • Location: 22 miles NE of Prospect (limited services), 65 miles NW of Klamath Falls • GPS: Lat 42.876344 Lon -122.338061 • Open: May-Oct • Stay limit: 14 days • Total sites: 25 • RV sites: 25 • Max RV Length: 16 • RV fee: Free • No water • Vault toilets • Elevation: 5467

## Richland

**Moonshine Mine RA - IP** • Agency: Utility Company • Tel: 541-785-7209 • Location: 13 miles S of Richland (limited services), 51 miles SE of Baker City • GPS: Lat 44.650403 Lon -117.102328 • Stay limit: 14 days • Total sites: Dispersed • RV sites: Undefined • RV fee: Free • No water • Vault toilets • Activities: Fishing, power boating • Elevation: 2100

**Swedes Landing** • Agency: Bureau of Land Management • Tel: 541-473-3144 • Location: 14 miles SE of Richland (limited services), 51 miles SE of Baker City • GPS: Lat 44.640762 Lon -117.106561 • Open: All year • Stay limit: 14 days • Total sites: 3 • RV sites: 3 • RV fee: Free • No water • Vault toilets • Activities: Hiking, mountain biking, fishing, power boating, hunting, non-power boating • Elevation: 2076

## Rogue River

**Elderberry Flat** • Agency: Bureau of Land Management • Tel: 541-618-2200 • Location: 21 miles N of Rogue River • GPS: Lat 42.662449 Lon -123.098957 • Open: Apr-Nov • Total sites: 11 • RV sites: 11 • RV fee: Free • No water • Vault toilets • Activities: Motor sports • Elevation: 2103

## Rome

**Rome Launch** • Agency: Bureau of Land Management • Tel: 541-473-3144 • Location: 1 mile E of Rome (limited services), 104 miles SE of Burns • GPS: Lat 42.835951 Lon -117.620959 • Open: Mar-Nov • Total sites: 5 • RV sites: 5 • RV fee: Free • Central water • Vault toilets • Elevation: 3387

## Rufus

**Giles French** • Agency: Corps of Engineers • Tel: 541-506-7819 • Location: 2 miles E of Rufus (limited services), 25 miles NE of The Dalles • GPS: Lat 45.708258 Lon -120.700583 • Stay limit: 14 days • Total sites: Dispersed • RV sites: Undefined • RV fee: Free • Flush toilets • Notes: Near RR tracks • Activities: Power boating • Elevation: 190

**Rufus Landing** • Agency: Corps of Engineers • Tel: 541-506-7819 • Location: 1 mile W of Rufus (limited services), 24 miles E of The Dalles • GPS: Lat 45.693131 Lon -120.755837 • Stay limit: 14 days • Total sites: Dispersed • RV sites: Undefined • RV fee: Free • No water • Vault toilets • Elevation: 179

## Seaside

**Saddle Mountain SNA** • Agency: State • Location: 13 miles SE of Seaside • GPS: Lat 45.908059 Lon -123.742723 • Total sites: Dispersed • RV sites: Undefined (dispersed sites along the road) • RV fee: Free • No water • No toilets • Elevation: 477

## Selma

**Briggs Creek** (Rogue River-Siskiyou NF) • Agency: US Forest Service • Tel: 541-471-6500 • Location: 18 miles NW of Selma (limited services), 26 miles NW of Cave Junction • GPS: Lat 42.377761 Lon -123.804198 • Open: May-Oct • Stay limit: 14 days • Total sites: 3 • RV sites: 3 • RV fee: Free • No water • Vault toilets • Activities: Hiking, fishing, swimming • Elevation: 891

**Secret Creek** (Rogue River-Siskiyou NF) • Agency: US Forest Service • Tel: 541-592-4000 • Location: 21 miles N of Selma (limited services), 26 miles W of Grants Pass • GPS: Lat 42.421799 Lon -123.688916 • Open: May-Sep • Stay limit: 14 days • Total sites: 4 • RV sites: 4 • RV fee: Free • No water • Vault toilets • Activities: Hiking, motor sports • Elevation: 2070

**Spalding Pond** (Rogue River-Siskiyou NF) • Agency: US Forest Service • Tel: 541-592-4000 • Location: 16 miles NW of Selma (limited services), 25 miles N of Cave Junction • GPS: Lat 42.346501 Lon -123.703682 • Open: May-Oct • Stay limit: 14 days • Total sites: 4 • RV sites: 4 • RV fee: Free • No water • No toilets • Activities: Fishing • Elevation: 3402

## Silver Lake

**Antler Horse Camp** (Fremont-Winema NF) • Agency: US Forest Service • Tel: 541-576-2107 • Location: 18 miles SW of Silver Lake (limited services), 66 miles S of LaPine • GPS: Lat 42.959185 Lon -121.247684 • Open: All year (limited services Sep-Jun) • Total sites: 5 • RV sites: 5 • RV fee: Free • Central water • Vault toilets • Activities: Mountain biking, equestrian area • Elevation: 6416

**Bunyard Crossing** (Fremont-Winema NF) • Agency: US Forest Service • Tel: 541-576-2107 • Location: 7 miles S of Silver Lake (limited services), 56 miles SE of LaPine • GPS: Lat 43.043797 Lon -121.081691 • Open: May-Nov • Total sites: 3 • RV sites: 3 • RV fee: Free • No water • Vault toilets • Activities: Hiking, fishing • Elevation: 4530

**Duncan Reservoir** • Agency: Bureau of Land Management • Tel: 541-947-2177 • Location: 10 miles SE of Silver Lake (limited services), 59 miles SE of LaPine • GPS: Lat 43.071274 Lon -120.945024 • Open: All year • Total sites: 4 • RV sites: 4 • RV fee: Free • No water • Vault toilets • Activities: Fishing, swimming, power boating, non-power boating • Elevation: 4850

**Farm Well Horse Camp Trailhead** (Fremont-Winema NF) • Agency: US Forest Service • Tel: 541-576-2107 • Location: 11 miles SE of Silver Lake (limited services), 59 miles SE of LaPine • GPS: Lat 43.026758 Lon -120.977777 • Open: All year (reduced services Sep-Jun) • Total sites: 5 • RV sites: 5 • RV fee: Free • No water • Vault toilets • Activities: Hiking, equestrian area • Elevation: 5058

**Lower Buck Creek Forest Camp** (Fremont-Winema NF) • Agency: US Forest Service • Tel: 541-576-2107 • Location: 15 miles SW of Silver Lake (limited services), 62 miles SE of LaPine • GPS: Lat 43.068544 Lon -121.246333 • Open: All year (reduced services Oct-May) • Total sites: 5 • RV sites: 5 • RV fee: Free • No water • Vault toilets • Activities: Fishing • Elevation: 4917

**Summer Lake SWA - CG 1** • Agency: State • Tel: 541-943-3152 • Location: 24 miles SE of Silver Lake (limited services), 73 miles NW of Lakeview • GPS: Lat 42.950266 Lon -120.763254 • Open: All year • Total sites: Dispersed • RV sites: Undefined • RV fee: Free • No water • No toilets • Activities: Hiking • Elevation: 4154

**Summer Lake SWA - CG 2** • Agency: State • Tel: 541-943-3152 • Location: 25 miles SE of Silver Lake (limited services), 74 miles NW of Lakeview • GPS: Lat 42.940555 Lon -120.767773 • Open: All year • Total sites: Dispersed • RV sites: Undefined • RV fee: Free • No water • No toilets • Activities: Hiking • Elevation: 4147

**Summer Lake SWA - CG 3** • Agency: State • Tel: 541-943-3152 • Location: 25 miles SE of Silver Lake (limited services), 74 miles NW of Lakeview • GPS: Lat 42.946617 Lon -120.742505 • Open: All year • Total sites: Dispersed • RV sites: Undefined • RV fee: Free • No water • No toilets • Activities: Hiking • Elevation: 4157

**Summer Lake SWA - CG 4** • Agency: State • Tel: 541-943-3152 • Location: 24 miles SE of Silver Lake (limited services), 73 miles SE of LaPine • GPS: Lat 42.961322 Lon -120.724871 • Open: All year • Total sites: Dispersed • RV sites: Undefined • RV fee: Free • No water • No toilets • Activities: Hiking • Elevation: 4163

**Upper Buck Creek** (Fremont-Winema NF) • Agency: US Forest Service • Tel: 541-576-2107 • Location: 17 miles SW of Silver Lake (limited services), 63 miles SE of LaPine • GPS: Lat 43.053408 Lon -121.266372 • Open: All year (reduced services Oct-May) • Total sites: 6 • RV sites: 6 • RV fee: Free • No water • Vault toilets • Activities: Fishing • Elevation: 5066

## Sisters

**Lava Camp Lake** (Deschutes NF) • Agency: US Forest Service • Tel: 541-549-7700 • Location: 14 miles W of Sisters • GPS: Lat 44.261227 Lon -121.785608 • Open: Jun-Oct • Total sites: 12 • RV sites: 12 • Max RV Length: 35 • RV fee: Free • No water • Vault toilets • Activities: Hiking • Elevation: 5312

**Sisters Cow Camp Horse Camp** (Deschutes NF) • Agency: US Forest Service • Tel: 541-383-5300 • Location: 4 miles W of Sisters • GPS: Lat 44.274196 Lon -121.615078 • Open: Apr-Oct • Total sites: 5 • RV sites: 5 • Max RV Length: 40 • RV fee: Free • No water • Vault toilets • Activities: Equestrian area • Elevation: 3432

## Spray

**Fairview** (Umatilla NF) • Agency: US Forest Service • Tel: 541-278-3716 • Location: 14 miles NE of Spray (limited services), 76 miles NW of John Day • GPS: Lat 44.955151 Lon -119.712474 • Open: All year (no services Nov-May) • Stay limit: 14 days • Total sites: 5 • RV sites: 5 • RV fee: Free • Central water • Vault toilets • Activities: Hunting, motor sports • Elevation: 4324

## Terrebonne

**Cyrus Horse Camp** (Ochoco NF) • Agency: US Forest Service • Tel: 541-416-6640 • Location: 11 miles NE of Terrebonne • GPS: Lat 44.447776 Lon -121.103144 • Stay limit: 14 days • Total sites: 5 • RV sites: 5 • RV fee: Free • No water • Vault toilets • Activities: Equestrian area • Elevation: 3350

## The Dalles

**Celilo** • Agency: Corps of Engineers • Tel: 541-506-7819 • Location: 9 miles E of The Dalles • GPS: Lat 45.650442 Lon -120.961022 • Total sites: Dispersed • RV sites: Undefined • RV fee: Free • Vault toilets • Notes: Near RR tracks • Activities: Fishing, power boating • Elevation: 167

## Tillamook

**Tillamook State Forest - Hollywood/Edwards Creek** • Agency: State • Tel: 503-842-2545 • Location: 17 miles SE of Tillamook • GPS: Lat 45.410176 Lon -123.611879 • Open: All year • Total sites: 3 • RV sites: 3 • RV fee: Free • No water • No toilets • Activities: Motor sports • Elevation: 435

**Tillamook State Forest - Jordan Creek 1-2** • Agency: State • Tel: 503-842-2545 • Location: 17 miles NE of Tillamook • GPS: Lat 45.538731 Lon -123.589473 • Open: All year • Total sites: Dispersed • RV sites: Undefined • RV fee: Free • No water • No toilets • Elevation: 442

**Tillamook State Forest - Jordan Creek 3** • Agency: State • Tel: 503-842-2545 • Location: 17 miles NE of Tillamook • GPS: Lat 45.544811 Lon -123.597048 • Open: All year • Total sites: Dispersed • RV sites: Undefined • RV fee: Free • No water • No toilets • Elevation: 410

**Tillamook State Forest - Jordan Creek 6-7** • Agency: State • Tel: 503-842-2545 • Location: 20 miles NE of Tillamook • GPS: Lat 45.533293 Lon -123.547985 • Open: All year • Total sites: Dispersed • RV sites: Undefined • RV fee: Free • No water • No toilets • Elevation: 607

**Tillamook State Forest - South Fork Trask** • Agency: State • Tel: 503-842-2545 • Location: 22 miles SE of Tillamook • GPS: Lat 45.371816 Lon -123.596855 • Open: All year • Total sites: 2 • RV sites: 2 • RV fee: Free • No water • No toilets • Elevation: 1699

## Ukiah

**Divide Well** (Umatilla NF) • Agency: US Forest Service • Tel: 541-278-3716 • Location: 17 miles W of Ukiah (limited services), 62 miles SW of Pendleton • GPS: Lat 45.102637 Lon -119.142102 • Open: All year • Stay limit: 14 days • Total sites: 11 • RV sites: 11 • RV fee: Free • No water • Vault toilets • Notes: Snow-mobile access only Nov-May - no services • Activities: Hunting • Elevation: 4747

**Drift Fence** (Umatilla NF) • Agency: US Forest Service • Tel: 541-278-3716 • Location: 8 miles SE of Ukiah (limited services), 55 miles S of Pendleton • GPS: Lat 45.071777 Lon -118.875732 • Open: May-Nov • Stay limit: 14 days • Total sites: 6 • RV sites: 4 • RV fee: Free • No water • Vault toilets • Activities: Fishing • Elevation: 4626

**Four Corners Sno-Park** (Umatilla NF) • Agency: US Forest Service • Tel: 541-278-3716 • Location: 19 miles E of Ukiah (limited services), 33 miles SW of La Grande • GPS: Lat 45.178511 Lon -118.606898 • Stay limit: 14 days • Total sites: 2 • RV sites: 2 • RV fee: Free • No water • Vault toilets • Elevation: 4442

**Umapine** (Wallowa-Whitman NF) • Agency: US Forest Service • Tel: 541-523-6391 • Location: 31 miles E of Ukiah (limited services), 37 miles SW of La Grande • GPS: Lat 45.114075 Lon -118.562078 • Open: May-Sep • Stay limit: 14 days • Total sites: 5 • RV sites: 5 • RV fee: Free • No water • Vault toilets • Activities: Motor sports • Elevation: 5079

## Wamic

**Little Badger** (Mt Hood NF) • Agency: US Forest Service • Tel: 503-668 1700 • Location: 12 miles NW of Wamic (limited services), 36 miles SW of The Dalles • GPS: Lat 45.281799 Lon -121.348385 • Open: May-Sep • Total sites: 3 • RV sites: 3 • Max RV Length: 16 • RV fee: Free • No water • Vault toilets • Activities: Hiking, fishing • Elevation: 2077

**Post Camp** (Mt Hood NF) • Agency: US Forest Service • Tel: 541-467-2291 • Location: 17 miles W of Wamic (limited services), 36 miles SE of Welches • GPS: Lat 45.216371 Lon -121.520079 • Open: May-Sep • Total sites: 4 • RV sites: 4 • Max RV Length: 16 • RV fee: Free • No water • Vault toilets • Activities: Fishing • Elevation: 4045

## Westport

**Clatsop State Forest - Kerry Road** • Agency: State • Tel: 503-325-5451 • Location: 6 miles NW of Westport (limited services), 15 miles NW of Clatskanie • GPS: Lat 46.145415 Lon -123.449054 • Open: All year • Total sites: 2 • RV sites: 2 • RV fee: Free • No water • Elevation: 1099

**Nicolai Mtn OHV Area - Shingle Mill - ODF** • Agency: State • Tel: 503-325-5451 • Location: 6 miles NW of Westport (limited services), 15 miles NW of Clatskanie • GPS: Lat 46.150815 Lon -123.452101 • Total sites: Dispersed • RV sites: Undefined • RV fee: Free • No water • Vault toilets • Activities: Motor sports • Elevation: 992

# Utah

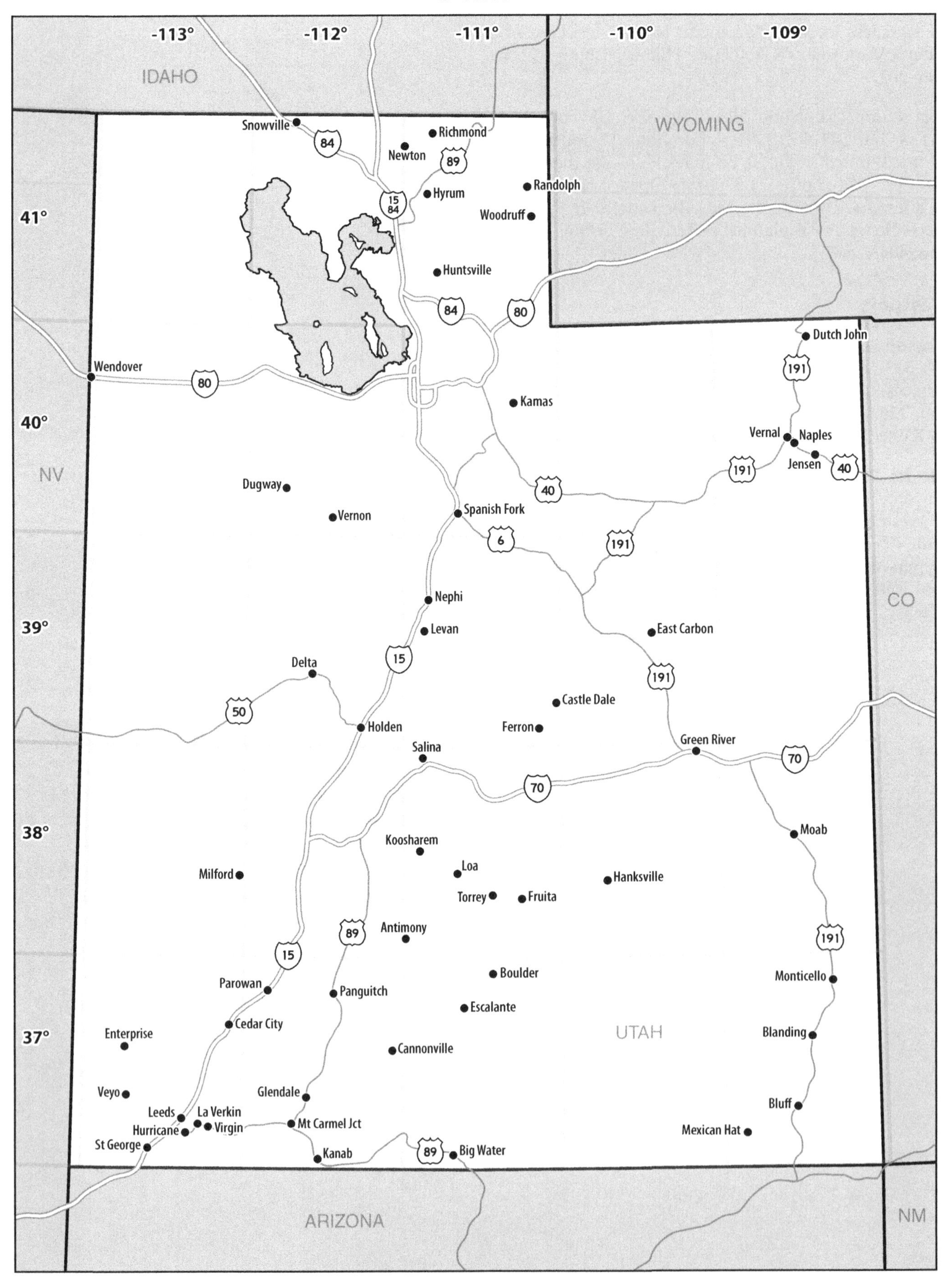

-113°
-112°
-111°
-110°
-109°
41°
40°
39°
38°
37°
IDAHO
WYOMING
NV
CO
ARIZONA
NM
UTAH
Snowville
Richmond
Newton
Hyrum
Randolph
Woodruff
Huntsville
Wendover
Kamas
Dutch John
Vernal
Naples
Jensen
Dugway
Vernon
Spanish Fork
Nephi
Levan
East Carbon
Delta
Castle Dale
Holden
Ferron
Salina
Green River
Moab
Koosharem
Loa
Milford
Hanksville
Torrey
Fruita
Antimony
Boulder
Monticello
Parowan
Panguitch
Escalante
Cedar City
Enterprise
Blanding
Cannonville
Veyo
Glendale
Bluff
Leeds
La Verkin
Virgin
Hurricane
Mt Carmel Jct
St George
Mexican Hat
Kanab
Big Water
84
89
15
80
191
40
6
50
70

# Utah — Camping Areas

| Abbreviation | Description |
|---|---|
| ATV | All Terrain Vehicle |
| DWR | Division of Wildlife Resources |
| NF | National Forest |
| NM | National Monument |
| NP | National Park |
| NRA | National Recreation Area |
| OHV | Off-Highway Vehicle |
| RA | Recreation Area |
| SFRD | Spanish Fork Ranger District |
| WMA | Wildlife Management Area |

## Antimony

**Otter Creek Reservoir - Fisherman's Bench** • Agency: Bureau of Land Management • Tel: 435-896-1500 • Location: 6 miles N of Antimony (limited services), 44 miles NE of Panguitch • GPS: Lat 38.180109 Lon -112.012049 • Total sites: Dispersed • RV sites: Undefined • RV fee: Free • No water • No toilets • Elevation: 6417

## Big Water

**Buckskin Gulch Trailhead** • Agency: Bureau of Land Management • Tel: 435-688-3200 • Location: 23 miles W of Big Water (limited services), 42 miles E of Kanab • GPS: Lat 37.067008 Lon -112.000579 • Total sites: Dispersed • RV sites: Undefined • RV fee: Free • No water • No toilets • Notes: Nearby BLM ranger station has maps and information on other camping areas • Activities: Hiking • Elevation: 4836

**Cottonwood Canyon Dispersed** • Agency: Bureau of Land Management • Location: 23 miles NW of Big Water (limited services), 59 miles NE of Kanab • GPS: Lat 37.240713 Lon -111.920923 • Total sites: Dispersed • RV sites: Undefined • RV fee: Free • No water • No toilets • Elevation: 4721

**Cottonwood Canyon Dispersed** • Agency: Bureau of Land Management • Location: 11 miles W of Big Water (limited services), 26 miles NW of Page, AZ • GPS: Lat 37.117754 Lon -111.853156 • Open: All year • Total sites: Dispersed • RV sites: Undefined • RV fee: Free • No water • No toilets • Notes: 2nd area .25 mile west at end of road • Elevation: 4784

**Cottonwood Canyon Dispersed** • Agency: Bureau of Land Management • Location: 11 miles W of Big Water (limited services), 26 miles NW of Page, AZ • GPS: Lat 37.119354 Lon -111.849618 • Open: All year • Total sites: Dispersed • RV sites: Undefined • RV fee: Free • No water • No toilets • Elevation: 4867

**Glen Canyon NRA - Alstrom Point** • Agency: National Park Service • Location: 25 miles E of Big Water (limited services), 40 miles NE of Page, AZ • GPS: Lat 37.059277 Lon -111.364684 • Total sites: Dispersed • RV sites: Undefined • RV fee: Free • No water • No toilets • Elevation: 4690

**Stateline** • Agency: Bureau of Land Management • Tel: 435-688-3200 • Location: 28 miles SW of Big Water (limited services), 47 miles E of Kanab • GPS: Lat 37.001113 Lon -112.035385 • Open: All year • Total sites: 4 • RV sites: 3 • RV fee: Free • No water • Vault toilets • Activities: Hiking • Elevation: 4977

## Blanding

**Arch Canyon/Comb Wash** • Agency: Bureau of Land Management • Tel: 435-587-1500 • Location: 18 miles SW of Blanding • GPS: Lat 37.507801 Lon -109.655044 • Open: All year • Total sites: Dispersed • RV sites: Undefined • RV fee: Free • No water • Vault toilets • Activities: Motor sports • Elevation: 4845

**Bailey S Lower Rd** • Agency: Bureau of Land Management • Location: 25 miles SW of Blanding • GPS: Lat 37.522409 Lon -109.748447 • Total sites: Dispersed • RV sites: Undefined • RV fee: Free • No water • No toilets • Elevation: 6099

**Blue Notch Road** • Agency: Bureau of Land Management • Location: 66 miles NW of Blanding • GPS: Lat 37.763527 Lon -110.293623 • Total sites: Dispersed • RV sites: Undefined • RV fee: Free • No water • No toilets • Elevation: 4831

**Clay Hills** • Agency: Bureau of Land Management • Location: 70 miles SW of Blanding • GPS: Lat 37.294118 Lon -110.397711 • Total sites: Dispersed • RV sites: Undefined • RV fee: Free • No water • Activities: Non-power boating • Elevation: 3721

**Jct 95-261** • Agency: Bureau of Land Management • Location: 32 miles W of Blanding • GPS: Lat 37.570625 Lon -109.882595 • Total sites: Dispersed • RV sites: Undefined • RV fee: Free • No water • No toilets • Activities: Hiking • Elevation: 6791

**Recapture Reservoir East Side** • Agency: Bureau of Land Management • Location: 4 miles N of Blanding • GPS: Lat 37.667694 Lon -109.437298 • Total sites: Dispersed • RV sites: Undefined • RV fee: Free • No water • No toilets • Activities: Power boating, non-power boating • Elevation: 6062

**Recapture Reservoir West Side** • Agency: Bureau of Land Management • Location: 4 miles N of Blanding • GPS: Lat

37.667068 Lon -109.443783 • Total sites: Dispersed • RV sites: Undefined • RV fee: Free • No water • No toilets • Elevation: 6076

## Bluff

**Valley of the Gods** • Agency: Bureau of Land Management • Tel: 435-587-1500 • Location: 23 miles W of Bluff (limited services), 49 miles SW of Blanding • GPS: Lat 37.316424 Lon -109.850376 • Total sites: Dispersed • RV sites: Undefined • RV fee: Free • No water • No toilets • Notes: No campfires • Elevation: 4997

## Boulder

**Escalante NM - Burr Trail Rd** • Agency: National Park Service • Location: 5 miles SE of Boulder (limited services), 32 miles NE of Escalante • GPS: Lat 37.848684 Lon -111.370475 • Total sites: Dispersed • RV sites: Undefined • RV fee: Free • No water • No toilets • Notes: Free permit required • Elevation: 5844

**Grand Staircase Escalante NM - Durffey Mesa** • Agency: Bureau of Land Management • Tel: 435-644-1200 • Location: 7 miles SE of Boulder (limited services), 33 miles NE of Escalante • GPS: Lat 37.862834 Lon -111.342453 • Total sites: Dispersed • RV sites: Undefined • RV fee: Free • No water • No toilets • Notes: Free permit required • Elevation: 5928

**Grand Staircase Escalante NM - Horse Canyon** • Agency: Bureau of Land Management • Tel: 435-644-1200 • Location: 20 miles E of Boulder (limited services), 46 miles NE of Escalante • GPS: Lat 37.922027 Lon -111.204368 • Total sites: Dispersed • RV sites: Undefined • RV fee: Free • No water • No toilets • Notes: Free permit required • Elevation: 5968

**Grand Staircase Escalante NM - North New Home Bench** • Agency: Bureau of Land Management • Tel: 435-644-1200 • Location: 3 miles SW of Boulder (limited services), 23 miles NE of Escalante • GPS: Lat 37.889317 Lon -111.460758 • Total sites: Dispersed • RV sites: Undefined • RV fee: Free • No water • No toilets • Notes: Free permit required • Activities: Hiking • Elevation: 6809

**Grand Staircase Escalante NM - Steep Creek Bench** • Agency: Bureau of Land Management • Tel: 435-644-1200 • Location: 8 miles SE of Boulder (limited services), 34 miles NE of Escalante • GPS: Lat 37.869709 Lon -111.336259 • Total sites: Dispersed • RV sites: Undefined • RV fee: Free • No water • No toilets • Notes: Free permit required • Elevation: 5961

**Grand Staircase Escalante NM - Stud Horse Peaks** • Agency: Bureau of Land Management • Tel: 435-644-1200 • Location: 29 miles E of Boulder (limited services), 55 miles NE of Escalante • GPS: Lat 37.868192 Lon -111.111702 • Total sites: Dispersed • RV sites: Undefined • RV fee: Free • No water • No toilets • Notes: Free permit required • Activities: Hiking • Elevation: 6782

## Cannonville

**Grand Staircase Escalante NM - Henrieville Creek** • Agency: Bureau of Land Management • Tel: 435-644-1200 • Location: 12 miles NE of Cannonville (limited services), 16 miles E of Tropic • GPS: Lat 37.617086 Lon -111.896804 • Total sites: Dispersed • RV sites: Undefined • RV fee: Free • No water • No toilets • Notes: Free permit required • Elevation: 6665

**Grand Staircase Escalante NM - Pump Canyon Springs** • Agency: Bureau of Land Management • Tel: 435-644-1200 • Location: 25 miles SE of Cannonville (limited services), 29 miles SE of Tropic • GPS: Lat 37.343314 Lon -111.870779 • Total sites: Dispersed • RV sites: Undefined • RV fee: Free • No water • No toilets • Notes: Free permit required • Activities: Hiking • Elevation: 5241

**Grand Staircase Escalante NM - Rock Springs Bench** • Agency: Bureau of Land Management • Tel: 435-644-1200 • Location: 8 miles SE of Cannonville (limited services), 13 miles SE of Tropic • GPS: Lat 37.494131 Lon -111.981379 • Total sites: Dispersed • RV sites: Undefined • RV fee: Free • No water • No toilets • Notes: Free permit required • Elevation: 5809

## Castle Dale

**San Rafael River** • Agency: Bureau of Land Management • Location: 29 miles SE of Castle Dale • GPS: Lat 39.058956 Lon -110.631925 • Total sites: Dispersed • RV sites: Undefined • RV fee: Free • No water • No toilets • Activities: Hiking, motor sports • Elevation: 5118

**The Wedge Overlook** • Agency: Bureau of Land Management • Location: 20 miles SE of Castle Dale • GPS: Lat 39.093267 Lon -110.758928 • Open: All year • Total sites: 6 • RV sites: 6 • RV fee: Free • No water • Vault toilets • Activities: Hiking, motor sports, equestrian area • Elevation: 6291

## Cedar City

**Kolob Reservoir Northwest** • Agency: County • Tel: 435-673-3617 • Location: 20 miles S of Cedar City • GPS: Lat 37.443101 Lon -113.052127 • Total sites: Dispersed • RV sites: Undefined • RV fee: Free • No water • Vault toilets • Activities: Hiking, mountain biking, fishing, motor sports, non-power boating • Elevation: 8140

**Kolob Reservoir Southeast** • Agency: County • Tel: 435-673-3617 • Location: 23 miles S of Cedar City • GPS: Lat 37.433086 Lon -113.045295 • Total sites: Dispersed • RV sites: Undefined • RV fee: Free • No water • Vault toilets • Activities: Hiking, mountain biking, fishing, power boating, motor sports, non-power boating • Elevation: 8154

**Kolob Reservoir West** • Agency: County • Tel: 435-673-3617 • Location: 21 miles S of Cedar City • GPS: Lat 37.438649 Lon -113.052481 • Total sites: Dispersed • RV sites: Undefined • RV fee: Free • No water • Vault toilets • Activities: Hiking, mountain biking, fishing, motor sports, non-power boating • Elevation: 8136

## Delta

**Amasa ATV Area** • Agency: Bureau of Land Management • Tel: 435-743-3123 • Location: 48 miles SW of Delta • GPS: Lat 39.141673 Lon -113.307273 • Total sites: Dispersed • RV sites: Undefined • RV fee: Free • No water • Vault toilets • Activities: Motor sports • Elevation: 6027

## Dugway

**White Rock** • Agency: Bureau of Land Management • Location: 13 miles NW of Dugway (limited services), 46 miles SW of Tooele • GPS: Lat 40.322602 Lon -112.905177 • Total sites: Dispersed • RV sites: Undefined • RV fee: Free • No water • No toilets • Activities: Rock climbing • Elevation: 5346

## Dutch John

**Bridgeport** • Agency: Bureau of Land Management • Tel: 435-781-4400 • Location: 31 miles SE of Dutch John (limited services), 74 miles NE of Vernal • GPS: Lat 40.879303 Lon -109.135604 • Total sites: Dispersed • RV sites: Undefined • Max RV Length: 18 • RV fee: Free • No water • No toilets • Activities: Hiking, mountain biking, fishing, power boating, non-power boating • Elevation: 5433

## East Carbon

**Mud Springs Plateau** • Agency: Bureau of Land Management • Location: 6 miles SW of East Carbon (limited services), 18 miles SE of Pine • GPS: Lat 39.513338 Lon -110.518894 • Total sites: Dispersed • RV sites: Undefined • RV fee: Free • No water • No toilets • Elevation: 5699

## Enterprise

**Newcastle Reservoir - DWR** • Agency: State • Location: 13 miles NE of Enterprise (limited services), 30 miles W of Cedar City • GPS: Lat 37.648156 Lon -113.527074 • Total sites: Dispersed • RV sites: Undefined • RV fee: Free • No water • No toilets • Activities: Fishing, power boating • Elevation: 5485

## Escalante

**Grand Staircase Escalante NM - Dance Hall Rock** • Agency: Bureau of Land Management • Tel: 435-644-1200 • Location: 41 miles SE of Escalante • GPS: Lat 37.356413 Lon -111.101489 • Total sites: Dispersed • RV sites: Undefined • RV fee: Free • No water • No toilets • Notes: Free permit required • Activities: Hiking • Elevation: 4618

**Grand Staircase Escalante NM - Forty Mile Spring** • Agency: Bureau of Land Management • Tel: 435-644-1200 • Location: 44 miles SE of Escalante • GPS: Lat 37.392523 Lon -111.048634 • Total sites: Dispersed • RV sites: Undefined • RV fee: Free • No water • Vault toilets • Notes: Free permit required • Elevation: 4793

**Grand Staircase Escalante NM - Harris Wash** • Agency: Bureau of Land Management • Tel: 435-644-1200 • Location: 15 miles SE of Escalante • GPS: Lat 37.605248 Lon -111.422393 • Total sites: Dispersed • RV sites: Undefined • RV fee: Free • No water • No toilets • Notes: Free permit required • Elevation: 5436

**Grand Staircase Escalante NM - Hole in the Rock** • Agency: Bureau of Land Management • Tel: 435-644-1200 • Location: 4 miles SE of Escalante • GPS: Lat 37.722533 Lon -111.527442 • Total sites: Dispersed • RV sites: Undefined • RV fee: Free • No water • No toilets • Notes: Free permit required • Elevation: 5738

**Grand Staircase Escalante NM - Sooner Rocks** • Agency: Bureau of Land Management • Tel: 435-644-1200 • Location: 45 miles SE of Escalante • GPS: Lat 37.32793 Lon -111.058817 • Total sites: Dispersed • RV sites: Undefined • RV fee: Free • No water • No toilets • Notes: Free permit required • Activities: Hiking • Elevation: 4356

**Grand Staircase Escalante NM - Spencer Flat** • Agency: Bureau of Land Management • Tel: 435-644-1200 • Location: 11 miles E of Escalante • GPS: Lat 37.726621 Lon -111.443822 • Total sites: Dispersed • RV sites: Undefined • RV fee: Free • No water • No toilets • Notes: Free permit required • Elevation: 5958

**Grand Staircase Escalante NM - Tin Can Flat** • Agency: Bureau of Land Management • Tel: 435-644-1200 • Location: 5 miles SE of Escalante • GPS: Lat 37.714589 Lon -111.514899 • Total sites: Dispersed • RV sites: Undefined • RV fee: Free • No water • No toilets • Notes: Free permit required • Activities: Hiking • Elevation: 5683

## Ferron

**Dutch Flat** • Agency: Bureau of Land Management • Location: 7 miles SE of Ferron (limited services), 15 miles S of Castle Dale • GPS: Lat 39.058163 Lon -111.040176 • Total sites: Dispersed • RV sites: Undefined • RV fee: Free • No water • No toilets • Elevation: 6079

**Justesen Flats ATV** • Agency: Bureau of Land Management • Location: 27 miles SE of Ferron (limited services), 47 miles W of Green River • GPS: Lat 38.842505 Lon -110.884172 • Total sites: Dispersed • RV sites: Undefined • RV fee: Free • No water • No toilets • Activities: Motor sports • Elevation: 7116

## Fruita

**Capitol Reef NP - Cedar Mesa** • Agency: National Park Service • Tel: 435-425-3791 • Location: 29 miles SE of Fruita (limited services), 106 miles SW of Green River • GPS: Lat 38.007 Lon -111.085 • Open: All year • Total sites: 5 • RV sites: 5 • RV fee: Free • No water • Vault toilets • Activities: Hiking • Elevation: 5610

## Glendale

**Grand Staircase Escalante NM - Skutumpah Terrace** • Agency: Bureau of Land Management • Tel: 435-644-1200 • Location: 16 miles SE of Glendale (limited services), 19 miles E of Orderville • GPS: Lat 37.268283 Lon -112.374518 • Total sites: Dispersed • RV sites: Undefined • RV fee: Free • No water • No toilets • Notes: Free permit required • Activities: Hiking • Elevation: 6018

## Green River

**Black Dragon Canyon** • Agency: Bureau of Land Management • Location: 15 miles W of Green River • GPS: Lat 38.937449 Lon -110.419039 • Total sites: Dispersed • RV sites: Undefined • RV fee: Free • No water • No toilets • Elevation: 4323

**Crystal Geyser** • Agency: Bureau of Land Management • Location: 8 miles S of Green River • GPS: Lat 38.937007 Lon -110.134721 • Total sites: Dispersed • RV sites: Undefined • RV fee: Free • No water • No toilets • Activities: Non-power boating • Elevation: 4058

**Dick Canyon** • Agency: Bureau of Land Management • Location: 103 miles NE of Green River, 47 miles NW of Fruita, CO • GPS: Lat 39.483769 Lon -109.090487 • Total sites: Dispersed • RV sites: Undefined • RV fee: Free • No water • No toilets • Activities: Hiking • Elevation: 8217

**Hastings Road** • Agency: Bureau of Land Management • Location: 10 miles N of Green River • GPS: Lat 39.122974 Lon -110.113897 • Total sites: Dispersed • RV sites: Undefined • RV fee: Free • No water • No toilets • Activities: Non-power boating • Elevation: 4128

**Nefertiti Rapids** • Agency: Bureau of Land Management • Location: 18 miles N of Green River • GPS: Lat 39.195279 Lon -110.077249 • Total sites: Dispersed • RV sites: Undefined • RV fee: Free • No water • Vault toilets • Activities: Hiking, non-power boating • Elevation: 4163

**The Wickiup** • Agency: Bureau of Land Management • Location: 30 miles W of Green River • GPS: Lat 38.893472 Lon -110.652176 • Total sites: Dispersed • RV sites: Undefined • RV fee: Free • No water • No toilets • Elevation: 6700

**Twin Knolls** • Agency: Bureau of Land Management • Location: 37 miles SW of Green River • GPS: Lat 38.788848 Lon -110.709829 • Total sites: Dispersed • RV sites: Undefined • RV fee: Free • No water • No toilets • Elevation: 6696

**White Wash Sand Dunes** • Agency: Bureau of Land Management • Tel: 435-259-2100 • Location: 26 miles SE of Green River • GPS: Lat 38.800522 Lon -110.033257 • Total sites: Dispersed • RV sites: Undefined • RV fee: Free • No water • No toilets (portable toilets required if not self-contained) • Elevation: 4147

## Hanksville

**Factory Butte - Swing Arm City OHV Area** • Agency: Bureau of Land Management • Tel: 435-896-1500 • Location: 12 miles W of Hanksville (limited services), 68 miles SW of Green River • GPS: Lat 38.365783 Lon -110.912165 • Total sites: Dispersed • RV sites: Undefined • RV fee: Free • No water • No toilets • Activities: Motor sports • Elevation: 4504

**McMillan Spring** • Agency: Bureau of Land Management • Tel: 435-542-3461 • Location: 32 miles SW of Hanksville (limited services), 51 miles SE of Torrey • GPS: Lat 38.072626 Lon -110.848074 • Total sites: 10 • RV sites: 10 • RV fee: Free (donation appreciated) • Central water • Vault toilets • Activities: Hunting, equestrian area • Elevation: 8412

**San Rafael Swell** • Agency: Bureau of Land Management • Location: 28 miles N of Hanksville (limited services), 45 miles SW of Green River • GPS: Lat 38.656072 Lon -110.710213 • Total sites: Dispersed • RV sites: Undefined • RV fee: Free • No water • No toilets • Activities: Hiking, motor sports • Elevation: 5600

**Sandthrax** • Agency: Bureau of Land Management • Tel: 435-542-3461 • Location: 28 miles S of Hanksville (limited services), 84 miles SW of Green River • GPS: Lat 38.016308 Lon -110.532063 • Total sites: 17 • RV sites: 7 • RV fee: Free • No water • No toilets • Notes: Beware of deep sand • Elevation: 4450

**South Temple Wash** • Agency: Bureau of Land Management • Location: 25 miles N of Hanksville (limited services), 42 miles SW of Green River • GPS: Lat 38.656662 Lon -110.661364 • Total sites: Dispersed • RV sites: Undefined • RV fee: Free • No water • Vault toilets • Notes: Jeep and ATV area • Activities: Hiking, mountain biking, motor sports • Elevation: 5318

**Taylor Flat** • Agency: Bureau of Land Management • Location: 37 miles N of Hanksville (limited services), 42 miles SW of Green River • GPS: Lat 38.753533 Lon -110.763605 • Total sites: Dispersed • RV sites: Undefined • RV fee: Free • No water • No toilets • Elevation: 6709

**Temple Mountaint** • Agency: Bureau of Land Management • Location: 27 miles N of Hanksville (limited services), 43 miles SW of Green River • GPS: Lat 38.667704 Lon -110.684824 • Total sites: Dispersed • RV sites: Undefined • RV fee: Free • No water • Vault toilets • Activities: Hiking • Elevation: 5453

**The Mix Pad** • Agency: Bureau of Land Management • Location: 19 miles W of Hanksville (limited services), 29 miles E of Torrey • GPS: Lat 38.339493 Lon -111.030876 • Total sites: Dispersed • RV sites: Undefined (dispersed sites along the road) • RV fee: Free • No water • No toilets • Notes: Subject to flooding • Activities: Motor sports • Elevation: 4665

**Wld Horse Road** • Agency: Bureau of Land Management • Location: 34 miles N of Hanksville (limited services), 51 miles SW of Green River • GPS: Lat 38.577351 Lon -110.772861 • Total sites: Dispersed • RV sites: Undefined (numerous sites) • RV fee: Free • No water • No toilets • Activities: Hiking • Elevation: 4879

## Holden

**Maple Hollow** (Fishlake NF) • Agency: US Forest Service • Tel: 435-743-5721 • Location: 7 miles SE of Holden (limited services), 22 miles NE of Fillmore • GPS: Lat 39.061151 Lon -112.170831 • Open: May-Sep • Total sites: 6 • RV sites: 4 • RV fee: Free • Central water • Vault toilets • Elevation: 7031

## Huntsville

**Ogden River Middle Fork** • Agency: County • Location: 2 miles N of Huntsville (limited services), 13 miles NE of Ogden • GPS: Lat 41.295605 Lon -111.754967 • Open: Apr-Dec • Total sites: Dispersed • RV sites: Undefined • RV fee: Free • No water • Vault toilets • Elevation: 5072

## Hurricane

**Hurricane Cliffs RA** • Agency: Bureau of Land Management • Tel: 435-688-3200 • Location: 5 miles E of Hurricane • GPS: Lat 37.187725 Lon -113.242263 • Total sites: 10 • RV sites: 2 • RV fee: Free • No water • No toilets • Elevation: 3756

**Hurricane Cliffs RA** • Agency: Bureau of Land Management • Tel: 435-688-3200 • Location: 5 miles E of Hurricane • GPS: Lat 37.182825 Lon -113.245121 • Total sites: 6 • RV sites: 1 • RV fee: Free • No water • No toilets • Elevation: 3787

**Hurricane Cliffs RA** • Agency: Bureau of Land Management • Tel: 435-688-3200 • Location: 4 miles E of Hurricane • GPS: Lat 37.165868 Lon -113.253745 • Total sites: 12 • RV sites: 2 • RV fee: Free • No water • No toilets • Elevation: 3882

**Hurricane Cliffs RA** • Agency: Bureau of Land Management • Tel: 435-688-3200 • Location: 6 miles E of Hurricane • GPS: Lat 37.187337 Lon -113.223551 • Total sites: 12 • RV sites: 3 • RV fee: Free • No water • No toilets • Notes: Rough access road • Elevation: 3647

## Hyrum

**Wapiti FA - DWR** • Agency: State • Tel: 801-538-4700 • Location: 14 miles E of Hyrum • GPS: Lat 41.605033 Lon -111.589521 • Total sites: Dispersed • RV sites: Undefined • RV fee: Free • No water • Vault toilets • Activities: Hiking, fishing • Elevation: 5474

## Jensen

**Cliff Ridge** • Agency: Bureau of Land Management • Tel: 435-781-4400 • Location: 21 miles E of Jensen (limited services), 30 miles E of Vernal • GPS: Lat 40.367685 Lon -109.119664 • Total sites: Dispersed • RV sites: Undefined • RV fee: Free • No water • No toilets • Notes: Hang-gliding area • Activities: Hiking, mountain biking, hunting, motor sports, equestrian area • Elevation: 8123

## Kamas

**East Fork Blacks Fork Trailhead** (Uinta-Wasatch-Cache NF) • Agency: US Forest Service • Location: 72 miles NE of Kamas, 37 miles SW of Mountain View, WY • GPS: Lat 40.884487 Lon -110.538462 • Total sites: 8 • RV sites: 8 • RV fee: Free • No water • Vault toilets • Activities: Hiking • Elevation: 9351

**Lower Canyon** (Fishlake NF) • Agency: US Forest Service • Tel: 435-783-4338 • Location: 6 miles E of Kamas • GPS: Lat 40.628795 Lon -111.177702 • Total sites: 6 • RV sites: 6 • RV fee: Free • No water • No toilets • Elevation: 7128

## Kanab

**Coral Pink Sand Dunes - Meadows** • Agency: Bureau of Land Management • Tel: 435-644-1200 • Location: 17 miles W of Kanab • GPS: Lat 37.067627 Lon -112.703822 • Total sites: Dispersed • RV sites: Undefined • RV fee: Free • No water • No toilets • Activities: Motor sports • Elevation: 6151

**Coral Pink Sand Dunes - Sand Spring** • Agency: Bureau of Land Management • Tel: 435-644-1200 • Location: 14 miles W of Kanab • GPS: Lat 37.077798 Lon -112.661815 • Total sites: Dispersed • RV sites: Undefined • RV fee: Free • No water • No toilets • Activities: Motor sports • Elevation: 6185

**Coral Pink Sand Dunes Dispersed** • Agency: Bureau of Land Management • Tel: 435-644-1200 • Location: 20 miles W of Kanab • GPS: Lat 37.033381 Lon -112.747553 • Total sites: Dispersed • RV sites: Undefined • RV fee: Free • No water • No toilets • Elevation: 5870

**Grand Staircase Escalante NM - Kitchen Corral Wash** • Agency: Bureau of Land Management • Tel: 435-644-1200 • Location: 27 miles E of Kanab • GPS: Lat 37.140117 Lon -112.091662 • Total sites: Dispersed • RV sites: Undefined • RV fee: Free • No water • No toilets • Notes: Free permit required • Elevation: 5371

**Peek-A-Boo ATV Area** • Agency: Bureau of Land Management • Location: 8 miles N of Kanab • GPS: Lat 37.154736 Lon -112.573671 • Open: All year • Total sites: Dispersed • RV sites: Undefined • RV fee: Free • No water • No toilets • Activities: Motor sports • Elevation: 5702

**The Arch site 1** • Agency: Bureau of Land Management • Location: 8 miles N of Kanab • GPS: Lat 37.142956 Lon -112.584759 • Total sites: Dispersed • RV sites: Undefined • RV fee: Free • No water • No toilets • Activities: Hiking • Elevation: 5657

**The Arch site 2** • Agency: Bureau of Land Management • Location: 8 miles N of Kanab • GPS: Lat 37.146552 Lon -112.582172 • Total sites: Dispersed • RV sites: Undefined • RV fee: Free • No water • No toilets • Activities: Hiking • Elevation: 5584

**The Arch site 3** • Agency: Bureau of Land Management • Location: 8 miles N of Kanab • GPS: Lat 37.147408 Lon -112.585359 • Total sites: Dispersed • RV sites: Undefined • RV fee: Free • No water • No toilets • Activities: Hiking • Elevation: 5611

## Koosharem

**Koosharem Reservoir** • Agency: Bureau of Land Management • Tel: 435-896-1500 • Location: 7 miles N of Koosharem (limited services), 23 miles SE of Richfield • GPS: Lat 38.60006 Lon -111.847175 • Total sites: Dispersed • RV sites: Undefined • RV fee: Free • No toilets • Activities: Hiking, fishing, motor sports • Elevation: 7014

## La Verkin

**Toquerville Falls** • Agency: Bureau of Land Management • Location: 9 miles N of La Verkin • GPS: Lat 37.299361 Lon -113.246888 • Total sites: Dispersed • RV sites: Undefined • RV fee: Free • No water • No toilets • Activities: Hiking, swimming • Elevation: 3764

**Virgin Dam Dispersed** • Agency: Bureau of Land Management • Location: 4 miles E of La Verkin • GPS: Lat 37.204937 Lon -113.231983 • Total sites: 1 • RV sites: 1 • RV fee: Free • No water • No toilets • Notes: Note private property boundaries • Elevation: 3584

**Virgin Dam Dispersed** • Agency: Bureau of Land Management • Location: 4 miles E of La Verkin • GPS: Lat 37.202553 Lon -113.231866 • Total sites: 1 • RV sites: 1 • RV fee: Free • No water • No toilets • Notes: Note private property boundaries • Elevation: 3587

**Virgin Dam Dispersed** • Agency: Bureau of Land Management • Location: 3 miles E of La Verkin • GPS: Lat 37.206323 Lon -113.240447 • Total sites: 5 • RV sites: 4 • RV fee: Free • No water • No toilets • Notes: Note private property boundaries • Elevation: 3620

## Leeds

**Red Cliffs Desert Reserve** • Agency: Bureau of Land Management • Location: 4 miles S of Leeds (limited services), 13 miles N of Hurricane • GPS: Lat 37.206654 Lon -113.330796 • Total sites: Dispersed • RV sites: Undefined • RV fee: Free • No water • No toilets • Activities: Hiking • Elevation: 3190

## Levan

**Chicken Creek** (Manti-La Sal NF) • Agency: US Forest Service • Location: 6 miles SE of Levan (limited services), 15 miles SE of Nephi • GPS: Lat 39.53 Lon -111.774 • Open: May-Nov • Total sites: 7 • RV sites: 7 • RV fee: Free • No water • Vault toilets • Activities: Fishing, motor sports • Elevation: 6125

## Loa

**Allred Point** • Agency: County • Location: 2 miles N of Loa (limited services), 46 miles SE of Richfield • GPS: Lat 38.433086 Lon -111.631621 • Total sites: Dispersed • RV sites: Undefined • RV fee: Free • Central water • No toilets • Activities: Fishing • Elevation: 7108

**Capitol Reef NP - Cathedral Valley** • Agency: National Park Service • Tel: 435-425-3791 • Location: 24 miles NE of Loa (limited services), 68 miles SE of Richfield • GPS: Lat 38.474731 Lon -111.367641 • Open: All year • Total sites: 6 • RV sites: 6 • RV fee: Free • No water • Vault toilets • Activities: Hiking • Elevation: 6939

## Mexican Hat

**Mexican Hat** • Agency: Bureau of Land Management • Location: 2 miles N of Mexican Hat (limited services), 48 miles SW of Blanding • GPS: Lat 37.171099 Lon -109.849266 • Total sites: Dispersed • RV sites: Undefined (numerous sites in area) • RV fee: Free • No water • No toilets • Elevation: 4234

**Muley Point** • Agency: Bureau of Land Management • Location: 18 miles NW of Mexican Hat (limited services), 59 miles SW of Blanding • GPS: Lat 37.235377 Lon -109.992191 • Total sites: Dispersed • RV sites: Undefined • RV fee: Free • No water • No toilets • Activities: Hiking • Elevation: 6194

## Milford

**Lions Club RV Park** • Agency: Municipal • Location: In Milford • GPS: Lat 38.40117 Lon -113.014436 • Total sites: 6 • RV sites: 6 • RV fee: Free (donation appreciated) • Central water • No toilets • Elevation: 5010

**Rock Corral** • Agency: Bureau of Land Management • Tel: 435-586-2401 • Location: 12 miles E of Milford • GPS: Lat 38.372466 Lon -112.834018 • Open: May-Nov • Total sites: Dispersed • RV sites: Undefined • RV fee: Free • No water • Vault toilets • Activities: Hiking • Elevation: 7093

## Moab

**Bride Canyon** • Agency: Bureau of Land Management • Tel: 435-259-2100 • Location: 12 miles NW of Moab • GPS: Lat 38.612017 Lon -109.666318 • Total sites: 6 • RV sites: 6 • RV fee: Free • No water • No toilets • Elevation: 4874

**Cisco Boat Ramp** • Agency: Bureau of Land Management • Location: 51 miles NE of Moab • GPS: Lat 38.969865 Lon -109.251941 • Total sites: Dispersed • RV sites: Undefined • RV fee: Free • No water • No toilets • Activities: Whitewater rafting • Elevation: 4163

**Copper Ridge Dinosaur Tracksite** • Agency: Bureau of Land Management • Location: 22 miles NW of Moab • GPS: Lat 38.829819 Lon -109.765039 • Open: All year • Stay limit: 14 days • Total sites: Dispersed • RV sites: Undefined (many sites along the road) • RV fee: Free • No water • Vault toilets • Activities: Hiking, mountain biking • Elevation: 4695

**Dalton Well Road Dispersed** • Agency: Bureau of Land Management • Location: 12 miles NW of Moab • GPS: Lat 38.716143 Lon -109.691953 • Total sites: Dispersed • RV sites: Undefined • RV fee: Free • No water • No toilets • Activities: Hiking, motor sports • Elevation: 4403

**Dalton Well Road Dispersed** • Agency: Bureau of Land Management • Location: 13 miles NW of Moab • GPS: Lat 38.722837 Lon -109.690397 • Open: All year • Total sites: Dispersed • RV sites: Undefined • RV fee: Free • No water • No toilets • Elevation: 4414

**Dubinky Well Road #1** • Agency: Bureau of Land Management • Tel: 435-259-2100 • Location: 18 miles NW of Moab • GPS: Lat 38.643814 Lon -109.819371 • Total sites: Dispersed • RV sites: Undefined • RV fee: Free • No water • No toilets • Elevation: 5298

**Dubinky Well Road #2** • Agency: Bureau of Land Management • Tel: 435-259-2100 • Location: 19 miles NW of Moab • GPS: Lat 38.656348 Lon -109.827185 • Total sites: Dispersed • RV sites: Undefined • RV fee: Free • No water • No toilets • Elevation: 5187

**Mill Canyon** • Agency: Bureau of Land Management • Tel: 435-259-2100 • Location: 15 miles NW of Moab • GPS: Lat 38.712414 Lon -109.739554 • Total sites: Dispersed • RV sites: Undefined • RV fee: Free • No water • No toilets • Activities: Hiking • Elevation: 4555

**Mineral Point Road** • Agency: Bureau of Land Management • Location: 22 miles W of Moab • GPS: Lat 38.585247 Lon -109.826302 • Open: All year • Total sites: 7 • RV sites: 2 • RV fee: Free • No water • No toilets • Activities: Hiking, motor sports • Elevation: 5775

**Spring Canyon Road - Site 1** • Agency: Bureau of Land Management • Location: 21 miles W of Moab • GPS: Lat 38.633541 Lon -109.871174 • Total sites: Dispersed • RV sites: Undefined • RV fee: Free • No water • No toilets • Activities: Hiking, motor sports • Elevation: 5111

**Spring Canyon Road - Site 2** • Agency: Bureau of Land Management • Location: 23 miles NW of Moab • GPS: Lat 38.634518 Lon -109.897116 • Total sites: Dispersed • RV sites: Undefined • RV fee: Free • No water • No toilets • Activities: Hiking, motor sports • Elevation: 5054

**Spring Canyon Road - Site 3** • Agency: Bureau of Land Management • Location: 25 miles W of Moab • GPS: Lat 38.622306 Lon -109.931642 • Total sites: Dispersed • RV sites: Undefined • RV fee: Free • No water • No toilets • Activities: Hiking, motor sports • Elevation: 5297

**Spring Canyon Road - Site 4** • Agency: Bureau of Land Management • Location: 26 miles W of Moab • GPS: Lat 38.630445 Lon -109.953867 • Total sites: Dispersed • RV sites: Undefined • RV fee: Free • No water • No toilets • Activities: Hiking, motor sports • Elevation: 5162

**Spring Canyon Road - Site 5** • Agency: Bureau of Land Management • Location: 28 miles NW of Moab • GPS: Lat 38.639143 Lon -109.976254 • Total sites: Dispersed • RV sites: Undefined • RV fee: Free • No water • No toilets • Activities: Hiking, motor sports • Elevation: 4830

**Willow Springs Trail Dispersed 1** • Agency: Bureau of Land Management • Location: 11 miles NW of Moab • GPS: Lat 38.697618 Lon -109.692145 • Open: All year • Total sites: Dispersed • RV sites: Undefined • RV fee: Free • No water • No toilets • Activities: Hiking • Elevation: 4443

**Willow Springs Trail Dispersed 2** • Agency: Bureau of Land Management • Location: 12 miles NW of Moab • GPS: Lat 38.696216 Lon -109.673125 • Open: All year • Total sites: Dispersed • RV sites: Undefined • RV fee: Free • No water • No toilets • Elevation: 4360

## Monticello

**Hart Point Road Dispersed** • Agency: Bureau of Land Management • Location: 27 miles NW of Monticello • GPS: Lat 38.069763 Lon -109.514162 • Total sites: Dispersed • RV sites: Undefined • RV fee: Free • No water • No toilets • Elevation: 6631

**Hart Point Road Dispersed** • Agency: Bureau of Land Management • Location: 27 miles NW of Monticello • GPS: Lat 38.064989 Lon -109.516922 • Total sites: Dispersed • RV sites: Undefined • RV fee: Free • No water • No toilets • Elevation: 6637

**Hart Point Road Dispersed** • Agency: Bureau of Land Management • Location: 24 miles NW of Monticello • GPS: Lat 38.018738 Lon -109.495227 • Total sites: Dispersed • RV sites: Undefined • RV fee: Free • No water • No toilets • Elevation: 6652

**Hart Point Road Dispersed** • Agency: Bureau of Land Management • Location: 25 miles NW of Monticello • GPS: Lat 38.034225 Lon -109.499171 • Total sites: Dispersed • RV sites: Undefined • RV fee: Free • No water • No toilets • Elevation: 6701

**Hart Point Road Dispersed** • Agency: Bureau of Land Management • Location: 26 miles NW of Monticello • GPS: Lat 38.048863 Lon -109.504119 • Total sites: Dispersed • RV sites: Undefined • RV fee: Free • No water • No toilets • Elevation: 6738

**Hart Point Road Dispersed** • Agency: Bureau of Land Management • Location: 23 miles NW of Monticello • GPS: Lat 38.011034 Lon -109.490983 • Total sites: Dispersed • RV sites: Undefined • RV fee: Free • No water • No toilets • Elevation: 6765

**Lloyd Lake** • Agency: Bureau of Land Management • Location: 2 miles SW of Monticello • GPS: Lat 37.855068 Lon -109.365275 • Total sites: Dispersed • RV sites: Undefined • RV fee: Free • No water • Vault toilets • Elevation: 7225

**Lockhart Rd South** • Agency: Bureau of Land Management • Location: 43 miles NW of Monticello • GPS: Lat 38.182475 Lon -109.668137 • Total sites: Dispersed • RV sites: Undefined • RV fee: Free • No water • No toilets • Elevation: 4914

## Mt Carmel Jct

**Mount Carmel** • Agency: Bureau of Land Management • Location: 2 miles S of Mt Carmel Jct (limited services), 6 miles S of Orderville • GPS: Lat 37.207169 Lon -112.675418 • Total sites: Dispersed • RV sites: Undefined • RV fee: Free • No water • No toilets • Elevation: 5500

**Mount Carmel Jct ATV** • Agency: Bureau of Land Management • Location: 1 mile S of Mt Carmel Jct (limited services), 16 miles NW of Knab • GPS: Lat 37.215127 Lon -112.684982 • Total sites: Dispersed • RV sites: Undefined • RV fee: Free • No water • No toilets • Activities: Motor sports • Elevation: 5177

**Twin Hollows Canyon** • Agency: Bureau of Land Management • Location: 1 mile S of Mt Carmel Jct (limited services), 16 miles NW of Knab • GPS: Lat 37.207192 Lon -112.689751 • Total sites: Dispersed • RV sites: Undefined • RV fee: Free • No water • No toilets • Activities: Motor sports • Elevation: 5139

**Yellowjacket Canyon** • Agency: Bureau of Land Management • Location: 7 miles S of Mt Carmel Jct (limited services), 16 miles NW of Kanab • GPS: Lat 37.144836 Lon -112.672894 • Total sites: Dispersed • RV sites: Undefined • RV fee: Free • No water • No toilets • Activities: Motor sports • Elevation: 5667

**Yellowjacket Spring** • Agency: Bureau of Land Management • Location: 11 miles S of Mt Carmel Jct (limited services), 20 miles NW of Kanab • GPS: Lat 37.089272 Lon -112.696388 • Total sites: Dispersed • RV sites: Undefined • RV fee: Free • No water • No toilets • Activities: Motor sports • Elevation: 6145

## Naples

**Atchee Ridge 1** • Agency: Bureau of Land Management • Location: 69 miles SE of Naples • GPS: Lat 39.660605 Lon -109.096294 • Total sites: Dispersed • RV sites: Undefined • RV fee: Free • No water • No toilets • Elevation: 7748

**Atchee Ridge 2** • Agency: Bureau of Land Management • Location: 65 miles SE of Naples • GPS: Lat 39.706875 Lon -109.143266 • Total sites: Dispersed • RV sites: Undefined • RV fee: Free • No water • No toilets • Elevation: 7243

## Nephi

**Cottonwood - SFRD** (Uinta-Wasatch-Cache NF) • Agency: US Forest Service • Tel: 801-798-3571 • Location: 10 miles

NE of Nephi • GPS: Lat 39.780366 Lon -111.723377 • Open: Apr-Oct • Stay limit: 7 days • Total sites: 18 • RV sites: 18 • RV fee: Free • No water • Vault toilets • Activities: Fishing • Elevation: 6594

**Little Sahara RA - Jericho** • Agency: Bureau of Land Management • Tel: 435-743-3100 • Location: 34 miles W of Nephi • GPS: Lat 39.686812 Lon -112.367833 • Open: All year • Total sites: 40 • RV sites: 40 • RV fee: Free • No toilets • Activities: Motor sports • Elevation: 5030

**Little Sahara RA - Oasis** • Agency: Bureau of Land Management • Tel: 435-743-3100 • Location: 34 miles W of Nephi • GPS: Lat 39.689381 Lon -112.353918 • Open: All year • Total sites: 115 • RV sites: 115 • RV fee: Free • Central water • No toilets • Activities: Motor sports • Elevation: 5019

**Little Sahara RA - Sand Mt** • Agency: Bureau of Land Management • Tel: 435-743-3100 • Location: 37 miles W of Nephi • GPS: Lat 39.639164 Lon -112.389114 • Open: All year • Total sites: Dispersed • RV sites: Undefined • RV fee: Free • Central water • No toilets • Activities: Motor sports • Elevation: 4928

**Little Sahara RA - White Sands** • Agency: Bureau of Land Management • Tel: 435-743-3100 • Location: 30 miles W of Nephi • GPS: Lat 39.740705 Lon -112.314718 • Open: All year • Total sites: 100 • RV sites: Undefined • RV fee: Free • Central water (no water in winter) • Vault toilets • Activities: Motor sports • Elevation: 5338

## Newton

**Newton Reservoir** • Agency: US Bureau of Reclamation • Tel: 801-379-1000 • Location: 3 miles N of Newton (limited services), 11 miles NW of Smithfield • GPS: Lat 41.89686 Lon -111.97806 • Open: May-Oct • Stay limit: 14 days • Total sites: Dispersed • RV sites: Undefined • RV fee: Free • No toilets • Activities: Fishing • Elevation: 4780

## Panguitch

**Casto Canyon** (Dixie NF) • Agency: US Forest Service • Tel: 435-676-2676 • Location: 7 miles SE of Panguitch • GPS: Lat 37.785266 Lon -112.339231 • Total sites: 5 • RV sites: 5 • Max RV Length: 35 • RV fee: Free • No water • No toilets • Activities: Hiking, mountain biking, motor sports, equestrian area • Elevation: 7028

## Parowan

**Paragonah(Red Creek) Reservoir WMA disbursed** • Agency: State • Location: 12 miles NE of Parowan • GPS: Lat 37.863395 Lon -112.676645 • Total sites: Dispersed • RV sites: Undefined • RV fee: Free • No toilets • Elevation: 7829

**Parowan Gap** • Agency: Bureau of Land Management • Location: 10 miles NW of Parowan • GPS: Lat 37.916884 Lon -112.978666 • Open: All year • Total sites: Dispersed • RV sites: Undefined • RV fee: Free • No water • No toilets • Notes: Near Parowan Gap Petroglyph Site • Elevation: 5710

## Randolph

**Crawford** • Agency: Bureau of Land Management • Location: 10 miles E of Randolph (limited services), 36 miles SE of Garden City • GPS: Lat 41.660204 Lon -111.095804 • Total sites: Dispersed • RV sites: Undefined • RV fee: Free • No water • No toilets • Elevation: 7608

## Richmond

**High Creek** (Uinta-Wasatch-Cache NF) • Agency: US Forest Service • Tel: 435-755-3620 • Location: 7 miles NE of Richmond • GPS: Lat 41.976 Lon -111.735 • Open: May-Oct • Stay limit: 7 days • Total sites: 2 • RV sites: 2 • RV fee: Free • No water • Vault toilets • Elevation: 5600

## Salina

**Cold Springs** (Fishlake NF) • Agency: US Forest Service • Tel: 435-896-9233 • Location: 21 miles SE of Salina • GPS: Lat 38.782456 Lon -111.643283 • Total sites: 9 • RV sites: 9 • RV fee: Free • No water • Vault toilets • Elevation: 9152

**Gooseberry I-70 Trailhead** (Fishlake NF) • Agency: US Forest Service • Tel: 435-896-9233 • Location: 8 miles E of Salina • GPS: Lat 38.915284 Lon -111.732219 • Total sites: 6 • RV sites: 4 • RV fee: Free • No water • Vault toilets • Activities: Motor sports, equestrian area • Elevation: 5766

**Salina Creek Second Crossing** (Fishlake NF) • Agency: US Forest Service • Tel: 435-896-9233 • Location: 24 miles E of Salina • GPS: Lat 38.937869 Lon -111.543251 • Open: Mar-Oct • Total sites: 28 • RV sites: 22 • RV fee: Free • No water • Vault toilets • Elevation: 7275

**Twin Ponds** (Fishlake NF) • Agency: US Forest Service • Tel: 435-896-9233 • Location: 21 miles SE of Salina • GPS: Lat 38.786458 Lon -111.640573 • Total sites: 13 • RV sites: 13 • RV fee: Free • No water • Vault toilets • Elevation: 9098

## Snowville

**Clear Creek** (Sawtooth NF) • Agency: US Forest Service • Tel: 208-678-0439 • Location: 36 miles W of Snowville (limited services), 69 miles NW of Tremonton • GPS: Lat 41.953483 Lon -113.321782 • Open: Jun-Oct • Stay limit: 14 days • Total sites: 12 • RV sites:

12 • RV fee: Free • Central water • Vault toilets • Activities: Hiking, motor sports • Elevation: 6312

## Spanish Fork

**Sawmill Hollow** (Uinta-Wasatch-Cache NF) • Agency: US Forest Service • Tel: 801-798-3571 • Location: 20 miles E of Spanish Fork • GPS: Lat 40.141 Lon -111.341 • Total sites: 6 • RV sites: 4 • Max RV Length: 30 • RV fee: Free • No water • Vault toilets • Activities: Hiking • Elevation: 6207

**Unicorn Ridge** (Uinta-Wasatch-Cache NF) • Agency: US Forest Service • Location: 24 miles SE of Spanish Fork • GPS: Lat 40.029454 Lon -111.281752 • Open: May-Oct • Total sites: 5 • RV sites: 5 • RV fee: Free • No water • Vault toilets • Activities: Motor sports • Elevation: 7591

## St George

**Road 033** • Agency: Bureau of Land Management • Location: 11 miles N of St George • GPS: Lat 37.273811 Lon -113.610736 • Total sites: Dispersed • RV sites: Undefined (large area) • RV fee: Free • No water • No toilets • Elevation: 4816

## Torrey

**Fremont River** • Agency: Bureau of Land Management • Location: 23 miles E of Torrey • GPS: Lat 38.275295 Lon -111.081531 • Total sites: Dispersed • RV sites: Undefined • RV fee: Free • No water • No toilets • Activities: Hiking • Elevation: 4827

**Highway 24** • Agency: Bureau of Land Management • Location: 4 miles NE of Torrey (limited services), 66 miles SE of Richfield • GPS: Lat 38.326759 Lon -111.364144 • Open: All year • Total sites: Dispersed • RV sites: Undefined • RV fee: Free • No water • No toilets • Activities: Hiking • Elevation: 6503

## Vernal

**Green River Bridge** • Agency: Bureau of Land Management • Tel: 435-636-3600 • Location: 9 miles S of Vernal • GPS: Lat 40.313971 Lon -109.482154 • Total sites: Dispersed • RV sites: Undefined • RV fee: Free • No water • No toilets • Activities: Fishing, power boating • Elevation: 4721

**Henrys Fork Horse Camp** (Uinta-Wasatch-Cache NF) • Agency: US Forest Service • Tel: 307-782-6555 • Location: 103 miles NW of Vernal, 38 miles S of Mountain View, WY • GPS: Lat 40.912636 Lon -110.327841 • Open: All year • Total sites: 3 • RV sites: 3 • RV fee: Free • No water • Vault toilets • Elevation: 9389

**Henrys Fork Trailhead** (Uinta-Wasatch-Cache NF) • Agency: US Forest Service • Tel: 307-782-6555 • Location: 104 miles NW of Vernal, 37 miles S of Mountain View, WY • GPS: Lat 40.909777 Lon -110.330552 • Open: All year • Total sites: 4 • RV sites: 4 • Max RV Length: 20 • RV fee: Free • No water • Vault toilets • Elevation: 9422

**Oaks Park** (Ashley NF) • Agency: US Forest Service • Tel: 435-789-1181 • Location: 32 miles N of Vernal • GPS: Lat 40.742089 Lon -109.623605 • Open: Jun-Sep • Total sites: 11 • RV sites: 11 • Max RV Length: 20 • RV fee: Free • Central water • Vault toilets • Elevation: 9262

**Pelican Lake** • Agency: Bureau of Land Management • Tel: 435-781-4400 • Location: 23 miles S of Vernal • GPS: Lat 40.181905 Lon -109.692984 • Open: May-Oct • Total sites: 13 • RV sites: 13 • RV fee: Free • No water • Vault toilets • Activities: Fishing, power boating, hunting • Elevation: 4817

**Seep Ridge** • Agency: Bureau of Land Management • Location: 83 miles S of Vernal, 49 miles NW of Fruita, CO • GPS: Lat 39.462642 Lon -109.283744 • Total sites: Dispersed • RV sites: Undefined (numerous sites along road) • RV fee: Free • No water • No toilets • Elevation: 8043

**South Fork** (Ashley NF) • Agency: US Forest Service • Location: 32 miles NW of Vernal • GPS: Lat 40.734967 Lon -109.739576 • Total sites: 6 • RV sites: 6 • RV fee: Free • No water • Vault toilets • Elevation: 9688

## Vernon

**Vernon Reservoir** (Uinta-Wasatch-Cache NF) • Agency: US Forest Service • Tel: 801-798-3571 • Location: 9 miles SE of Vernon (limited services), 39 miles S of Tooele • GPS: Lat 39.991743 Lon -112.385556 • Open: Apr-Dec • Stay limit: 16 days • Total sites: 10 • RV sites: 10 • RV fee: Free • No water • Vault toilets • Activities: Fishing • Elevation: 6191

## Veyo

**Horseman Park Rd Dispersed** • Agency: Bureau of Land Management • Location: 4 miles SE of Veyo (limited services), 13 miles N of St George • GPS: Lat 37.294358 Lon -113.650176 • Total sites: Dispersed • RV sites: Undefined • RV fee: Free • No water • No toilets • Elevation: 4754

**Horseman Park Rd Dispersed** • Agency: Bureau of Land Management • Location: 5 miles SE of Veyo (limited services), 13 miles N of St George • GPS: Lat 37.295666 Lon -113.647955 • Total sites: Dispersed • RV sites: Undefined • RV fee: Free • No water • No toilets • Elevation: 4792

**Horseman Park Rd Dispersed** • Agency: Bureau of Land Management • Location: 5 miles SE of Veyo (limited services), 14 miles N of St George • GPS: Lat 37.299309 Lon -113.649016 • Total sites: Dispersed • RV sites: Undefined • RV fee: Free • No water • No toilets • Elevation: 4800

**Horseman Park Rd Dispersed** • Agency: Bureau of Land Management • Location: 5 miles SE of Veyo (limited services), 14 miles N of St George • GPS: Lat 37.300549 Lon -113.647938 • Total sites: Dispersed • RV sites: Undefined • RV fee: Free • No water • No toilets • Elevation: 4818

**Horseman Park Rd Dispersed** • Agency: Bureau of Land Management • Location: 6 miles SE of Veyo (limited services), 14 miles N of St George • GPS: Lat 37.305408 Lon -113.642457 • Total sites: Dispersed • RV sites: Undefined • RV fee: Free • No water • No toilets • Elevation: 4883

## Virgin

**Kolob Creekside** • Agency: Bureau of Land Management • Location: 2 miles NE of Virgin (limited services), 8 miles E of La Verkin • GPS: Lat 37.220358 Lon -113.161699 • Total sites: Dispersed • RV sites: Undefined • RV fee: Free • No water • No toilets • Elevation: 3610

**Zion NP - Lava Point** • Agency: National Park Service • Tel: 435-772-3256 • Location: 22 miles NE of Virgin (limited services), 27 miles NE of La Verkin • GPS: Lat 37.383707 Lon -113.032797 • Open: Jun-Oct • Total sites: 6 • RV sites: 6 • Max RV Length: 19 • RV fee: Free • No water • Vault toilets • Activities: Hiking • Elevation: 7917

**Zion View** • Agency: Bureau of Land Management • Location: 7 miles N of Virgin (limited services), 11 miles NE of La Verkin • GPS: Lat 37.266967 Lon -113.176154 • Total sites: Dispersed • RV sites: Undefined • RV fee: Free • No water • No toilets • Elevation: 5594

## Wendover

**Bonneville Salt Flats** • Agency: Bureau of Land Management • Location: 6 miles NE of Wendover • GPS: Lat 40.771949 Lon -113.981459 • Total sites: Dispersed • RV sites: Undefined • RV fee: Free • No water • No toilets • Elevation: 4285

## Woodruff

**Birch Creek** • Agency: Bureau of Land Management • Tel: 801-977-4300 • Location: 9 miles W of Woodruff (limited services), 48 miles S of Garden City • GPS: Lat 41.505868 Lon -111.317264 • Open: May-Oct • Total sites: Dispersed • RV sites: Undefined • RV fee: Free • No water • Vault toilets • Activities: Fishing, power boating • Elevation: 6929

# Washington

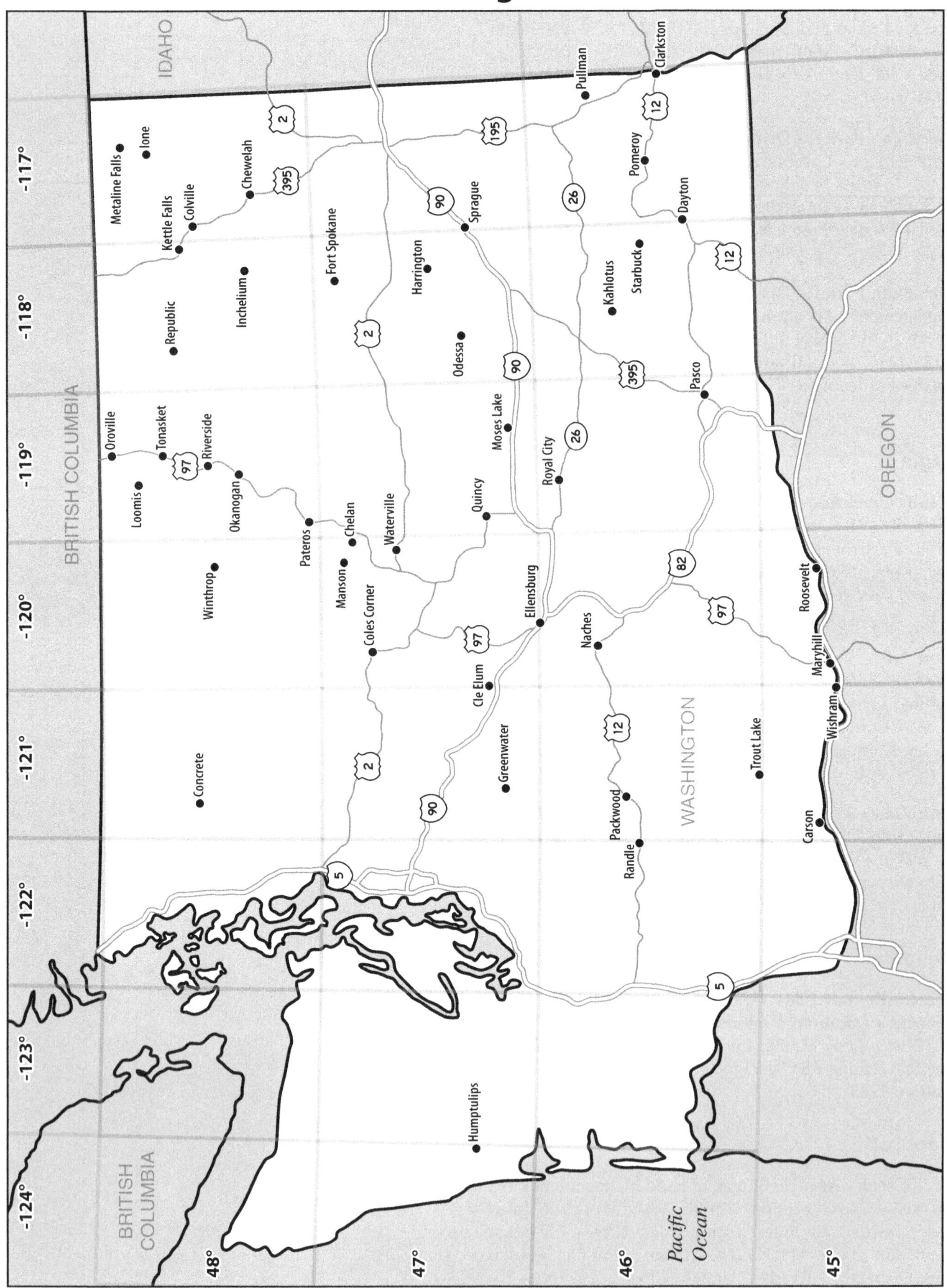
IDAHO
BRITISH COLUMBIA
OREGON
WASHINGTON
Pacific Ocean
-117°
-118°
-119°
-120°
-121°
-122°
-123°
-124°
48°
47°
46°
45°
Metaline Falls
Ione
Kettle Falls
Colville
Chewelah
Fort Spokane
Harrington
Sprague
Pullman
Clarkston
Pomeroy
Dayton
Starbuck
Kahlotus
Inchelium
Republic
Odessa
Pasco
Oroville
Tonasket
Riverside
Loomis
Okanogan
Pateros
Chelan
Manson
Waterville
Quincy
Moses Lake
Royal City
Winthrop
Coles Corner
Ellensburg
Naches
Roosevelt
Maryhill
Wishram
Cle Elum
Greenwater
Trout Lake
Concrete
Packwood
Randle
Carson
Humptulips
2
395
195
90
26
12
97
82
5

# Washington — Camping Areas

| Abbreviation | Description |
|---|---|
| CG | Campground |
| NF | National Forest |
| NRA | National Recreation Area |
| NWR | National Wildlife Refuge |
| RA | Recreation Area |
| WA | Wildlife Area |
| WDFW | Washington Department of Fish & Wildlife |

## Carson

**Falls Creek Horse Camp** (Gifford Pinchot NF) • Agency: US Forest Service • Tel: 509-395-3402 • Location: 21 miles N of Carson (limited services), 25 miles N of Stevenson • GPS: Lat 45.966551 Lon -121.846105 • Open: Jun-Sep • Total sites: 4 • RV sites: 4 (large RV's not recommended) • RV fee: Free • No water • Vault toilets • Activities: Hiking, mountain biking, equestrian area • Elevation: 3602

## Chelan

**Gallagher Flat Wildlife RA** • Agency: State • Location: 7 miles NE of Chelan • GPS: Lat 47.855822 Lon -119.943358 • Total sites: Dispersed • RV sites: Undefined • RV fee: Free • No water • No toilets • Elevation: 719

## Chewelah

**Little Pend Oreille NWR - Bayley Lake** • Agency: US Fish & Wildlife • Tel: 509-684-8384 • Location: 15 miles N of Chewelah • GPS: Lat 48.425513 Lon -117.663476 • Open: Apr-Dec • Total sites: Dispersed • RV sites: Undefined • RV fee: Free • No water • Vault toilets • Elevation: 2347

**Little Pend Oreille NWR - Bear Creek CG** • Agency: US Fish & Wildlife • Tel: 509-684-8384 • Location: 16 miles N of Chewelah • GPS: Lat 48.441607 Lon -117.674909 • Open: Apr-Dec • Total sites: Dispersed • RV sites: Undefined • RV fee: Free • No water • Vault toilets • Elevation: 2255

## Clarkston

**Blyton Landing** (Lower Granite Lake) • Agency: Corps of Engineers • Tel: 509-751-0240 • Location: 18 miles NW of Clarkston • GPS: Lat 46.559246 Lon -117.270804 • Open: All year • Total sites: Dispersed • RV sites: Undefined • RV fee: Free • No water • Vault toilets • Activities: Power boating • Elevation: 761

**Nisqually John Landing** (Lower Granite Lake) • Agency: Corps of Engineers • Tel: 509-751-0240 • Location: 11 miles NW of Clarkston • GPS: Lat 46.476857 Lon -117.23506 • Open: All year • Total sites: Dispersed • RV sites: Undefined • RV fee: Free • No water • Vault toilets • Activities: Power boating • Elevation: 764

## Cle Elum

**Liberty** • Agency: Bureau of Land Management • Tel: 509-536-1200 • Location: 15 miles NE of Cle Elum • GPS: Lat 47.253323 Lon -120.670489 • Total sites: Dispersed • RV sites: Undefined • RV fee: Free • No water • No toilets • Activities: Hiking • Elevation: 2730

**Williams Creek** (Okanogan-Wenatchee NF) • Agency: US Forest Service • Location: 15 miles NE of Cle Elum • GPS: Lat 47.246208 Lon -120.682756 • Total sites: 16 • RV sites: 16 • RV fee: Free • No water • Vault toilets • Activities: Hiking • Elevation: 2546

## Coles Corner

**Highway 207** • Agency: State • Location: 1 mile NE of Coles Corner (limited services), 15 miles N of Leavenworth • GPS: Lat 47.765781 Lon -120.727979 • Total sites: Dispersed • RV sites: Undefined • RV fee: Free • No water • No toilets • Elevation: 1949

**Meadow Creek** (Okanogan-Wenatchee NF) • Agency: US Forest Service • Tel: 509-548-2550 • Location: 10 miles N of Coles Corner (limited services), 25 miles N of Leavenworth • GPS: Lat 47.867438 Lon -120.693655 • Total sites: 4 • RV sites: 4 • Max RV Length: 30 • RV fee: Free • No water • No toilets • Elevation: 2280

**White Pine** (Okanogan-Wenatchee NF) • Agency: US Forest Service • Tel: 509-548-2550 • Location: 7 miles W of Coles Corner (limited services), 21 miles NW of Leavenworth • GPS: Lat 47.789091 Lon -120.872694 • Open: May-Sep • Total sites: 5 • RV sites: 5 • RV fee: Free • No water • Vault toilets • Elevation: 2369

## Colville

**Little Pend Oreille NWR - Cottonwood CG** • Agency: US Fish & Wildlife • Tel: 509-684-8384 • Location: 12 miles SE of Colville • GPS: Lat 48.456481 Lon -117.718168 • Open: Apr-Dec • Total sites: Dispersed • RV sites: Undefined • RV fee: Free • No water • Vault toilets • Elevation: 2046

**Little Pend Oreille NWR - Horse Camp** • Agency: US Fish & Wildlife • Tel: 509-684-8384 • Location: 12 miles SE of Colville • GPS: Lat 48.478187 Lon -117.689729 • Open: Apr-Dec • Total sites: Dispersed • RV sites: Undefined • RV fee: Free • No water • Vault toilets • Activities: Equestrian area • Elevation: 2372

**Little Pend Oreille NWR - River Camp** • Agency: US Fish & Wildlife • Tel: 509-684-8384 • Location: 12 miles SE of Colville • GPS: Lat 48.475245 Lon -117.685826 • Open: Apr-Dec • Total sites: Dispersed • RV sites: Undefined • RV fee: Free • No water • Vault toilets • Elevation: 2327

**Little Twin Lakes** (Colville NF) • Agency: US Forest Service • Tel: 509-738-7700 • Location: 17 miles E of Colville • GPS: Lat 48.574777 Lon -117.645809 • Open: May-Sep • Total sites: 20 • RV sites: 20 • RV fee: Free • No water • Vault toilets • Activities: Fishing, power boating, non-power boating • Elevation: 3750

## Concrete

**Park Butte Trailhead** (Schrieber's Meadow, Mt Baker-Snoqualmie NF) • Agency: US Forest Service • Tel: 360-856-5700 x515 • Location: 18 miles N of Concrete (limited services), 36 miles NE of Sedro-Woolley • GPS: Lat 48.707103 Lon -121.812416 • Stay limit: 1 day • Total sites: 6 • RV sites: 6 • RV fee: Free • No water • Vault toilets • Activities: Hiking • Elevation: 3419

## Dayton

**Godman** (Umatilla NF) • Agency: US Forest Service • Tel: 509-843-1891 • Location: 26 miles SE of Dayton • GPS: Lat 46.1 Lon -117.786 • Total sites: 8 • RV sites: 3 • RV fee: Free • No water • Vault toilets • Activities: Hiking • Elevation: 5702

## Ellensburg

**Lion Rock Spring** (Okanogan-Wenatchee NF) • Agency: US Forest Service • Tel: 509-852-1100 • Location: 23 miles N of Ellensburg • GPS: Lat 47.251369 Lon -120.581709 • Open: Jun-Oct • Total sites: 3 • RV sites: 3 • Max RV Length: 22 • RV fee: Free • No water • Vault toilets • Activities: Hiking • Elevation: 6260

**Quartz Mt** (Okanogan-Wenatchee NF) • Agency: US Forest Service • Location: 31 miles NW of Ellensburg • GPS: Lat 47.076645 Lon -121.079628 • Total sites: 3 • RV sites: 3 • Max RV Length: 22 • RV fee: Free • Elevation: 6116

## Fort Spokane

**Lake Roosevelt NRA - Pierre** (Lake Roosevelt NRA) • Agency: National Park Service • Tel: 509-633-3830 • Location: 10 miles NE of Fort Spokane (limited services), 33 miles N of Davenport • GPS: Lat 47.946948 Lon -118.243883 • Open: All year • Total sites: Dispersed • RV sites: Undefined • RV fee: Free • No water • Vault toilets • Activities: Power boating • Elevation: 1339

## Greenwater

**Half Camp Horse Camp** (Mt Baker-Snoqualmie NF) • Agency: US Forest Service • Tel: 360-825-6585 • Location: 18 miles SE of Greenwater (limited services), 35 miles SE of Enumclaw • GPS: Lat 46.974083 Lon -121.496039 • Total sites: 9 • RV sites: 9 • RV fee: Free • No water • Vault toilets • Activities: Hiking, equestrian area • Elevation: 3927

## Harrington

**Twin Lakes** • Agency: Bureau of Land Management • Tel: 509-536-1200 • Location: 21 miles NW of Harrington (limited services), 26 miles SW of Davenport • GPS: Lat 47.53033 Lon -118.50583 • Open: All year • Total sites: 5 • RV sites: 5 • RV fee: Free • No water • Vault toilets • Activities: Hiking, mountain biking, fishing, non-power boating • Elevation: 1890

## Humptulips

**Campbell Tree Grove** (Olympic NF) • Agency: US Forest Service • Tel: 360-288-2525 • Location: 25 miles NE of Humptulips (limited services), 46 miles NE of Hoquiam • GPS: Lat 47.480937 Lon -123.688034 • Open: May-Sep • Total sites: 31 • RV sites: 21 • Max RV Length: 16 • RV fee: Free • No water • Vault toilets • Activities: Fishing • Elevation: 1188

## Inchelium

**Colville Reservation - Rogers Bar** • Agency: Indian Reservation • Tel: 509-633-3830 • Location: 22 miles S of Inchelium (limited services), 52 miles SW of Kettle Falls • GPS: Lat 48.066847 Lon -118.252172 • Open: May-Oct • Total sites: Dispersed • RV sites: Undefined (large area with many sites) • RV fee: Free • Vault toilets • Notes: Permit required • Activities: Swimming, power boating, non-power boating • Elevation: 1309

## Ione

**Big Meadow Lake** (Colville NF) • Agency: US Forest Service • Tel: 509-738-7700 • Location: 9 miles W of Ione (limited services), 26 miles NE of Colville • GPS: Lat 48.726164 Lon -117.562668 • Open: May-Sep • Stay limit: 14 days • Total sites: 17 • RV sites: 17 • RV fee: Free • Central water • Vault toilets • Activities: Hiking, fishing, power boating • Elevation: 3428

## Kahlotus

**Devil's Bench** (Lake West) • Agency: Corps of Engineers • Tel: 509-282-3219 • Location: 6 miles S of Kahlotus (limited services), 22 miles SE of Connell • GPS: Lat 46.567474 Lon -118.537404 • Open: All year • Total sites: 6 • RV sites: 6 • RV fee: Free • No water • Vault toilets • Activities: Power boating • Elevation: 584

## Kettle Falls

**Davis Lake** (Colville NF) • Agency: US Forest Service • Tel: 509-738-7700 • Location: 19 miles NW of Kettle Falls • GPS: Lat 48.738738 Lon -118.228761 • Open: All year • Stay limit: 14 days • Total sites: 4 • RV sites: 4 • RV fee: Free • No water • Vault toilets • Activities: Hiking, fishing, non-power boating • Elevation: 4528

## Loomis

**Chopaka Lake** • Agency: Bureau of Land Management • Tel: 509-536-1200 • Location: 10 miles N of Loomis (limited services), 29 miles NW of Tonasket • GPS: Lat 48.916938 Lon -119.702052 • Open: All year (road may be inaccessible in winter) • Total sites: 8 • RV sites: 8 • RV fee: Free • No water • Vault toilets • Activities: Fishing, power boating, non-power boating • Elevation: 2920

## Manson

**South Navarre** (Okanogan-Wenatchee NF) • Agency: US Forest Service • Tel: 509-682-4900 • Location: 34 miles NW of Manson • GPS: Lat 48.107487 Lon -120.339647 • Total sites: 4 • RV sites: 4 • RV fee: Free • No water • Vault toilets • Activities: Hiking, motor sports • Elevation: 6463

## Maryhill

**Cliffs Park** • Agency: Corps of Engineers • Tel: 503-296-1181 • Location: 5 miles NE of Maryhill (limited services), 20 miles SE of Goldendale • GPS: Lat 45.712095 Lon -120.718019 • Stay limit: 14 days • Total sites: Dispersed • RV sites: Undefined • RV fee: Free • No water • No toilets • Elevation: 180

**Rock Creek Park** • Agency: Corps of Engineers • Tel: 541-506-7819 • Location: 22 miles E of Maryhill (limited services), 31 miles SE of Goldendale • GPS: Lat 45.719417 Lon -120.460817 • Open: All year • Stay limit: 14 days • Total sites: Dispersed • RV sites: Undefined • RV fee: Free • No water • Vault toilets • Activities: Power boating • Elevation: 269

## Metaline Falls

**Boundary Dam - Seattle City Power** (Colville NF) • Agency: Utility Company • Tel: 509-446-3083 • Location: 12 miles N of Metaline Falls (limited services), 59 miles NE of Colville • GPS: Lat 48.985224 Lon -117.352616 • Stay limit: 6 days • Total sites: 22 • RV sites: 12 • RV fee: Free • No water • Flush toilets • Activities: Fishing, power boating • Elevation: 2028

**Crescent Lake** (Colville NF) • Agency: US Forest Service • Tel: 509-446-7500 • Location: 12 miles N of Metaline Falls (limited services), 60 miles NE of Colville • GPS: Lat 48.988564 Lon -117.311432 • Open: May-Sep • Stay limit: 14 days • Total sites: 3 • RV sites: 3 • RV fee: Free • No water • Vault toilets • Activities: Fishing, power boating, non-power boating • Elevation: 2713

## Moses Lake

**Moses Lake** • Agency: Bureau of Land Management • Location: 6 miles S of Moses Lake • GPS: Lat 47.062779 Lon -119.320773 • Open: All year • Total sites: Dispersed • RV sites: Undefined • RV fee: Free • No water • No toilets • Activities: Motor sports • Elevation: 1043

## Naches

**Cash Prairie Trailhead** (Okanogan-Wenatchee NF) • Agency: US Forest Service • Tel: 509-653-1401 • Location: 30 miles W of Naches • GPS: Lat 46.716617 Lon -121.164099 • Total sites: 1 • RV sites: Undefined • RV fee: Free • No water • No toilets • Activities: Hiking • Elevation: 6298

**Crow Lake Way Trailhead** (Okanogan-Wenatchee NF) • Agency: US Forest Service • Location: 39 miles NW of Naches • GPS: Lat 46.952111 Lon -121.307065 • Total sites: 5 • RV sites: 5 • RV fee: Free • No water • Vault toilets • Activities: Hiking, equestrian area • Elevation: 3395

**FSR 1500** (Mt. Baker-Snoqualmie NF) • Agency: State • Location: 14 miles NW of Naches • GPS: Lat 46.816355 Lon -120.943028 • Total sites: Dispersed • RV sites: Undefined • RV fee: Free • No water • No toilets • Elevation: 2044

**Milk Pond** (Okanogan-Wenatchee NF) • Agency: US Forest Service • Tel: 509-653-1401 • Location: 29 miles NW of Naches • GPS: Lat 46.987 Lon -121.063 • Total sites: 5 • RV sites: 5 • RV fee: Free • No water • Vault toilets • Elevation: 2989

**Rattlesnake Trailhead** (Okanogan-Wenatchee NF) • Agency: US Forest Service • Tel: 509 996-4000 • Location: 24 miles NW of Naches • GPS: Lat 46.795487 Lon -121.100495 • Total sites: 3 • RV sites: 3 • RV fee: Free • Activities: Hiking • Elevation: 3100

## Odessa

**Coffeepot Lake** • Agency: Bureau of Land Management • Tel: 509-536-1200 • Location: 18 miles NE of Odessa • GPS: Lat 47.500043 Lon -118.556805 • Open: All year • Total sites: Dispersed • RV sites: Undefined • RV fee: Free • No water • Vault toilets • Activities: Hiking, fishing, power boating, non-power boating • Elevation: 1844

**Pacific Lake** • Agency: Bureau of Land Management • Tel: 509-536-1200 • Location: 8 miles N of Odessa • GPS: Lat 47.415097 Lon -118.732898 • Open: All year • Total sites: Dispersed • RV sites: Undefined • RV fee: Free • Vault toilets • Activities: Hiking, mountain biking, motor sports • Elevation: 1604

## Okanogan

**Buzzard Lake - WDFW** • Agency: State • Tel: 509-223-3358 • Location: 13 miles NW of Okanogan • GPS: Lat 48.419368 Lon -119.712874 • Total sites: Dispersed • RV sites: Undefined • RV fee: Free • No water • No toilets • Activities: Fishing, hunting • Elevation: 3387

## Oroville

**Loomis Loop** • Agency: Bureau of Land Management • Location: 8 miles NW of Oroville • GPS: Lat 48.986518 Lon -119.569832 • Total sites: Dispersed • RV sites: Undefined • RV fee: Free • No water • No toilets • Activities: Power boating, non-power boating • Elevation: 1131

**Scotch Creek WA - Eder Unit** • Agency: State • Tel: 509-826-4430 • Location: 3 miles NE of Oroville • GPS: Lat 48.968668 Lon -119.401089 • Total sites: Dispersed • RV sites: Undefined • RV fee: Free • No water • No toilets • Notes: Camping limited to reader board site at entrance • Elevation: 1297

## Packwood

**Cat Creek** (Gifford Pinchot NF) • Agency: US Forest Service • Tel: 360-497-1100 • Location: 25 miles S of Packwood • GPS: Lat 46.348408 Lon -121.624807 • Open: May-Sep • Total sites: 5 • RV sites: 5 • RV fee: Free • No water • Vault toilets • Activities: Hiking, fishing, motor sports • Elevation: 2753

**Chain of Lakes Trailhead** (Gifford Pinchot NF) • Agency: US Forest Service • Tel: 360-497-1100 • Location: 36 miles S of Packwood • GPS: Lat 46.293498 Lon -121.595741 • Open: Jul-Sep • Total sites: 3 • RV sites: 3 • Max RV Length: 16 • RV fee: Free • No water • Vault toilets • Activities: Hiking, fishing, motor sports, non-power boating • Elevation: 4386

**Cody Horse Camp** (Gifford Pinchot NF) • Agency: US Forest Service • Tel: 360-497-1100 • Location: 25 miles S of Packwood • GPS: Lat 46.364328 Lon -121.566356 • Total sites: 16 • RV sites: 16 • Max RV Length: 35 • RV fee: Free • Central water • Vault toilets • Activities: Hiking, equestrian area • Elevation: 3150

**Indian Creek Trailhead** (Okanogan-Wenatchee NF) • Agency: US Forest Service • Location: 26 miles E of Packwood • GPS: Lat 46.664767 Lon -121.285207 • Total sites: 6 • RV sites: 6 • RV fee: Free • No water • No toilets • Activities: Hiking, equestrian area • Elevation: 3360

**Mesatchee Creek Horse Camp** (Okanogan-Wenatchee NF) • Agency: US Forest Service • Tel: 509-653-1401 • Location: 34 miles NE of Packwood • GPS: Lat 46.912788 Lon -121.405879 • Total sites: 3 • RV sites: 3 • RV fee: Free • No water • Vault toilets • Activities: Hiking, equestrian area • Elevation: 3664

**Sand Ridge Trailhead** (Okanogan-Wenatchee NF) • Agency: US Forest Service • Tel: 509-653-1401 • Location: 26 miles E of Packwood • GPS: Lat 46.651026 Lon -121.279787 • Total sites: 2 • RV sites: 2 • RV fee: Free • No water • Vault toilets • Activities: Hiking, equestrian area • Elevation: 3550

**Soda Springs** (Gifford Pinchot NF) • Agency: US Forest Service • Tel: 360-497-1100 • Location: 14 miles NE of Packwood • GPS: Lat 46.704269 Lon -121.481736 • Open: All year (no services in winter) • Total sites: 6 • RV sites: 6 • Max RV Length: 18 • RV fee: Free • No water • No toilets • Elevation: 3224

## Pasco

**Big Flat HMU** (Lake Sacajawea) • Agency: Corps of Engineers • Tel: 509-547-2048 • Location: 15 miles E of Pasco • GPS: Lat 46.294521 Lon -118.792344 • Open: All year • Total sites: Dispersed • RV sites: Undefined • RV fee: Free • No water • Vault toilets • Activities: Power boating, non-power boating • Elevation: 502

## Pateros

**Highway 153** • Agency: State • Location: 1 mile SW of Pateros (limited services), 19 miles NE of Chelan • GPS: Lat 48.046116 Lon -119.915991 • Total sites: Dispersed • RV sites: Undefined • RV fee: Free • No water • No toilets • Elevation: 789

## Pomeroy

**Alder Thicket** (Umatilla NF) • Agency: US Forest Service • Tel: 509-843-1891 • Location: 18 miles S of Pomeroy • GPS: Lat 46.258932 Lon -117.567041 • Open: May-Oct • Total sites: 5 • RV sites: 5 • RV fee: Free • No water • Vault toilets • Activities: Hiking • Elevation: 5141

**Big Springs** (Umatilla NF) • Agency: US Forest Service • Tel: 541-278-3716 • Location: 22 miles S of Pomeroy • GPS: Lat 46.231099 Lon -117.543764 • Open: All year • Total sites: 10 • RV sites: 5 • RV fee: Free • No water • Vault toilets • Activities: Hiking, hunting • Elevation: 5066

**Forest Boundary** (Umatilla NF) • Agency: US Forest Service • Tel: 541-278-3716 • Location: 15 miles S of Pomeroy • GPS: Lat 46.293 Lon -117.557 • Total sites: 6 • RV sites: 6 • RV fee: Free • No water • Vault toilets • Activities: Motor sports • Elevation: 4465

**Illia Landing** (Lake Bryan) • Agency: Corps of Engineers • Tel: 509-843-2214 • Location: 24 miles N of Pomeroy • GPS: Lat 46.696473 Lon -117.471492 • Open: All year • Total sites: Dispersed • RV sites: Undefined • RV fee: Free • Central water • Vault toilets • Activities: Power boating • Elevation: 643

**Lambi Creek** • Agency: Corps of Engineers • Location: 21 miles N of Pomeroy • GPS: Lat 46.680028 Lon -117.501517 • Open: All year • Total sites: 6 • RV sites: 6 • Max RV Length: 18 • RV fee: Free • No water • Vault toilets • Activities: Fishing, power boating • Elevation: 660

**Offield Landing** (Lower Granite Lake) • Agency: Corps of Engineers • Tel: 509-397-6413 • Location: 25 miles NE of Pomeroy • GPS: Lat 46.652655 Lon -117.418236 • Open: All year • Total sites: Dispersed • RV sites: Undefined • RV fee: Free • No water • Vault toilets • Elevation: 748

**Pataha** (Umatilla NF) • Agency: US Forest Service • Tel: 509-843-1891 • Location: 17 miles S of Pomeroy • GPS: Lat 46.292 Lon -117.514 • Open: All year (no services Dec-Mar) • Total sites: 3 • RV sites: 2 • RV fee: Free • No water • Vault toilets • Activities: Fishing • Elevation: 3993

**Wickiup** (Umatilla NF) • Agency: US Forest Service • Tel: 509-843-1891 • Location: 34 miles SE of Pomeroy • GPS: Lat 46.137 Lon -117.435 • Open: All year (no services Dec-Mar) • Total sites: 7 • RV sites: 7 • RV fee: Free • No water • Vault toilets • Elevation: 5968

**Willow Landing** (Lake Bryan) • Agency: Corps of Engineers • Tel: 509-751-0240 • Location: 24 miles NW of Pomeroy • GPS: Lat 46.681858 Lon -117.749517 • Open: All year • Total sites: Dispersed • RV sites: Undefined • RV fee: Free • No water • Vault toilets • Activities: Power boating • Elevation: 633

## Pullman

**Lower Granite Lock and Dam** (Lower Granite Lake) • Agency: Corps of Engineers • Tel: 509-843-1493 • Location: 26 miles SW of Pullman • GPS: Lat 46.664922 Lon -117.433902 • Total sites: Dispersed • RV sites: Undefined • RV fee: Free • No water • Vault toilets • Elevation: 655

**Wawawai Landing** (Snake River) • Agency: Corps of Engineers • Tel: 509-751-0240 • Location: 18 miles SW of Pullman • GPS: Lat 46.630525 Lon -117.379952 • Open: All year • Total sites: Dispersed • RV sites: Undefined • RV fee: Free • No water • Vault toilets • Activities: Power boating • Elevation: 745

## Quincy

**Quincy Wildlife Recreation Area** • Agency: US Bureau of Reclamation • Tel: 509-765-6641 • Location: 9 miles SW of Quincy • GPS: Lat 47.140025 Lon -119.924338 • Total sites: Dispersed • RV sites: Undefined • RV fee: Free • No water • No toilets • Elevation: 1192

## Randle

**Green River Horse Camp** (Gifford Pinchot NF) • Agency: US Forest Service • Tel: 360-497-1100 • Location: 22 miles SW of Randle (limited services), 30 miles SE of Morton • GPS: Lat 46.349505 Lon -122.084408 • Total sites: 8 • RV sites: 8 • Max RV Length: 40 • RV fee: Free • No water • Vault toilets • Activities: Equestrian area • Elevation: 2887

**Mount Adams Veneer County Mill Pond** • Agency: State • Location: 1 mile S of Randle (limited services), 17 miles SW of Packwood • GPS: Lat 46.516087 Lon -121.952928 • Total sites: Dispersed • RV sites: Undefined • RV fee: Free • No water • No toilets • Elevation: 885

## Republic

**Jungle Hill Horse Camp** (Colville NF) • Agency: US Forest Service • Location: 15 miles E of Republic • GPS: Lat 48.633257 Lon -118.545341 • Total sites: 5 • RV sites: 5 • RV fee: Free • No water • Vault toilets • Activities: equestrian area • Elevation: 4118

**Kettle Crest** (Colville NF) • Agency: US Forest Service • Tel: 509-447-3129 • Location: 17 miles E of Republic • GPS: Lat 48.608652 Lon -118.476856 • Open: All year • Stay limit: 14 days • Total sites: 2 • RV sites: 2 • RV fee: Free • No water • Vault toilets • Notes: Sno-Park permit required if camping between 11/01 and 05/01 • Activities: Skiing, hiking, equestrian area • Elevation: 5467

**Lambert Creek Horse Camp** (Colville NF) • Agency: US Forest Service • Tel: 509-775-7400 • Location: 18 miles NE of Republic • GPS: Lat 48.728711 Lon -118.522669 • Total sites: 5 • RV sites: 5 • RV fee: Free • No water (water for stock) • Vault toilets • Activities: equestrian area • Elevation: 3889

**Wapaloosie Horse Camp** (Colville NF) • Agency: US Forest Service • Location: 24 miles E of Republic • GPS: Lat 48.662933 Lon -118.439506 • Open: All year (no services in winter) • Stay limit: 14 days • Total sites: 5 • RV sites: 5 • RV fee: Free • No water • Vault toilets • Activities: Equestrian area • Elevation: 5007

## Riverside

**Crawfish Lake** (Okanogan-Wenatchee NF) • Agency: US Forest Service • Tel: 509-486-2186 • Location: 20 miles E of Riverside (limited services), 27 miles NE of Omak • GPS: Lat 48.484619 Lon -119.216064 • Open: May-Sep • Total sites: 19 • RV sites: 14 • Max RV Length: 18 • RV fee: Free • No water • Vault toilets • Activities: Fishing, power boating, non-power boating • Elevation: 4547

## Roosevelt

**Roosevelt Park** • Agency: Corps of Engineers • Tel: 541-506-7819 • Location: 1 mile S of Roosevelt (limited services), 42 miles SE of Goldendale • GPS: Lat 45.731855 Lon -120.222176 • Open: All year • Stay limit: 14 days • Total sites: Dispersed • RV sites: Undefined • RV fee: Free • Central water • Vault toilets • Activities: Fishing, swimming, power boating • Elevation: 266

**Sundale Park** • Agency: Corps of Engineers • Tel: 503-296-1181 • Location: 5 miles W of Roosevelt (limited services), 37 miles SE of Goldendale • GPS: Lat 45.719066 Lon -120.315282 • Open: All year • Stay limit: 14 days • Total sites: Dispersed • RV sites: Undefined • RV fee: Free • No water • Vault toilets • Activities: Fishing, power boating • Elevation: 269

## Royal City

**John Wayne Pioneer Trail** • Agency: State • Location: 10 miles SW of Royal City • GPS: Lat 46.838173 Lon -119.704116 • Total sites: Dispersed • RV sites: Undefined • RV fee: Free • No water • No toilets • Elevation: 554

## Sprague

**Escure Ranch** • Agency: Bureau of Land Management • Location: 23 miles S of Sprague (limited services), 31 miles SE of Ritzville • GPS: Lat 47.015048 Lon -117.943425 • Total sites: 15 • RV sites: 15 • RV fee: Free • Vault toilets • Activities: Hiking • Elevation: 1459

## Starbuck

**Ayer Boat Basin** (Lake West) • Agency: Corps of Engineers • Tel: 509-282-3219 • Location: 15 miles NW of Starbuck (limited services), 38 miles NW of Dayton • GPS: Lat 46.585975 Lon -118.367966 • Open: All year • Total sites: Dispersed • RV sites: Undefined • Max RV Length: 40 • RV fee: Free • No water • Vault toilets • Activities: Power boating • Elevation: 545

**Little Goose Dam North** • Agency: Corps of Engineers • Tel: 509-751-0240 • Location: 10 miles NE of Starbuck (limited services), 33 miles N of Dayton • GPS: Lat 46.587083 Lon -118.035968 • Open: All year • Total sites: Dispersed • RV sites: Undefined • RV fee: Free • No water • Vault toilets • Activities: Fishing, power boating • Elevation: 547

**Little Goose Landing** (Lake Bryan) • Agency: Corps of Engineers • Tel: 509-751-0240 • Location: 10 miles NE of Starbuck (limited services), 33 miles N of Dayton • GPS: Lat 46.585664 Lon -118.006097 • Open: All year • Total sites: 4 • RV sites: 4 • RV fee: Free • No water • Vault toilets • Activities: Fishing, power boating • Elevation: 607

**Riparia Park** (Lake West) • Agency: Corps of Engineers • Tel: 509-282-3219 • Location: 14 miles NE of Starbuck (limited services), 36 miles NW of Dayton • GPS: Lat 46.577182 Lon -118.090553 • Open: All year • Total sites: Dispersed • RV sites: Undefined • Max RV Length: 40 • RV fee: Free • No water • Vault toilets • Notes: No wood fires Jun-Oct • Elevation: 538

**Texas Rapids** • Agency: Corps of Engineers • Tel: 509-282-3219 • Location: 12 miles NE of Starbuck (limited services), 34 miles NW of Dayton • GPS: Lat 46.578826 Lon -118.058079 • Open: All year • Total sites: Dispersed • RV sites: Undefined • RV fee: Free • No water • Flush toilets • Activities: Power boating • Elevation: 581

## Tonasket

**Lyman Lake** (Okanogan-Wenatchee NF) • Agency: US Forest Service • Tel: 509-486-2186 • Location: 28 miles SE of Tonasket • GPS: Lat 48.526111 Lon -119.024979 • Open: Jun-Sep • Total sites: 4 • RV sites: 4 • RV fee: Free • No water • Vault toilets • Activities: Fishing • Elevation: 2930

## Trout Lake

**Cold Spring Indian** (Gifford Pinchot NF) • Agency: US Forest Service • Tel: 509-395-3400 • Location: 17 miles NW of Trout Lake (limited services), 39 miles NW of White Salmon • GPS: Lat 46.084754 Lon -121.758225 • Total sites: 12 • RV sites: 12 • RV fee: Free • No water • Vault toilets • Activities: Hiking, fishing • Elevation: 4185

**Huckleberry Access** (Gifford Pinchot NF) • Agency: US Forest Service • Tel: 509-395-3400 • Location: 22 miles NW of Trout Lake (limited services), 44 miles NW of White Salmon • GPS: Lat 46.091084 Lon -121.799871 • Open: May-Oct • Total sites: 3 • RV sites: 3 • Max RV Length: 32 • RV fee: Free • Central water • Vault toilets • Activities: Hiking • Elevation: 4216

**Little Goose Horse Camp** (Gifford Pinchot NF) • Agency: US Forest Service • Tel: 509-395-3400 • Location: 12 miles NW of Trout Lake (limited services), 34 miles NW of White Salmon • GPS: Lat 46.034912 Lon -121.715088 • Total sites: 7 • RV sites: 7 • Max RV Length:

24 • RV fee: Free • No water • Vault toilets • Activities: Equestrian area • Elevation: 4088

**Meadow Creek Indian** (Gifford Pinchot NF) • Agency: US Forest Service • Tel: 509-395-3400 • Location: 16 miles NW of Trout Lake (limited services), 38 miles NW of White Salmon • GPS: Lat 46.069309 Lon -121.756569 • Total sites: 3 • RV sites: 3 • RV fee: Free • No water • Vault toilets • Elevation: 4139

## Waterville

**Douglas Creek** • Agency: Bureau of Land Management • Tel: 509-536-1200 • Location: 17 miles SE of Waterville (limited services), 43 miles NE of Wenatchee • GPS: Lat 47.484562 Lon -119.898208 • Open: Mar-Nov • Total sites: Dispersed • RV sites: Undefined • RV fee: Free • No water • No toilets • Activities: Hiking, fishing, swimming, hunting • Elevation: 1488

## Winthrop

**Andrews Creek** (Okanogan-Wenatchee NF) • Agency: US Forest Service • Tel: 509-996-4003 • Location: 23 miles N of Winthrop • GPS: Lat 48.78346 Lon -120.108347 • Total sites: 4 • RV sites: 2 • RV fee: Free • No water • Vault toilets • Elevation: 3037

## Wishram

**Avery Park** • Agency: Corps of Engineers • Tel: 541-506-7819 • Location: 4 miles W of Wishram (limited services), 10 miles NE of The Dalles • GPS: Lat 45.662814 Lon -121.036197 • Open: All year • Total sites: Dispersed • RV sites: Undefined • RV fee: Free • No water • Vault toilets • Elevation: 210

# Wyoming

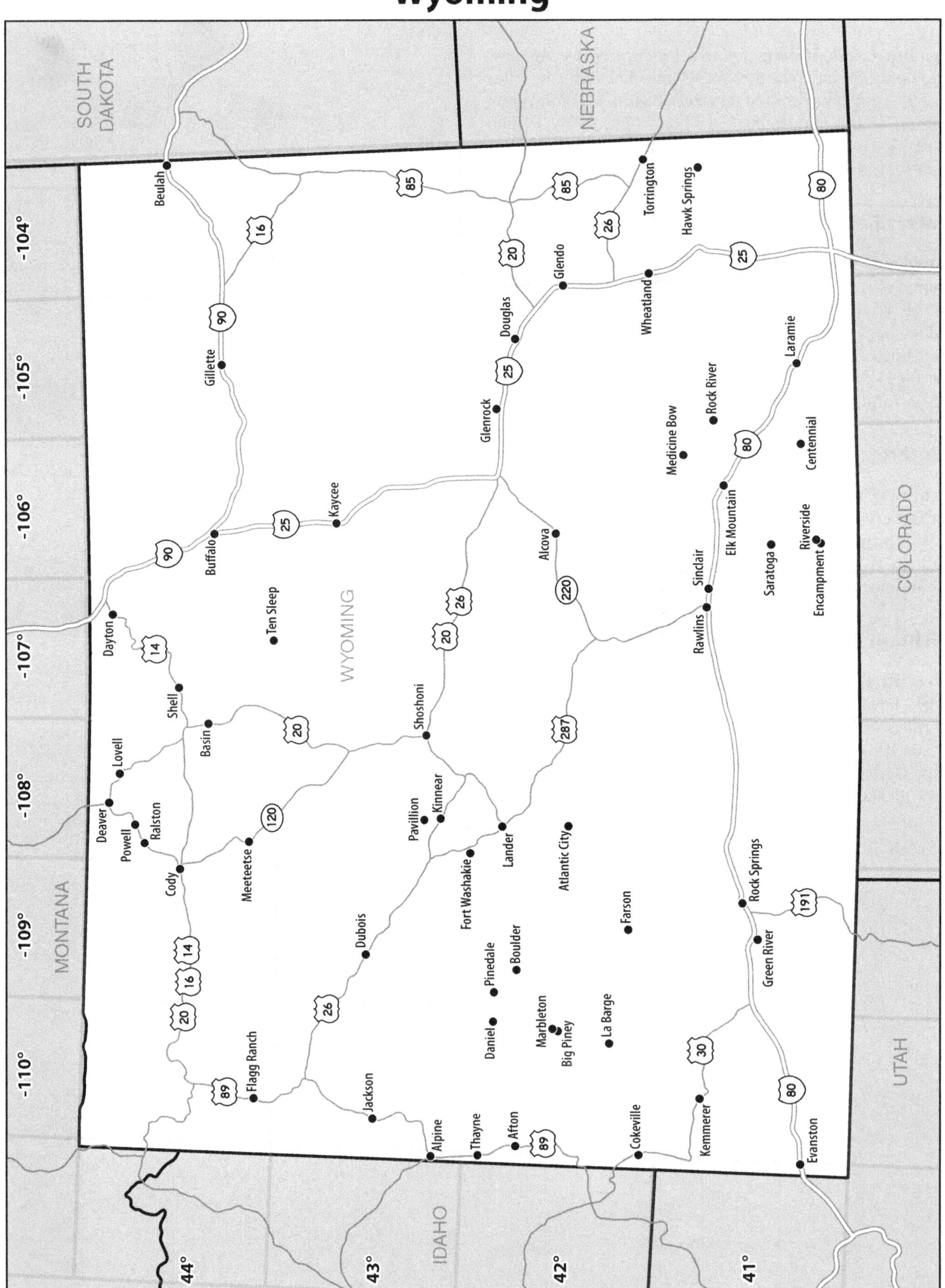

SOUTH DAKOTA
NEBRASKA
MONTANA
IDAHO
UTAH
COLORADO
WYOMING
-104°
-105°
-106°
-107°
-108°
-109°
-110°
44°
43°
42°
41°
Beulah
Torrington
Hawk Springs
Glendo
Wheatland
Douglas
Gillette
Glenrock
Laramie
Rock River
Medicine Bow
Centennial
Kaycee
Buffalo
Alcova
Elk Mountain
Riverside
Encampment
Saratoga
Sinclair
Rawlins
Ten Sleep
Dayton
Shell
Shoshoni
Basin
Lovell
Deaver
Powell
Ralston
Cody
Meeteetse
Pavillion
Kinnear
Fort Washakie
Lander
Atlantic City
Dubois
Farson
Rock Springs
Green River
Pinedale
Boulder
Daniel
Marbleton
Big Piney
La Barge
Flagg Ranch
Jackson
Alpine
Thayne
Afton
Cokeville
Kemmerer
Evanston
90
85
16
20
26
25
80
14
120
220
287
89
30
191

# Wyoming — Camping Areas

| Abbreviation | Description |
|---|---|
| CG | Campground |
| NF | National Forest |
| NP | National Park |
| RA | Recreation Area |
| WGF | Wyoming Game & Fish |
| WHMA | Wildlife Habitat Management Area |
| WMA | Wildlife Management Area |

## Afton

**Salt River Public Access - A/G Lane** • Agency: State • Location: 6 miles NW of Afton • GPS: Lat 42.794403 Lon -110.975483 • Total sites: Dispersed • RV sites: Undefined • RV fee: Free • No water • Activities: Fishing • Elevation: 6031

## Alcova

**Chalk Bluffs** • Agency: Bureau of Land Management • Tel: 307-261-7600 • Location: 11 miles NE of Alcova (limited services), 23 miles SW of Casper • GPS: Lat 42.675737 Lon -106.623692 • Total sites: 8 • RV sites: 8 • RV fee: Free • No water • Vault toilets • Activities: Fishing • Elevation: 5268

**North Platte River - Miracle Mile #1 Public Access - WGF** • Agency: State • Location: 32 miles SW of Alcova (limited services), 49 miles NE of Rawlins • GPS: Lat 42.225484 Lon -106.877822 • Total sites: Dispersed • RV sites: Undefined • RV fee: Free • No water • Vault toilets • Activities: Fishing, power boating, non-power boating • Elevation: 5876

**North Platte River - Miracle Mile #2 Public Access - WGF** • Agency: State • Location: 31 miles SW of Alcova (limited services), 47 miles NE of Rawlins • GPS: Lat 42.214664 Lon -106.876284 • Total sites: Dispersed • RV sites: Undefined • RV fee: Free • No water • Vault toilets • Activities: Fishing, power boating, non-power boating • Elevation: 5882

## Alpine

**Murphy Lake Access - WGF** • Agency: State • Location: 16 miles SE of Alpine • GPS: Lat 43.057434 Lon -110.863335 • Total sites: Dispersed • RV sites: Undefined • RV fee: Free • No water • No toilets • Activities: Fishing • Elevation: 6624

**Salt River Access - WGF** • Agency: State • Location: 3 miles S of Alpine • GPS: Lat 43.126428 Lon -111.030789 • Total sites: Dispersed • RV sites: Undefined • RV fee: Free • No water • No toilets • Activities: Fishing, power boating • Elevation: 5620

**Salt River Public Access - Perkes'** • Agency: State • Location: 6 miles S of Alpine • GPS: Lat 43.087474 Lon -111.043581 • Total sites: Dispersed • RV sites: Undefined • RV fee: Free • No water • Activities: Fishing, power boating • Elevation: 5713

## Atlantic City

**No Name** • Agency: Bureau of Land Management • Location: 10 miles SE of Atlantic City (limited services), 40 miles S of Lander • GPS: Lat 42.392749 Lon -108.624442 • Total sites: Dispersed • RV sites: Undefined • RV fee: Free • No water • Vault toilets • Activities: Fishing • Elevation: 7246

**No Name** • Agency: Bureau of Land Management • Location: 21 miles W of Atlantic City (limited services), 47 miles SW of Lander • GPS: Lat 42.519618 Lon -109.048365 • Total sites: 10 • RV sites: 7 • RV fee: Free • No water • Vault toilets • Elevation: 7888

## Basin

**Harrington Reservoir - WGF** • Agency: State • Tel: 307-777-4600 • Location: 16 miles W of Basin (limited services), 17 miles SW of Greybull • GPS: Lat 44.358963 Lon -108.316075 • Total sites: Dispersed • RV sites: Undefined • RV fee: Free • No water • Activities: Fishing • Elevation: 4290

## Beulah

**Sand Creek Public Access - East Oxbow - WGF** • Agency: State • Location: 3 miles S of Beulah (limited services), 19 miles NE of Sundance • GPS: Lat 44.516808 Lon -104.083653 • Open: All year • Total sites: Dispersed • RV sites: Undefined • RV fee: Free • No water • Vault toilets • Activities: Fishing, hunting • Elevation: 3592

**Sand Creek Public Access - Road and Gun - WGF** • Agency: State • Location: 3 miles S of Beulah (limited services), 20 miles NE of Sundance • GPS: Lat 44.51605 Lon -104.09773 • Open: All year • Total sites: Dispersed • RV sites: Undefined • RV fee: Free • No water • Vault toilets • Activities: Fishing, hunting • Elevation: 3622

**Sand Creek Public Access - Rogers - WGF** • Agency: State • Location: 3 miles S of Beulah (limited services), 20 miles NE of Sundance • GPS: Lat 44.515484 Lon -104.089056 • Open: All year • Total sites: Dispersed • RV sites: Undefined • RV fee: Free • No water • Vault toilets • Activities: Fishing, hunting • Elevation: 3606

**Sand Creek Public Access -West Oxbow - WGF** • Agency: State • Location: 4 miles S of Beulah (limited services), 21 miles NE of Sundance • GPS: Lat 44.512896 Lon -

104.102737 • Open: All year • Total sites: Dispersed • RV sites: Undefined • RV fee: Free • No water • Vault toilets • Activities: Fishing, hunting • Elevation: 3652

## Big Piney

**Green River - Ferry Island Access - WGF** • Agency: State • Tel: 307-777-4600 • Location: 11 miles SE of Big Piney (limited services), 68 miles NE of Kemmerer • GPS: Lat 42.518435 Lon -110.072857 • Total sites: Dispersed • RV sites: Undefined • RV fee: Free • No water • Vault toilets • Activities: Fishing, power boating, non-power boating • Elevation: 6801

**Green River - Reardon Draw Access - WGF** • Agency: State • Tel: 307-777-4600 • Location: 8 miles S of Big Piney (limited services), 60 miles NE of Kemmerer • GPS: Lat 42.423455 Lon -110.103733 • Total sites: Dispersed • RV sites: Undefined • RV fee: Free • No water • Vault toilets • Activities: Fishing, power boating, non-power boating • Elevation: 6676

**South Piney Creek - WGF** • Agency: State • Tel: 307-777-4600 • Location: 18 miles W of Big Piney (limited services), 54 miles SW of Pinedale • GPS: Lat 42.507315 Lon -110.451232 • Total sites: Dispersed • RV sites: Undefined • RV fee: Free • No water • No toilets • Activities: Fishing • Elevation: 7715

## Boulder

**Blucher Creek** • Agency: Bureau of Land Management • Tel: 307-352-0256 • Location: 43 miles SE of Boulder (limited services), 55 miles SE of Pinedale • GPS: Lat 42.561771 Lon -109.141683 • Stay limit: 14 days • Total sites: Dispersed • RV sites: Undefined • RV fee: Free • No water • Vault toilets • Activities: Hiking • Elevation: 8577

**Scab Creek** • Agency: Bureau of Land Management • Tel: 307-367-5300 • Location: 15 miles NE of Boulder (limited services), 26 miles SE of Pinedale • GPS: Lat 42.820904 Lon -109.553253 • Open: May-Nov • Stay limit: 14 days • Total sites: 9 • RV sites: 9 • Max RV Length: 31 • RV fee: Free • No water • Vault toilets • Activities: Hiking, fishing, hunting, rock climbing, equestrian area • Elevation: 8255

**Stokes Crossing** • Agency: Bureau of Land Management • Tel: 307-367-5300 • Location: 9 miles N of Boulder (limited services), 21 miles SE of Pinedale • GPS: Lat 42.819321 Lon -109.715796 • Total sites: 2 • RV sites: 2 • RV fee: Free • No water • Vault toilets • Activities: Fishing, swimming, power boating, non-power boating • Elevation: 7201

## Buffalo

**Bud Love Wildlife Habitat Mgmt Area - Taylor Pond - WGF** • Agency: State • Tel: 307-777-4600 • Location: 13 miles NW of Buffalo • GPS: Lat 44.412846 Lon -106.887311 • Open: May-Dec • Stay limit: 14 days • Total sites: Dispersed • RV sites: Undefined • RV fee: Free • No water • Activities: Fishing • Elevation: 5724

**Bud Love Wildlife Habitat Mgmt Area - WGF** • Agency: State • Tel: 307-777-4600 • Location: 11 miles NW of Buffalo • GPS: Lat 44.420283 Lon -106.853475 • Open: May-Dec • Stay limit: 14 days • Total sites: Dispersed • RV sites: Undefined • RV fee: Free • No water • No toilets • Activities: Hiking, fishing, hunting • Elevation: 5308

**Healey Reservoir - WGF** • Agency: State • Location: 5 miles NE of Buffalo • GPS: Lat 44.403276 Lon -106.616918 • Total sites: Dispersed • RV sites: Undefined • RV fee: Free • No water • No toilets • Activities: Fishing • Elevation: 4386

**South Sayles Reservoir - WGF** • Agency: State • Location: 12 miles NW of Buffalo • GPS: Lat 44.409788 Lon -106.869045 • Total sites: Dispersed • RV sites: Undefined • RV fee: Free • No water • No toilets • Activities: Fishing • Elevation: 5482

**Tie Hack Reservoir** • Agency: State • Tel: 307-777-4600 • Location: 16 miles SW of Buffalo • GPS: Lat 44.287754 Lon -106.923787 • Total sites: Dispersed • RV sites: Undefined • RV fee: Free • No water • No toilets • Activities: Fishing • Elevation: 7511

## Centennial

**Fishhook Lake - WGF** • Agency: State • Location: 12 miles NW of Centennial (limited services), 39 miles W of Laramie • GPS: Lat 41.358649 Lon -106.266982 • Total sites: Dispersed • RV sites: Undefined • RV fee: Free • No water • Vault toilets • Activities: Fishing • Elevation: 10600

## Cody

**Clark's Fork River, Upper - WGF** • Agency: State • Tel: 307-777-4600 • Location: 52 miles NW of Cody • GPS: Lat 44.858036 Lon -109.568076 • Total sites: Dispersed • RV sites: Undefined • RV fee: Free • No water • No toilets • Activities: Fishing • Elevation: 6066

**Deer Creek** (Shoshone NF) • Agency: US Forest Service • Tel: 307-527-6921 • Location: 40 miles SW of Cody • GPS: Lat 44.158457 Lon -109.619461 • Open: All year • Stay limit: 16 days • Total sites: 6 • RV sites: 6 • Max RV Length: 16 • RV fee: Free (donation appreciated) • No water • Vault toilets • Notes: Food storage order 04-00-104 • Activities: Hiking, fishing • Elevation: 6447

**Hogan - Luce CG** • Agency: Bureau of Land Management • Tel: 307-578-5900 • Location: 24 miles NW of Cody • GPS: Lat 44.787463 Lon -109.257649 • Open: All year • Total sites: 5 • RV sites: 5 • RV fee: Free • Vault toilets • Activities: Hiking, fishing, power boating, hunting, equestrian area • Elevation: 4826

**Lily Lake** (Shoshone NF) • Agency: US Forest Service • Tel: 307-527-6921 • Location: 65 miles NW of Cody • GPS: Lat 44.945 Lon -109.714 • Open: All year • Stay limit: 16 days • Total sites: 8 • RV sites: 8 • Max RV Length: 22 • RV fee: Free (donation appreciated) • No water • Vault toilets • Activities: Hiking, mountain biking, non-power boating, equestrian area • Elevation: 7700

**Little Sunlight** (Shoshone NF) • Agency: US Forest Service • Tel: 307-527-6921 • Location: 50 miles NW of Cody • GPS: Lat 44.718 Lon -109.591 • Stay limit: 16 days • Total sites: 5 • RV sites: 5 • RV fee: Free • No water • Vault toilets • Activities: Hiking, equestrian area • Elevation: 6952

**Sunlight WHMA - Grizzly** • Agency: State • Tel: 307-777-4600 • Location: 48 miles NW of Cody • GPS: Lat 44.737729 Lon -109.555765 • Open: May-Dec • Stay limit: 14 days • Total sites: Dispersed • RV sites: Undefined • RV fee: Free • No water • Elevation: 6801

**Sunlight WHMA - Sunlight** • Agency: State • Tel: 307-777-4600 • Location: 45 miles NW of Cody • GPS: Lat 44.739734 Lon -109.529498 • Open: May-Dec • Stay limit: 14 days • Total sites: Dispersed • RV sites: Undefined • RV fee: Free • No water • Elevation: 6752

## Cokeville

**Pine Creek** • Agency: Bureau of Land Management • Tel: 307-828-4500 • Location: 7 miles E of Cokeville (limited services), 50 miles NW of Kemmerer • GPS: Lat 42.104735 Lon -110.828238 • Total sites: 7 • RV sites: 7 • RV fee: Free • No water • Vault toilets • Notes: Near ski area • Activities: Hunting, motor sports • Elevation: 6868

## Daniel

**Warren Bridge/Green River Access #1** • Agency: Bureau of Land Management • Tel: 307-367-5300 • Location: 13 miles N of Daniel (limited services), 21 miles NW of Pinedale • GPS: Lat 43.024467 Lon -110.103173 • Total sites: 5 • RV sites: 5 • RV fee: Free • No water • No toilets • Activities: Hiking, fishing, swimming, power boating, non-power boating • Elevation: 7498

**Warren Bridge/Green River Access #2** • Agency: Bureau of Land Management • Tel: 307-367-5300 • Location: 13 miles N of Daniel (limited services), 22 miles NW of Pinedale • GPS: Lat 43.033077 Lon -110.101697 • Total sites: Dispersed • RV sites: Undefined • RV fee: Free • No water • No toilets • Activities: Hiking, fishing, swimming, power boating, non-power boating • Elevation: 7514

**Warren Bridge/Green River Access #3** • Agency: Bureau of Land Management • Tel: 307-367-5300 • Location: 16 miles N of Daniel (limited services), 24 miles NW of Pinedale • GPS: Lat 43.060059 Lon -110.085445 • Total sites: 3 • RV sites: 3 • RV fee: Free • No water • No toilets • Activities: Hiking, fishing, swimming, power boating, non-power boating • Elevation: 7559

**Warren Bridge/Green River Access #4** • Agency: Bureau of Land Management • Tel: 307-367-5300 • Location: 16 miles N of Daniel (limited services), 24 miles NW of Pinedale • GPS: Lat 43.065721 Lon -110.081076 • Total sites: 4 • RV sites: 4 • RV fee: Free • No water • Vault toilets • Activities: Hiking, fishing, swimming, power boating, non-power boating • Elevation: 7562

**Warren Bridge/Green River Access #5** • Agency: Bureau of Land Management • Tel: 307-367-5300 • Location: 17 miles N of Daniel (limited services), 25 miles NW of Pinedale • GPS: Lat 43.072302 Lon -110.074066 • Total sites: 2 • RV sites: 2 • RV fee: Free • No water • No toilets • Activities: Hiking, fishing, swimming, power boating, non-power boating • Elevation: 7575

**Warren Bridge/Green River Access #6** • Agency: Bureau of Land Management • Tel: 307-367-5300 • Location: 17 miles N of Daniel (limited services), 25 miles NW of Pinedale • GPS: Lat 43.080704 Lon -110.066597 • Total sites: 3 • RV sites: 3 • RV fee: Free • No water • Vault toilets • Activities: Hiking, fishing, swimming, power boating, non-power boating • Elevation: 7587

**Warren Bridge/Green River Access #7** • Agency: Bureau of Land Management • Tel: 307-367-5300 • Location: 18 miles N of Daniel (limited services), 26 miles NW of Pinedale • GPS: Lat 43.089371 Lon -110.066434 • Total sites: 7 • RV sites: 7 • RV fee: Free • No water • No toilets • Activities: Hiking, fishing, swimming, power boating, non-power boating • Elevation: 7592

**Warren Bridge/Green River Access #8** • Agency: Bureau of Land Management • Tel: 307-367-5300 • Location: 18 miles N of Daniel (limited services), 26 miles NW of Pinedale • GPS: Lat 43.098339 Lon -110.063323 • Total sites: Dispersed • RV sites: Undefined • RV fee: Free • No water • No toilets • Activities: Hiking, fishing, swimming, power boating, non-power boating • Elevation: 7608

## Dayton

**Amsden Creek WMA - Amsden Meadows** • Agency: State • Tel: 307-777-4600 • Location: 5 miles W of Dayton (limited services), 23 miles W of Sheridan • GPS: Lat 44.877766 Lon -107.339481 • Open: May-Oct • Total sites: Dispersed • RV sites: Undefined • RV fee: Free • No toilets • Elevation: 4511

**Amsden Creek WMA - Tongue Canyon** • Agency: State • Tel: 307-777-4600 • Location: 5 miles SW of Dayton (limited services), 23 miles W of Sheridan • GPS: Lat 44.847014 Lon -107.329811 • Open: May-Oct • Total sites: Dispersed • RV sites: Undefined • RV fee: Free • No toilets • Elevation: 4341

**Amsden Creek WMA - Tongue River** • Agency: State • Tel: 307-777-4600 • Location: 4 miles SW of Dayton (limited services), 22 miles W of Sheridan • GPS: Lat 44.848391 Lon -107.306006 • Open: May-Oct • Total sites: Dispersed • RV sites: Undefined • RV fee: Free • No toilets • Elevation: 4101

**Bull Creek Access - WGF** • Agency: State • Location: 27 miles SW of Dayton (limited services), 47 miles W of Sheridan • GPS: Lat 44.768161 Lon -107.566966 • Total sites: Dispersed • RV sites: Undefined • RV fee: Free • No water • No toilets • Activities: Fishing • Elevation: 7989

**Kerns WHMA - Gay Creek** • Agency: State • Tel: 307-777-4600 • Location: 21 miles NW of Dayton (limited services), 35 miles NW of Sheridan • GPS: Lat 44.969285 Lon -107.530598 • Open: Jun-Nov • Stay limit: 14 days • Total sites: Dispersed • RV sites: Undefined • RV fee: Free • No water • No toilets • Activities: Fishing, power boating, non-power boating • Elevation: 5123

## Deaver

**Deaver Reservoir - WGF** • Agency: State • Tel: 307-261-5628 • Location: 4 miles NW of Deaver (limited services), 15 miles NW of Lovell • GPS: Lat 44.903302 Lon -108.638743 • Total sites: Dispersed • RV sites: Undefined • RV fee: Free • No water • Vault toilets • Activities: Fishing, power boating, non-power boating • Elevation: 4311

## Douglas

**Ayers Natural Bridge** • Agency: County • Tel: 307-358-3532 • Location: 16 miles W of Douglas • GPS: Lat 42.733872 Lon -105.611915 • Open: Apr-Oct • Total sites: 12 • RV sites: 12 • Max RV Length: 30 • RV fee: Free • Notes: No pets • Elevation: 5344

**Riverside City Park** • Agency: Municipal • Tel: 307-358-9750 • Location: In Douglas • GPS: Lat 42.762937 Lon -105.391996 • Stay limit: 2 days • Total sites: 20 • RV sites: 20 • RV fee: Free • Central water • Flush toilets • Elevation: 4805

## Dubois

**Dubois** • Agency: Bureau of Land Management • Location: 12 miles SE of Dubois • GPS: Lat 43.432689 Lon -109.445977 • Total sites: 6 • RV sites: 6 • RV fee: Free • No water • No toilets • Activities: Fishing • Elevation: 6371

**Spence and Moriarity WHMA - Long Meadow - WGF** • Agency: State • Tel: 307-777-4600 • Location: 18 miles E of Dubois • GPS: Lat 43.563287 Lon -109.459723 • Open: May-Nov • Stay limit: 14 days • Total sites: Dispersed • RV sites: Undefined • RV fee: Free • No water • No toilets • Activities: Hiking, fishing, swimming, power boating, hunting, non-power boating • Elevation: 6867

**Spence and Moriarity WHMA - Thunderhead - WGF** • Agency: State • Tel: 307-777-4600 • Location: 20 miles NE of Dubois • GPS: Lat 43.583012 Lon -109.458322 • Open: May-Nov • Stay limit: 14 days • Total sites: Dispersed • RV sites: Undefined • RV fee: Free • No water • No toilets • Activities: Hiking, fishing, swimming, power boating, hunting, non-power boating • Elevation: 6962

**Spence and Moriarity WHMA - Zeng's Hideaway - WGF** • Agency: State • Tel: 307-777-4600 • Location: 15 miles E of Dubois • GPS: Lat 43.515069 Lon -109.468109 • Open: May-Nov • Stay limit: 14 days • Total sites: Dispersed • RV sites: Undefined • RV fee: Free • No water • Vault toilets • Activities: Hiking, fishing, swimming, power boating, hunting, non-power boating • Elevation: 6648

**Whiskey Basin WMA - Glacier Trail** • Agency: State • Tel: 307-777-4600 • Location: 13 miles SE of Dubois • GPS: Lat 43.425925 Lon -109.572226 • Open: All year (access restricted Dec-May) • Stay limit: 14 days • Total sites: Dispersed • RV sites: Undefined • RV fee: Free • No water • Activities: Hiking • Elevation: 7612

**Whiskey Basin WMA - Ring Lake** • Agency: State • Tel: 307-777-4600 • Location: 10 miles SE of Dubois • GPS: Lat 43.450039 Lon -109.541219 • Open: All year (access restricted Dec-May) • Stay limit: 14 days • Total sites: Dispersed • RV sites: Undefined • RV fee: Free • No water • Activities: Fishing, power boating, non-power boating • Elevation: 7415

**Whiskey Basin WMA - Torrey Creek** • Agency: State • Tel: 307-777-4600 • Location: 10 miles SE of Dubois • GPS: Lat 43.443809 Lon -109.537977 • Open: All year (access restricted Dec-May) • Stay limit: 14 days • Total sites: Dispersed • RV sites: Undefined • RV fee: Free • No water • Activities: Fishing, power boating, non-power boating • Elevation: 7431

**Whiskey Basin WMA - Trail Lake** • Agency: State • Tel: 307-777-4600 • Location: 11 miles SE of Dubois • GPS: Lat 43.437087 Lon -109.539912 • Open: All year (access restricted Dec-May) • Stay limit: 14 days • Total sites: Dispersed • RV sites: Undefined • RV fee: Free • No water • Activities: Fishing, power boating, non-power boating • Elevation: 7411

**Whiskey Basin WMA - Trail Meadow** • Agency: State • Tel: 307-777-4600 • Location: 12 miles SE of Dubois • GPS: Lat 43.424911 Lon -109.566899 • Open: All year (access restricted Dec-May) • Stay limit: 14 days • Total sites: Dispersed • RV sites: Undefined • RV fee: Free • No water • Activities: Hiking • Elevation: 7500

## Elk Mountain

**Beumee WHMA - Site 2** • Agency: State • Tel: 307-777-4600 • Location: 10 miles SE of Elk Mountain (limited services), 44 miles NW of Laramie • GPS: Lat 41.638851 Lon -106.273586 • Stay limit: 14 days • Total sites: Dispersed • RV sites: Undefined • RV fee: Free • No water • No toilets • Elevation: 7559

**Wagonhound** • Agency: Bureau of Land Management • Location: 11 miles SE of Elk Mountain (limited services), 45 miles NW of Laramie • GPS: Lat 41.623326 Lon -106.291714 • Total sites: Dispersed • RV sites: Undefined • RV fee: Free • No water • No toilets • Elevation: 7595

**Wick WHMA - Site 1** • Agency: State • Tel: 307-777-4600 • Location: 13 miles SE of Elk Mountain (limited services), 47 miles NW of Laramie • GPS: Lat 41.609486 Lon -106.310087 • Open: May-Nov • Stay limit: 14 days • Total sites: Dispersed • RV sites: Undefined • RV fee: Free • No water • No toilets • Elevation: 7667

**Wick WHMA - Site 2** • Agency: State • Tel: 307-777-4600 • Location: 13 miles SE of Elk Mountain (limited services), 47 miles NW of Laramie • GPS: Lat 41.607351 Lon -106.313008 • Open: May-Nov • Stay limit: 14 days • Total sites: Dispersed • RV sites: Undefined • RV fee: Free • No water • No toilets • Elevation: 7707

## Encampment

**Encampment City Park** • Agency: Municipal • Tel: 307 327-5501 • Location: In Encampment (limited services), 18 miles S of Saratoga • GPS: Lat 41.211165 Lon -106.792195 • Stay limit: 3 days • Total sites: 9 • RV sites: 9 • Max RV Length: 50 • RV fee: Free (donation appreciated) • Electric sites: 8 • Water at site • Flush toilets • Notes: 3-day limit • Elevation: 7274

**Encampment River - WGF** • Agency: State • Tel: 307-777-4600 • Location: 3 miles N of Encampment (limited services), 20 miles S of Saratoga • GPS: Lat 41.249132 Lon -106.759569 • Total sites: Dispersed • RV sites: Undefined • RV fee: Free • No water • No toilets • Activities: Fishing • Elevation: 7976

**Pickaroon** (Medicine Bow-Routt NF) • Agency: US Forest Service • Tel: 307-745-2300 • Location: 24 miles SE of Encampment (limited services), 42 miles SE of Saratoga • GPS: Lat 41.126 Lon -106.431 • Open: Jun-Sep • Stay limit: 14 days • Total sites: 8 • RV sites: 8 • Max RV Length: 16 • RV fee: Free • No toilets • Activities: Hiking, fishing, equestrian area • Elevation: 7448

## Evanston

**Bear River - WGF** • Agency: State • Tel: 307-777-4600 • Location: 19 miles N of Evanston • GPS: Lat 41.506258 Lon -111.011686 • Total sites: Dispersed • RV sites: Undefined • RV fee: Free • No water • Vault toilets • Activities: Fishing • Elevation: 6416

**Woodruff Narrows Reservoir - WGF** • Agency: State • Tel: 307-777-4600 • Location: 17 miles N of Evanston • GPS: Lat 41.485147 Lon -111.026982 • Total sites: Dispersed • RV sites: Undefined • RV fee: Free • No water • Vault toilets • Activities: Fishing • Elevation: 6469

**Woodruff Narrows/Bear River Access - WGF** • Agency: State • Location: 18 miles N of Evanston • GPS: Lat 41.505514 Lon -111.023478 • Total sites: Dispersed • RV sites: Undefined • RV fee: Free • Central water • Vault toilets • Activities: Hiking, fishing, non-power boating • Elevation: 6475

## Farson

**Big Sandy Reservoir** • Agency: US Bureau of Reclamation • Tel: 801-379-1000 • Location: 11 miles N of Farson (limited services), 51 miles N of Rock Springs • GPS: Lat 42.245522 Lon -109.433356 • Total sites: 11 • RV sites: 11 • RV fee: Free • No water • Activities: Fishing, power boating, non-power boating • Elevation: 6762

**Sweetwater River** • Agency: Bureau of Land Management • Tel: 307-352-0256 • Location: 56 miles NE of Farson (limited services), 64 miles SE of Pinedale • GPS: Lat 42.562074 Lon -109.062969 • Total sites: 10 • RV sites: 10 • RV fee: Free • No water • Vault toilets • Activities: Hiking, mountain biking, fishing • Elevation: 8287

## Flagg Ranch

**Grand Teton NP - Flagg Ranch Rd Site #4** • Agency: National Park Service • Location: 3 miles SW of Flagg Ranch (limited services), 58 miles N of Jackson • GPS: Lat 44.086294 Lon -110.699272 • Stay limit: 14 days • Total sites: 2 • RV sites: 2 • Max RV Length: 18 • RV fee: Free • No water • Vault toilets • Elevation: 6866

## Fort Washakie

**Dickinson Creek** (Shoshone NF) • Agency: US Forest Service • Tel: 307-332-5460 • Location: 23 miles SW of Fort Washakie (limited services), 35 miles W of Lander • GPS: Lat 42.835693 Lon -109.057617 • Open: Apr-Oct • Stay limit: 16 days • Total sites: 15 • RV sites: 15 • Max RV

Length: 20 • RV fee: Free • No water • Vault toilets • Notes: Tribal fishing license required if on nearby reservation land • Activities: Hiking, fishing • Elevation: 9354

## Gillette

**Weston Hills RA** • Agency: Bureau of Land Management • Tel: 307-684-1100 • Location: 35 miles NE of Gillette • GPS: Lat 44.635982 Lon -105.355455 • Total sites: Dispersed • RV sites: Undefined • RV fee: Free • No water • No toilets • Activities: Hiking, mountain biking, fishing, hunting, equestrian area • Elevation: 3900

## Glendo

**North Platte River - Glendo Public Access - WGF** • Agency: State • Location: 7 miles SE of Glendo (limited services), 38 miles N of Wheatland • GPS: Lat 42.464995 Lon -104.954805 • Total sites: Dispersed • RV sites: Undefined • RV fee: Free • No toilets • Activities: Fishing, power boating, non-power boating • Elevation: 4508

## Glenrock

**North Platte River - Bixby Public Access - WGF** • Agency: State • Location: 11 miles E of Glenrock • GPS: Lat 42.856762 Lon -105.668736 • Total sites: Dispersed • RV sites: Undefined • RV fee: Free • No water • No toilets • Activities: Fishing, power boating, non-power boating • Elevation: 4928

**North Platte River - Pacificorp Public Access - WGF** • Agency: State • Location: 7 miles E of Glenrock • GPS: Lat 42.841366 Lon -105.740056 • Total sites: Dispersed • RV sites: Undefined • RV fee: Free • No water • No toilets • Activities: Fishing, power boating, non-power boating • Elevation: 4929

**South Recreation Complex** • Agency: Municipal • Tel: 307-436-9294 • Location: 3 miles S of Glenrock • GPS: Lat 42.835782 Lon -105.873727 • Total sites: 4 • RV sites: 4 • RV fee: Free • Flush toilets • Elevation: 5033

## Green River

**White Mountain Road** • Agency: Bureau of Land Management • Location: 3 miles NE of Green River • GPS: Lat 41.548516 Lon -109.421571 • Open: All year • Total sites: Dispersed • RV sites: Undefined • RV fee: Free • No water • No toilets • Activities: Motor sports, equestrian area • Elevation: 7165

## Hawk Springs

**Springer/Bump Sulllivan WHMA - Bump Sullivan Reservoir** • Agency: State • Tel: 307-777-4600 • Location: 8 miles NW of Hawk Springs (limited services), 17 miles SW of Torrington • GPS: Lat 41.861609 Lon -104.311394 • Stay limit: 14 days • Total sites: Dispersed • RV sites: Undefined • RV fee: Free • No water • No toilets • Activities: Hiking, fishing, swimming, power boating, hunting, non-power boating • Elevation: 4300

**Springer/Bump Sulllivan WHMA - Goshen Hole Reservoir** • Agency: State • Tel: 307-777-4600 • Location: 10 miles N of Hawk Springs (limited services), 17 miles SW of Torrington • GPS: Lat 41.892742 Lon -104.287288 • Stay limit: 14 days • Total sites: Dispersed • RV sites: Undefined • RV fee: Free • No water • Vault toilets • Activities: Hiking, fishing, swimming, power boating, hunting, non-power boating • Elevation: 4278

## Jackson

**Gros Ventre River Access - WGF** • Agency: State • Tel: 307-777-4600 • Location: 8 miles N of Jackson • GPS: Lat 43.584231 Lon -110.713394 • Total sites: Dispersed • RV sites: Undefined • RV fee: Free • No water • No toilets • Activities: Fishing • Elevation: 6474

## Kaycee

**Kaycee Town Park** • Agency: Municipal • Tel: 307-738-2301 • Location: In Kaycee (limited services), 45 miles S of Buffalo • GPS: Lat 43.713383 Lon -106.630616 • Total sites: 10 • RV sites: 3 • Max RV Length: 30 • RV fee: Free • Central water • No toilets • Elevation: 4695

**Middle Fork of the Powder River** • Agency: Bureau of Land Management • Tel: 307-684-1100 • Location: 38 miles SW of Kaycee (limited services), 66 miles SE of Worland • GPS: Lat 43.577034 Lon -107.142292 • Total sites: 5 • RV sites: 5 • Max RV Length: 20 • RV fee: Free • No water • Vault toilets • Elevation: 7323

**Middle Fork Powder River** • Agency: Bureau of Land Management • Location: 20 miles SW of Kaycee (limited services), 65 miles SW of Buffalo • GPS: Lat 43.597122 Lon -106.911523 • Total sites: Dispersed • RV sites: Undefined • RV fee: Free • No water • Vault toilets • Activities: Hiking • Elevation: 5505

## Kemmerer

**Fossil Butte** • Agency: Bureau of Land Management • Location: 13 miles W of Kemmerer • GPS: Lat 41.828991 Lon -110.781379 • Total sites: Dispersed • RV sites: Undefined • RV fee: Free • No water • No toilets • Elevation: 6760

**Lake Viva Naughton Public Access** • Agency: State • Location: 17 miles NW of Kemmerer • GPS: Lat 41.998811 Lon -110.656838 • Total sites: Dispersed • RV sites: Undefined • RV fee: Free • No water • Vault toilets • Activities: Fishing • Elevation: 7275

**Lake Viva Naughton Public Access - Dempsey Point** • Agency: State • Location: 21 miles NW of Kemmerer • GPS: Lat 41.997892 Lon -110.671752 • Total sites: Dispersed • RV sites: Undefined • RV fee: Free • No water • Vault toilets • Activities: Fishing, power boating, non-power boating • Elevation: 7251

**Lake Viva Naughton Public Access - Marina Area** • Agency: State • Location: 16 miles NW of Kemmerer • GPS: Lat 41.981553 Lon -110.654223 • Total sites: Dispersed • RV sites: Undefined • RV fee: Free • No water • Vault toilets • Activities: Fishing, power boating, non-power boating • Elevation: 7316

## Kinnear

**Ocean Lake WHMA - Lindholm** • Agency: State • Location: 3 miles NE of Kinnear (limited services), 17 miles NW of Riverton • GPS: Lat 43.171473 Lon -108.644396 • Open: All year • Stay limit: 14 days • Total sites: Dispersed • RV sites: Undefined • RV fee: Free • No water • Vault toilets • Activities: Fishing, power boating, non-power boating • Elevation: 5246

**Ocean Lake WHMA - Long Point Area - WGF** • Agency: State • Location: 3 miles NE of Kinnear (limited services), 17 miles NW of Riverton • GPS: Lat 43.174876 Lon -108.630556 • Open: All year • Stay limit: 14 days • Total sites: Dispersed • RV sites: Undefined • RV fee: Free • No water • Vault toilets • Activities: Fishing, power boating, non-power boating • Elevation: 5253

**Ocean Lake WHMA - South Cove Area - WGF** • Agency: State • Location: 3 miles NE of Kinnear (limited services), 17 miles NW of Riverton • GPS: Lat 43.165415 Lon -108.632626 • Open: All year • Stay limit: 14 days • Total sites: Dispersed • RV sites: Undefined • RV fee: Free • No water • Vault toilets • Activities: Fishing • Elevation: 5245

**Pilot Butte Reservoir - WGF** • Agency: State • Location: 6 miles NW of Kinnear (limited services), 21 miles NW of Riverton • GPS: Lat 43.201348 Lon -108.758799 • Total sites: Dispersed • RV sites: Undefined • RV fee: Free • No water • Vault toilets • Activities: Hiking, fishing, swimming, power boating, non-power boating • Elevation: 5472

## La Barge

**Gypsum Creek Access - WGF** • Agency: State • Location: 16 miles NE of La Barge (limited services), 58 miles NE of Kemmerer • GPS: Lat 42.322327 Lon -109.997978 • Total sites: Dispersed • RV sites: Undefined • RV fee: Free • No water • No toilets • Activities: Fishing • Elevation: 7244

**LaBarge Creek** • Agency: Bureau of Land Management • Tel: 307-777-4600 • Location: 16 miles NW of La Barge (limited services), 62 miles N of Kemmerer • GPS: Lat 42.293963 Lon -110.440055 • Total sites: Dispersed • RV sites: Undefined • RV fee: Free • No water • Activities: Fishing • Elevation: 7299

**Slate CreeK** • Agency: Bureau of Land Management • Tel: 307-828-4500 • Location: 27 miles SE of La Barge (limited services), 33 miles NE of Kemmerer • GPS: Lat 41.983962 Lon -110.044609 • Total sites: 8 • RV sites: 8 • RV fee: Free • No water • Vault toilets • Activities: Fishing, motor sports • Elevation: 6381

**Tail Race** • Agency: Bureau of Land Management • Tel: 307-828-4500 • Location: 23 miles SE of La Barge (limited services), 34 miles NE of Kemmerer • GPS: Lat 42.024968 Lon -110.061183 • Total sites: 9 • RV sites: 9 • RV fee: Free • No water • Vault toilets • Activities: Fishing • Elevation: 6417

**Weeping Rock** • Agency: Bureau of Land Management • Tel: 307-828-4500 • Location: 24 miles SE of La Barge (limited services), 35 miles NE of Kemmerer • GPS: Lat 42.020655 Lon -110.047654 • Open: All year • Total sites: 10 • RV sites: 10 • RV fee: Free • No water • Vault toilets • Activities: Hiking, mountain biking, fishing, hunting, equestrian area • Elevation: 6447

## Lander

**Hugh Otte** (Shoshone NF) • Agency: US Forest Service • Tel: 307-332-5460 • Location: 9 miles SW of Lander • GPS: Lat 42.732432 Lon -108.849298 • Stay limit: 16 days • Total sites: 8 • RV sites: 8 • RV fee: Free • No water • Vault toilets • Activities: Hiking, equestrian area • Elevation: 7056

**Little Popo Agie** (Shoshone NF) • Agency: US Forest Service • Tel: 307-332-5460 • Location: 25 miles SW of Lander • GPS: Lat 42.607848 Lon -108.857318 • Stay limit: 16 days • Total sites: 4 • RV sites: 1 • Max RV Length: 16 • RV fee: Free • No water • Vault toilets • Activities: Hiking, fishing • Elevation: 8802

## Laramie

**Forbes/Sheep Mountain WMA** • Agency: State • Tel: 307-777-4600 • Location: 30 miles SW of Laramie • GPS: Lat 41.171347 Lon -106.068281 • Open: May-Dec • Stay limit: 14 days • Total sites: Dispersed • RV sites: Undefined • RV fee: Free • No water • No toilets • Activities: Hiking, hunting • Elevation: 8189

**Gelatt Lake Public Access - WGF** • Agency: State • Location: 13 miles SW of Laramie • GPS: Lat 41.236717 Lon -105.836579 • Total sites: Dispersed • RV sites: Undefined • RV fee: Free • No water • Vault toilets • Activities: Fishing, power boating, non-power boating • Elevation: 7247

**Jelm WMA** • Agency: State • Tel: 307-777-4600 • Location: 26 miles SW of Laramie • GPS: Lat 41.099516 Lon -106.013248 • Open: All year • Stay limit: 5 days • Total sites: Dispersed • RV sites: Undefined • RV fee: Free • No water • No toilets • Activities: Fishing, hunting • Elevation: 7618

**Lake Hattie Public Access Area - WGF** • Agency: State • Location: 18 miles SW of Laramie • GPS: Lat 41.236694 Lon -105.900698 • Total sites: Dispersed • RV sites: Undefined • RV fee: Free • No water • No toilets • Activities: Fishing, power boating, non-power boating • Elevation: 7284

**Meeboer Lake Access Area - WGF** • Agency: State • Location: 14 miles SW of Laramie • GPS: Lat 41.214229 Lon -105.823297 • Total sites: Dispersed • RV sites: Undefined • RV fee: Free • Central water • Vault toilets • Activities: Fishing, power boating, non-power boating • Elevation: 7241

**Twin Buttes Reservoir Public Access - WGF** • Agency: State • Location: 14 miles SW of Laramie • GPS: Lat 41.233729 Lon -105.853308 • Total sites: Dispersed • RV sites: Undefined • RV fee: Free • No water • No toilets • Activities: Fishing, power boating, non-power boating • Elevation: 7264

## Lovell

**Cottonwood** • Agency: Bureau of Land Management • Tel: 307-578-5900 • Location: 16 miles E of Lovell • GPS: Lat 44.869417 Lon -108.071986 • Total sites: 5 • RV sites: 5 • Max RV Length: 20 • RV fee: Free • Vault toilets • Activities: Hiking • Elevation: 4836

**Lovell Camper Park** • Agency: Municipal • Tel: 307-548-6551 • Location: In Lovell • GPS: Lat 44.841517 Lon -108.383533 • Total sites: 15 • RV sites: 15 • Max RV Length: 32 • RV fee: Free • Central water • Flush toilets • Notes: 3-day limit • Elevation: 3819

**Yellowtail WMA - Site 1** • Agency: State • Tel: 307-777-4600 • Location: 11 miles NE of Lovell • GPS: Lat 44.877284 Lon -108.208718 • Open: All year • Stay limit: 14 days • Total sites: Dispersed • RV sites: Undefined • RV fee: Free • No water • No toilets • Activities: Hiking, fishing, hunting, non-power boating • Elevation: 3649

**Yellowtail WMA - Site 10** • Agency: State • Tel: 307-777-4600 • Location: 11 miles NE of Lovell • GPS: Lat 44.887777 Lon -108.202497 • Open: All year • Stay limit: 14 days • Total sites: Dispersed • RV sites: Undefined • RV fee: Free • No water • No toilets • Activities: Hiking, fishing, hunting, non-power boating • Elevation: 3678

**Yellowtail WMA - Site 11** • Agency: State • Tel: 307-777-4600 • Location: 11 miles NE of Lovell • GPS: Lat 44.910034 Lon -108.208898 • Open: All year • Stay limit: 14 days • Total sites: Dispersed • RV sites: Undefined • RV fee: Free • No water • Vault toilets • Activities: Hiking, fishing, hunting, non-power boating • Elevation: 3659

**Yellowtail WMA - Site 2** • Agency: State • Tel: 307-777-4600 • Location: 10 miles NE of Lovell • GPS: Lat 44.871426 Lon -108.221924 • Open: All year • Stay limit: 14 days • Total sites: Dispersed • RV sites: Undefined • RV fee: Free • No water • No toilets • Activities: Hiking, fishing, hunting, non-power boating • Elevation: 3664

**Yellowtail WMA - Site 3** • Agency: State • Tel: 307-777-4600 • Location: 11 miles NE of Lovell • GPS: Lat 44.884037 Lon -108.200512 • Open: All year • Stay limit: 14 days • Total sites: Dispersed • RV sites: Undefined • RV fee: Free • No water • No toilets • Activities: Hiking, fishing, hunting, non-power boating • Elevation: 3657

**Yellowtail WMA - Site 4** • Agency: State • Tel: 307-777-4600 • Location: 19 miles E of Lovell • GPS: Lat 44.806365 Lon -108.168313 • Open: All year • Stay limit: 14 days • Total sites: Dispersed • RV sites: Undefined • Max RV Length: 25 • RV fee: Free • No water • No toilets • Activities: Hiking, fishing, hunting, non-power boating • Elevation: 3658

**Yellowtail WMA - Site 5** • Agency: State • Tel: 307-777-4600 • Location: 13 miles E of Lovell • GPS: Lat 44.834506 Lon -108.160265 • Open: All year • Stay limit: 14 days • Total sites: Dispersed • RV sites: Undefined • RV fee: Free • No water • No toilets • Activities: Hiking, fishing, hunting, non-power boating • Elevation: 3659

**Yellowtail WMA - Site 6** • Agency: State • Tel: 307-777-4600 • Location: 10 miles E of Lovell • GPS: Lat 44.843454 Lon -108.198504 • Open: All year • Stay limit: 14 days • Total sites: Dispersed • RV sites: Undefined • RV fee: Free • No water • No toilets • Activities: Hiking, fishing, hunting, non-power boating • Elevation: 3659

**Yellowtail WMA - Site 7** • Agency: State • Tel: 307-777-4600 • Location: 10 miles E of Lovell • GPS: Lat 44.843344 Lon -108.202263 • Open: All year • Stay limit: 14 days • Total sites: Dispersed • RV sites: Undefined • RV fee: Free • No water • No toilets • Notes: Near RR tracks • Activities: Hiking, fishing, hunting, non-power boating • Elevation: 3685

**Yellowtail WMA - Site 8** • Agency: State • Tel: 307-777-4600 • Location: 9 miles E of Lovell • GPS: Lat 44.856284 Lon -108.209709 • Open: All year • Stay limit: 14 days • Total sites: Dispersed • RV sites: Undefined • RV fee: Free • No water • No toilets • Notes: Near RR tracks • Activities: Hiking, fishing, hunting, non-power boating • Elevation: 3661

**Yellowtail WMA - Site 9** • Agency: State • Tel: 307-777-4600 • Location: 10 miles E of Lovell • GPS: Lat

44.855893 Lon -108.176557 • Open: All year • Stay limit: 14 days • Total sites: Dispersed • RV sites: Undefined • RV fee: Free • No water • No toilets • Activities: Hiking, fishing, hunting, non-power boating • Elevation: 3652

## Marbleton

**New Fork River - W-351 Bridge** • Agency: Bureau of Land Management • Tel: 307-367-5300 • Location: 15 miles E of Marbleton (limited services), 26 miles S of Pinedale • GPS: Lat 42.606199 Lon -109.855856 • Total sites: 2 • RV sites: 2 • RV fee: Free • No water • Vault toilets • Activities: Fishing, power boating, non-power boating • Elevation: 6847

## Medicine Bow

**East Allen Lake Public Access - WGF** • Agency: State • Tel: 307-777-4600 • Location: 4 miles S of Medicine Bow (limited services), 59 miles NW of Laramie • GPS: Lat 41.870969 Lon -106.221928 • Total sites: Dispersed • RV sites: Undefined • RV fee: Free • No water • Vault toilets • Activities: Fishing, power boating, non-power boating • Elevation: 6543

**Prior Flat** • Agency: Bureau of Land Management • Tel: 307-328-4200 • Location: 40 miles NW of Medicine Bow (limited services), 63 miles S of Casper • GPS: Lat 42.241569 Lon -106.584398 • Open: Jun-Nov • Total sites: 15 • RV sites: 15 • RV fee: Free • No water • Vault toilets • Activities: Hiking • Elevation: 7733

## Meeteetse

**Lower Sunshine Reservoir - WGF** • Agency: State • Tel: 307-777-4600 • Location: 8 miles SW of Meeteetse (limited services), 37 miles S of Cody • GPS: Lat 44.097303 Lon -108.984914 • Total sites: Dispersed • RV sites: Undefined • RV fee: Free • No water • No toilets • Activities: Fishing, power boating • Elevation: 6299

**Upper Sunshine Reservoir - WGF** • Agency: State • Tel: 307-777-4600 • Location: 15 miles SE of Meeteetse (limited services), 45 miles S of Cody • GPS: Lat 44.053986 Lon -109.076777 • Total sites: Dispersed • RV sites: Undefined • RV fee: Free • No water • No toilets • Activities: Fishing, power boating • Elevation: 6629

**Wood River** (Shoshone NF) • Agency: US Forest Service • Tel: 307-527-6921 • Location: 23 miles SE of Meeteetse (limited services), 53 miles S of Cody • GPS: Lat 43.931703 Lon -109.132183 • Open: May-Sep • Stay limit: 16 days • Total sites: 5 • RV sites: 5 • Max RV Length: 30 • RV fee: Free (donation appreciated) • No water • Vault toilets • Notes: Food storage order • Activities: Hiking, fishing, equestrian area • Elevation: 7316

## Pavillion

**Ocean Lake WHMA - Dickinson Park Area - WGF** • Agency: State • Location: 9 miles SE of Pavillion (limited services), 19 miles NW of Riverton • GPS: Lat 43.204772 Lon -108.577213 • Open: All year • Stay limit: 14 days • Total sites: Dispersed • RV sites: Undefined • RV fee: Free • No water • Vault toilets • Activities: Fishing, power boating, non-power boating • Elevation: 5262

**Ocean Lake WHMA - Stultz Area - WGF** • Agency: State • Location: 6 miles SE of Pavillion (limited services), 20 miles NW of Riverton • GPS: Lat 43.212584 Lon -108.618723 • Open: All year • Stay limit: 14 days • Total sites: Dispersed • RV sites: Undefined • RV fee: Free • No water • Vault toilets • Activities: Fishing, power boating, non-power boating • Elevation: 5253

## Pinedale

**Fall Creek WHMA - WGF** • Agency: State • Tel: 307-777-4600 • Location: 12 miles E of Pinedale • GPS: Lat 42.867122 Lon -109.666768 • Open: May-Nov • Stay limit: 14 days • Total sites: Dispersed • RV sites: Undefined • RV fee: Free • No water • No toilets • Activities: Hiking, fishing, hunting • Elevation: 7930

**Green River - Daniel Access - WGF** • Agency: State • Location: 17 miles NW of Pinedale • GPS: Lat 42.944198 Lon -110.131613 • Total sites: Dispersed • RV sites: Undefined • RV fee: Free • No water • No toilets • Activities: Fishing • Elevation: 7362

**Half Moon WHMA - Pole Creek** • Agency: State • Tel: 307-777-4600 • Location: 10 miles E of Pinedale • GPS: Lat 42.880858 Lon -109.717391 • Open: May-Nov • Stay limit: 14 days • Total sites: Dispersed • RV sites: Undefined • RV fee: Free • No water • No toilets • Activities: Hiking, fishing, hunting • Elevation: 7484

**North Boulder Lake** • Agency: Bureau of Land Management • Tel: 307-367-5300 • Location: 15 miles E of Pinedale • GPS: Lat 42.841404 Lon -109.702373 • Open: Jun-Sep • Total sites: 5 • RV sites: 5 • RV fee: Free • No water • Vault toilets • Activities: Fishing, swimming, power boating, non-power boating • Elevation: 7323

**Soda Lake WHMA - Aspen** • Agency: State • Tel: 307-777-4600 • Location: 8 miles N of Pinedale • GPS: Lat 42.964529 Lon -109.832177 • Open: May-Nov • Stay limit: 14 days • Total sites: Dispersed • RV sites: Undefined • RV fee: Free • No water • No toilets • Activities: Hiking, fishing, power boating, hunting, non-power boating • Elevation: 7625

**Soda Lake WHMA - East Boat Ramp - WGF** • Agency: State • Tel: 307-777-4600 • Location: 8 miles N of Pinedale • GPS: Lat 42.965253 Lon -109.840235 • Open:

May-Nov • Stay limit: 14 days • Total sites: Dispersed • RV sites: Undefined • RV fee: Free • No water • No toilets • Activities: Hiking, fishing, power boating, hunting, non-power boating • Elevation: 7576

**Soda Lake WHMA - East Point** • Agency: State • Tel: 307-777-4600 • Location: 8 miles N of Pinedale • GPS: Lat 42.969286 Lon -109.841896 • Open: May-Nov • Stay limit: 14 days • Total sites: Dispersed • RV sites: Undefined • RV fee: Free • No water • No toilets • Activities: Hiking, fishing, power boating, hunting, non-power boating • Elevation: 7562

**Soda Lake WHMA - Horse Pasture** • Agency: State • Tel: 307-777-4600 • Location: 8 miles N of Pinedale • GPS: Lat 42.962646 Lon -109.849104 • Open: May-Nov • Stay limit: 14 days • Total sites: Dispersed • RV sites: Undefined • RV fee: Free • No water • No toilets • Activities: Hiking, fishing, power boating, hunting, non-power boating • Elevation: 7562

**Soda Lake WHMA - Inlet** • Agency: State • Tel: 307-777-4600 • Location: 8 miles N of Pinedale • GPS: Lat 42.962912 Lon -109.845647 • Open: May-Nov • Stay limit: 14 days • Total sites: Dispersed • RV sites: Undefined • RV fee: Free • No water • No toilets • Activities: Hiking, fishing, power boating, hunting, non-power boating • Elevation: 7562

**Soda Lake WHMA - North Thumb** • Agency: State • Tel: 307-777-4600 • Location: 8 miles N of Pinedale • GPS: Lat 42.968512 Lon -109.845432 • Open: May-Nov • Stay limit: 14 days • Total sites: Dispersed • RV sites: Undefined • RV fee: Free • No water • No toilets • Activities: Hiking, fishing, power boating, hunting, non-power boating • Elevation: 7562

**Soda Lake WHMA - South Bench** • Agency: State • Tel: 307-777-4600 • Location: 8 miles N of Pinedale • GPS: Lat 42.955251 Lon -109.852771 • Open: May-Nov • Stay limit: 14 days • Total sites: Dispersed • RV sites: Undefined • RV fee: Free • No water • No toilets • Activities: Hiking, fishing, power boating, hunting, non-power boating • Elevation: 7585

**Soda Lake WHMA - Spawning Camp** • Agency: State • Tel: 307-777-4600 • Location: 7 miles N of Pinedale • GPS: Lat 42.959489 Lon -109.839112 • Open: May-Nov • Stay limit: 14 days • Total sites: Dispersed • RV sites: Undefined • RV fee: Free • No water • No toilets • Activities: Hiking, fishing, power boating, hunting, non-power boating • Elevation: 7572

**Soda Lake WHMA - West Bench** • Agency: State • Tel: 307-777-4600 • Location: 7 miles N of Pinedale • GPS: Lat 42.959404 Lon -109.857034 • Open: May-Nov • Stay limit: 14 days • Total sites: Dispersed • RV sites: Undefined • RV fee: Free • No water • No toilets • Activities: Hiking, fishing, power boating, hunting, non-power boating • Elevation: 7569

**Soda Lake WHMA - West Boat Ramp - WGF** • Agency: State • Tel: 307-777-4600 • Location: 8 miles N of Pinedale • GPS: Lat 42.961455 Lon -109.854722 • Open: May-Nov • Stay limit: 14 days • Total sites: Dispersed • RV sites: Undefined • RV fee: Free • No water • No toilets • Activities: Hiking, fishing, power boating, hunting, non-power boating • Elevation: 7576

**Soda Lake WHMA - West Thumb** • Agency: State • Tel: 307-777-4600 • Location: 8 miles N of Pinedale • GPS: Lat 42.965619 Lon -109.844653 • Open: May-Nov • Stay limit: 14 days • Total sites: Dispersed • RV sites: Undefined • RV fee: Free • No water • No toilets • Activities: Hiking, fishing, power boating, hunting, non-power boating • Elevation: 7552

**Soda Lake WHMA - Wetlands** • Agency: State • Tel: 307-777-4600 • Location: 8 miles N of Pinedale • GPS: Lat 42.972974 Lon -109.849085 • Open: May-Nov • Stay limit: 14 days • Total sites: Dispersed • RV sites: Undefined • RV fee: Free • No water • No toilets • Activities: Hiking, fishing, power boating, hunting, non-power boating • Elevation: 7602

**Willow Lake** (Bridger-Teton NF) • Agency: US Forest Service • Tel: 307-739-5500 • Location: 12 miles N of Pinedale • GPS: Lat 42.990811 Lon -109.900115 • Open: Jun-Sep • Total sites: 19 • RV sites: 17 • RV fee: Free • No water • Vault toilets • Notes: Food storage order 04-00-104 • Activities: Fishing, swimming, power boating, non-power boating • Elevation: 7707

## Powell

**Shoshone River - WGF** • Agency: State • Tel: 307-777-4600 • Location: 10 miles SW of Powell • GPS: Lat 44.659605 Lon -108.931305 • Total sites: Dispersed • RV sites: Undefined • RV fee: Free • No water • No toilets • Activities: Fishing, power boating • Elevation: 4543

## Ralston

**Clark's Fork River, Lower - WGF** • Agency: State • Tel: 307-777-4600 • Location: 23 miles NW of Ralston (limited services), 26 miles NW of Powell • GPS: Lat 44.885763 Lon -109.138864 • Total sites: Dispersed • RV sites: Undefined • RV fee: Free • No water • Vault toilets • Activities: Fishing • Elevation: 4170

## Rawlins

**Teton Reservoir** • Agency: Bureau of Land Management • Tel: 307-828-4500 • Location: 14 miles S of Rawlins • GPS: Lat 41.603208 Lon -107.255528 • Open: All year • Total sites: 5 • RV sites: 5 • RV fee: Free • No water • Vault toilets • Activities: Fishing, non-power boating • Elevation: 7021

## Riverside

**Corral Creek** • Agency: Bureau of Land Management • Tel: 307-328-4200 • Location: 22 miles NE of Riverside (limited services), 39 miles SE of Saratoga • GPS: Lat 41.261296 Lon -106.572779 • Open: Jun-Nov • Total sites: 6 • RV sites: 6 • RV fee: Free • No water • Vault toilets • Activities: Fishing, non-power boating • Elevation: 7224

## Rock River

**Beumee WHMA - Site 1** • Agency: State • Tel: 307-777-4600 • Location: 16 miles SW of Rock River (limited services), 46 miles NW of Laramie • GPS: Lat 41.669309 Lon -106.169029 • Stay limit: 14 days • Total sites: Dispersed • RV sites: Undefined • RV fee: Free • No water • No toilets • Elevation: 7418

**Beumee WHMA - Site 5** • Agency: State • Tel: 307-777-4600 • Location: 16 miles SW of Rock River (limited services), 48 miles NW of Laramie • GPS: Lat 41.689103 Lon -106.170932 • Stay limit: 14 days • Total sites: Dispersed • RV sites: Undefined • RV fee: Free • No water • Vault toilets • Activities: Hiking, fishing, hunting • Elevation: 7462

**Beumee WHMA - Site 7** • Agency: State • Tel: 307-777-4600 • Location: 16 miles SW of Rock River (limited services), 48 miles NW of Laramie • GPS: Lat 41.681986 Lon -106.119062 • Stay limit: 14 days • Total sites: Dispersed • RV sites: Undefined • RV fee: Free • No water • No toilets • Activities: Hiking, fishing, hunting • Elevation: 7116

**Diamond Lake Public Access Area - North** • Agency: State • Location: 17 miles SW of Rock River (limited services), 36 miles NW of Laramie • GPS: Lat 41.611925 Lon -106.094564 • Total sites: Dispersed • RV sites: Undefined • RV fee: Free • No water • Vault toilets • Elevation: 7373

**Diamond Lake Public Access Area - South** • Agency: State • Location: 16 miles SW of Rock River (limited services), 36 miles NW of Laramie • GPS: Lat 41.603661 Lon -106.091323 • Total sites: Dispersed • RV sites: Undefined • RV fee: Free • No water • Vault toilets • Elevation: 7376

**Wheatland Reservoir #3 Access - WGF** • Agency: State • Location: 19 miles NE of Rock River (limited services), 49 miles SW of Wheatland • GPS: Lat 41.888266 Lon -105.728882 • Total sites: Dispersed • RV sites: Undefined • RV fee: Free • No water • Vault toilets • Activities: Fishing, power boating, non-power boating • Elevation: 6962

## Rock Springs

**Killpecker Sand Dunes** • Agency: Bureau of Land Management • Tel: 307-352-0256 • Location: 32 miles N of Rock Springs • GPS: Lat 41.993126 Lon -109.124915 • Total sites: Dispersed • RV sites: Undefined • RV fee: Free • No water • No toilets • Activities: Motor sports • Elevation: 6923

## Saratoga

**Frazier Public Access** • Agency: State • Location: 12 miles NW of Saratoga • GPS: Lat 41.548148 Lon -106.903823 • Total sites: Dispersed • RV sites: Undefined • RV fee: Free • No water • No toilets • Activities: Fishing • Elevation: 6703

**North Platte River - Foote Public Access - WGF** • Agency: State • Location: 5 miles N of Saratoga • GPS: Lat 41.509115 Lon -106.838114 • Total sites: Dispersed • RV sites: Undefined • RV fee: Free • No water • No toilets • Activities: Fishing • Elevation: 6752

**North Platte River - Pick Bridge Rd Access - WGF** • Agency: State • Location: 10 miles NW of Saratoga • GPS: Lat 41.538911 Lon -106.881001 • Total sites: Dispersed • RV sites: Undefined • RV fee: Free • No water • Vault toilets • Activities: Fishing, power boating, non-power boating • Elevation: 6696

**North Platte River - Sanger Public Access - WGF** • Agency: State • Location: 13 miles NW of Saratoga • GPS: Lat 41.557391 Lon -106.919688 • Total sites: Dispersed • RV sites: Undefined • RV fee: Free • No water • Vault toilets • Activities: Fishing, power boating, non-power boating • Elevation: 6676

**North Platte River - Treasure Island Access - WGF** • Agency: State • Location: 9 miles S of Saratoga • GPS: Lat 41.331809 Lon -106.727662 • Total sites: Dispersed • RV sites: Undefined • RV fee: Free • No water • Vault toilets • Activities: Fishing, power boating, non-power boating • Elevation: 6939

## Shell

**Calvin Lake - WGF** • Agency: State • Location: 29 miles NE of Shell (limited services), 44 miles NE of Greybull • GPS: Lat 44.622947 Lon -107.414345 • Total sites: Dispersed • RV sites: Undefined • RV fee: Free • No water • Vault toilets • Activities: Fishing • Elevation: 9449

## Shoshoni

**Sand Mesa WHMA - Alkali Bay** • Agency: State • Tel: 307-777-4600 • Location: 16 miles NW of Shoshoni (limited services), 27 miles NE of Riverton • GPS: Lat 43.294927 Lon -108.242448 • Open: All year • Stay limit: 14

days • Total sites: Dispersed • RV sites: Undefined • RV fee: Free • No water • Vault toilets • Activities: Fishing, power boating, non-power boating • Elevation: 4823

**Sand Mesa WHMA - Bass Lake** • Agency: State • Tel: 307-777-4600 • Location: 16 miles NW of Shoshoni (limited services), 26 miles NE of Riverton • GPS: Lat 43.294333 Lon -108.246792 • Open: All year • Stay limit: 14 days • Total sites: Dispersed • RV sites: Undefined • RV fee: Free • No water • Vault toilets • Activities: Fishing, power boating, non-power boating • Elevation: 4810

**Sand Mesa WHMA - Beach** • Agency: State • Tel: 307-777-4600 • Location: 17 miles NW of Shoshoni (limited services), 27 miles NE of Riverton • GPS: Lat 43.298207 Lon -108.233717 • Open: All year • Stay limit: 14 days • Total sites: Dispersed • RV sites: Undefined • RV fee: Free • No water • Vault toilets • Activities: Fishing, power boating, non-power boating • Elevation: 4829

**Sand Mesa WHMA - Drainfield** • Agency: State • Tel: 307-777-4600 • Location: 17 miles NW of Shoshoni (limited services), 27 miles NE of Riverton • GPS: Lat 43.303433 Lon -108.231555 • Open: All year • Stay limit: 14 days • Total sites: 3 • RV sites: 3 • RV fee: Free • No water • Vault toilets • Activities: Fishing, power boating, non-power boating • Elevation: 4826

## Sinclair

**Dugway** • Agency: Bureau of Land Management • Tel: 307-328-4200 • Location: 8 miles NE of Sinclair (limited services), 13 miles NE of Rawlins • GPS: Lat 41.860593 Lon -107.054107 • Open: All year • Total sites: 5 • RV sites: 5 • RV fee: Free • No water • Vault toilets • Activities: Fishing, non-power boating • Elevation: 6440

**Kortes Dam Campground** • Agency: US Bureau of Reclamation • Tel: 307-261-5628 • Location: 44 miles NE of Sinclair (limited services), 49 miles NE of Rawlins • GPS: Lat 42.193015 Lon -106.86921 • Total sites: Dispersed • RV sites: Undefined • RV fee: Free • No toilets • Activities: Hiking, fishing, hunting, equestrian area • Elevation: 5945

**North Platte River - Miracle Mile #3 Public Access - WGF** • Agency: State • Location: 43 miles NE of Sinclair (limited services), 49 miles NE of Rawlins • GPS: Lat 42.190826 Lon -106.870105 • Total sites: 10 • RV sites: 10 • RV fee: Free • No water • Vault toilets • Activities: Fishing, power boating, non-power boating • Elevation: 5934

**North Platte River - Miracle Mile #4 Public Access - WGF** • Agency: State • Location: 43 miles NE of Sinclair (limited services), 49 miles NE of Rawlins • GPS: Lat 42.221201 Lon -106.876058 • Total sites: Dispersed • RV sites: Undefined • RV fee: Free • No water • Vault toilets • Activities: Fishing • Elevation: 5873

## Ten Sleep

**Battle Park Trailhead** (Bighorn NF) • Agency: US Forest Service • Location: 33 miles NE of Ten Sleep (limited services), 59 miles NE of Worland • GPS: Lat 44.306587 Lon -107.310747 • Stay limit: 14 days • Total sites: 15 • RV sites: 15 (camping allowed only across road from the TH parking area) • RV fee: Free (donation appreciated) • Central water • Vault toilets • Activities: Hiking, equestrian area • Elevation: 9134

**Buffalo Creek** • Agency: Bureau of Land Management • Tel: 307-587-9227 • Location: 55 miles S of Ten Sleep (limited services), 80 miles SE of Worland • GPS: Lat 43.437912 Lon -107.223752 • Open: May-Sep • Total sites: 4 • RV sites: 4 • RV fee: Free • No water • Vault toilets • Activities: Fishing, hunting • Elevation: 8159

**Carter/Billy Miles - WGF** • Agency: State • Location: 7 miles NE of Ten Sleep (limited services), 33 miles NE of Worland • GPS: Lat 44.104861 Lon -107.378798 • Total sites: Dispersed • RV sites: Undefined • RV fee: Free • No water • No toilets • Activities: Hiking • Elevation: 5663

**Grave Springs** • Agency: Bureau of Land Management • Tel: 307-261-7600 • Location: 54 miles S of Ten Sleep (limited services), 79 miles SE of Worland • GPS: Lat 43.464031 Lon -107.228659 • Open: All year (limited winter access) • Total sites: 12 • RV sites: 10 • RV fee: Free • No water • Vault toilets • Activities: Fishing, hunting • Elevation: 8268

**Renner WHMA** • Agency: State • Tel: 307-777-4600 • Location: 13 miles N of Ten Sleep (limited services), 38 miles NE of Worland • GPS: Lat 44.17625 Lon -107.50283 • Open: All year • Stay limit: 14 days • Total sites: Dispersed • RV sites: Undefined • RV fee: Free • Activities: Hiking, fishing, power boating, hunting, non-power boating • Elevation: 4780

**Tensleep Canyon** (Bighorn NF) • Agency: US Forest Service • Location: 5 miles NE of Ten Sleep (limited services), 30 miles NE of Worland • GPS: Lat 44.068419 Lon -107.368815 • Total sites: 5 • RV sites: 5 • RV fee: Free • No water • No toilets • Activities: Swimming, rock climbing • Elevation: 4892

## Thayne

**Salt River Public Access - Diversion** • Agency: State • Location: 2 miles S of Thayne (limited services), 12 miles N of Afton • GPS: Lat 42.881602 Lon -110.998313 • Total sites: Dispersed • RV sites: Undefined • RV fee: Free • No water • Activities: Fishing • Elevation: 5937

## Torrington

**Packer Lake Access Area - WGF** • Agency: State • Location: 15 miles SE of Torrington • GPS: Lat 41.896684 Lon -104.052875 • Stay limit: 5 days • Total sites: Dispersed • RV sites: Undefined • RV fee: Free • No water • No toilets • Activities: Fishing • Elevation: 4078

## Wheatland

**Cottonwood Draw WHMA - Site 1** • Agency: State • Tel: 307-777-4600 • Location: 15 miles NE of Wheatland • GPS: Lat 42.129525 Lon -104.737071 • Open: All year • Stay limit: 7 days • Total sites: Dispersed • RV sites: Undefined • RV fee: Free • No water • No toilets • Elevation: 4457

**Cottonwood Draw WHMA - Site 2** • Agency: State • Tel: 307-777-4600 • Location: 15 miles NE of Wheatland • GPS: Lat 42.126067 Lon -104.736423 • Open: All year • Stay limit: 7 days • Total sites: Dispersed • RV sites: Undefined • RV fee: Free • No water • No toilets • Elevation: 4511

**Grayrocks Reservoir Public Access 1** • Agency: State • Location: 18 miles NE of Wheatland • GPS: Lat 42.160997 Lon -104.69326 • Total sites: Dispersed • RV sites: Undefined (numerous sites along SE shore) • RV fee: Free • No water • Vault toilets • Activities: Fishing, power boating, non-power boating • Elevation: 4455

**Grayrocks Reservoir Public Access 10** • Agency: State • Location: 15 miles NE of Wheatland • GPS: Lat 42.136757 Lon -104.737176 • Total sites: Dispersed • RV sites: Undefined • RV fee: Free • No water • No toilets • Activities: Fishing, power boating, non-power boating • Elevation: 4413

**Grayrocks Reservoir Public Access 11** • Agency: State • Location: 15 miles NE of Wheatland • GPS: Lat 42.135862 Lon -104.739903 • Total sites: Dispersed • RV sites: Undefined • RV fee: Free • No water • No toilets • Activities: Fishing, power boating, non-power boating • Elevation: 4413

**Grayrocks Reservoir Public Access 12** • Agency: State • Location: 15 miles NE of Wheatland • GPS: Lat 42.134896 Lon -104.749493 • Total sites: Dispersed • RV sites: Undefined • RV fee: Free • No water • No toilets • Activities: Fishing, power boating, non-power boating • Elevation: 4414

**Grayrocks Reservoir Public Access 2** • Agency: State • Location: 17 miles NE of Wheatland • GPS: Lat 42.152581 Lon -104.705667 • Total sites: Dispersed • RV sites: Undefined • RV fee: Free • No water • No toilets • Activities: Fishing, power boating, non-power boating • Elevation: 4415

**Grayrocks Reservoir Public Access 3** • Agency: State • Location: 17 miles NE of Wheatland • GPS: Lat 42.149639 Lon -104.707694 • Total sites: Dispersed • RV sites: Undefined • RV fee: Free • No water • No toilets • Activities: Fishing, power boating, non-power boating • Elevation: 4420

**Grayrocks Reservoir Public Access 4** • Agency: State • Location: 17 miles NE of Wheatland • GPS: Lat 42.146064 Lon -104.715715 • Total sites: Dispersed • RV sites: Undefined • RV fee: Free • No water • No toilets • Activities: Fishing, power boating, non-power boating • Elevation: 4414

**Grayrocks Reservoir Public Access 5** • Agency: State • Location: 16 miles NE of Wheatland • GPS: Lat 42.144166 Lon -104.719294 • Total sites: Dispersed • RV sites: Undefined • RV fee: Free • No water • No toilets • Activities: Fishing, power boating, non-power boating • Elevation: 4414

**Grayrocks Reservoir Public Access 6** • Agency: State • Location: 16 miles NE of Wheatland • GPS: Lat 42.142194 Lon -104.723657 • Total sites: Dispersed • RV sites: Undefined • RV fee: Free • No water • No toilets • Activities: Fishing, power boating, non-power boating • Elevation: 4413

**Grayrocks Reservoir Public Access 7** • Agency: State • Location: 16 miles NE of Wheatland • GPS: Lat 42.140933 Lon -104.727319 • Total sites: Dispersed • RV sites: Undefined • RV fee: Free • No water • No toilets • Activities: Fishing, power boating, non-power boating • Elevation: 4414

**Grayrocks Reservoir Public Access 8** • Agency: State • Location: 16 miles NE of Wheatland • GPS: Lat 42.139092 Lon -104.728698 • Total sites: Dispersed • RV sites: Undefined • RV fee: Free • No water • No toilets • Activities: Fishing, power boating, non-power boating • Elevation: 4415

**Grayrocks Reservoir Public Access 9** • Agency: State • Location: 16 miles NE of Wheatland • GPS: Lat 42.137644 Lon -104.731303 • Total sites: Dispersed • RV sites: Undefined • RV fee: Free • No water • No toilets • Activities: Fishing, power boating, non-power boating • Elevation: 4413

**Lewis Park** • Agency: Municipal • Tel: 307-322-2962 • Location: In Wheatland • GPS: Lat 42.048131 Lon -104.954783 • Total sites: 15 • RV sites: 10 • RV fee: Free (donation appreciated) • Electric sites: 10 • Central water • Flush toilets • Notes: 3-days free • Elevation: 4760

**Tom Thorn - Beth Williams WHMA - CG A** • Agency: State • Tel: 307-777-4600 • Location: 34 miles SW of Wheatland • GPS: Lat 41.778559 Lon -105.372641 • Stay limit: 14 days • Total sites: Dispersed • RV sites: Undefined • RV fee: Free • No water • No toilets • Activities: Hiking, fishing, hunting • Elevation: 6220

**Tom Thorn - Beth Williams WHMA - CG B** • Agency: State • Tel: 307-777-4600 • Location: 34 miles SW of Wheatland • GPS: Lat 41.779227 Lon -105.371712 • Stay limit: 14 days • Total sites: Dispersed • RV sites: Undefined • RV fee: Free • No water • No toilets • Activities: Hiking, fishing, hunting • Elevation: 6230

**Tom Thorn - Beth Williams WHMA - CG C** • Agency: State • Tel: 307-777-4600 • Location: 34 miles SW of Wheatland • GPS: Lat 41.778794 Lon -105.367632 • Stay limit: 14 days • Total sites: Dispersed • RV sites: Undefined • RV fee: Free • No water • No toilets • Activities: Hiking, fishing, hunting • Elevation: 6260

**Wheatland Reservoir #1 Access - WGF** • Agency: State • Location: 9 miles SW of Wheatland • GPS: Lat 41.995297 Lon -105.031391 • Total sites: Dispersed • RV sites: Undefined • RV fee: Free • Vault toilets • Activities: Fishing, power boating, non-power boating • Elevation: 4915